Dai[ly Telegraph]
CRICKET YEAR BOOK 86

**Michael Melford
Bill Frindall**

Consultant editor Michael Melford
Statistics Bill Frindall
Special articles E.W. Swanton
Other contributors
George Abbott, Rajan Bala (India), Mike Beddow, Tony Cozier (West Indies), Rachael Flint, John Fogg, David Green, Neil Hallam, Derek Hodgson, Doug Ibbotson, David Leggat (New Zealand), Andy Lloyd (Zimbabwe tour), Michael Owen-Smith (South Africa), Qamar Ahmed (Pakistan), D.J. Rutnagur, Alan Shiell (Australia), Sa'adi Thawfeeq (Sri Lanka), A.S.R. Winlaw.

Editor: Norman Barrett
Designer Martin Bronkhorst
Illustrator Dennis Curran

Acknowledgements Thanks are due to David Armstrong and Mike Gear for supplying the statistics for the Minor Counties and Second XI championships, respectively, and to the TCCB for making the first-class fixtures available. The English Schools' Cricket Association material was kindly supplied by Cyril J. Cooper.

Most of the photographs appearing in this book are reproduced by permission of Adrian Murrell/All-Sport. Other pictures were provided by Bill Smith, Associated Sports Photography, Michael King and Simon Miles (All-Sport), and Syndication International.

The editors particularly wish to thank Radford Barrett, Daily Telegraph Sports Editor, for his generous help.

Published by Telegraph Publications
135 Fleet Street, London EC4P 4BL

First Published 1985
© Daily Telegraph 1985
Scorecharts © Bill Frindall 1985

British Library Cataloguing in Publication Data
Daily Telegraph cricket year book. ―― '86
 1. Cricket – Periodicals
 796.35'8'05 GV911

 ISBN 0-86367-063-6
 ISBN 0-86367-062-8 Pbk

Conditions of Sale:
This book is sold subject to the conditions that it shall not, by way of trade or otherwise, be lent, re-sold, hired out or otherwise circulated without the publisher's prior consent in any form of binding or cover other than that in which it is published.

Printed in Great Britain
by Redwood Burn Limited, Trowbridge, Wiltshire
Typeset by Thomas/Weintroub Associates, Wembley.

Contents

- 5 Foreword, by Mike Brearley
- **9 Looking Back**
- 10 A Triumphant Summer
  by Michael Melford
- 14 Australian Viewpoint
  by Alan Shiell
- 16 Daily Telegraph 'Twin Hundreds',
  by E.W. Swanton
- 17 Daily Telegraph Cricketers of the Year,
  by E.W. Swanton
- **19 England's Winter Tour 1984-85**
- 20 England in India
- 32 Tour Statistical Summary
- **33 Overseas Cricket 1984-85**
- 34 Pakistan v India
- 38 India v Australia (1-day)
- 39 Australia v West Indies
- 48 Pakistan v New Zealand
- 55 New Zealand v Pakistan
- 62 West Indies v New Zealand
- 70 Benson & Hedges World Series Cup
- 73 World Championship of Cricket
- 75 Other Overseas Results
- 76 Cricket in Australia
- 80 Cricket in South Africa
- 84 Cricket in the West Indies
- 86 Cricket in New Zealand
- 88 Cricket in India
- 91 Cricket in Pakistan
- 93 Cricket in Sri Lanka
- **95 Tours to England 1985**
- 96 Australia in England
- 131 Texaco Trophy
- 135 Zimbabwe in England
- **137 English Season 1985**
- 138 Britannic Assurance Championship
- 142 Review of the Counties
- 142 Derbyshire
- 144 Essex
- 146 Glamorgan
- 148 Gloucestershire
- 150 Hampshire
- 152 Kent
- 154 Lancashire
- 156 Leicestershire
- 158 Middlesex
- 160 Northamptonshire
- 162 Nottinghamshire
- 164 Somerset
- 166 Surrey
- 168 Sussex
- 170 Warwickshire
- 172 Worcestershire
- 174 Yorkshire
- 176 University Cricket
- 179 First-Class Averages
- 187 Benson & Hedges Cup
- 190 NatWest Bank Trophy
- 194 John Player League
- 196 Second XI County Championship
  and Under-25 Competition
- 198 Minor Counties
- 200 Village and Club Cricket
- 201 Schools Cricket
- 202 Women's Cricket
- **205 Extras**
- 206 Test Career Records
- 214 Guide to Newcomers
- 218 Obituary 1984-85
- **221 Looking Forward**
- 222 England on Tour 1985-86
- 223 England 'B' Tour
- 225 The 1986 Season
- 226 Fixtures 1986

Foreword

In a newspaper article on the Lord's Test, I said, 'If there had been two umpire Birds standing in this match England could well have scored 400 in the first innings: if two umpire Evanses, 150.'

I realized from the response to this remark that it was assumed that I was criticizing the umpires. Brian Walden, for instance, wrote, 'Tut! Tut! And this from a member of the MCC. Don't tell me the cricketing establishment are going to start telling the truth to the vulgar rabble? Jim Swanton will die of fright.'

I began to wonder if what I said really did take the lid off some popular view of judicial infallibility. Other questions occurred to me, too. How far *should* umpires be criticized, and by whom?

To return to the first question. If what I said about umpires Bird and Evans is true, does it follow that one or other must be in the wrong? I think not. The law states that umpires must be convinced that certain conditions have been met before they give a batsman out. But some people need more convincing than others. Take lbws. A right-arm bowler who delivers the ball from close to the stumps bowls a ball that moves in to the right-handed batsman. The batsman pushes half forward, and the ball hits his front leg in line with the off-stump. Let us suppose that the ball keeps low, so there is no question of its going over the top. Now, some umpires, of whom Dickie Bird is one, would almost never give the batsman out. They would argue that though such a ball might hit leg-and-middle, or leg-stump, they could not be certain that it would not miss.

Their criteria for certainty are high. I once said to Dickie, half joking, 'There's no such thing as absolute certainty, only the certainty that befits the subject.' As Aristotle said, 'What is certain or accurate for a carpenter is not certain or accurate for a geometer.' Bird, incidentally, sometimes smiles as he gives you out: not sadistically; it is the smile of a man who feels he has seen the truth.

Other umpires – probably David Evans falls into this category – might be less stringent; and by that I do not mean less good. For it might be that these umpires are braver and do not take the easy way out. Certainly it is a bad thing for the game if batsmen can be absolutely safe from lbws if they push six inches forward.

On some pitches, especially when the ball moves off the seam and keeps low, the character of the umpire makes an enormous difference to the pattern of the game. If the sequence that I describe above happens just four times in one innings, and if umpire Bird gives each decision not out while umpire Evans gives them all out –

and if, further, the four players are front-line batsmen – then the average difference in each one's score may be 40 or 50. So the overall difference to the total may well be 200 or even more, as it is notorious that success breeds success, among bowlers and batsmen alike.

What players ask of the umpire is, above all, consistency. Bird is (with lbws though not with run-outs) a 'not-outer' and very consistent. Evans is also a fine umpire; but he is a consistent 'outer'.

My remark did not cast doubt on the umpires' capabilities; only on an illusion of uniformity, of justice as an all-seeing mechanical eye. There are limits, naturally, to the range that is acceptable. Some decisions are plain wrong, either way.

But then another question arises. Who is entitled to criticize umpires, and in what sort of terms? I am a firm believer in the old-fashioned idea that players should not show dissent from an umpire's decision. Of course they do, in the heat of the moment. But it should never be prolonged, and the captain must intervene to control it. Frank Keating wrote recently that after watching John McEnroe he was not sorry that the Americans stuck to baseball and tennis. It is remarkable that in cricket, where the umpire's decision makes, on average, far more difference to the course of a match and to the individual's success than in tennis, acceptance by the players is so frequently gracious.

What about commentators? Here the case is different. Their job is to describe the scene as knowledgeably as they can. They are entitled to criticize as well as praise; targets include players, groundsmen, administrators, and other pressmen. I do not see why umpires alone should be exempt. So I would be prepared to state, along with others, that I thought Evans was wrong to give Gooch out lbw at Lord's, Alan Whitehead *perhaps* wrong to give Ritchie not out at Nottingham.

Nevertheless, the media have a duty to be restrained in such critical comment. Firstly, they should not take into account in their judgement the opportunities afforded to them, but not to the umpire, of seeing the incident replayed time after time on TV. They should bear in mind the fact that the umpire sees the delivery once only.

Secondly, they should remember how fallible and conflictual people's judgements often are. There were many occasions on the field when I discovered that those in the best possible positions to see what happened – for instance, when there was an appeal for bat-pad catches, the close fielders themselves – disagreed. Players close to the scene of the crime would differ about whether a ball was too high for an lbw, or whether it passed inside or outside the bat. Batsmen themselves are notoriously bad judges of where they put their feet; and occasionally they are mistaken even about whether they edged a ball. All this ought to lead to reticence amongst those, of whom I am now one, seated some hundred yards away, rarely behind the line, and only occasionally able to see a TV screen – and that is usually blurred. Where the camera can sometimes *prove* a point is with run-outs. And again it is easy for eye-witnesses to be wrong. I remember a Middlesex match at Leeds in which Clive Radley, sauntering in, was given run-out. We, including Clive, were convinced that the decision was a travesty of justice – until a photo appeared in the morning paper showing conclusively that the batsman was out.

Either way, whether the camera suggests a mistake (say lbw) or whether the camera-less naked eye is convinced of one, the spectator should be cautious.

Much criticism of umpires ultimately rests on the reactions of players. When Border was given out, caught off bat and pad, at Nottingham, he stood, presumably in disbelief, for a second or two before walking off. It was that hesitation alone that led the observer to question the decision, and for one reporter to write that the bat was not near the ball. In my opinion, Border's bat was extremely close to the ball, and it was impossible for anyone to tell, by watching from the boundary (or probably from silly-mid-off even) or by seeing it on TV, whether or not the ball touched the edge of the bat on the way through.

Because the player concerned was Border, the best batsman in the match, the dismissal became a Big Incident, which would have been even Bigger had Australia lost. I have little sympathy with the star players in such situations. In my view, they often get the benefit of borderline decisions simply because the umpire is so conscious of their bearing on a match. And when they allow the world to see their disagreement, they cause greater pressures to fall on umpires. Though I did not always live up to this standard myself (and nor did he), I admire Ian Chappell's example: in a Test at Melbourne in 1974-75 he was, I am told, given out caught behind in each innings when both times the ball merely touched his pad. Yet each time he marched off in a way that let no one know that he had been badly treated.

Finally, it is all too easy to attribute dubious motives to an umpire. In the same article on 14 July, 1985, the reporter mentioned above in effect accused umpire Whitehead not only of a mistake with regard to Border, and another about Ritchie's lbw, but with a third, more inexcusable fault. He said that the latter was probably a make-up for the former. Yet what is the basis for this claim? We come back, again, to Border's reaction on being given out, and the interpretation put on his hesitation by the reporter. Like players, writers, too, should show restraint.

Looking back

A Triumphant Summer

A season at the mercy of an admittedly overdue wet summer survived the handicaps imposed by the weather remarkably well. England won back the Ashes with an admirable exhibition of positive cricket and it was watched by big crowds. It was a refreshing confirmation that Test cricket, especially when it is against Australia, is still the highlight of the season in England, and it should have saved the counties from what otherwise might have been awkward financial problems. In the John Player League, generally a useful source of income, 20 per cent of the matches produced no result because of rain.

Apart from the luck that it did not rain more during the hours of play, the triumph of the Test series over the weather derived from several factors, notably the outstanding work of ground staffs toiling long hours in drying out grounds. Two special Test regulations also played their part, the requirement of 90 overs per day and the addition of an extra hour to a day's play if an hour or more has been lost earlier.

This last playing condition has had an uneasy history. It is still not simple to interpret, for there will be times when the umpires have to decide between resuming play after the loss of 55 minutes when they believe the ground will be fit and delaying another five minutes which would enable the whole hour to be made up. In the past, a dark wet afternoon has often become a darker wetter evening, so that the extra hour was of no use. This year, however, it was taken successfully on four occasions. The day's play ended in evening sunshine, the crowd departed feeling that they had had their money's worth, and something had been done to keep the match up to schedule.

Indeed, at Edgbaston on the fourth evening, the extra hour was crucial, for in it Richard Ellison took his four wickets in 15 balls, reducing Australia to 37 for five. Without that start, they must have batted comfortably through the limited amount of play possible when the next day's rain stopped. This squared an old account, for it was at Edgbaston in 1975 that England, having just started their innings when heavy rain fell on an uncovered pitch, lost valuable wickets when the weather perversely allowed the extra hour rule to come into force.

The 90 overs requirement meant that play ran as much as 45 minutes over time on occasion, but was a great help towards the reaching of a definite result in four of the six Tests. It also meant that slow bowling, even though in short supply on the Australian side, was sometimes employed more than it would otherwise have been. The success of the 90 overs in this series will no doubt strengthen the resolve of the TCCB to persuade all other touring teams to agree to at least this figure, even though West Indies have hitherto been deeply shocked by the idea and will not accept that spectators are being deprived of entertainment by seeing only 12 or 13 overs an hour throughout the day.

The stirring finish to the Britannic Assurance County Championship sustained interest right up to the last day of the season, on September 17. As five of the Middlesex side had also taken part in recovering the Ashes, they could be accounted unusually worthy winners. Mike Gatting had the dual distinction of captaining the champion county and heading the Test batting averages, which not even Peter May quite achieved in the same season.

The NatWest Trophy final, as in 1984, went to the very last ball, before Essex beat Nottinghamshire by one run. I understand the selectivity of one spectator who, knowing the sameness and predictability of many long-drawn-out limited-overs matches, makes a habit of looking in just for the last half-hour. But this one, in which only five wickets fell to the bowlers, produced much fine batting on a splendid pitch. The Lord's square in September 1985 was green and little scarred, as seldom before at that time of year, a reflection of the persistent rain and reduced amount of cricket, perhaps, but also of the work of the new MCC head groundsman, Mike Hunt.

Behaviour. One of the less agreeable topics of the summer was that of bad behaviour on the field, not a frequent occurrence but exposed to harsh publicity when it happens in front of television cameras. The TCCB is, very properly, tough on misconduct and dissent. If it were not, it would be performing a long-term disservice to the game by condoning behaviour which is a thoroughly bad example to the impressionable young watchers, who are the players of the future.

Sometimes the players may feel aggrieved because they have not said anything outrageous or indeed made any gesture that was obvious to spectators watching from a distance. They may think, in fact, that they have done nothing to which exception would have been taken before the days of television close-ups and replays.

That is not the point. Television is a part of modern cricket. It helps to provide players, especially Test players, with extra income, and it builds them up as 'personalities' who as a result have a greater market value off the field. Much as one winces at the old tag about 'justice being seen to be done', it can be appropriately adapted here to read 'behaviour must be seen to be good'.

Covering. The debate about whether pitches should be covered or not, and to what extent, is never dormant for long in English cricket. Full covering came in in 1981, and for Test matches in England in 1979, accelerated perhaps by the unfortunate experience of the New Zealanders in a Test match at Trent Bridge in 1978, when the compromise of leaving pitches uncovered during the hours of play was in being. It was clear that heavy rain was going to fall at any moment, but strictly at the scheduled hour of starting play was possible. After two balls had been bowled, it was stopped; a good dry batting pitch, which now had to be left open to the skies, was turned into a less straightforward one; and New Zealand were put under what must have been a particularly galling handicap.

This was especially unfortunate because it underlined a weakness in a compromise that went some way towards satisfying the demands of both coverers and anti-coverers. The basic arguments remain the same:

In favour of covering – it provides more play, gives the batsman more confidence to play strokes, makes the bowler work harder for his wickets, and puts England on a par with other countries. Moreover, the domestic game in England is now played at a brisker tempo – in terms of scoring rate, not bowling rate – than in the days of uncovered pitches.

Against covering – it can lead to sweating, it takes the pace out of pitches and breeds medium-pace bowlers, it provides fewer opportunities for spinners, it puts less of a premium on the batsman's all-round skill, and it means that time is made up through the artificial forfeiture of innings and the like rather than through the influence of nature on the pitch. Most of all, it detracts from the variety and character of the game.

The last point seems particularly valid at a time when the variety and character are under threat, though less in England than overseas, from a surfeit of limited-overs cricket. Perhaps the time has come for another compromise.

The England B tour. A secondary tour, at just below Test level, has long been thought desirable, and the one to be made by an England B team to Bangladesh, Sri Lanka, and Zimbabwe early in 1986 is on a larger scale than anything attempted previously. Never before has a genuine England second team, carefully picked by Test selectors, been sent abroad. The last side to go on a tour with the same purpose of giving promising players overseas experience was that captained by Mike Brearley in Pakistan in 1966-67. But that was an under-25 side.

What makes the winter's tour particularly interesting is that the second team looks stronger than any that might have been picked in the 1970s. Several of its members must have been close to being chosen for the main tour in West Indies. Still more intriguing is that the opposition is now strong enough to make this far from a semi-social, semi-missionary tour. It is to be expected that England B will lose a few matches.

Sri Lanka took most of the honours from their Test match at Lord's in 1984, and in September 1985 won a short home series against India. Zimbabwe are producing players of a high calibre in Curran and Hick. They beat Australia in a World Cup match in 1983, and are thought by those who have played against them recently to be a very formidable limited-overs side. The England B side, coming from an English mid-winter, will have the usual problems of acclimatization – three to four weeks seems to be the usual time needed to have everyone near his best – and they will have to cope with two other changes of climate and playing conditions later.

Before its independence, Bangladesh used to have only the odd player in Pakistan teams and they may not have the same strength as the two other countries to be visited later, but the tour provides an opportunity for the TCCB to make up for the failure of David Gower's side to go to Bangladesh last winter. The Bangladesh section of the tour of India had to be omitted when the assassination of Mrs Gandhi necessitated a shortening of the programme.

The tour may cost the Board as much as £100,000, but it is seen by the counties as a sound investment, which will bring dividends both for the counties themselves and for England at Test level, with the improvement in playing standards that experience of cricket overseas against fairly strong opposition ought to inspire.

One other reason that the tour is at last able to be undertaken is that the host countries are now in a better position to bear a share of the cost themselves. The recent success of Sri Lankan and Zimbabwean sides should help in generating funds and enthusiasm. They will not pay for the travel or salaries of the English team, but they will look after various local expenses, an arrangement that, in view of the traditional problems experienced by many countries in laying their hands on foreign currency, will be a blessing to one and all.

The Battle for the Ashes

When, on September 2, 1985, David Gower held aloft a replica of the famous Ashes urn on the pavilion balcony at the Oval, he was not just celebrating victory over our oldest Test opponents. He was signalling the re-emergence of English pride after the humiliating defeat by the West Indies the previous summer. Leading by example, David Gower succeeded in moulding his side into a team to be reckoned with, which finally routed the Australians, despite Allan Border's authoritative captaincy. Follow the changing fortunes of the fascinating series with *The Battle for the Ashes*. Michael Carey unfolds the full story, Alan Shiell gives the Australian viewpoint and Bill Frindall provides wide-ranging and statistical analysis.

Available through leading bookshops, the Telegraph Bookshop at 130 Fleet Street, price £5.95 paperback and £8.95 hardback, or by post from Department TBFA, Daily Telegraph, 135 Fleet Street, London EC4P 4BL (please add 55p for postage and packing).

Australian Viewpoint
by Alan Shiell

The sports editor asked me for some impressions of English cricket; a reasonable request, of course, but not necessarily an easy one, coming, as it has, immediately after Australia have lost the Ashes at the Oval.

In every way, except one, I'm among the luckiest of the 15 million people in the Lucky Country, because I have spent 15 months of my 40 years in the dear old Mother Country, on three five-month cricket tours – 1977, 1981, and 1985. The exception is that Australia have won only two of the 17 Tests on those tours, losing 0-3 in 1977, 1-3 in 1981, and 1-3 again in 1985. So Trent Bridge 1981 and Lord's 1985 hold special memories.

Right now, as the disc jockeys say, my impressions might be dimmed somewhat by the shadow of defeat, particularly so soon after England's other 'important' victory over Australia in the Press match on a lovely little ground opposite an even lovelier little pub just out of Birmingham, on the rest day of the fifth Test. It's hard for an Australian to live with himself when he has been involved with the losing of the Ashes and seen the real players lose the Ashes in the space of 16 days.

In this sort of mood, I have to say that if you want a colonial's overriding general impression of English cricket it is that it smacks of an Old Boys' club; of older men, wearing grey suits or dark blue blazers and club ties, drinking pints of bitter or gin-and-tonics and saying 'jolly good show' or 'absolutely'. Where are the women and children?

A marketing man from Sydney told me that, whereas 74 per cent of Australian cricket spectators were under the age of 35, a comparable majority of English crowds was aged more than 45. Women and children comprised about 60 per cent (half each) of Australian audiences, whose interest in the game had been either generated or increased by Channel 9's snappy television coverage and the hustle and bustle and razzamatazz – including coloured clothes and white balls – of the World Series Cup limited-overs competition, many matches of which are played under lights. The very thought of that does not please everyone in English and Australian cricket, but facts are facts. In Australia, five-day Test matches uphold the game's glorious traditions, but one-day fixtures are the real money-spinners, even if they are not real cricket.

The marketing man was surprised by the 'one-sided make-up of the mostly male crowds' and also by what he called 'the genteel nature of the presentation of cricket in England'. And he was alarmed by the 'poor facilities' at English grounds. He wondered about the game's future in England, because he did not believe it was attracting a new audience; its committed followers were getting older and older and he could not see evidence of cricket attempting changes to comply with life in the 1980s.

Women and children caused quite a change on the Australians' 1985 tour of England. It was a somewhat unique tour in that it was the first of the 'travelling creche', or the first such family-orientated Australian tour of England, in the mould of England's ill-fated 'mothers and babies' tour of Australia under 'father' Mike Denness in 1974-75.

No fewer than 13 of the 17 Australians (the exceptions were Bob Holland, Greg Matthews, Dave Gilbert, and Ray Phillips) and manager Bob Merriman and assistant manager Geoff Dymock had their wives, fiancées, or girlfriends, and children living with them for all, most, or part of the tour. (So, too, I must add, did most of the seven Australian Pressmen.)

It is an emotional issue. The ayes say it is essential in these days of 'professionalism' because the affluent players are away from home so often that their women deserve a trip and they help to provide a more natural, harmonious way of life. The noes say the women are something of a disruptive influence on team spirit, preventing the players from being together often enough and turning a working tour into a social holiday. Certainly there was evidence of this in the rather indifferent attitude of the Australians as they folded so meekly in their second innings of the last Test, at the Oval, which, incidentally, surely is the most claustrophobic of Test venues.

It was, though, the happiest, friendliest, and most pleasant and obliging touring team with which I have been associated, so maybe the ayes have it. I just wish I hadn't seen one of the players crawling around a cocktail bar in a Nottingham hotel, searching for his crying daughter's dummy. Or was it the teat off her bottle?

On the field, I will remember the consummate skill of David Gower, the belligerence of Ian Botham, the artistry of John Emburey and Phil Edmonds, the courage and defiance of Allan Border, and the dignified manner in which two teams played and mixed. Away from it, I will recall, with the fondest of memories, travelling more than 5,000 miles around Britain, enjoying the hospitality of its people. And I will never forget the magnificent men of Belfast.

Daily Telegraph 'Twin Hundreds'
by E.W. Swanton

Nothing could be less surprising than that **Ian Terence Botham** should have won the Walter Lawrence Trophy for 1985, nor more so than that the award with which my name is associated, for the winner of the race to a hundred wickets, should have gone to **Neal Victor Radford**, a 28-year-old discard from Lancashire, born in Northern Rhodesia (now Zambia), and South African educated, who after five unproductive summers at Old Trafford had sought pastures new with Worcestershire.

After two years when the Walter Lawrence Trophy was won against bowlers who were not trying, it is at least a comfort to announce that in 1985 the award has gone to Botham in healthier circumstances. True, it was against a largely inexperienced reserve attack and was made when, on the third afternoon, the match had become a certain draw that he reached his hundred from 50 balls against Warwickshire on July 26. There was, however, no suggestion of collusion as he hammered 138 not out in 67 minutes from 65 balls, including 13 sixes and 12 fours.

If these runs at Edgbaston were cheaply bought, it had not been so when Hampshire came to Taunton in late May. Somerset were 58 for four against Marshall and Tremlett when Botham arrived. Missed at third slip when 5, he went carefully until lunch, but afterwards launched forth, reaching his hundred off 76 balls and the last 133 of his 149 in only 80 balls. Oddly, he had needed just 76 balls to make another transforming, devastating hundred, also at Taunton, against Glamorgan earlier in the month.

Somerset's headquarters is a small ground, and it must have seemed like a tennis court to the suffering bowlers when this immensely powerful man, wielding a bat of awesome weight, put them to the sword.

For the latter part of the summer the bowling race was as close as could be, with young Lawrence of Gloucestershire and the formidable Malcolm Marshall jostling along with Radford, and Courtenay Walsh not far behind. Finally, in mid-September, Radford reached three figures, 101 wickets in all for 24.68 a time, 6 ahead of Marshall, who was one of only four bowlers in the country who took their wickets at less than 20 runs each.

Radford, as I write, is a stand-by choice for England's tour of West Indies in the New Year. He is a wiry fellow, strong, not tall, who can keep going all day. He bowled more first-class overs (779.4) than any save for four spinners, and his pace is generally lively and at most decidedly quick. Whether he opts to remain eligible for England or whether he prefers to play, if chosen, for South Africa remains to be seen.

Daily Telegraph Cricketers of the Year
by E.W. Swanton

In this fourth annual selection by *Daily Telegraph* correspondents of Cricketers of the Year, it is once again evident how rapidly, in this age of almost perpetual Test cricket, the cast changes, how swiftly reputations are made. There could be no better illustration of this fact than the choice (made by Michael Melford and me) of **Robert Timothy Robinson** as England's man of the year – that is of the period from October to October – even (marginally) above Mike Gatting. It took Robinson five summers to win a cap for his native Notts, and twelve months ago he had yet to put on his pads for England. Now, aged 27, he prepares to tackle the West Indian bowlers fortified by all but a thousand Test runs at an average of 62. To each of the Tests won by England, at Delhi, Headingley, and Edgbaston, he contributed innings of 150-odd. There is a determination and solidity about his batting that warms the heart.

Alan Shiell's nomination of **Kepler Christoffel Wessels** has it in common with the case of Robinson that he, too, had to wait until he was 27 to become established as a Test batsman, in his case left-handed. The circumstances were, however, different in that Wessels, an Afrikaner by birth and an itinerant by ambition, reached his goal via three South African provinces, a five-year apprenticeship with Sussex, followed by eventual domicile in Queensland and consequent Australian citizenship. Where all around him were confounded in Australia last winter by West Indian speed, Wessels survived criticism of the rawest Australian brand, confronting it to the extent of averaging 80 in his last six Test innings. Resolution and defiance, as with Robinson, were the keys to success.

Tony Cozier had no difficulty in again choosing **Malcolm Denzil Marshall**, as he explains: 'In the year under review, Marshall collected 79 wickets at 18.69 runs each in 13 Tests in England, Australia, and at home against New Zealand. Seldom did opposing batsmen appear comfortable against him and, whatever the conditions, wherever the venue, he was able to strike fire from the pitch. Valuable innings in the lower order and athletic fielding in any position enhanced his value and earned him the Man of the Series awards in successive series against Australia and New Zealand.'

In this fourth year of publication only three others have been nominated more than once: Imran Khan, Richard Hadlee, and Peter Kirsten.

By contrast with the English and Australian choices, **Ravishankar Jayadritha Shastri** was playing for India as a teenage prodigy. Today, at the age of 23, he has five Test hundreds and seven fifties to his credit, plus 73 rather expensive wickets with his slow left-arm spin. Rajan Bala believes that 'it is his unusual cricket intelligence that sets him apart,' while I see that Christopher Martin-Jenkins described him in the 'World Championship', so called, at Melbourne in March, as calm, stately and beyond his years. No one seems to doubt that this personable young man is a future captain of his country.

The selection by David Leggat of **John Reid** as New Zealand's star of 1984-85 brings us back to another batsman in his late twenties, a grafting left-hander (no relation to his namesake and former Test captain) who with an average of 85 had most to do with the home victory over Pakistan. Reid is unusual among current cricketers in that to him, despite the five Test Hundreds to his name, cricket is 'just a hobby'. Hence his declining what turned out to be a tour in the West Indies spoiled by vehement and apparently well-founded New Zealand accusations of intimidation.

Qamar Ahmed has named as Pakistan's man of the year **Wasim Akram,** almost wholly on the strength of the Test at Dunedin wherein this well-built 18-year-old left-arm medium-pacer took five wickets in each innings – clearly a youngster to be watched.

The Sri Lankan nomination, through Sa'adi Thawfeeq, of **Aravinda de Silva** likewise rewards promise rather than fulfilment. Aged 20, he was blooded against England at Lord's. I can find little statistical support for the view that he is 'Sri Lanka's most exciting batting discovery since Duleep Mendis'. We shall see.

To complete the list, we have as the South African picked by Michael Owen-Smith a name well respected in England, **Clive Edward Butler Rice.** The Notts captain, who also leads Transvaal, is rated the best in his own country. He topped the Currie Cup batting averages in 1984-85, and is reckoned to be the obvious choice as national captain against the Australian team this winter.

England's winter tour 1984-85

England in India

It is to be hoped that there will never be another tour like England's of India in 1984-85, beginning as it did with Mrs Gandhi's assassination within a few hours of their arrival in New Delhi and barely two miles from their hotel. Within a month they had had the more personal shock of the early-morning assassination in Bombay of the British Deputy High Commissioner, Mr Percy Norris, their host of the night before.

Yet the young team overcame the effects of these terrible events, and with their 2-1 Test victory made the most successful tour by an England side for many years. They were, in fact, the first team ever to come from behind to win a series in India.

The first problem which David Gower and the very able manager Tony Brown had to tackle was what to do with the England team in Delhi, where security and national mourning kept them from fitting in the practice so badly needed by a side coming out of an English winter. They went to Sri Lanka, where they were warmly welcomed and accommodated until they could start a patched-up itinerary in India.

The second blow, the assassination of Mr Norris, took place on the day before the first Test. But although England were always losing that from the first day, not a word of excuse was offered.

First meetings with a good leg-spinner can always be difficult, and the 18-year-old Sivaramakrishnan emerged with 12 wickets from the match. England's only consolation was Mike Gatting's fine 136, his first Test hundred and an innings of significance, for he was to prove the outstanding batsman, averaging nearly 100 in the series.

Before the second Test, England's revival started in the first one-day international, in Puna. Again it was Gatting who inspired it. Needing 215 to win, England were at one time 129 for six, but Gatting made 115 not out and with Downton won victory by four wickets.

For a long time in the second Test in Delhi it looked as if England would merely have the better of a draw. But after Tim Robinson's splendid 160, made with great composure and self-discipline, had earned a lead, the spin of Pat Pocock and Phil Edmonds won a largely unexpected victory on the last afternoon.

They could not yet put the one-day series out of mind, for the second of the five matches was due at Cuttack after a six-day break for Christmas and a General Election. It needed another lively effort by Downton, this time with Marks and Ellison, to win it. The Indian batting helped by losing pace after the start of 188 in 37 overs given them by Shastri and Srikkanth.

Even at this stage there were signs that, while England's morale was high, India's team spirit was threatened by internal differences. The dropping for the third Test of Kapil Dev, the much publicized disagreements between Gavaskar, Kapil Dev, and the selectors, and India's subsequent performance in the rain-affected third Test were not likely to raise India's morale. Only remonstrations from the crowd forced Gavaskar into declaring the first innings of the match on the fourth afternoon. The farcical draw on this dead pitch in Calcutta was no hardship to an England side that had just squared the series and could await its chance with confidence.

The chance came in the fourth Test in Madras. The victory there was one of England's best for many years, achieved as it was on an excellent pitch. Throughout the tour India had a depth of batting that seemed capable of swamping the slender English bowling. But Gavaskar was probably past his best and, like Kapil Dev, was never more than a potential threat. Somehow England stemmed the flood of runs that could have drowned them – agile fielding helped – and they made runs quickly enough to provide a winning platform twice. The start usually given in India by Fowler and Robinson was a refreshing change. Lamb played well and Cowdrey, Downton, and Edmonds made useful contributions. Gower was out of form, but played an invaluable innings in the final Test.

The major role, however, was played by Gatting, for it was he who snatched the initiative from the youthful Sivaramakrishnan. After his 12 for 181 in the first Test, Sivara took six for 99 in the first innings at Delhi, but the lessons were learnt from Gatting's playing of him, and from then on he took only another five wickets for 443 runs.

The double hundreds in Madras by Fowler and Gatting and the innings of Robinson and Lamb gave the England bowlers time in which to work. Hard toil lay ahead, but the job was done, largely through Neil Foster, who in taking 11 wickets in the match looked a fast-medium bowler of genuine Test class.

With this victory the series was, in effect, won – if the Kanpur mud was anything like as flat and lifeless as in former years. Though England lost the toss and had to face a huge score, they played with sense and with a spirit that never suggested they would throw away the series. The one-day series had been won 4-1 between the last two Tests, India winning only the fourth match.

The benefits from the tour included a timely boost for English cricket and for Gower's captaincy. He put his faith in his vice-captain's undoubted talents, and Gatting, given the opportunity by a captain who believed in him, produced the goods. So did Edmonds, for long a high-class all-rounder but the sort of mystic whom some captains are glad to avoid. Gower and the selectors could also be congratulated for having picked Robinson, and indeed such a happy and well-knit team overall.

The tour, of course, did little for England's fast-bowling future. But no one goes to the slow mud pitches of the subcontinent to make a name for himself as a fast bowler, and Foster's development could be looked on as a bonus.

ENGLAND'S WINTER TOUR 1984-85 / IN INDIA

First Test: Bombay, 28, 29 November, 1, 2, 3 December.
India won by 8 wickets.

England made a start from which they never recovered, though the match lasted into the fifth day. Batting with little confidence against the young leg-spinner Sivaramakrishnan, they lost eight wickets for 190 on the first day. Their bowlers did unexpectedly well in taking five wickets for 156, but by the time a seventh-wicket stand of 235 between Shastri and Kumani finished on the third afternoon and India declared with a lead of 270, there was little hope for England's survival with the ball turning inconsistently.

A second-wicket stand of 135 between Fowler and Gatting gave them a respectable start to the second innings, and Gatting's splendidly made 136 illustrated how the spin could be played. But of the later batsmen, some not too lucky with umpiring decisions, only Downton provided much resistance.

Second Test: Delhi, 12, 13, 15, 16, 17 December.
England won by 8 wickets.

Few had confidence in the lasting qualities of a slow pitch and when India recovered from a start of 140 for six to reach 307, they looked well placed. But though the bounce remained uneven and the ball turned throughout, the pitch, like so many in India, never became much worse, England batted enterprisingly, with Robinson holding one end and his partners, notably Lamb and Gatting, playing boldly at the other end. Robinson batted through the whole of the third day's play, for nine and three-quarter hours in all, and Downton led the later batsmen to a score that gave England a first innings lead of 111.

They took two wickets on the fourth day but, when at lunch on the final day India led by 93 with six wickets still standing, a draw seemed certain. However, Pocock and Edmonds brought a swift and decisive collapse as the last six wickets fell for 28 runs.

England needed 125 in what proved to be 32 overs. Never allowing India to recover the initiative, Fowler, Robinson, Gatting, and Lamb made the runs with eight overs to spare.

Third Test: Calcutta, 31 December, 1, 3, 4, 5 January.
Drawn.

After the unusually small crowds of the first two Tests, public enthusiasm was back to normal in Calcutta, but the 75,000 odd who turned up daily saw a miserable cricket match. Rain was partly to blame, for only four overs were bowled on the second day, but India's turgid progress in a first innings that lasted until the fourth afternoon – for 200 overs – completed the destruction of the match as a competitive contest. The fifth-wicket stand of 214 between Shastri and Azharuddin took seven hours, though it was given some interest by the obvious promise of the young Azharuddin. As it proved, he was making the first of three hundreds in his first three Tests, a feat never before achieved.

When Gavaskar at last declared – after the police had warned that they could not control an increasingly unruly crowd otherwise – England batted enterprisingly, Gatting making a brilliant 48 in 45 minutes and Lamb following with much the same robustness. Lacking incentive, England lost wickets but won popular acclaim.

Fourth Test: Madras, 13, 14, 15, 17, 18 January.
England won by 9 wickets.

England won a famous victory by positive batting and by twice bowling out a batting side of considerable depth on a good pitch. They may have been lucky to lose the toss, for the pitch had a quicker bounce on the first day, but India helped their downfall by an over-boisterous approach which gave them a run-rate of over four an over, but which, against the lively Neil Foster, meant that they were all out for 272 before the end of the first day.

Fowler and Robinson played safely through that evening and, though Robinson was out on the second afternoon after a fine opening stand of 178, his was the only wicket lost that day. Foster, though dropped four times, reached 149 by the second evening, and continued his stand next day with Gatting until it reached 241. Fowler's 201 was the highest by an England batsman in a Test in India, but Gatting had passed him by the time he was out on the third evening, when England were 604 for five, already 332 ahead.

They batted on next morning for five overs before starting on the tough task of bowling India out in the remaining 10½ hours. Foster immediately made a hugely important breakthrough with the new ball, removing Gavaskar, Srikkanth, and Vengsarkar in eight deliveries. Though only one more wicket fell on the fourth day, that of Mohinder Amarnath after his stand of 100 with Azharuddin, India started the last day still 134 behind. On the last morning, the spinners removed Azharuddin and Shastri. Two more wickets fell to the new ball, Foster bringing his match tally up to 11, and eventually, after a last-wicket stand of 51 between Kumani and Chetan Sharma, England needed 33 to win. They made them in eight overs with 22 overs to spare.

Fifth Test: Kanpur, 31 January, 1, 3, 4, 5 February.
Drawn

Defending their 2-1 lead was never a great problem for England on a typically lifeless Kanpur pitch, though, having lost the toss, they began their innings on the third day needing 354 to avoid the follow-on. An opening stand of 156 between Fowler and Robinson provided a suitably determined start, Gatting carried on, and, when a slightly awkward situation developed at 286 for six, Gower, in his highest innings of the series, and Edmonds soon sorted it out. On the last day, the Indian batsmen attacked violently in a desperate effort to save the series, but England had no trouble in weathering the 36 overs before India gave it up.

India v England 1984-85 1st Test
India won by 8 wickets
Played at Wankhede Stadium, Bombay, 28, 29 November, 1, 2, 3 December
Toss: England. Umpires: B. Ganguli and Swaroop Kishen
Debuts: England – C.S. Cowdrey and R.T. Robinson

England

G. Fowler	c and b Sivaramakrishnan	28	lbw b Sivaramakrishnan	55
R.T. Robinson	c Kirmani b Sivaramakrishnan	22	lbw b Kapil Dev	1
M.W. Gatting	c and b Sivaramakrishnan	15	c Patil b Sivarama	136
D.I. Gower*	b Kapil Dev	13	c Vengsarkar b Shastri	2
A.J. Lamb	c Shastri b Kapil Dev	9	st Kirmani b Sivaramakrishnan	1
C.S. Cowdrey	c Kirmani b Yadav	13	c Vengsarkar b Yadav	14
R.M. Ellison	b Sivaramakrishnan	1	(8) c Vengsarkar b Yadav	0
P.R. Downton†	not out	37	(7) lbw b Sivaramakrishnan	62
P.H. Edmonds	c Gaekwad b Shastri	48	c Kapil Dev b Sivaramakrishnan	8
P.I. Pocock	c Kirmani b Sivaramakrishnan	8	not out	22
N.G. Cowans	c Shastri b Sivaramakrishnan	0	c Vengsarkar b Sivaramakrishnan	0
Extras	(B1)	1	(B4, LB8, NB4)	16
		195		**317**

India

S.M. Gavaskar*	c Downton b Cowans	27	c Gower b Cowans	5
A.D. Gaekwad	run out	24	st Downton b Edmonds	1
D.B. Vengsarkar	c Lamb b Cowans	34	not out	21
M. Amarnath	c Cowdrey b Pocock	49	not out	22
S.M. Patil	c Gower b Edmonds	20		
R.J. Shastri	c Lamb b Pocock	142		
Kapil Dev	b Cowdrey	42		
S.M.H. Kirmani†	c Lamb b Pocock	102		
C. Sharma	not out	5		
N.S. Yadav	not out	7		
L. Sivaramakrishnan	did not bat			
Extras	(B4, LB2, NB7)	13	(B2)	2
	(8 wkts dec)	**465**	(2 wkts)	**51**

India	O	M	R	W	O	M	R	W
Kapil Dev	22	8	44	2	21	8	34	1
Sharma	11	4	28	0	9	2	39	0
Shastri	17	8	23	1	29	8	50	1
Amarnath	3	2	1	0				
Sivarama	31.2	10	64	6	46	10	117	6
Yadav	12	2	34	1	29	9	64	2
Gaekwad					1	0	1	0

England	O	M	R	W	O	M	R	W
Ellison	18	3	85	0				
Cowans	28	6	109	2	5	2	18	1
Edmonds	33	6	82	1	8	3	21	1
Pocock	46	10	133	3	2.1	0	10	0
Cowdrey	5	0	30	1				
Gatting	7	0	20	0				

Fall of Wickets

Wkt	E 1st	I 1st	E 2nd	I 2nd
1st	46	47	3	5
2nd	51	59	138	7
3rd	78	116	145	–
4th	78	156	152	–
5th	93	156	199	–
6th	94	218	222	–
7th	114	453	228	–
8th	175	453	255	–
9th	193	–	317	–
10th	195	–	317	–

ENGLAND'S WINTER TOUR 1984-85/IN INDIA

India v England 1984-85 2nd Test
England won by 8 wickets
Played at Feroz Shah Kotla, Delhi, 12, 13, 15, 16, 17 December
Toss: India. Umpires: D.N. Dotiwalla and P.D. Reporter
Debuts: India – M. Prabhakar

India

S.M. Gavaskar*	c Downton b Ellison	1	b Pocock	65
A.D. Gaekwad	b Pocock	28	(8) c Downton b Edmonds	0
D.B. Vengsarkar	st Downton b Edmonds	24	b Cowans	1
M. Amarnath	c Gower b Pocock	42	b Edmonds	64
S.M. Patil	c Pocock b Edmonds	30	c Lamb b Edmonds	41
R.J. Shastri	c Fowler b Pocock	2	not out	25
Kapil Dev	c Downton b Ellison	60	c Lamb b Pocock	7
S.M.H. Kirmani†	c Gatting b Ellison	27	(9) b Pocock	6
M. Prabhakar	c Downton b Ellison	25	(2) c Downton b Cowans	5
N.S. Yadav	not out	28	c Lamb b Edmonds	1
L. Sivaramakrishnan	run out	25	c and b Pocock	0
Extras	(B1, LB12, NB2)	15	(B6, LB10, W1, NB3)	20
		307		**235**

England

G. Fowler	c Gaekwad b Prabhakar	5	c Vengsarkar b Sivaramakrishnan	29
R.T. Robinson	c Gavaskar b Kapil Dev	160	run out	18
M.W. Gatting	b Yadav	26	not out	30
A.J. Lamb	c Vengsarkar b Yadav	52	not out	37
D.I. Gower*	lbw b Sivaramakrishnan	5		
C.S. Cowdrey	c Gavaskar b Sivaramakrishnan	38		
P.R. Downton†	c Kapil Dev b Sivaramakrishnan	74		
P.H. Edmonds	c Shastri b Sivaramakrishnan	26		
R.M. Ellison	b Sivaramakrishnan	10		
P.I. Pocock	b Sivaramakrishnan	0		
N.G. Cowans	not out	0		
Extras	(B6, LB13, NB3)	22	(B4, LB7, W2)	13
		418	(2 wkts)	**127**

England	O	M	R	W	O	M	R	W
Cowans	20	5	70	0	13	2	43	2
Ellison	26	6	66	4	7	1	20	0
Edmonds	44.2	16	83	2	44	24	60	4
Pocock	33	8	70	3	38.4	4	93	4
Gatting	2	0	5	0	1	0	3	0

India	O	M	R	W	O	M	R	W
Kapil Dev	32	5	87	1	6	0	20	0
Prabhakar	21	3	68	1	3	0	18	0
Sivaramakrishnan	49.1	17	99	6	8	0	41	1
Yadav	36	6	95	2	2	0	7	0
Shastri	29	4	44	0	4	0	20	0
Amarnath	2	0	6	0				
Gavaskar					0.4	0	10	0

Fall of Wickets

Wkt	I 1st	E 1st	I 2nd	E 2nd
1st	3	15	12	41
2nd	56	60	15	68
3rd	68	170	136	–
4th	129	181	172	–
5th	131	237	207	–
6th	140	343	214	–
7th	208	398	216	–
8th	235	411	225	–
9th	258	415	234	–
10th	307	418	235	–

India v England 1984-85 3rd Test
Match Drawn
Played at Eden Gardens, Calcutta, 31 December, 1, 3, 4, 5 January
Toss: India. Umpires: B. Ganguli and V. Raju
Debuts: India – M. Azharuddin

India

S.M. Gavaskar*	c Gatting b Edmonds	13		
A.D. Gaekwad	c Downton b Cowans	18		
D.B. Vengsarkar	b Edmonds	48		
M. Amarnath	c Cowdrey b Edmonds	42		
M. Azharuddin	c Gower b Cowans	110		
R.J. Shastri	b Cowans	111	(1) not out	7
S.M.H. Kirmani†	c Fowler b Pocock	35		
M. Prabhakar	not out	35	(2) lbw b Lamb	21
C. Sharma	not out	13		
N.S. Yadav	did not bat		(3) not out	0
L. Sivaramakrishnan				
Extras	(LB8, W1, NB3)	12	(NB1)	1
	(7 wkts dec)	437	(1 wkt)	29

England

G. Fowler	c Vengsarkar b Sivaramakrishnan	49
R.T. Robinson	b Yadav	36
D.I. Gower*	c Shastri b Yadav	19
P.I. Pocock	c Azhuruddin b Sivaramakrishnan	5
M.W. Gatting	b Yadav	48
A.J. Lamb	c Kirmani b Sharma	67
C.S. Cowdrey	lbw b Yadav	27
P.R. Downton†	not out	6
P.H. Edmonds	c Gavaskar b Sharma	8
R.M. Ellison	c and b Sharma	1
N.G. Cowans	b Sharma	1
Extras	(LB2, NB7)	9
		276

England	O	M	R	W	O	M	R	W
Cowans	41	12	103	3	4	1	6	0
Ellison	53	14	117	0	1	0	1	0
Edmonds	47	22	72	3	4	3	2	0
Pocock	52	14	108	1	2	1	4	0
Gatting	2	1						
Cowdrey	2	0	15	0	4	0	10	–
Gower	3	0	13	0				
Fowler					1	1	0	0
Robinson					1	1	0	0
Lamb					1	0	6	1

India	O	M	R	W
Sharma	12.3	0	38	4
Prabhakar	5	1	16	0
Sivaramakrishnan	28	7	90	2
Yadav	32	10	86	4
Shastri	23	6	44	0

Fall of Wickets

Wkt	I 1st	E 1st	I 2nd
1st	28	71	29
2nd	35	98	–
3rd	126	110	–
4th	127	152	–
5th	341	163	–
6th	356	229	–
7th	407	261	–
8th	–	270	–
9th	–	273	–
10th	–	276	–

Robinson retired hurt at 31 and resumed at 71.

India v England 1984-85 4th Test
England won by 9 wickets
Played at Chidambaram Stadium, Chepauk, Madras, 13, 14, 15, 17, 18 January
Toss: India. Umpires: M.Y. Gupte and V.K. Ramaswamy
Debuts: nil

India

S.M. Gavaskar*	b Foster	17		c Gatting b Foster	3
K. Srikkanth	c Downton b Cowans	0		c Cowdrey b Foster	16
D.B. Vengsarkar	c Lamb b Foster	17		c Downton b Foster	2
M. Amarnath	c Downton b Foster	78		c Cowans b Foster	95
M. Azharuddin	b Cowdrey	48		c Gower b Pocock	105
R.J. Shastri	c Downton b Foster	2		c Cowdrey b Edmonds	33
Kapil Dev	c Cowans b Cowdrey	53		c Gatting b Cowans	49
S.M.H. Kirmani†	not out	30		c Lamb b Edmonds	75
N.S. Yadav	b Foster	2	(10)	c Downton b Cowans	5
L. Sivaramakrishnan	c Cowdrey b Foster	13	(9)	lbw b Foster	5
C. Sharma	c Lamb b Cowans	5		not out	17
Extras	(LB3, NB4)	7		(B1, LB4, NB2)	7
		272			**412**

England

G. Fowler	c Kirmani b Kapil Dev	201
	c Kirmani b Sivaramakrishnan	2
R.T. Robinson	c Kirmani b Sivaramakrishnan	74
	not out	21
M.W. Gatting	c sub (Gopal Sharma) b Shastri	207
	not out	10
A.J. Lamb	b Amarnath	62
P.H. Edmonds	lbw b Shastri	36
N.A. Foster	b Amarnath	5
D.I. Gower*	b Kapil Dev	18
C.S. Cowdrey	not out	3
P.R. Downton†	not out	3
P.I. Pocock	did not bat	
N.G. Cowans	"	
Extras	(B7, LB19, NB17)	43
	(LB1, W1)	2
	(7 wkts dec)	**652**
	(1 wkt)	**35**

England	O	M	R	W	O	M	R	W
Cowans	12.5	3	39	2	15	1	73	2
Foster	23	2	104	6	28	8	59	5
Edmonds	6	1	33	0	41.5	13	119	2
Cowdrey	19	1	65	2	5	0	26	0
Pocock	7	1	28	0	33	8	130	1

India	O	M	R	W	O	M	R	W
Kapil Dev	36	5	131	2	3	0	20	0
Sharma	18	0	95	0				
Sivaramakrishnan	44	6	145	1	4	0	12	1
Yadav	23	4	76	0				
Shastri	42	7	143	2	1	0	2	0
Amarnath	12	1	36	2				

Fall of Wickets

Wkt	I 1st	E 1st	I 2nd	E 2nd
1st	17	178	7	7
2nd	17	419	19	–
3rd	45	563	22	–
4th	155	599	212	–
5th	167	604	259	–
6th	167	640	259	–
7th	241	646	341	–
8th	243	–	350	–
9th	263	–	361	–
10th	272	–	412	–

India v England 1984-85 5th Test
Match Drawn
Played at Green Park, Kanpur, 31 January, 1, 3, 4, 5 February
Toss: India. Umpires: V.K. Ramaswamy and P.D. Reporter
Debuts: India – Gopal Sharma

India

S.M. Gavaskar*	b Cowans	9		
K. Srikkanth	c Downton b Foster	84	not out	41
M. Azharuddin	c sub (R.M. Ellison) b Cowdrey	122	not out	54
M. Amarnath	b Cowans	15		
D.B. Vengsarkar	c Downton b Foster	137		
A. Malhotra	lbw b Pocock	27		
R.J. Shastri	b Edmonds	59	(1) run out	2
Kapil Dev	c Gower b Foster	42		
S.M.H. Kirmani†	not out	16		
L. Sivaramakrishnan	not out	16		
G. Sharma	did not bat			
Extras	(B9, LB12, W5)	26		
	(8 wkts dec)	553	(1 wkt dec)	97

England

G. Fowler	c Kirmani b Shastri	69		
R.T. Robinson	lbw b Kapil Dev	96	retired hurt	16
M.W. Gatting	c and b Sharma	62	not out	41
A.J. Lamb	c Srikkanth b Shastri	13		
D.I. Gower*	lbw b Shastri	78	(1) not out	32
C.S. Cowdrey	c Kirmani b Sharma	1		
P.R. Downton†	b Sharma	1		
P.H. Edmonds	lbw b Kapil Dev	49		
N.A. Foster	c Kirmani b Kapil Dev	8		
P.I. Pocock	not out	4		
N.G. Cowans	b Kapil Dev	9		
Extras	(B10, LB17)	27	(LB2)	2
		417	(0 wkt)	91

England	O	M	R	W	O	M	R	W
Cowans	36	9	115	2	7	0	51	0
Foster	36	8	123	3				
Pocock	24	2	79	1				
Edmonds	48	16	112	1				
Cowdrey	21	1	103	1	5	0	39	0
Gatting					1	0	7	0

India	O	M	R	W	O	M	R	W
Kapil Dev	36.5	7	81	4	5	0	19	0
Amarnath	4	1	6	0				
Sharma	60	16	115	3	11	4	17	0
Sivaramakrishnan	54	11	133	0	10	2	22	0
Shastri	32	13	52	3	7	2	12	0
Malhotra	2	0	3	0				
Srikkanth					2	0	11	0
Azharuddin					1	0	8	0

Fall of Wickets

Wkt	I 1st	E 1st	I 2nd	E 2nd
1st	19	156	2	–
2nd	169	196	–	–
3rd	209	222	–	–
4th	277	276	–	–
5th	362	278	–	–
6th	457	286	–	–
7th	511	386	–	–
8th	533	402	–	–
9th	–	404	–	–
10th	–	417	–	–

Robinson retired hurt at 36

Test Match Averages: India v England 1984-85

India

Batting and Fielding	M	I	NO	HS	R	Avge	100	50	Ct/St
M. Azharuddin	3	5	1	122	439	109.75	3	1	1
S.M.H. Kirmani	5	7	2	102	291	58.20	1	1	10/1
M. Amarnath	5	8	1	95	407	58.14	–	3	–
R.J. Shastri	5	9	2	142	383	54.71	2	1	4
K. Srikkanth	2	4	1	84	141	47.00	–	1	1
Kapil Dev	4	6	0	60	253	42.16	–	2	2
D.B. Vengsarkar	5	8	1	137	284	40.57	1	–	7
C. Sharma	3	4	3	17*	40	40.00	–	–	1
S.M. Patil	2	3	0	41	91	30.33	–	–	1
M. Prabhakar	2	4	1	35*	86	28.66	–	–	–
S.M. Gavaskar	5	8	0	65	140	17.50	–	1	3
L. Sivaramakrishnan	5	5	1	25	59	14.75	–	–	2
N.S. Yadav	4	6	3	28*	43	14.33	–	–	–
A.D. Gaekwad	3	5	0	28	71	14.20	–	–	2

Played in one Test: A. Malhotra 27; G. Sharma (1 ct) did not bat.

Bowling	O	M	R	W	Avge	Best	5wI	10wM
L. Sivaramakrishnan	274.3	63	723	23	31.43	6-64	3	1
N.S. Yadav	134	31	362	9	40.22	4-86	–	–
Kapil Dev	161.5	33	436	10	43.60	4-81	–	–
R.J. Shastri	184	48	390	7	55.71	3-52	–	–

Also bowled: M. Azharuddin 1-0-8-0; M. Amarnath 21-4-49-2; C. Sharma 50.3-6-200-4; A.D. Gaekwad 1-0-1-0; S.M. Gavaskar 0.4-0-10-0; G. Sharma 71-20-132-3; A. Malhotra 2-0-3-0; M. Prabhakar 29-4-102-1; K. Srikkanth 2-0-11-0.

England

Batting and Fielding	M	I	NO	HS	R	Avge	100	50	Ct/St
M.W. Gatting	5	9	3	207	575	95.83	2	1	4
R.T. Robinson	5	9	2	160	444	63.42	1	2	–
P.R. Downton	5	6	3	74	183	61.00	–	2	14/2
G. Fowler	5	8	0	201	438	54.75	1	2	2
A.J. Lamb	5	7	1	67	241	40.16	–	3	9
P.H. Edmonds	5	6	0	49	175	29.16	–	–	–
D.I. Gower	5	7	1	78	167	27.83	–	1	6
C.S. Cowdrey	5	6	1	38	96	19.20	–	–	5
P.I. Pocock	5	5	2	22*	39	13.00	–	–	2
N.A. Foster	2	2	0	8	13	6.50	–	–	–
R.M. Ellison	3	4	0	10	12	3.00	–	–	–
N.G. Cowans	5	5	1	9	10	2.50	–	–	2

Bowling	O	M	R	W	Avge	Best	5wI	10wM
N.A. Foster	87	18	286	14	20.42	6-104	2	1
P.H. Edmonds	276.1	104	584	14	41.71	4-60	–	–
N.G. Cowans	181.5	41	627	14	44.78	3-103	–	–
P.I. Pocock	237.5	53	655	13	50.38	4-93	–	–

Also bowled: C.S. Cowdrey 61-2-288-4; R.M. Ellison 105-24-289-4; G. Fowler 1-1-0-0; M.W. Gatting 13-1-36-0; D.I. Gower 3-0-13-0; A.J. Lamb 1-0-6-1; R.T. Robinson 1-1-0-0.

Statistical Highlights of the Tests

1st Test, Bombay. India's win ended a sequence of 31 matches without success and extended a similar spell by England to a record 13 Tests. It was England's eighth defeat in 1984, equalling the unprecedented fate of India in 1959. The selection of Christopher Cowdrey enabled Pocock to become only the second England Player after Wilfred Rhodes (who appeared with Fred and Maurice Tate) to take the field with two generations of the same family. Cowdrey bowled Kapil Dev with his fourth ball in Test cricket and caused his father, Colin, listening in London to the 'Test Match Special' commentary, to drive in the wrong direction along a one-way street. Kapil Dev became the second Indian after Bishan Bedi to take 250 Test wickets. The partnership of 235 between Shastri and Kirmani, who both registered their highest Test scores, established a seventh-wicket record for India against all countries. Gavaskar completed 1,000 runs in Tests at the Wankhede Stadium. Downton's 62 was his highest innings in Tests. Sivaramakrishnan (12 for 181) returned the second-best Indian match analysis against England after 'Vinoo' Mankad's 12 for 108 at Madras in 1951-52.

2nd Test, Delhi. Gower led England to victory for the first time in 11 attempts. This success enabled them to end their worst sequence of 13 matches without a win. Playing in only his second Test, Robinson recorded the 100th century in this series. His partnership of 110 with Lamb was England's first of three figures for the third wicket in India. Downton (74) registered his highest Test score for the second innings in succession. Amarnath completed 3,000 runs in his 46th Test.

3rd Test, Calcutta. Sunil Gavaskar appeared in his 88th successive Test to claim the world record from his brother-in-law, Gundappa Viswanath. Mohammad Azharuddin (21) became the seventh batsman to score a century in his first Test for India. He reached it off 288 balls, in 382 minutes, with 8 fours. Shastri's fifth Test hundred took 422 minutes (330 balls) and was the second-slowest in all Tests for India after Vengsarkar's 437-minute epic against Pakistan at Delhi in 1979-80. Within a week, Shastri was to score the fastest 200 in all first-class cricket and equal another world record by hitting six sixes in one over. His partnership of 214 with Azharuddin was India's highest for the fifth wicket against England, beating 190 by the Nawab of Pataudi and Chandu Borde at Delhi in 1963-64. Shastri was the fourth batsman after M.L. 'Jai' Jaisimha, Geoffrey Boycott, and Kim Hughes to bat on all five days of a Test match. Fowler scored his 1,000th run in 19 Tests.

4th Test, Madras. For the first time a visiting team in India led the rubber after being a match down. England's total of 652-7 declared was their highest against India (beating 633-5d at Edgbaston in 1979), the highest in any Test in India, their fourth-highest against all countries, and their highest since 1938-39. Fowler (201) and Gatting (207) were the first pair to score double hundreds in the same innings for England in 610 Test matches since 1877; it was the sixth such instance in all Test cricket. The previous highest score for England in India was 179 by Dennis Amiss at Delhi in 1976-77. Fowler shared in record England partnerships for this series of 178 with Robinson and 241 with Gatting. Azharuddin was only the fourth batsman after Bill Ponsford, Doug Walters and Alvin Kallicharran to score hundreds in each of his first two Tests. The tenth-wicket partnership of 51 between Kirmani and Chetan Sharma equalled India's record against England set in 1963-64 by Nadkarni and Chandrasekhar at Calcutta. Foster (11 for 163) achieved the best match analysis of his first-class career; he was the second bowler after Alec Bedser (Lord's 1946) to take 11 wickets in his first Test against India.

5th Test, Kanpur. Gower became the third captain after Douglas Jardine and Tony Greig to lead England to victory in India, and the first to do so from any country after being a match down. Not since 1954-55 in Australia had England won a rubber overseas after losing the first Test. It was England's first victorious expedition overseas since they beat Australia in 1978-79. Azharuddin, whose second fifty occupied only 38 balls, bacame the first batsman to score hundreds in each of his first three Test matches. India's total of 553-8 declared was their highest against England, exceeding 510 at Leeds in 1967. Gopal Sharma was the first Uttar Pradesh cricketer to represent India since 1936, when the Maharajkumar of Vizianagram led his country in their first three-match rubber in England. Vengsarkar scored his ninth hundred in 124 innings (76 Tests), while Srikkanth (84) recorded his highest score at this level.

One-Day Internationals

5 December at Nehru Stadium, Poona. ENGLAND won by 4 wickets. Toss: England. India 214-6 closed (45 overs) (K. Srikkanth 50, D.B. Vengsarkar 105). England 215-6 (43.2 overs) (M.W. Gatting 115*). Awards: D.B. Vengsarkar (105) and M.W. Gatting (115*).

27 December at Baribati Stadium, Cuttack. ENGLAND won on scoring rate (bad light). Toss: England. India 252-5 closed (49 overs) (K. Srikkanth 99, R.J. Shastri 102). England 241-6 (46 overs) (M.W. Gatting 59). Award: R.J. Shastri (102, 10-0-48-0, and 1 ct).

20 January at Chinnaswamy Stadium, Bangalore. ENGLAND won by 3 wickets. Toss: England. India 205-6 closed (46 overs). England 206-7 (45 overs) (A.J. Lamb 59*). Award: A.J. Lamb (59*).

23 January at Vidarbha C.A. Ground, Nagpur. INDIA won by 3 wickets. Toss: India. England 240-7 closed (50 overs) (M.D. Moxon 70; R.J. Shastri 10-1-40-4). India 241-7 (47.4 overs) (S.M. Gavaskar 52, Kapil Dev 54). Award: Kapil Dev (54 and 10-1-42-1).

27 January at Sector 16 Stadium, Chandigarh. ENGLAND won by 7 runs. Toss: India. England 121-6 closed (15 overs). India 114-5 closed (15 overs) (R.J. Shastri 53). Award: R.J. Shastri (53 and 3-0-30-1).

Tour Statistical Summary

England Tour of India and Sri Lanka 1984-85

First-Class Matches: Played 12; Won 3, Lost 2, Drawn 7
All Matches: Played 18; Won 7, Lost 3, Drawn 8

First-Class Averages

Batting and Fielding	M	I	NO	HS	R	Avge	100	50	Ct/St
M.W. Gatting	11	17	5	207	1029	85.75	3	4	10
M.D. Moxon	3	4	0	153	231	57.75	1	–	2
R.T. Robinson	11	18	3	160	861	57.40	3	3	1
G. Fowler	10	15	0	201	727	48.46	3	2	3
A.J. Lamb	10	14	2	67	441	36.75	–	4	13
D.I. Gower	11	15	1	86	482	34.42	–	4	10
N.A. Foster	7	8	4	29	128	32.00	–	–	2
P.R. Downton	9	11	3	74	238	29.75	–	2	20/3
C.S. Cowdrey	9	11	1	70	211	21.10	–	1	9
V.J. Marks	6	8	1	66	142	20.28	–	1	1
P.H. Edmonds	11	12	0	49	241	20.08	–	–	5
R.M. Ellison	8	10	1	83*	152	16.88	–	1	2
P.J.W. Allott	3	3	1	14	29	14.50	–	–	–
B.N. French	4	5	0	19	63	12.60	–	–	12/2
P.I. Pocock	8	9	3	22*	48	8.00	–	–	2
N.G. Cowans	10	8	1	10	21	3.00	–	–	3

Played in one match: J.P. Agnew 12*.

Bowling	O	M	R	W	Avge	Best	5wI	10wM
N.A. Foster	230.1	58	655	29	22.58	6-104	2	1
J.P. Agnew	45	4	205	7	29.28	5-102	1	–
P.H. Edmonds	498.1	184	1019	32	31.84	4-13	–	–
N.G. Cowans	267.5	60	916	25	36.64	3-59	–	–
P.I. Pocock	321.1	73	932	23	40.52	4-57	–	–
V.J. Marks	121	28	321	7	45.85	4-48	–	–
C.S. Cowdrey	114	12	442	9	49.11	3-61	–	–
R.M. Ellison	210.1	57	550	11	50.00	4-66	–	–

Also bowled: P.J.W. Allott 62.1-11-209-2; G. Fowler 1-1-0-0; M.W. Gatting 34-2-90-1; D. Gower 3-0-13-0; A.J. Lamb 2-1-6-1; R.T. Robinson 1-1-0-0.

Overseas cricket
1984-85

Pakistan v India

India's tour of Pakistan, due to last a month from mid-October 1984, was cut short by the assassination of Mrs Gandhi which led the Indian team to return home after two of the scheduled three Test matches had been played.

The premature end of the series was largely unregretted. There was little public interest, even in the first Test, in Lahore, and two drawn Tests did little to stimulate it. Nor did a bitter attack launched on certain Pakistan umpires by the Indian captain Sunil Gavaskar create a congenial atmosphere for a third Test, which would have been played in the often turbulent setting of Karachi.

Pakistan could be said to have had the better of the two Tests as they made India follow on in the first and led on the first and only innings in the second. At Lahore, their captain Zaheer Abbas sustained his side's innings for nine hours until he declared at 428 for nine. India then collapsed on the third afternoon from 112 for two, losing their last eight wickets for 44 runs to the young left-arm fast-medium bowler Azeem Hafeez, who plays under the disadvantage of a deformed right hand, and a steady partner in Mudassar. Though making no secret that they were unhappy about the umpiring, India cleared off the deficit of 272 for the loss of four wickets, and Amarnath batted through for a draw, making 101 not out.

At Faisalabad, the second Test was predictably drawn on one of the easiest batting pitches in the world. With a hundred apiece for Patil and Shastri, India mustered exactly 500.

Kapil Dev was soon prevented from bowling by a back injury, and they had small chance of restricting the Pakistan batsmen, of whom Mudassar, 199, Qasim Omar, 210, and Saleem Malik, 102 not out, were the most prolific. In the match, 1,174, runs were scored for the loss of only 16 wickets, one of those run out.

Of the two one-day internationals played, Pakistan, put in by Gavaskar, did well to make 199 for seven in difficult conditions in distant Quetta and won by 46 runs. By contrast, on an excellent pitch in Rawalpindi two days later India made 260 for two in only 39 overs and won by 57 runs.

Pakistan v India 1984-85 1st Test
Match Drawn
Played at Gaddafi Stadium, Lahore, 17, 18, 19, 21, 22 October
Toss: Pakistan. Umpires: Khizer Hayat and Shakoor Rana
Debuts: India – Chetan Sharma

Pakistan

Mohsin Khan	b Sharma	4
Mudassar Nazar	c Gavaskar b Sharma	15
Qasim Omar	c Amarnath b Shastri	46
Javad Miandad	c Amarnath b Sharma	34
Zaheer Abbas*	not out	168
Salim Malik	c and b Shastri	45
Wasim Raja	c Amarnath b Kapil Dev	3
Ashraf Ali†	c Gavaskar b Gaekwad	65
Tausif Ahmed	c Gavaskar b Maninder	10
Jalaluddin	lbw b Shastri	2
Azeem Hafeez	not out	17
Extras	(LB7, W1, NB11)	19
	(9 wickets declared)	**428**

India

S.M. Gavaskar*	c Salim b Azeem	48		lbw b Jalaluddin	37
A.D. Gaekwad	b Jalaluddin	4		c Salim b Tausif	60
D.B. Vengsarkar	c Ashraf b Azeem	41		c Mudassar b Azeem	28
M. Amarnath	b Wasim	36		not out	101
S.M. Patil	c Salim b Azeem	0		b Jalaluddin	7
R.J. Shastri	lbw b Azeem	0		lbw b Salim	71
Kapil Dev	lbw b Azeem	3	(8)	not out	33
R.M.H. Binny	lbw b Mudassar	0	(7)	lbw b Wasim	13
S.M.H. Kirmani†	c sub (Ramiz Raja) b Mudassar	2			
C. Sharma	b Azeem	4			
Maninder Singh	not out	4			
Extras	(B2, LB7, W1, NB4)	14		(B6, LB7, W4, NB4)	21
		156		(6 wickets)	**371**

India	O	M	R	W
Kapil Dev	30	4	104	1
Sharma	29	2	94	3
Binny	8	1	20	0
Maninder	40	10	90	1
Shastri	46	13	90	3
Amarnath	4	0	19	0
Gaekwad	1	0	4	1

Pakistan	O	M	R	W	O	M	R	W
Jalaluddin	17	5	41	1	24	3	61	2
Azeem Hafeez	23	7	46	6	43	12	114	1
Mudassar Nawaz	16	2	31	2	14	3	34	0
Tausif Ahmed	13	3	19	0	50	19	93	1
Wasim Raja	5.3	0	10	1	19	4	46	1
Salim Malik					5	2	6	1
Javed Miandad					1	0	4	0

Fall of Wickets

Wkt	P 1st	I 1st	I 2nd
1st	6	7	85
2nd	54	94	114
3rd	100	112	148
4th	110	114	164
5th	195	114	290
6th	212	119	315
7th	354	120	–
8th	394	130	–
9th	397	135	–
10th	–	156	–

Pakistan v India 1984-85 2nd Test
Match Drawn
Played at Iqbal Stadium, Faisalabad, 24, 25, 26, 28, 29 October
Toss: India. Umpires: Amanullah Hussain and Mahboob Shah
Debuts: Pakistan – Manzoor Elahi

India

S.M. Gavaskar*	c Omar b Qadir	35
A.D. Gaekwad	c and b Manzoor	74
D.B. Vengsarkar	c Mohsin b Qadir	5
M. Amarnath	hit wkt b Azeem	37
S.M. Patil	c Zaheer b Mudassar	127
R.J. Shastri	c Ashraf b Qadir	139
Kapil Dev	c Ashraf b Azeem	16
Madan Lal	c Ashraf b Azeem	0
S.M.H. Kirmani†	c sub (Shoaib Mohammad) b Azeem	6
N.S. Yadav	c Salim b Qadir	29
C. Sharma	not out	18
Extras	(B1, LB6, NB7)	14
		500

Pakistan

Mohsin Khan	c Gavaskar b Sharma	59
Mudassar Nazar	c Kirmani b Yadav	199
Qasim Omar	c Yadav b Gaekwad	210
Javad Miandad	st Kirmani b Shastri	16
Zaheer Abbas*	c Kirmani b Madan Lal	26
Salim Malik	not out	102
Manzoor Elahi	run out	26
Ashraf Ali†	not out	9
Abdul Qadir	did not bat	
Jalaluddin	"	
Azeem Hafeez	"	
Extras	(B7, LB6, W1, NB13)	27
	(6 wickets)	**674**

Pakistan	O	M	R	W
Jalaluddin	34	5	103	0
Azeem Hafeez	44	9	137	4
Mudassar Nazar	21	3	74	1
Manzoor Elahi	25	5	74	1
Abdul Qadir	38	8	104	4
Salim Malik	1	0	1	0

India	O	M	R	W
Kapil Dev	5	0	22	0
Sharma	32	0	139	1
Madan Lal	27	2	94	1
Yadav	74	16	196	1
Shastri	50	14	99	1
Gaekwad	27	5	75	1
Amarnath	8.5	0	36	0

Fall of Wickets

	I	P
Wkt	1st	1st
1st	88	141
2nd	100	391
3rd	148	430
4th	170	494
5th	370	608
6th	412	650
7th	420	–
8th	441	–
9th	461	–
10th	500	–

Statistical Highlights of the Tests

1st Test, Lahore. Sunil Gavaskar (35) became the fourth and youngest player after Colin Cowdrey, Geoffrey Boycott, and Clive Lloyd to play in 100 Test matches. Chetan Sharma, aged 18 years 288 days, bowled Mohsin with his fifth ball in Test cricket – the third Indian to take a wicket in his first over at this level. Zaheer and Amarnath each recorded their third hundreds at Lahore in this series; Zaheer's was his 12th in Tests (equalling Hanif Mohammad's Pakistan record) and sixth against India, while Amarnath's eighth Test century was his fourth against Pakistan. Zaheer's partnership of 142 with Ashraf Ali was Pakistan's highest for the seventh wicket against India, beating 88 by Mushtaq Mohammad and Intikhab Alam at Calcutta in 1960-61. Azeem's analysis of 6 for 46 was his best in Test cricket and included a spell of 4 for 5.

2nd Test, Faisalabad. Only 16 wickets fell in five days of uninterrupted play at an average cost of 73 runs. Gavaskar became the first batsman to score 8,500 in Tests. Abdul Qadir took his 100th Test wicket in 28 matches when he dismissed Salim. He was the sixth Pakistan bowler to achieve this feat. India recorded their highest score in Pakistan (previously 465 at Lahore in 1978-79). It included a fifth-wicket partnership of 200 between Patil and Shastri – the highest by India for any wicket against Pakistan. Pakistan gained a first innings lead on the last day, their total of 674-6 being their highest in Test cricket (previously 657-8 against West Indies at Bridgetown in 1957-58). Qasim Omar (675 minutes, 442 balls, 27 fours) compiled the highest score by a Kenyan in Test cricket, his partnership of 250 with Mudassar Nazar being the highest for the second wicket by either side in this series (beating 246 by Hanif Mohammad and Saeed Ahmed at Bombay in 1960-61). Mudassar (552 minutes, 408 balls, 24 fours) registered his seventh century in Tests and his sixth against India, while Salim Malik's fourth Test hundred was his third at the Iqbal Stadium. This was the 35th encounter between these countries and the 25th to be drawn.

One-Day Internationals

12 October at Ayub Stadium, Quetta. PAKISTAN won by 46 runs. Toss: India. Pakistan 199-7 closed (40 overs) (Zaheer Abbas 55). India 153 (37.1 overs). Award: Manzoor Elahi (36 and 4-0-18-2).

31 October at Jinnah Stadium, Sialkot. NO RESULT (this match and the remainder of the tour were abandoned following news of the assassination of Mrs Gandhi). Toss: Pakistan. India 210-3 closed (40 overs) (D.B. Vengsarkar 94*, S.M. Patil 59). No award.

India v Australia (1-day)

Australia won a one-day series in India 3-0, but the experiment was not a success overall. Two matches had to be abandoned through rain, the itinerary was a hectic one involving five matches in different parts of India within nine days, and the lorry carrying the Australian team's kit arrived late, causing a two-hour delay to the start of the unofficial third match in Jamshedpur. The onset of rain then restricted play to 5.1 overs (during which India made 21-2). As a result of the Jamshedpur farce, the arrangements for the tour came under criticism, not least in the Indian Press.

The tour, beginning in late September, was not considered a good augury for the holding of the World Cup in India and Pakistan in October and November 1987, though a fairer comment at this stage was that it provided the World Cup organizers with useful experience of the practical difficulties. Doubts about the weather for the 1987 tournament were not strictly relevant, for the World Cup will begin much later in October, when the last effects of the monsoon should have died away.

On the playing side, Australia, captained by Kim Hughes, had good reason to be pleased with their pre-season trip. India were not disgraced, but gave no hint that by the end of the season they would have found a team to win the 'Mini-World Cup' in Australia.

One-Day Internationals

28 September at Jawaharlal Nehru Stadium, New Delhi (floodlit). AUSTRALIA won by 48 runs. Toss: Australia. Australia 220-9 closed (48 overs) (K.C. Wessels 107, K.J. Hughes 72). India 171 (40.5 overs) (C.G. Rackemann 10-1-41-4). Award: K.C. Wessels (107).

1 October at University Stadium, Trivandrum. NO RESULT (rain). Toss: Australia. India 175 (37 overs) (D.B. Vengsarkar 77; T.G. Hogan 8-0-33-4). Australia 29-1 (7.4 overs). No award.

5 October at Sardar Patel Stadium, Ahmedabad. AUSTRALIA won by 7 wickets. Toss: Australia. India 206-6 closed (46 overs) (R.M.H. Binny 57). Australia 210-3 (43.5 overs) (A.R. Border 62*). Award: G.F. Lawson (10-2-25-3).

6 October at Nehru Stadium, Indore. AUSTRALIA won by 6 wickets. Toss: Australia. India 235-5 closed (44 overs) (R.J. Shastri 102). Australia 236-4 (40.1 overs) (S.B. Smith 56, G.M. Ritchie 59*). Award: R.J. Shastri (102 and 6-0-35-0).

Australia v West Indies

The West Indies' emphatic 3-1 win in this inaptly billed 'Showdown for the Crown' series completed for Clive Hubert Lloyd the revenge he had been seeking in Australia since his team was thrashed 5-1 by Ian Chappell's side in 1975-76. Yet it was cruelly ironic that the most successful captain in the history of Test cricket should lose his last match after the West Indies had gone a record 27 Tests without defeat.

The West Indies retained the Frank Worrell Trophy through winning the first three Tests by wide margins. Lloyd's curious decision to delay his second innings' declaration enabled Australia to scramble a draw in Melbourne (with only two wickets in hand, they still were 171 runs behind), and Australia pulled off a stunning victory in Sydney.

Australia used 19 players in the series, with only four – batsmen Kepler Wessels, Allan Border, and Graeme Wood and fast bowler Geoff Lawson – appearing in all five Tests. The West Indies needed only 12 players; their one change being the inclusion of off-spinning all-rounder Roger Harper for injured speedster Michael Holding in Adelaide and Melbourne.

The West Indies fast bowlers dominated the series, collecting 75 of Australia's 87 wickets. They were assisted by an extraordinarily high standard of fielding and catching, particularly by acrobatic wicketkeeper Jeff Dujon and the glue-fingered slips cordon of Lloyd, Viv Richards, Richie Richardson, and Gordon Greenidge.

Australian fast bowlers suffered because of probably the worst collective catching effort ever produced by an Australian team. No fewer than 26 catches were missed, and this had a demoralizing effect on players already haunted and taunted by the West Indies' incessant pace-bowling barrage.

Kim Hughes resigned as Australian captain after the second Test, the fifth in succession he had lost to Lloyd. Hughes had led Australia in 28 Tests – for 4 wins, 13 losses, and 11 draws. In tears at an emotion-charged Press conference, Hughes could not read all of a prepared statement, which said, in part: 'The constant speculation, criticism, and innuendo by former players and sections of the media have finally taken their toll.' Hughes's confidence and form deserted him, and he was not chosen for the fifth Test, following scores of 4, 37, 34, 4, 0, 2, 0, and 0.

Border settled into the captaincy quickly and comfortably enough, helped by his own grim determination, the dual success (70 and 113) of new opening batsman Andrew Hilditch in Melbourne (he had been recalled after five years), the belligerent quick bowling of youngster McDermott in Melbourne and Sydney, and the fairytale performances of home-state spinners Holland and Bennett in Sydney.

Slow over rates by both teams caused considerable dissatisfaction among Australian administrators: some on-the-field disagreements prompted Wes Hall, the West Indies' team manager, to express his regret at the deterioration in relations between the teams; and the aggregate crowd of 339,933 was well below that expected, even allowing for Australia's losing the first three Tests so convincingly. The breakdown was: 49,592 (Perth), 35,313 (Brisbane), 56,558 (Adelaide), 97,271 (Melbourne), and 101,199 (Sydney).

Australia v West Indies 1984-85 1st Test
West Indies won by an innings and 112 runs
Played at WACA Ground, Perth, 9, 10, 11, 12 November
Toss: West Indies. Umpires: A.R. Crafter and P.J. McConnell
Debuts: West Indies – C.A. Walsh

West Indies

C.G. Greenidge	c Rackemann b Alderman	30
D.L. Haynes	c Yallop b Hogg	56
R.B. Richardson	b Alderman	0
H.A. Gomes	b Hogg	127
I.V.A. Richards	c Phillips b Alderman	10
C.H. Lloyd*	c Phillips b Alderman	0
P.J.L. Dujon†	c Phillips b Alderman	139
M.D. Marshall	c Hughes b Hogg	21
M.A. Holding	c Wood b Alderman	1
J. Garner	c Phillips b Hogg	17
C.A. Walsh	not out	9
Extras	(B1, LB1, NB4)	6
		416

Australia

K.C. Wessels	c Holding b Garner	13	c Lloyd b Garner		0
J. Dyson	c Lloyd b Marshall	0	b Marshall		30
G.M. Wood	c Lloyd b Garner	6	c Richardson b Walsh		56
A.R. Border	c Dujon b Holding	15	c Haynes b Marshall		6
K.J. Hughes*	c Marshall b Holding	4	lbw b Marshall		37
G.N. Yallop	c Greenidge b Holding	2	c Haynes b Walsh		1
W.B. Phillips†	c Marshall b Holding	22	c Dujon b Garner		16
G.F. Lawson	c Dujon b Marshall	1	not out		38
R.M. Hogg	b Holding	0	b Marshall		0
C.G. Rackemann	c Richardson b Holding	0	b Garner		0
T.M. Alderman	not out	0	c Richardson b Holding		23
Extras	(B4, LB2, NB7)	13	(LB7, NB14)		21
		76			**228**

Australia	O	M	R	W				
Lawson	24	3	79	0				
Rackemann	28	3	106	0				
Hogg	32	6	101	4				
Alderman	39	12	128	6				

West Indies	O	M	R	W	O	M	R	W
Marshall	15	7	25	2	21	4	68	4
Garner	7	0	24	2	16	5	52	3
Holding	9.2	3	21	6	11.3	1	53	1
Walsh					20	4	43	2
Gomes					1	0	1	0
Richards					1	0	4	0

Fall of Wickets

Wkt	WI 1st	A 1st	A 2nd
1st	83	1	4
2nd	83	18	94
3rd	89	28	107
4th	104	40	107
5th	104	46	124
6th	186	55	166
7th	335	58	168
8th	337	63	168
9th	387	63	169
10th	416	76	228

Dujon retired hurt at 155 and resumed at 186.

Australia v West Indies 1984-85 2nd Test
West Indies won by 8 wickets
Played at Woolloongabba, Brisbane, 23, 24, 25, 26 November
Toss: West Indies. Umpires: R.A. French and M.W. Johnson
Debuts: Australia – D.C. Boon, R.G. Holland

Australia

J. Dyson	c Dujon b Holding	13	c Dujon b Marshall	21
K.C. Wessels	b Garner	0	c Gomes b Walsh	61
G.M. Wood	c Marshall b Walsh	20	c Richardson b Holding	3
A.R. Border	c Lloyd b Marshall	17	c sub (R.A. Harper) b Holding	24
K.J. Hughes*	c Marshall b Garner	34	lbw b Holding	4
D.C. Boon	c Richardson b Marshall	11	c Holding b Marshall	51
W.B. Phillips†	c Dujon b Walsh	44	(8) c sub (R.A. Harper) b Holding	54
G.F. Lawson	b Garner	14	(9) c Richards b Marshall	14
T.M. Alderman	c Lloyd b Walsh	0	(7) c Richardson b Marshall	1
R.G. Holland	c Dujon b Garner	6	b Marshall	0
R.M. Hogg	not out	0	not out	21
Extras	(B4, LB1, NB11)	16	(B4, LB5, NB8)	17
		175		**271**

West Indies

C.G. Greenidge	c Border b Lawson	44		
D.L. Haynes	b Alderman	21	(1) b Lawson	7
R.B. Richardson	c Phillips b Alderman	138	(2) c Alderman b Hogg	5
H.A. Gomes	b Holland	13	(3) not out	9
I.V.A. Richards	c Boon b Lawson	6	(4) not out	3
P.J.L. Dujon†	c Phillips b Holland	14		
C.H. Lloyd*	c Hughes b Alderman	114		
M.D. Marshall	b Lawson	57		
M.A. Holding	b Lawson	1		
J. Garner	not out	0		
C.A. Walsh	c Phillips b Lawson	0		
Extras	(B2, LB6, NB8)	16	(LB2)	2
		424	(2 wkts)	**26**

West Indies	O	M	R	W	O	M	R	W
Garner	18.4	5	67	4	20	4	80	0
Marshall	14.4	5	39	2	34	7	82	5
Holding	6.2	2	9	1	30	7	92	4
Walsh	16	5	55	3	5	2	7	1
Richards					1	0	1	0

Australia	O	M	R	W	O	M	R	W
Lawson	30.4	8	116	5	5	0	10	1
Alderman	29	10	107	3				
Hogg	21	3	71	0	4.1	0	14	1
Holland	27	5	97	2				
Border	5	0	25	0				

Fall of Wickets

Wkt	A 1st	WI 1st	A 2nd	WI 2nd
1st	1	36	88	6
2nd	33	99	88	18
3rd	33	129	99	–
4th	81	142	106	–
5th	97	184	131	–
6th	102	336	212	–
7th	122	414	236	–
8th	136	423	236	–
9th	173	424	271	–
10th	175	424	271	–

Australia v West Indies 1984-85 3rd Test
West Indies won by 191 runs
Played at Adelaide Oval, 7, 8, 9, 10, 11 December
Toss: West Indies. Umpires: A.R. Crafter and M.W. Johnson
Debuts: nil

West Indies

C.G. Greenidge	c Hogg b Lawson	95	lbw b Lawson	4
D.L. Haynes	c Hughes b Hogg	0	c Wood b Lawson	50
R.B. Richardson	c Border b Lawson	8	(4) lbw b Hogg	3
H.A. Gomes	c Rixon b Lawson	60	(5) not out	120
I.V.A. Richards	c Rixon b Lawson	0	(6) c Rixon b Hogg	42
C.H. Lloyd*	b Lawson	78	(7) c Rixon b Lawson	6
P.J.L. Dujon†	lbw b Lawson	77	(8) c Boon b Holland	32
M.D. Marshall	c Rixon b Lawson	9		
R.A. Harper	c Rixon b Lawson	9	(3) c Rixon b Hogg	26
J. Garner	not out	8		
C.A. Walsh	b Holland	0		
Extras	(B5, LB4, NB3)	12	(LB2, NB7)	9
		356	(7 wkts dec)	292

Australia

G.M. Wood	c Greenidge b Harper	41	(7) c Dujon b Harper	19
J. Dyson	c Dujon b Walsh	8	lbw b Marshall	5
K.C. Wessels	b Marshall	98	(1) c Dujon b Harper	70
S.J. Rixon†	c Richards b Marshall	0	(6) lbw b Harper	16
K.J. Hughes	c Dujon b Garner	0	(4) b Marshall	2
A.R. Border*	c Garner b Marshall	21	(3) b Marshall	18
D.C. Boon	c Dujon b Marshall	12	(5) c Harper b Garner	9
G.F. Lawson	c Dujon b Garner	49	c Dujon b Marshall	2
R.G. Holland	c Haynes b Walsh	2	not out	7
R.M. Hogg	not out	7	b Harper	7
T.M. Alderman	c Richardson b Marshall	10	b Marshall	0
Extras	(B2, LB8, NB26)	36	(B7, LB7, NB4)	18
		284		173

Australia	O	M	R	W	O	M	R	W
Lawson	40	7	112	8	24	6	69	3
Hogg	28	7	75	1	21	2	77	3
Alderman	19	8	38	0	12	1	66	0
Holland	30.2	5	109	1	18.1	1	54	1
Wessels	5	0	13	0				
Border					4	0	24	0

West Indies	O	M	R	W	O	M	R	W
Marshall	26	8	69	5	15.5	4	38	5
Garner	26	5	61	2	16	2	58	1
Walsh	24	8	88	2	4	0	20	0
Harper	21	4	56	1	15	6	43	4

Fall of Wickets

Wkt	WI 1st	A 1st	WI 2nd	A 2nd
1st	4	28	4	22
2nd	25	91	39	70
3rd	157	91	45	78
4th	157	122	121	97
5th	172	138	218	126
6th	322	145	225	150
7th	331	232	292	153
8th	348	241	–	153
9th	355	265	–	170
10th	356	284	–	173

Wessels retired hurt at 90 in the first innings and resumed at 138.

Australia v West Indies 1984-85 4th Test
Match Drawn
Played at Melbourne Cricket Ground, 22, 23, 24, 26, 27 December
Toss: Australia. Umpires: P.J. McConnell and S.G. Randall
Debuts: Australia – M.J. Bennett

West Indies

C.G. Greenidge	c Bennett b Lawson	10	lbw b Lawson	1
D.L. Haynes	c Border b Lawson	13	b McDermott	63
R.B. Richardson	b McDermott	51	b Lawson	3
H.A. Gomes	c Matthews b McDermott	68	c Bennett b McDermott	18
I.V.A. Richards	c Hughes b Matthews	208	lbw b McDermott	0
P.J.L. Dujon†	b McDermott	0	not out	49
C.H. Lloyd*	c Lawson b Matthews	19	not out	34
M.D. Marshall	c Rixon b Hogg	55		
R.A. Harper	c and b Hogg	5		
J. Garner	lbw b Lawson	8		
C.A. Walsh	not out	18		
Extras	(B1, LB11, NB12)	24	(B4, LB9, NB5)	18
		479	(5 wkts dec)	**186**

Australia

G.M. Wood	lbw b Garner	12	c Dujon b Garner	5
A.M.J. Hilditch	b Harper	70	b Gomes	113
K.C. Wessels	c Dujon b Marshall	90	b Garner	0
K.J. Hughes	c Dujon b Walsh	0	lbw b Garner	0
A.R. Border*	c Richards b Walsh	35	c Dujon b Richards	41
G.R.J. Matthews	b Marshall	5	b Harper	2
S.J. Rixon†	c Richardson b Marshall	0	c Richardson b Harper	17
M.J. Bennett	not out	22	not out	3
G.F. Lawson	c Walsh b Garner	8	b Walsh	0
C.J. McDermott	b Marshall	0		
R.M. Hogg	lbw b Marshall	19		
Extras	(B5, LB7, W1, NB22)	35	(B6, LB2, NB9)	17
		296	(8 wkts)	**198**

Australia	O	M	R	W	O	M	R	W
Lawson	37	9	108	3	19	4	54	2
Hogg	27	2	96	2	14	3	40	0
McDermott	27	2	118	3	21	6	65	3
Bennett	20	0	78	0	3	0	12	0
Matthews	14.3	2	67	2				
Wessels					1	0	2	0

West Indies	O	M	R	W	O	M	R	W
Marshall	31.5	6	86	5	20	4	36	0
Garner	24	6	74	2	19	1	49	3
Walsh	21	5	57	2	18	4	44	1
Harper	14	1	58	1	22	4	54	2
Richards	1	0	9	0	6	2	7	1
Gomes					2	2	0	1

Fall of Wickets

Wkt	WI 1st	A 1st	WI 2nd	A 2nd
1st	27	38	2	17
2nd	30	161	12	17
3rd	153	163	63	17
4th	154	220	63	128
5th	154	238	100	131
6th	223	238	–	162
7th	362	240	–	198
8th	376	253	–	198
9th	426	253	–	–
10th	479	296	–	–

Australia v West Indies 1984-85 5th Test
Australia won by an innings and 55 runs
Played at Sydney Cricket Ground, 30, 31 December, 1, 2 January
Toss: Australia. Umpires: R.C. Isherwood and M.W. Johnson
Debuts: nil

Australia

A.M.J. Hilditch	c Dujon b Holding	2
G.M. Wood	c Haynes b Gomes	45
K.C. Wessels	b Holding	173
G.M. Ritchie	run out	37
A.R. Border*	c Greenidge b Walsh	69
D.C. Boon	b Garner	49
S.J. Rixon†	c Garner b Holding	20
M.J. Bennett	c Greenidge b Garner	23
G.F. Lawson	not out	5
C.J. McDermott	c Greenidge b Walsh	4
R.G. Holland	did not bat	
Extras	(B7, LB20, NB17)	44
	(9 wkts dec)	**471**

West Indies

C.G. Greenidge	c Rixon b McDermott	18	b Holland		12
D.L. Haynes	c Wessels b Holland	34	lbw b McDermott		3
R.B. Richardson	b McDermott	2	c Wood b Bennett		26
H.A. Gomes	c Bennett b Holland	28	c Wood b Lawson		8
I.V.A. Richards	c Wessels b Holland	15	b Bennett		58
C.H. Lloyd*	c Wood b Holland	33	c Border b McDermott		72
P.J.L. Dujon†	c Hilditch b Bennett	22	c and b Holland		8
M.D. Marshall	st Rixon b Holland	0	not out		32
M.A. Holding	c McDermott b Bennett	0	c Wessels b Holland		0
J. Garner	c Rixon b Holland	0	c Rixon b Bennett		8
C.A. Walsh	not out	1	c Bennett b Holland		4
Extras	(LB3, NB7)	10	(B2, LB12, NB8)		22
		163			**253**

West Indies	O	M	R	W				
Marshall	37	2	111	0				
Garner	31	5	101	2				
Holding	31	7	74	3				
Walsh	38.2	1	118	2				
Gomes	12	2	29	1				
Richards	7	2	11	0				

Australia	O	M	R	W	O	M	R	W
Lawson	9	1	27	0	6	1	14	1
McDermott	9	0	34	2	12	0	56	2
Bennett	22.4	7	45	2	33	9	79	3
Holland	22	7	54	6	33	8	90	4

Fall of Wickets

Wkt	A 1st	WI 1st	WI 2nd
1st	12	26	7
2nd	126	34	31
3rd	338	72	46
4th	342	103	93
5th	350	106	153
6th	392	160	180
7th	450	160	231
8th	463	160	231
9th	471	160	244
10th	–	163	253

Ritchie retired hurt at 194 and resumed at 342.

OVERSEAS CRICKET 1984-85/AUSTRALIA v WEST INDIES

Test Match Averages: Australia v West Indies 1984-85

Australia

Batting and Fielding	M	I	NO	HS	R	Avge	100	50	Ct/St
A.M.J. Hilditch	2	3	0	113	185	61.66	1	1	1
K.C. Wessels	5	9	0	173	505	56.11	1	4	3
M.J. Bennett	2	3	2	23	48	48.00	–	–	4
W.B. Phillips	2	4	0	54	136	34.00	–	1	7
A.R. Border	5	9	0	69	246	27.33	–	1	4
D.C. Boon	3	5	0	51	132	26.40	–	1	2
G.M. Wood	5	9	0	56	207	23.00	–	1	5
G.F. Lawson	5	9	2	49	131	18.71	–	–	1
R.M. Hogg	4	7	3	21*	54	13.50	–	–	2
J. Dyson	3	6	0	30	77	12.83	–	–	–
S.J. Rixon	3	5	0	20	53	10.60	–	–	11/1
K.J. Hughes	4	8	0	37	81	10.12	–	–	4
T.M. Alderman	3	6	1	23	34	6.80	–	–	1
R.G. Holland	3	4	1	7*	15	5.00	–	–	1
C.J. McDermott	2	2	0	4	4	2.00	–	–	1

Played in one Test: G.R.J. Matthews 5, 2 (1ct); C.G. Rackemann 0, 0 (1 ct); G.M. Ritchie 37; G.N. Yallop 2, 1 (1 ct).

Bowling	O	M	R	W	Avge	Best	5wI	10wM
G.F. Lawson	194.4	39	589	23	25.60	8-112	2	1
C.J. McDermott	69	8	273	10	27.30	3-65	–	–
R.G. Holland	130.3	26	404	14	28.85	6-54	1	1
T.M. Alderman	99	31	339	9	37.66	6-128	1	–
M.J. Bennett	78.5	16	214	5	42.80	3-79	–	–
R.M. Hogg	147.1	23	474	11	43.09	4-101	–	–

Also bowled: A.R. Border 9-0-49-0; G.R.J. Matthews 14.3-2-67-2; C.G. Rackemann 28-3-106-0; K.C. Wessels 6-0-15-0.

West Indies

Batting and Fielding	M	I	NO	HS	R	Avge	100	50	Ct/St
H.A. Gomes	5	9	2	127	451	64.42	2	2	1
C.H. Lloyd	5	8	1	114	356	50.85	1	2	5
P.J.L. Dujon	5	8	1	139	341	48.71	1	1	19
I.V.A. Richards	5	9	1	208	342	42.75	1	1	3
M.D. Marshall	5	6	1	57	174	34.80	–	2	4
D.L. Haynes	5	9	0	63	247	27.44	–	3	4
C.G. Greenidge	5	8	0	95	214	26.75	–	1	5
R.B. Richardson	5	9	0	138	236	26.22	1	1	9
R.A. Harper	2	3	0	26	40	13.33	–	–	1
C.A. Walsh	5	6	3	18*	32	10.66	–	–	1
J. Garner	5	6	2	17	41	10.25	–	–	2
M.A. Holding	3	4	0	1	2	0.50	–	–	2

Bowling	O	M	R	W	Avge	Best	5wI	10wM
M.A. Holding	88.1	20	249	15	16.60	6-21	1	–
M.D. Marshall	215.2	45	554	28	19.78	5-38	4	1
R.A. Harper	72	15	211	8	26.37	4-43	–	–
J. Garner	177.4	33	566	19	29.78	4-67	–	–
C.A. Walsh	146.2	29	432	13	33.23	3-55	–	–

Also bowled: H.A. Gomes 15-4-30-2; Richards 16-4-32-1.

Statistical Highlights of the Tests

1st Test, Perth. With only their fourth victory by an innings in 58 Tests against Australia (completed with a day and two sessions in hand), West Indies became the first side to win nine Test matches in succession. Gomes registered his eighth century in 41 Tests and his fifth against Australia, while Dujon achieved the highest of his four hundreds in his 25th match. Australia followed on 340 runs in arrears after being dismissed in 100 minutes for 76, their lowest total against West Indies (beating 82 at Adelaide in 1951-52). It was also the lowest total of this series, surpassing 78 by West Indies at Sydney in 1951-52. Alderman's analysis of 6 for 128 was his best in 20 Tests.

2nd Test, Brisbane. Clive Lloyd scored the last of his 19 Test hundreds and exceeded Walter Hammond's total of 7,249 runs to claim fifth place in the list of Test cricket's highest career aggregates (behind Gavaskar, Boycott, Sobers, and Cowdrey). He also became the first West Indian to score six hundreds against Australia. Richardson scored his third hundred in only his ninth Test innings and hit 24 fours. Playing his 44th Test, Garner became the fifth West Indian after Gibbs, Sobers, Roberts, and Holding to take 200 wickets. Lawson took his 100th Test wicket in 25 matches. West Indies thus extended their record number of consecutive wins to ten. Hughes resigned the captaincy after leading Australia to only four victories in 28 matches during an intermittent reign that began in 1979-80.

3rd Test, Adelaide. Six minutes before tea on the fifth day, West Indies celebrated the centenary of Test cricket at the Adelaide Oval by gaining their 36th victory in 72 Tests under the leadership of Clive Lloyd. This result extended their world record of successive wins to eleven and equalled England's record of 26 matches without defeat (set between 1968 and 1971). It also ensured their retention of the Frank Worrell Trophy, regained in 1977-78 and now successfully defended for the fourth time. Lawson's analysis of 8 for 112 was his best in first-class cricket. Gomes became the seventh West Indian to score 1,000 runs against Australia and emulated Lloyd by scoring his sixth hundred against them. Marshall, who took five wickets in an innings for the tenth time, reached 150 wickets in his 34th Test.

4th Test, Melbourne. Although a defiant 339-minute vigil by Hilditch ended their record run of victories, West Indies set a world record by avoiding defeat for the 27th consecutive match. After debutant McDermott (19) had taken the wickets of Richardson, Gomes, and Dujon for one run in seven balls, Richards, who scored his 18th Test hundred, went on to record the third double century of his Test career and the first for West Indies in Australia. Their previous highest innings was 169 by Roy Fredericks at Perth in 1975-76. Garner was no-balled seven times by umpire Randell in his second over, which lasted 10 minutes. Marshall gained five wickets for the fourth successive time.

5th Test, Sydney. West Indies suffered their first defeat since December 1981, when Australia beat them at Melbourne. Their last defeat by an innings had been at Melbourne in 1968-69. It was only Clive Lloyd's 11th defeat in a record 74 Tests as captain. He retired after amassing 7,515 runs (average 46.68), with 19 hundreds, in 110 Tests. Only Colin Cowdrey (114) had appeared in more matches. Wessels made his fourth hundred in 17 Tests. Holland, a 38-year-old leg-spinner playing in only his third Test, returned match figures of 10 for 144, a record against West Indies at Sydney. Marshall's 28 wickets established a West Indies record for a rubber in Australia.

West Indies Tour of Australia 1984-85

First-Class Matches: Played 11; Won 4, Lost 2, Drawn 5
All Matches: Played 34; Won 24, Lost 4, Drawn 6

First-Class Averages

Batting and Fielding	M	I	NO	HS	R	Avge	100	50	Ct/St
C.H. Lloyd	10	16	2	114	732	52.28	1	5	7
H.A. Gomes	10	15	3	127	621	51.75	2	3	2
P.J.L. Dujon	9	13	2	151*	536	48.72	2	1	27
D.L. Haynes	10	17	1	155	635	39.68	1	5	5
I.V.A. Richards	10	17	1	208	606	37.87	2	2	9
A.L. Logie	5	7	0	134	250	35.71	1	–	–
R.B. Richardson	10	17	1	145	557	34.81	2	3	14
C.G. Greenidge	9	15	0	95	469	31.26	–	3	9
M.D. Marshall	7	9	2	57	212	30.28	–	2	4
W.W. Davis	5	7	2	50	110	22.00	–	1	1
T.R.O. Payne	3	5	0	55	93	18.60	–	1	9
E.A.E. Baptiste	4	6	0	54	107	17.83	–	1	1
C.A. Walsh	9	10	6	18*	55	13.75	–	–	2
R.A. Harper	6	9	1	38*	104	13.00	–	–	6
J. Garner	8	9	4	17	58	11.60	–	–	3
M.A. Holding	6	7	0	21	49	7.00	–	–	6

Bowling	O	M	R	W	Avge	Best	5wI	10wM
M.D. Marshall	267.3	59	699	36	19.41	5-38	4	1
M.A. Holding	161.3	40	410	20	20.50	6-21	1	–
I.V.A. Richards	94	26	175	7	25.00	4-18	–	–
C.A. Walsh	311.1	68	946	37	25.56	6-119	2	–
J. Garner	237.4	58	668	25	26.72	4-19	–	–
E.A.E. Baptiste	121.2	28	350	11	31.81	4-67	–	–
R.A. Harper	253.5	56	658	17	38.70	5-72	1	–
W.W. Davis	117.4	24	421	8	52.62	3-58	–	–

Also bowled: P.J.L. Dujon 9-3-43-1; H.A. Gomes 68-17-137-3; C.G. Greenidge 3-0-7-0; D.L. Haynes 6-0-27-0; A.L. Logie 10-1-29-1; R.B. Richardson 10-1-40-0.

Pakistan v New Zealand

Within three weeks of their home series against India, Pakistan had started another against New Zealand. Proving better equipped with spin, they won it 2-0, taking the first two Tests, in Lahore and Hyderabad, by six wickets and seven wickets, respectively. New Zealand, captained by Jeremy Coney and lacking not only Howarth but Hadlee, topped 300 for the only time in the third and last Test, and their open disagreement with the umpiring reflected their failure to do themselves justice. They also lost the one-day series 3-1.

The Lahore pitch for the first Test took spin to an unusual extent and Pakistan, having added overnight a third spinner, the left-arm Iqbal Qasim, had the upper hand throughout. It was Mudassar, however, who struck a blow from which New Zealand never really recovered when he removed Jeff Crowe, Edgar, and Reid for eight runs with the new ball on the first morning. Qasim took four wickets in each innings, and despite Chatfield's accuracy Pakistan comfortably made the 178 needed to win by six wickets.

At Hyderabad, the left-handed John Reid made 106, and though Miandad responded with 104, an equally outstanding innings in a low-scoring match, New Zealand led on first innings by 37 runs. They now had an off-spinner John Bracewell in support of Boock who took seven for 87. Their batsmen struggled against Qasim and Qadir in the second innings but left Pakistan to make 229, a stiff task in the context of the match to date.

Martin Crowe soon removed Mohsin and Qasim Omar, but from 14 for two Mudassar and Miandad settled the match with a fine bold piece of batting. In a stand of 212 each made a hundred, Miandad his second of the match.

The third Test started with a piece of history. Pakistan's opening pair, Mudassar Nazar and Shoaib Mohammad, were respectively the sons of Nazar Mohammad and Hanif Mohammad who opened together in their country's first series against India 32 years before.

Pakistan were at one time 124 for five but reached 328. New Zealand replied with enterprising batting against the spinners by Wright, Reid, and the Crowe brothers. They led by 98 runs, and on the last morning, when they had Pakistan 130 for five, had some chance of winning. But the 21-year-old Saleem Malik played with much brilliance, Wasim Raja held steady, and no more wickets fell.

Pakistan v New Zealand 1984-85 1st Test
Pakistan won by 6 wickets
Played at Gaddafi Stadium, Lahore, 16, 17, 18, 19, 20 November
Toss: New Zealand. Umpires: Mahboob Shah and Shakil Khan
Debuts: New Zealand – D.A. Stirling

New Zealand

J.J. Crowe	c Dalpat b Mudassar	0	(5) c Dalpat b Qasim		43
B.A. Edgar	b Mudassar	3	lbw b Azeem		26
M.D. Crowe	c Omar b Qadir	55	c sub (Ramiz Raja) b Qasim		33
J.G. Wright	c Dalpat b Azeem	1	(1) run out		65
J.F. Reid	lbw b Mudassar	2	(4) b Qadir		6
J.V. Coney*	c Mohsin b Qasim	7	c Dalpat b Azeem		26
E.J. Gray	c sub (Ramiz Raja) b Qasim	12	(8) c Mudassar b Qadir		6
I.D.S. Smith†	c Qasim b Azeem	41	(9) not out		11
D.A. Stirling	b Qasim	16	(10) c Dalpat b Qasim		10
S.L. Boock	c Miandad b Qasim	13	c Miandad b Qadir		0
E.J. Chatfield	not out	6	c Omar b Qasim		0
Extras	(B1)	1	(B8, LB2, W1, NB4)		15
		157			**241**

Pakistan

Mudassar Nazar	c Reid b Stirling	26
Mohsin Khan	c Reid b Gray	58
Qasim Omar	c J.J. Crowe b Boock	13
Javed Miandad	c Reid b Gray	11
Zaheer Abbas*	c M.D. Crowe b Boock	43
Salim Malik	lbw b Stirling	10
Abdul Qadir	c Coney b Chatfield	14
Anil Dalpat†	b M.D. Crowe	11
Iqbal Qasim	c Coney b Chatfield	22
Azeem Hafeez	c Boock b Chatfield	11
Tausif Ahmed	not out	0
Extras	(NB2)	2
		221

b Boock		16
c and b Gray		38
lbw b Stirling		20
not out		48
c Smith b Gray		31
not out		24
(LB4)		4
(4 wkts)		**181**

Pakistan

	O	M	R	W	O	M	R	W
Mudassar Nazar	11	5	8	3	10	1	30	0
Azeem Hafeez	18	9	40	2	13	5	37	2
Abdul Qadir	21	6	58	1	26	4	82	3
Iqbal Qasim	22.4	10	41	4	29.5	10	65	4
Tausif Ahmed	2	0	9	0	4	0	17	0

New Zealand

	O	M	R	W	O	M	R	W
Stirling	27	7	71	2	15.1	2	60	1
M.D. Crowe	7	1	21	1				
Gray	8	1	19	2	18	0	45	2
Chatfield	28.2	7	57	3	13	7	12	0
Boock	24	7	53	2	17	2	56	1
Coney					2	1	4	0

Fall of Wickets

Wkt	NZ 1st	P 1st	NZ 2nd	P 2nd
1st	0	54	66	33
2nd	11	84	123	77
3rd	28	103	138	77
4th	31	114	140	138
5th	50	144	208	–
6th	76	165	209	–
7th	120	188	220	–
8th	124	189	220	–
9th	146	212	235	–
10th	157	221	241	–

Pakistan v New Zealand 1984-85 2nd Test
Pakistan won by 7 wickets
Played at Niaz Stadium, Hyderabad, 25, 26, 27, 29 November
Toss: New Zealand. Umpires: Khizer Hayat and Mian Aslam
Debuts: nil

New Zealand

J.G. Wright	c Dalpat b Qasim	18	c Dalpat b Qasim	22
B.A. Edgar	c Salim b Qadir	11	lbw b Mudassar	1
M.D. Crowe	b Qadir	19	(4) st Dalpat b Quasim	21
J.F. Reid	b Azeem	106	(3) lbw b Qadir	21
J.V. Coney*	c Manzoor b Qadir	6	b Qasim	5
J.J. Crowe	c Salim b Zaheer	39	lbw b Qasim	57
I.D.S. Smith†	c Qasim b Zaheer	6	c Mudassar b Azeem	34
E.J. Gray	lbw b Mudassar	25	c Omar b Qasim	5
J.G. Bracewell	c Mudassar b Qadir	0	c and b Qadir	0
D.A. Stirling	not out	11	b Qadir	11
S.L. Boock	lbw b Qadir	12	not out	4
Extras	(B13, NB1)	14	(B1, LB4, NB3)	8
		267		189

Pakistan

Mudassar Nazar	c M.D. Crowe b Bracewell	28	c Coney b Boock	106
Mohsin Khan	c Gray b Boock	9	b M.D. Crowe	2
Qasim Omar	c Coney b Boock	45	lbw b M.D. Crowe	0
Javed Miandad	c J.J. Crowe b Boock	104	not out	103
Anil Dalpat†	b Bracewell	1		
Zaheer Abbas*	st Smith b Boock	2		
Salim Malik	b Boock	1		
Manzoor Elahi	c J.J. Crowe b Boock	19	(5) not out	4
Abdul Qadir	lbw b Boock	11		
Iqbal Qasim	c J.J. Crowe b Bracewell	8		
Azeem Hafeez	not out	0		
Extras	(LB2)	2	(B5, LB7, W3)	15
		230	(3 wkts)	230

Pakistan	O	M	R	W	O	M	R	W
Mudassar Nazar	7	4	14	1	5	2	8	1
Azeem Hafeez	18	4	29	1	8	3	33	1
Iqbal Qasim	33	6	80	1	24.1	7	79	5
Abdul Qadir	40.3	11	108	5	18	3	59	3
Manzoor Elahi	2	1	2	0				
Zaheer Abbas	8	1	21	2	1	0	5	0

New Zealand	O	M	R	W	O	M	R	W
Stirling	3	1	11	0	4	0	26	0
M.D. Crowe	3	0	8	0	8	1	29	2
Coney	10	4	8	0	4	1	9	0
Boock	37	12	87	7	23.4	4	69	1
Bracewell	16.1	3	44	3	13	2	36	0
Gray	22	4	70	0	11	0	49	0

Fall of Wickets

Wkt	NZ 1st	P 1st	NZ 2nd	P 2nd
1st	30	26	2	14
2nd	30	50	34	14
3rd	74	153	58	226
4th	88	154	71	–
5th	150	159	80	–
6th	164	169	125	–
7th	237	191	149	–
8th	239	215	149	–
9th	243	230	167	–
10th	267	230	189	–

Pakistan v New Zealand 1984-85 3rd Test
Match Drawn
Played at National Stadium, Karachi, 10, 11, 12, 14, 15, December
Toss: Pakistan. Umpires: Javed Akhtar and Shakoor Rana
Debuts: Nil

Pakistan

Mudassar Nazar	c Smith b Stirling	5	c McEwan b Stirling	0
Shoaib Mohammad	c Smith b Stirling	31	c McEwan b Boock	34
Qasim Omar	lbw b Boock	45	c and b M.D. Crowe	17
Javed Miandad	c Smith b M.D. Crowe	13	c J.J. Crowe b Boock	58
Zaheer Abbas*	c Smith b Stirling	14	c Smith b Bracewell	3
Salim Malik	c and b M.D. Crowe	50	not out	119
Wasim Raja	lbw b Stirling	51	not out	60
Abdul Qadir	c Wright b Boock	7		
Anil Dalpat†	b Boock	52		
Iqbal Qasim	not out	45		
Azeem Hafeez	lbw b Boock	0		
Extras	(B5, LB6, W1, NB3)	15	(B2, LB8, NB7)	17
		328	(5 wkts)	308

New Zealand

J.G. Wright	c Dalpat b Qasim	107
B.A. Edgar	run out	15
J.F. Reid	c Qasim b Azeem	97
M.D. Crowe	lbw b Wasim	45
J.J. Crowe	c Miandad b Azeem	62
J.V. Coney*	c and b Qasim	16
P.E. McEwan	not out	40
I.D.S. Smith†	c Salim b Qasim	0
D.A. Stirling	c Omar b Qasim	7
J.G. Bracewell	c Dalpat b Azeem	30
S.L. Boock	c Dalpat b Azeem	0
Extras	(B1, LB5, NB1)	7
		426

New Zealand	O	M	R	W	O	M	R	W
Stirling	29	5	88	4	14	1	82	1
M.D. Crowe	21	4	81	2	10	3	26	1
McEwan	4	1	6	0	2	0	7	0
Boock	41	19	83	4	30	10	83	2
Coney	5	3	5	0				
Bracewell	20	5	54	0	33	11	83	1
J.J. Crowe					2	0	9	0
Wright					1	0	1	0
Reid					2	0	7	0

Pakistan	O	M	R	W
Mudassar Nazar	15.4	4	45	0
Azeem Hafeez	46.4	9	132	4
Iqbal Qasim	57	13	133	4
Wasim Raja	33	8	97	1
Zaheer Abbas	5.2	1	13	0

Fall of Wickets

Wkt	P 1st	NZ 1st	P 2nd
1st	14	83	5
2nd	80	163	37
3rd	92	258	119
4th	102	292	126
5th	124	338	130
6th	204	352	–
7th	226	353	–
8th	315	361	–
9th	319	426	–
10th	328	426	–

Test Match Averages: Pakistan v New Zealand 1984-85

Pakistan

Batting and Fielding	M	I	NO	HS	R	Avge	100	50	Ct/St
Javed Miandad	3	6	2	104	337	84.25	2	1	3
Salim Malik	3	5	2	119*	204	68.00	1	1	3
Iqbal Qasim	3	3	1	45*	75	37.50	–	–	4
Mudassar Nazar	3	6	0	106	181	30.16	1	–	3
Mohsin Khan	2	4	0	58	107	26.75	–	1	1
Qasim Omar	3	6	0	45	140	23.33	–	–	4
Anil Dalpat	3	3	0	52	64	21.33	–	–	10/1
Zaheer Abbas	3	5	0	43	93	18.60	–	–	–
Abdul Qadir	3	3	0	14	32	10.66	–	–	1
Azeem Hafeez	3	3	1	11	11	5.50	–	–	–

Played in one match: Manzoor Elahi 19, 4* (1 ct); Shoaib Mohammad 31, 34; Tausif Ahmed 0*; Wasim Raja 51, 60*.

Bowling	O	M	R	W	Avge	Best	5wI	10wM
Mudassar Nazar	48.4	14	105	5	21.00	3-8	–	–
Iqbal Qasim	166.5	46	398	18	22.11	5-79	1	–
Abdul Qadir	105.3	24	307	12	25.58	5-108	1	–
Azeem Hafeez	103.4	30	271	10	27.10	4-132	–	–

Also bowled: Manzoor Elahi 2-1-2-0; Tausif Ahmed 6-0-26-0; Wasim Raja 33-8-97-1; Zaheer Abbas 14.2-2-39-2.

New Zealand

Batting and Fielding	M	I	NO	HS	R	Avge	100	50	Ct/St
J.F. Reid	3	5	0	106	232	46.40	1	1	3
J.G. Wright	3	5	0	107	213	42.60	1	1	1
J.J. Crowe	3	5	0	62	201	40.20	–	2	5
M.D. Crowe	3	5	0	55	173	34.60	–	1	4
I.D.S. Smith	3	5	1	41	92	23.00	–	–	6/1
D.A. Stirling	3	5	1	16	55	13.75	–	–	–
J.V. Coney	3	5	0	26	60	12.00	–	–	4
E.J. Gray	2	4	0	25	48	12.00	–	–	2
B.A. Edgar	3	5	0	26	56	11.20	–	–	–
J.G. Bracewell	2	3	0	30	30	10.00	–	–	–
S.L. Boock	3	5	1	13	29	7.25	–	–	1

Played in one Test: E.J. Chatfield 6*, 0; P.E. McEwan 40* (2 ct).

Bowling	O	M	R	W	Avge	Best	5wI	10wM
S.L. Boock	172.4	54	431	17	25.35	7-87	1	–
M.D. Crowe	49	9	165	6	27.50	2-29	–	–
D.A. Stirling	92.1	16	338	8	42.25	4-88	–	–

Also bowled: J.G. Bracewell 82.1-21-217-4; E.J. Chatfield 41.2-14-69-3; J.V. Coney 21-9-26-0; J.J. Crowe 2-0-9-0; E.J. Gray 59-5-183-4; P.E. McEwan 6-1-13-0; J.F. Reid 2-0-7-0; J.G. Wright 1-0-1-0.

Statistical Highlights of the Tests

1st Test, Lahore. Pakistan completed their ninth victory in 22 Tests against New Zealand after just 20 minutes of play on the fifth day. Coney captained New Zealand for the first time, Howarth being unavailable for the tour. Iqbal Qasim, although not included among the originally selected 16 players, was recalled from Karachi on the eve of the match after missing 13 Tests. On a grassless pitch, his left-arm legbreaks returned match figures of 8 for 106. In his 72nd match, Zaheer became the first Pakistani to score 5,000 runs in Test cricket.

2nd Test, Hyderabad. Pakistan celebrated staging Test cricket's 1,000th match by clinching the rubber with more than a day to spare. Javed Miandad became the second Pakistani after Hanif Mohammad (v England at Dacca in 1961-62) to score a century in each innings of a Test. This feat took his tally of hundreds to 13, five of them against New Zealand. With Mudassar, who scored his eighth century, Miandad shared a partnership of 212 – a record for the third wicket by either country in this series. For New Zealand, Reid scored his third hundred and Boock (7 for 87) returned his best analysis.

3rd Test, Karachi. Salim Malik completed 1,000 runs in the first innings of his 21st Test before scoring the highest of his five centuries in the second. He reached his hundred in 173 minutes – the fastest century of the rubber. The stand of 89 between Anil Dalpat and Iqbal Qasim was a Pakistan eighth-wicket record for this series. Wright scored his fourth hundred in 34 Tests, Boock took his 50th wicket and Smith his 50th catch.

One-Day Internationals

12 November at Shahi Bagh Stadium, Peshawar. PAKISTAN won by 46 runs. Toss: New Zealand. Pakistan 191-5 closed (39 overs) (Javed Miandad 80*). New Zealand 145 (36.2 overs) (I.D.S. Smith 59; Zakir Khan 8-2-19-4). Award: Zakir Khan (8-2-19-4).

23 November at Iqbal Stadium, Faisalabad. PAKISTAN won by 5 runs. Toss: New Zealand. Pakistan 157-5 closed (20 overs). New Zealand 152-7 closed (20 overs) (J.G. Wright 55; Mudassar Nazar 4-0-27-4). Award: Salim Malik (41 and 1 ct).

2 December at Jinnah Park Stadium, Sialkot. NEW ZEALAND won by 34 runs. Toss: Pakistan. New Zealand 187-9 closed (36 overs) (M.D. Crowe 67; Tausif Ahmed 6-0-38-4). Pakistan 153-8 closed (36 overs). Award: M.D. Crowe (67 and 5-0-21-2).

7 December at Ibn-e-Qasim Bagh Stadium, Multan. PAKISTAN won by 1 wicket. Toss: New Zealand. New Zealand 213-8 closed (35 overs). Pakistan 214-9 (35 overs) (Zaheer Abbas 73). Award: Zaheer Abbas (73 and 6-0-35-1).

New Zealand Tour of Sri Lanka and Pakistan 1984-85

First-Class Matches: Played 5; Won 0, Lost 1, Drawn 4
All Matches: Played 11; Won 2, Lost 5, Drawn 4

First-Class Averages

Batting and Fielding	M	I	NO	HS	R	Avge	100	50	Ct/St
P.E. McEwan	2	3	2	44	117	117.00	–	–	2
M.D. Crowe	4	7	1	71	294	49.00	–	3	5
J.G. Wright	4	7	0	107	309	44.14	1	2	1
J.F. Reid	5	9	2	106	301	43.00	1	2	4
J.J. Crowe	5	8	0	62	298	37.25	–	2	7
B.A. Edgar	5	9	0	75	224	24.88	–	2	–
J.V. Coney	4	6	0	79	139	23.16	–	1	4
I.D.S. Smith	4	7	1	41	133	22.16	–	–	8/2
E.J. Gray	4	7	0	56	133	19.00	–	1	3
J.G. Bracewell	4	5	1	30	55	13.75	–	–	–
D.A. Stirling	4	6	1	16	55	11.00	–	–	–
S.L. Boock	5	6	1	13	30	6.00	–	–	1

Also batted: B.L. Cairns (2 matches) 7,10* (3 ct); E.J. Chatfield (2 matches) 6*, 0. M.C. Snedden (1 match) (2 ct) did not bat.

Bowling	O	M	R	W	Avge	Best	5wI	10wM
S.L. Boock	221.4	75	501	21	23.85	7-87	1	–
E.J. Gray	90	12	253	10	25.30	3-24	–	–
M.D. Crowe	55	11	181	6	30.16	2-29	–	–
D.A. Stirling	111.5	19	392	9	43.55	4-88	–	–
J.G. Bracewell	117.1	31	294	6	49.00	3-44	–	–

Also bowled: B.L. Cairns 17-5-75-3; E.J. Chatfield 51.2-17-93-4; J.V. Coney 21-9-26-0; J.J. Crowe 2-0-9-0; P.E. McEwan 6-1-13-0; J.F. Reid 2-0-7-0; M.C. Snedden 11-1-52-2; J.G. Wright 1-0-1-0.

New Zealand v Pakistan

For the New Zealand players who had experienced the particular demands of the tour to Pakistan, the 2-0 win in the return series at home was indeed sweet revenge. Gone was the brittle batting of Lahore and Hyderabad. Instead, there was strength and solidity right down the order. The bowling was generally demanding, with the spearhead, Richard Hadlee, returning to take 16 wickets in the five Pakistani innings. New Zealand also won the one-day series 3-0, with one match unfinished.

Pakistan had pinned much of their hopes on the skills of its mercurial leg-spinner Abdul Qadir. However, he picked up only two wickets in 81 overs in the first two Tests, and was sent home on the morning of the third one-day international for 'disciplinary reasons'.

Only six times in the series did a Pakistan batsman pass 50, and none carried on to three figures. Only once, in the first Test on a good batting strip, did the total reach 300. In Wasim Akram and, to a lesser extent and in the one-day internationals, Rameez Raja, the tour did throw up two players who should play significant roles in Pakistan's cricket future.

The first Test could have had a most interesting conclusion, had the final day not been rained out. John Reid's patient 148 in 572 minutes was the cornerstone on which New Zealand produced their best score against Pakistan. Reid's stand with Hadlee, 145 for the sixth wicket, was a record between the countries. Pakistan saved the match on the fourth morning, when Qadir's fighting 54 took them past the follow-on mark. The final day would have begun with Pakistan requiring 374 for victory, beyond their grasp, but with time to be dismissed.

Bad batting cost Pakistan the second Test in Auckland. They were dismissed for 169 and 183 and only Mudassar Nazar showed the necessary technique and application against bowling that used the greenish pitch and humid conditions admirably. Reid's fifth century in 12 Tests, along with meaty contributions from John Wright and Martin Crowe, enabled New Zealand to pass 450 for the second time in the series.

The third Test was one of the most thrilling in New Zealand's cricket history. Inspired work by Hadlee late on the first day, a marvellous display of sustained seam bowling by Akram, earning him 10 wickets in his second Test, a fine double, 96 and 89, from little Qasim Omar, and a nail-biting 50-run stand from Coney and Chatfield to win the match by two wickets – in effect, one wicket, for Cairns was absent with concussion – made it a memorable contest.

New Zealand v Pakistan 1984-85 1st Test
Match Drawn
Played at Basin Reserve, Wellington, 18, 19, 20, 21, 22 (no play) January
Toss: New Zealand. Umpires: G.C. Morris and S.J. Woodward
Debuts: nil

New Zealand

G.P. Howarth*	run out	33	c Dalpat b Azeem	17
J.G. Wright	c Shoaib b Azeem	11	lbw b Mudassar	11
J.F. Reid	b Azeem	148	c Qadir b Qasim	3
M.D. Crowe	c Dalpat b Qasim	37	c Qadir b Qasim	33
J.J. Crowe	c Shoaib b Qasim	4	not out	19
J.V. Coney	b Qadir	48	not out	18
R.J. Hadlee	c Miandad b Azeem	89		
I.D.S. Smith†	c and b Mudassar	65		
B.L. Cairns	b Azeem	36		
S.L. Boock	c Dalpat b Azeem	0		
E.J. Chatfield	not out	3		
Extras	(B5, LB12, NB1)	18	(LB2)	2
		492	(4 wkts)	**103**

Pakistan

Mudassar Nazar	c and b Boock	38
Mohsin Khan	c Wright b Boock	40
Shoaib Mohammad	run out	7
Qasim Omar	b Boock	8
Javed Miandad*	c Smith b Boock	30
Salim Malik	c Cairns b Hadlee	66
Wasim Raja	c M.D. Crowe b Boock	14
Abdul Qadir	c Smith b Hadlee	54
Anil Dalpat†	c Smith b Chatfield	15
Iqbal Qasim	not out	27
Azeem Hafeez	c Boock b Cairns	3
Extras	(B9, LB9, NB2)	20
		322

Pakistan	O	M	R	W	O	M	R	W
Mudassar Nazar	29	5	80	1	6	3	13	1
Azeem Hafeez	48	12	127	5	15	3	51	1
Abdul Qadir	51	13	142	1	8	1	18	0
Iqbal Qasim	41	5	105	2	16	8	19	2
Wasim Raja	2	0	10	0				
Shoaib Mohammad	1	0	4	0				
Javed Miandad	3	1	7	0				

New Zealand	O	M	R	W
Hadlee	32	11	70	2
Cairns	27.4	5	65	1
Chatfield	25	10	52	1
Boock	45	18	117	5

Fall of Wickets

Wkt	NZ 1st	P 1st	NZ 2nd
1st	24	62	24
2nd	61	85	30
3rd	126	95	42
4th	138	102	73
5th	230	161	–
6th	375	187	–
7th	414	223	–
8th	488	288	–
9th	488	309	–
10th	492	322	–

New Zealand v Pakistan 1984-85 2nd Test
New Zealand won by an innings and 99 runs
Played at Eden Park, Auckland, 25, 26, 27, 28 January
Toss: New Zealand. Umpires: F.R. Goodall and S.J. Woodward
Debuts: Pakistan – Wasim Akram

Pakistan

Mudassar Nazar	lbw b Hadlee	12	b Cairns	89
Mohsin Khan	c Coney b Cairns	26	c Coney b Hadlee	1
Qasim Omar	c M.D. Crowe b Cairns	33	c Cairns b Chatfield	22
Zaheer Abbas	c J.J. Crowe b Cairns	6	(6) c sub b Hadlee	12
Javed Miandad*	c Smith b Chatfield	26	c Smith b Chatfield	1
Wasim Raja	c Smith b Chatfield	4	(7) c Wright b Boock	11
Abdul Qadir	run out	0	(8) lbw b Cairns	10
Salim Malik	not out	41	(4) c Cairns b Chatfield	0
Anil Dalpat†	c J.J. Crowe b Hadlee	7	lbw b Cairns	6
Wasim Akram	c M.D. Crowe b Hadlee	0	(11) not out	0
Azeem Hafeez	c Boock b Hadlee	6	(10) lbw b Cairns	17
Extras	(LB5, NB3)	8	(LB11, NB3)	14
		169		**183**

New Zealand

G.P. Howarth*	c Miandad b Mudassar	13
J.G. Wright	c Salim b Wasim Akram	66
J.F. Reid	not out	158
M.D. Crowe	c sub b Qadir	84
S.L. Boock	c Wasim Raja b Azeem	10
J.J. Crowe	run out	30
J.V. Coney	c Dalpat b Mudassar	25
R.J. Hadlee	c Mohsin b Azeem	13
I.D.S. Smith†	c Miandad b Wasim Akram	7
B.L. Cairns	b Azeem	23
E.J. Chatfield	not out	1
Extras	(B6, LB9, NB6)	21
	(9 wkts dec)	**451**

New Zealand	O	M	R	W	O	M	R	W
Hadlee	19.5	3	60	4	17	1	66	2
Cairns	29	10	73	3	19.4	8	49	4
Chatfield	14	5	24	2	19	5	47	3
Coney	4	1	7	0				
Boock					4	2	10	1

Pakistan	O	M	R	W
Azeem Hafeez	47	10	157	3
Wasim Akram	34.4	4	105	2
Mudassar	34	5	85	2
Abdul Qadir	22	5	52	1
Wasim Raja	1	0	3	0
Salim Malik	8.2	2	34	0

Fall of Wickets

Wkt	P 1st	NZ 1st	P 2nd
1st	33	60	13
2nd	58	108	54
3rd	93	245	54
4th	105	278	57
5th	111	359	79
6th	115	366	122
7th	123	387	140
8th	147	411	152
9th	151	447	178
10th	169	–	183

New Zealand v Pakistan 1984-85 3rd Test
New Zealand won by 2 wickets
Played at Carisbrook, Dunedin, 9, 10, 11, 13, 14 February
Toss: New Zealand. Umpires: F.R. Goodall and G.C. Morris
Debuts: nil

Pakistan

Mudassar Nazar	c J.J. Crowe b Hadlee	18	c Coney b Bracewell	5
Mohsin Khan	run out	39	c M.D. Crowe b Hadlee	27
Qasim Omar	c J.J. Crowe b Coney	96	c Smith b Chatfield	89
Javed Miandad*	c Smith b Hadlee	79	c Reid b Hadlee	2
Zaheer Abbas	c Reid b Hadlee	6	lbw b Cairns	0
Rashid Khan	c M.D. Crowe b Hadlee	0	(9) b Bracewell	37
Anil Dalpat†	b Bracewell	16	b Chatfield	21
Salim Malik	lbw b Hadlee	0	(6) b Cairns	9
Tahir Naqqash	c Wright b Hadlee	0	(8) run out	1
Azeem Hafeez	c Smith b Bracewell	4	b Chatfield	7
Wasim Akram	not out	1	not out	8
Extras	(B1, LB2, NB12)	15	(B1, LB9, NB7)	17
		274		**223**

New Zealand

G.P. Howarth*	b Wasim	23	c Mohsin b Wasim	17
J.G. Wright	c Omar b Azeem	32	c Mohsin b Azeem	1
J.F. Reid	b Wasim	24	c Dalpat b Wasim	0
M.D. Crowe	c Miandad b Wasim	57	c Mudassar b Tahir	84
J.J. Crowe	lbw b Wasim	6	lbw b Wasim	0
J.V. Coney	c Dalpat b Rashid	24	not out	111
R.J. Hadlee	c Dalpat b Rashid	18	b Azeem	11
I.D.S. Smith†	lbw b Tahir	12	c Miandad b Wasim	6
B.L. Cairns	c Dalpat b Wasim	6	retired hurt	0
B.P. Bracewell	c Rashid b Tahir	3	c Tahir b Wasim	4
E.J. Chatfield	not out	2	not out	21
Extras	(B7, LB5, NB1)	13	(B5, LB6, W1, NB11)	23
		220	(8 wkts)	**278**

New Zealand	O	M	R	W	O	M	R	W
Hadlee	24	5	51	6	26	9	59	2
Bracewell	18.2	1	81	2	14.4	2	48	2
Cairns	22	0	77	0	22	5	41	2
Chatfield	24	6	46	0	26	5	65	3
Coney	6	1	16	1				

Pakistan	O	M	R	W	O	M	R	W
Rashid Khan	23	7	64	2	9	2	33	0
Azeem Hafeez	20	6	65	1	32	9	84	2
Wasim Akram	26	7	56	5	33	10	72	5
Tahir Naqqash	16.4	4	23	2	16.4	1	58	1
Mudassar Nazar					9	2	20	0

Fall of Wickets

Wkt	P 1st	NZ 1st	P 2nd	NZ 2nd
1st	25	41	5	4
2nd	100	81	72	5
3rd	241	84	75	23
4th	243	92	76	23
5th	245	149	103	180
6th	251	185	157	208
7th	251	203	166	216
8th	255	205	169	228
9th	273	216	181	–
10th	274	220	223	–

Test Match Averages: New Zealand v Pakistan 1984-85

New Zealand

Batting and Fielding	M	I	NO	HS	R	Avge	100	50	Ct/St
J.F. Reid	3	5	1	158*	333	83.25	2	–	2
J.V. Coney	3	5	2	111*	226	75.33	1	–	3
M.D. Crowe	3	5	0	84	295	59.00	–	3	5
R.J. Hadlee	3	4	0	89	131	32.75	–	1	5
E.J. Chatfield	3	4	4	21*	27	–	–	–	–
J.G. Wright	3	5	0	66	121	24.20	–	1	3
I.D.S. Smith	3	4	0	65	90	22.50	–	1	9
B.L. Cairns	3	4	1	36	65	21.66	–	–	3
G.P. Howarth	3	5	0	33	103	20.60	–	–	–
J.J. Crowe	3	5	1	30	59	14.75	–	–	4
S.L. Boock	2	2	0	10	10	5.00	–	–	3

Played in one Test: B.P. Bracewell 3, 4.

Bowling	O	M	R	W	Avge	Best	5wI	10wM
R.J. Hadlee	118.5	29	306	16	19.12	6-51	1	–
S.L. Boock	49	20	127	6	21.16	5-117	1	–
E.J. Chatfield	108	31	234	9	26.00	3-47	–	–
B.L. Cairns	120.2	28	305	10	30.50	4-49	–	–

Also bowled: B.P. Bracewell 33-3-129-4; J.V. Coney 10-2-23-1.

Pakistan

Batting and Fielding	M	I	NO	HS	R	Avge	100	50	Ct/St
Qasim Omar	3	5	0	96	248	49.60	–	2	1
Mudassar Nazar	3	5	0	89	162	32.40	–	1	2
Salim Malik	3	5	1	66	116	29.00	–	1	1
Javed Miandad	3	5	0	79	138	27.60	–	1	5
Mohsin Khan	3	5	0	40	133	26.60	–	–	3
Abdul Qadir	2	3	0	54	64	21.33	–	1	2
Anil Dalpat	3	5	0	21	65	13.00	–	–	8
Wasim Raja	2	3	0	14	29	9.66	–	–	1
Wasim Akram	2	4	3	8*	9	9.00	–	–	–
Azeem Hafeez	3	5	0	17	37	7.40	–	–	–
Zaheer Abbas	2	4	0	12	24	6.00	–	–	–

Played in one Test: Iqbal Qasim 27*; Rashid Khan 0, 37 (1 ct); Shoaib Mohammad 7 (2 ct); Tahir Naqqash 0, 1 (1 ct).

Bowling	O	M	R	W	Avge	Best	5wI	10wM
Wasim Akram	93.4	21	233	12	19.41	5-56	2	1
Azeem Hafeez	162	40	484	12	40.33	5-127	1	–

Also bowled: Abdul Qadir 81-19-212-2; Iqbal Qasim 57-13-124-4; Javed Miandad 3-1-7-0; Mudassar Nazar 78-15-198-4; Rashid Khan 32-9-97-2; Salim Malik 8.2-2-34-0; Shoaib Mohammad 1-0-4-0; Tahir Naqqash 33.2-5-81-3; Wasim Raja 3-0-13-0.

Statistical Highlights of the Tests

1st Test, Wellington. New Zealand's total of 492 was their highest against Pakistan, beating 482-6 declared at Lahore in 1964-65. Reid batted 551 minutes for his 148, his partnership of 145 with Hadlee setting a New Zealand sixth-wicket record against Pakistan. Abdul Qadir's 54 was his highest innings in Test cricket. Torrential rain flooded parts of the Basin Reserve and prevented play on the last day.

2nd Test, Auckland. Just before tea on the fourth day, New Zealand gained their first victory in 11 home Tests against Pakistan. It was only their second win in 26 contests in this series and their first by an innings. Mudassar completed 3,000 runs in 51 Tests and Chatfield, playing in his 22nd match, took his 50th Test wicket. Reid's fifth hundred (his second in successive innings) took him past 1,000 runs in just 20 innings. He continued after having five stitches inserted in his chin – gashed by a bouncer from Azeem when he had scored 123.

3rd Test, Dunedin. Test cricket returned to Carisbrook for the first time since 1980. New Zealand's margin of victory was just one wicket in reality as Cairns had been hospitalized with a suspected hairline fracture of the skull. They thus narrowly avenged their recent identical 2-0 defeat in the rubber in Pakistan. Javed Miandad completed 5,000 runs in his 68th Test – four matches fewer than Zaheer, the only other batsman to achieve this aggregate for Pakistan. Hadlee (53 Tests) became the first bowler to take 250 wickets for New Zealand. Wasim Akram, an 18-year-old left-arm fast-medium bowler playing in only his second Test, almost snatched victory for Pakistan with an analysis of 5 for 72 in 33 overs.

One-Day Internationals

12 January at McLean Park, Napier. NEW ZEALAND won by 110 runs. Toss: New Zealand. New Zealand 277-6 closed (50 overs) (G.P. Howarth 68). Pakistan 167-9 closed (50 overs). Award: R.J. Hadlee (34*, 8-0-30-2, and 1 ct).

15 January at Seddon Park, Hamilton. NEW ZEALAND won by 4 wickets. Toss: Pakistan. Pakistan 221-4 closed (50 overs) (Javed Miandad 90*). New Zealand 222-6 (48.5 overs) (M.D. Crowe 59). Award: Javed Miandad (90* and 1 ct).

6 February at Lancaster Park, Christchurch. NEW ZEALAND won by 13 runs. Toss: New Zealand. New Zealand 264-8 closed (50 overs) (J.G. Wright 65, J.F. Reid 88). Pakistan 251 (49.4 overs) (Zaheer Abbas 58, Ramiz Raja 75). Award: J.F. Reid (88).

17 February at Eden Park, Auckland. NO RESULT (rain). Toss: Pakistan. Pakistan 189 (49.1 overs) (Ramiz Raja 59, Tahir Naqqash 61). No award.

OVERSEAS CRICKET 1984-85 / NEW ZEALAND v PAKISTAN

Pakistan Tour of New Zealand 1984-85

First-Class Matches: Played 5; Won 1, Lost 2, Drawn 2
All Matches: Played 9; Won 1, Lost 5, Drawn 3

First-Class Averages

Batting and Fielding	M	I	NO	HS	R	Avge	100	50	Ct/St
Qasim Omar	5	9	1	114*	464	58.00	1	3	4
Ramiz Raja	2	3	1	70*	81	40.50	–	1	2
Mudassar Nazar	4	6	0	89	237	39.50	–	2	2
Javed Miandad	4	7	0	112	267	38.14	1	1	5
Salim Malik	5	9	2	66	229	32.71	–	2	1
Mohsin Khan	5	9	0	71	244	27.11	–	1	3
Zaheer Abbas	3	5	0	92	116	23.20	–	1	–
Abdul Qadir	3	4	0	54	70	17.50	–	1	3
Wasim Akram	3	5	4	8*	15	15.00	–	–	1
Wasim Raja	4	6	1	19	56	11.20	–	–	1
Anil Dalpat	5	7	0	21	77	11.00	–	–	10/1
Tahir Naqqash	3	4	0	20	35	8.75	–	–	2
Azeem Hafeez	3	5	0	17	37	7.40	–	–	–

Also batted: Iqbal Qasim (2 matches) 16*, 27* (1 ct); Mohsin Kamal (2 matches) 0, 8* (1 ct); Rashid Khan (1 match) 0, 37 (1 ct); Shoaib Mohammad (1 match) 7 (2 ct).

Bowling	O	M	R	W	Avge	Best	5wI	10wM
Wasim Raja	24.3	3	92	6	15.33	2-27	–	–
Wasim Akram	122.4	30	302	12	25.16	5-56	2	1
Tahir Naqqash	83.2	16	217	6	36.16	2-11	–	–
Mohsin Kamal	40.4	4	192	5	38.40	2-28	–	–
Azeem Hafeez	162	40	484	12	40.33	5-127	1	–
Mudassar Nazar	106	16	275	5	55.00	2-85	–	–
Abdul Qadir	112	28	285	5	57.00	3-71	–	–

Also bowled: Iqbal Qasim 90-23-191-4; Javed Miandad 7-1-23-1; Qasim Omar 4-1-8-0; Ramiz Raja 2-1-4-0; Rashid Khan 32-9-97-2; Salim Malik 16.4-4-65-0; Shoaib Mohammad 1-0-4-0.

West Indies v New Zealand

New Zealand endured a difficult and unsuccessful time in 1985 on their second tour of the West Indies. With a team which, by its captain's admission, was a year or two past its peak, without their most reliable batsman of the recent past – the left-handed John Reid, who was unavailable – and against confident, powerful opponents, the New Zealanders were outclassed. Their record at the end of a seven-week tour was two heavy Test defeats and two draws, defeats in all five one-day internationals, and three hard-fought draws against combined teams in the three-day first-class matches. They did not win a single match, and never came close to winning one.

New Zealand depended too heavily on too few players, and the performance lacked consistency. The batting suffered greatly through the failure to get a solid start. The new 19-year-old opener, Ken Rutherford, clearly was not yet ready to cope with the demands of Test cricket. The experienced left-hander John Wright and captain Geoff Howarth were far below their best.

This put great strain on the middle order and, although the Crowe brothers each scored a century – Martin a marathon 188 in the high-scoring second Test, the elder Jeff in the fourth in a record second-wicket partnership with Howarth – they achieved little else besides. Only the tall, correct vice-captain Jeremy Coney scored with any frequency, until he had his left forearm fractured while batting in the first innings of the fourth Test.

Richard Hadlee confirmed his reputation as one of the game's outstanding fast bowlers and, during his match-saving innings in the first Test, joined the elite group of players to have scored over 2,000 runs and taken more than 200 wickets in Tests. Yet he lacked penetrative support, although the fast-medium Ewan Chatfield always bowled steadily.

The West Indies were playing for the first time since Clive Lloyd's retirement. Vivian Richards succeeded him as captain, but the formula for success remained the same.

Richards himself, Richie Richardson, who made a big century in the second Test, and the openers Gordon Greenidge and Desmond Haynes all averaged over 50.

The most telling individual contribution was, yet again, provided by Malcolm Marshall, who was Man of the Series for the second successive time. He spearheaded the incisive bowling with 27 wickets at 18, creating problems with his speed and hostility, more often than not delivering from round the wicket. In addition, he played an important innings in the third Test in which he also took 11 wickets.

At times, particularly during one period late on the second day of the final Test, Marshall and his fellow fast bowlers taxed the umpires' interpretation of Law 42 dealing with intimidatory bowling. Yet the series, the first between the teams since the disagreeable West Indies tour of Australia and New Zealand five years earlier, was played in equitable spirits throughout.

West Indies v New Zealand 1984-85 1st Test
Match Drawn
Played at Queen's Park Oval, Port-of-Spain, Trinidad, 29, 30, 31 March, 2, 3 April
Toss: West Indies. Umpires: D.M. Archer and C.E. Cumberbatch
Debuts: New Zealand – K.R. Rutherford

West Indies

C.G. Greenidge	b Boock	100			
D.L. Haynes	c Rutherford b Hadlee	0	(1) c M.D. Crowe b Chatfield	78
H.A. Gomes	c Smith b Hadlee	0	c and b Chatfield	25
R.B. Richardson	c Hadlee b Coney	78	(2) c Smith b Chatfield	3
I.V.A. Richards*	b Hadlee	57	(4) b Cairns	78
A.L. Logie	b Chatfield	24	(5) b Cairns	42
P.J.L. Dujon†	b Chatfield	15	(6) b Chatfield	5
M.D. Marshall	c sub (J.G. Bracewell) b Chatfield	0	(7) c Coney b Chatfield	1
R.A. Harper	c Howarth b Chatfield	0	(8) not out	11
M.A. Holding	lbw b Hadlee	12	(9) c J.J. Crowe b Chatfield	8
J. Garner	not out	0		
Extras	(B1, LB16, NB4)	21	(LB3, NB7)	10
		307	(8 wickets declared)	**261**

New Zealand

J.G. Wright	c Richardson b Harper	40	lbw b Holding	19
K.R. Rutherford	c Haynes b Marshall	0	run out	0
J.J. Crowe	c and b Harper	64	c Garner b Marshall	27
M.D. Crowe	lbw b Holding	3	c Haynes b Marshall	2
G.P. Howarth*	c sub (P.V. Simmons) b Holding	45	b Marshall	14
J.V. Coney	lbw b Marshall	25	c Dujon b Marshall	44
R.J. Hadlee	c Garner b Holding	18	not out	39
I.D.S. Smith†	c Logie b Holding	10	not out	11
B.L. Cairns	c Harper b Garner	8		
S.L. Boock	c sub (P.V. Simmons) b Garner	3		
E.J. Chatfield	not out	4		
Extras	(B12, LB11, NB19)	42	(B17, LB6, NB8)	31
		262	(6 wickets)	**187**

New Zealand	O	M	R	W	O	M	R	W
Hadlee	24.3	6	82	4	17	2	58	0
Chatfield	28	11	51	4	22	4	73	6
Cairns	26	3	93	0	19	2	70	2
Boock	19	5	47	1	14	4	57	0
Coney	9	3	17	1				

West Indies	O	M	R	W	O	M	R	W
Marshall	25	3	78	2	26	4	65	4
Garner	21.3	8	41	2	18	2	41	0
Holding	29	8	79	4	17	6	36	1
Harper	22	11	33	2	14	7	19	0
Richards	2	0	7	0	2	1	1	0
Gomes	1	0	1	0	2	1	2	0
Richardson					1	1	0	0
Logie					1	1	0	0

Fall of Wickets

Wkt	WI 1st	NZ 1st	WI 2nd	NZ 2nd
1st	5	0	10	0
2nd	9	110	58	40
3rd	194	113	172	59
4th	196	132	226	76
5th	236	182	239	83
6th	267	223	240	158
7th	267	225	241	–
8th	269	248	261	–
9th	302	250	–	–
10th	307	262	–	–

West Indies v New Zealand 1984-85 2nd Test
Match Drawn
Played at Bourda, Georgetown, Guyana, 6, 7, 8, 10, 11 April
Toss: West Indies. Umpires: L.H. Barker and D.J. Narine
Debuts: West Indies – C.G. Butts

West Indies

C.G. Greenidge	b Chatfield	10	c and b Coney		69
D.L. Haynes	b Hadlee	90	c Smith b Hadlee		9
R.B. Richardson	run out	185	(4) c J.J. Crowe b Cairns		60
H.A. Gomes	lbw b Cairns	53	(5) c sub (J.G. Bracewell) b Rutherford		35
I.V.A. Richards*	st Smith b Coney	40	(8) not out		7
A.L. Logie	c Howarth b Hadlee	52	not out		41
P.J.L. Dujon†	not out	60	b Cairns		3
C.G. Butts	did not bat		(3) c Smith b Hadlee		9
M.D. Marshall	"				
M.A. Holding	"				
J. Garner	"				
Extras	(B1, LB16, W1, NB3)	21	(B7, LB25, W1, NB2)		35
	(6 wickets declared)	**511**	(6 wickets)		**268**

New Zealand

J.G. Wright	run out	27
K.R. Rutherford	c Dujon b Garner	4
J.J. Crowe	b Marshall	22
M.D. Crowe	lbw b Garner	188
G.P. Howarth*	c Haynes b Marshall	4
J.V. Coney	c Richards b Holding	73
R.J. Hadlee	c Dujon b Marshall	16
I.D.S. Smith†	lbw b Marshall	53
B.L. Cairns	b Holding	3
S.L. Boock	b Holding	0
E.J. Chatfield	not out	3
Extras	(B12, LB2, W6, NB27)	47
		440

New Zealand	O	M	R	W	O	M	R	W
Hadlee	25.5	5	83	2	16	3	32	2
Chatfield	30	3	122	1	16	3	43	0
Cairns	32	5	105	1	18	4	47	2
Boock	43	11	107	0	18	3	52	0
Coney	18	2	62	1	10	3	20	1
Howarth	4	1	15	0	5	4	2	0
Rutherford					9	1	38	1
Wright					3	1	2	0

West Indies	O	M	R	W
Marshall	33	3	110	4
Garner	27.4	5	72	2
Holding	28	6	89	3
Butts	47	12	113	0
Richards	8	1	22	0
Gomes	8	2	20	0

Fall of Wickets

Wkt	WI 1st	NZ 1st	WI 2nd
1st	30	8	22
2nd	221	45	46
3rd	327	81	150
4th	394	98	191
5th	407	240	207
6th	511	261	225
7th	–	404	–
8th	–	415	–
9th	–	415	–
10th	–	440	–

OVERSEAS CRICKET 1984-85/WEST INDIES v NEW ZEALAND

West Indies v New Zealand 1984-85 3rd Test
West Indies won by 10 wickets
Played at Kensington Oval, Bridgetown, Barbados, 26, 27, 28, 30 April, 1 May
Toss: West Indies. Umpires: D.M. Archer and L.H. Barker
Debuts: Nil

New Zealand

G.P. Howarth*	c Greenidge b Garner	1	c Haynes b Marshall	5
J.G. Wright	c Dujon b Marshall	0	c Richardson b Davis	64
K.R. Rutherford	c Richards b Marshall	0	c Holding b Marshall	2
M.D. Crowe	hit wkt b Holding	14	c Dujon b Marshall	2
J.J. Crowe	c Dujon b Davis	21	b Davis	4
J.V. Coney	c Richardson b Marshall	12	c Logie b Marshall	83
I.D.S. Smith†	c Greenidge b Marshall	2	c and b Marshall	26
R.J. Hadlee	c Logie b Davis	29	c Greenidge b Davis	3
D.A. Stirling	c Logie b Davis	6	b Marshall	3
S.L. Boock	c Dujon b Garner	1	c Haynes b Marshall	22
E.J. Chatfield	not out	0	not out	4
Extras	(NB8)	8	(B8, LB1, W2, NB19)	30
		94		**248**

West Indies

C.G. Greenidge	c J.J. Crowe b Hadlee	2	not out	4
D.L. Haynes	c Smith b Hadlee	62	not out	5
R.B. Richardson	lbw b M.D. Crowe	22		
H.A. Gomes	c J.J.Crowe b M.D.Crowe	0		
W.W. Davis	c Smith b Stirling	16		
I.V.A. Richards*	c M.D. Crowe b Boock	105		
A.L. Logie	c J.J. Crowe b Chatfield	7		
P.J.L. Dujon†	b Hadlee	3		
M.D. Marshall	c J.J. Crowe b Chatfield	63		
J. Garner	not out	37		
M.A. Holding	c Smith b Stirling	1		
Extras	(B2, LB8, W6, NB2)	18	(W1)	1
		336	(0 wkt)	**10**

West Indies	O	M	R	W	O	M	R	W
Marshall	15	3	40	4	25.3	6	80	7
Garner	15	9	14	2	19	5	56	0
Holding	7	4	12	1	1	0	2	0
Davis	10.4	5	28	3	18	0	66	3
Richards					13	3	25	0
Gomes					4	0	10	0

New Zealand	O	M	R	W	O	M	R	W
Hadlee	26	5	86	3				
Chatfield	28	10	57	2				
Stirling	14.1	0	82	2				
M.D. Crowe	10	2	25	2				
Boock	15	1	76	1	1	1	0	0
Rutherford					0.4	0	10	0

Fall of Wickets

Wkt	NZ 1st	WI 1st	NZ 2nd	WI 2nd
1st	1	12	26	–
2nd	1	91	35	–
3rd	1	91	45	–
4th	18	95	60	–
5th	37	142	108	–
6th	44	161	141	–
7th	80	174	149	–
8th	87	257	226	–
9th	90	327	235	–
10th	94	336	248	–

OVERSEAS CRICKET 1984-85 / WEST INDIES v NEW ZEALAND

West Indies v New Zealand 1984-85 4th Test
West Indies won by 10 wickets
Played at Sabina Park, Kingston, Jamaica, 4, 5, 6, 8, 9 May
Toss: New Zealand. Umpires: D.M. Archer and J.R. Gayle
Debuts: Nil

West Indies

Batsman	Dismissal	Score	2nd innings	Score
C.G. Greenidge	c J.J. Crowe b M.D. Crowe	46	not out	33
D.L. Haynes	c J.J. Crowe b Coney	76	not out	24
R.B. Richardson	c M.D. Crowe b Coney	30		
H.A. Gomes	c Wright b Hadlee	45		
I.V.A. Richards*	lbw b Hadlee	23		
A.L. Logie	c M.D. Crowe b Hadlee	0		
P.J.L. Dujon†	c Bracewell b Troup	70		
M.D. Marshall	lbw b Bracewell	26		
W.W. Davis	c M.D. Crowe b Troup	0		
J. Garner	c M.D. Crowe b Hadlee	12		
C.A. Walsh	not out	12		
Extras	(B7, LB9, W1, NB6)	23	(B1, LB1)	2
		363	(0 wkt)	**59**

New Zealand

Batsman	Dismissal	Score	2nd innings	Score
G.P. Howarth*	c Gomes b Marshall	5	c Gomes b Walsh	84
J.G. Wright	b Davis	53	c Dujon b Garner	10
J.J. Crowe	c Richardson b Garner	2	c Marshall b Richards	112
M.D. Crowe	c Davis b Walsh	6	c Dujon b Walsh	1
J.V. Coney	retired hurt	4	absent hurt	–
K.R. Rutherford	c Dujon b Marshall	1	(5) lbw b Marshall	5
I.D.S. Smith†	b Garner	0	(6) b Marshall	9
R.J. Hadlee	c Dujon b Davis	18	(7) c Walsh b Marshall	14
J.G. Bracewell	not out	25	(8) c Gomes b Marshall	27
G.B. Troup	c Marshall b Davis	0	(9) c Richardson b Garner	2
E.J. Chatfield	b Davis	2	(10) not out	0
Extras	(B4, LB1, W2, NB15)	22	(B4, LB7, NB8)	19
		138		**283**

New Zealand Bowling

Bowler	O	M	R	W	O	M	R	W
Hadlee	28.4	11	53	4	5	1	15	0
Troup	17	1	87	2	3	0	13	0
Chatfield	26	5	85	0	2	0	10	0
M.D. Crowe	10	2	30	1				
Bracewell	21	5	54	1	4	0	14	0
Coney	14	3	38	2				
Smith					3	1	5	0

West Indies Bowling

Bowler	O	M	R	W	O	M	R	W
Marshall	17	3	47	2	28.4	8	66	4
Garner	16	0	37	2	19	8	41	2
Davis	13.5	5	19	4	21	1	75	0
Walsh	9	1	30	1	16	4	45	2
Richards					14	2	34	1
Gomes					3	0	11	0
Richardson					1	1	0	0

Fall of Wickets

Wkt	WI 1st	NZ 1st	NZ 2nd	WI 2nd
1st	82	11	13	–
2nd	144	15	223	–
3rd	164	37	223	–
4th	207	65	228	–
5th	207	68	238	–
6th	273	106	242	–
7th	311	113	259	–
8th	311	122	281	–
9th	339	138	283	–
10th	363	–	–	–

Test Match Averages: West Indies v New Zealand 1984-85

West Indies

Batting and Fielding	M	I	NO	HS	R	Avge	100	50	Ct/St
R.B. Richardson	4	6	0	185	378	63.00	1	2	5
I.V.A. Richards	4	6	1	105	310	62.00	1	2	2
D.L. Haynes	4	8	2	90	344	57.33	–	4	5
C.G. Greenidge	4	7	2	100	264	52.80	1	1	3
J. Garner	4	3	2	37*	49	49.00	–	–	3
A.L. Logie	4	6	1	52	166	33.20	–	1	4
P.J.L. Dujon	4	6	1	70	156	31.20	–	2	11
H.A. Gomes	4	6	0	53	158	26.33	–	1	2
M.D. Marshall	4	4	0	63	90	22.50	–	1	3
M.A. Holding	3	3	0	12	21	7.00	–	–	1

Also batted: C.G. Butts (1 match) 9; W.W. Davis (2 matches) 16, 0 (1 ct); R.A. Harper (1 match) 0, 11* (2 ct); C.A. Walsh (1 match) 12* (1 ct).

Bowling	O	M	R	W	Avge	Best	5wI	10wM
M.D. Marshall	170.1	30	486	27	18.00	7-80	1	1
W.W. Davis	63.3	11	188	10	18.80	4-19	–	–
M.A. Holding	82	24	218	9	24.22	4-79	–	–
J. Garner	136.1	37	302	10	30.20	2-14	–	–

Also bowled: C.G. Butts 47-12-113-0; H.A. Gomes 18-3-44-0; R.A. Harper 36-18-52-2; A.L. Logie 1-1-0-0; I.V.A. Richards 39-7-89-1; R.B. Richardson 2-2-0-0; C.A. Walsh 25-5-75-3.

New Zealand

Batting and Fielding	M	I	NO	HS	R	Avge	100	50	Ct/St
J.V. Coney	4	6	1	83	241	48.20	–	2	2
J.J. Crowe	4	7	0	112	252	36.00	1	1	8
M.D. Crowe	4	7	0	188	216	30.85	1	–	6
J.G. Wright	4	7	0	64	213	30.42	–	2	1
R.J. Hadlee	4	7	1	39*	137	22.83	–	–	1
G.P. Howarth	4	7	0	84	158	22.57	–	1	2
I.D.S. Smith	4	7	1	53	111	18.50	–	1	7/1
E.J. Chatfield	4	6	5	4*	13	13.00	–	–	1
S.L. Boock	3	4	0	22	26	6.50	–	–	–
K.R. Rutherford	4	7	0	5	12	1.71	–	–	1

Also batted: J.G. Bracewell (1 match) 25*, 27 (1 ct); B.L. Cairns (2 matches) 8, 3; D.A. Stirling (1 match) 6, 3; G.B. Troup (1 match) 0, 2.

Bowling	O	M	R	W	Avge	Best	5wI	10wM
R.J. Hadlee	143	31	409	15	27.26	4-53	–	–
J.V. Coney	51	11	137	5	27.40	2-38	–	–
E.J. Chatfield	152	35	441	13	33.92	6-73	1	1
B.L. Cairns	95	14	315	5	63.00	2-47	–	–

Also bowled: S.L. Boock 110-25-339-2; J.G. Bracewell 25-5-68-1; M.D. Crowe 20-4-55-3; G.P. Howarth 9-5-17-0; K.R. Rutherford 9.4-1-48-1; I.D.S. Smith 3-1-5-0; D.A. Stirling 14.1-0-82-2; G.B. Troup 20-1-100-2; J.G. Wright 3-1-2-0.

Statistical Highlights of the Tests

1st Test, Port-of-Spain. New Zealand paid only their second visit to the Caribbean 13 years after their first. The partnership of 185 between Greenidge, who compiled his 12th Test hundred, and Richardson was a third-wicket record for this series. Almost four hours was lost on the third day when rain seeped through a frayed tarpaulin covering the pitch. New Zealand were set 307 to win in a minimum of five hours. During his match-saving partnership with Coney, Hadlee became the sixth player and first New Zealander to complete the Test double double of 2,000 runs and 200 wickets.

2nd Test, Georgetown. Richardson's fourth and highest Test hundred dominated the second-highest West Indies total in a home Test against New Zealand (after 564-8 at Bridgetown in 1971-72). During his innings of 188, his second Test hundred, Martin Crowe completed 1,000 runs in 21 Tests. His partnerships with Coney (142) and Smith (143) were fifth- and seventh-wicket New Zealand records for this series.

3rd Test, Bridgetown. New Zealand (94) were dismissed for their lowest total in the Caribbean (previously 162 at Port-of-Spain in 1971-72). Richards included 3 sixes and 13 fours in his 19th Test hundred – his first as captain. Before returning his best match analysis of 11 for 120 (a West Indies record v New Zealand), Marshall shared in record West Indies eighth- and ninth-wicket partnerships against New Zealand with Richards (83) and Garner (70) respectively. Greenidge made the winning hit 37 minutes into the fifth day to secure the first outright result in eight Tests between these teams in the Caribbean.

4th Test, Kingston. West Indies, undefeated at home since 1978, gained their second successive victory by ten wickets, this time with more than a day to spare. After New Zealand had followed on, Howarth, playing possibly his final Test innings, and Jeff Crowe added 210 to set a New Zealand second-wicket record for this series (previously 139 by Glenn Turner and Bevan Congdon at Port-of-Spain in 1971-72). Marshall's tally of 27 wickets in the rubber equalled the record set by Bruce Taylor for New Zealand in 1971-72.

One-Day Internationals

20 March at Recreation Ground, St John's, Antigua. WEST INDIES won by 23 runs. Toss: New Zealand. West Indies 231-8 closed (46 overs) (D.L. Haynes 54, I.V.A. Richards 70). New Zealand 208-8 closed (46 overs) (J.J. Crowe 53). Award: R.A. Harper (45*, 8-0-34-2, and 1 ct).

27 March at Queen's Park Oval, Port-of-Spain, Trinidad. WEST INDIES won by 6 wickets. Toss: West Indies. New Zealand 51-3 closed (22 overs). West Indies 55-4 (17 overs). Award: W.W. Davis (6-2-7-3).

14 April at Albion Sports Complex, Berbice, Guyana. WEST INDIES won by 130 runs. Toss: New Zealand. West Indies 259-5 closed (50 overs) (D.L. Haynes 146*, I.V.A. Richards 51). New Zealand 129 (48.1 overs). Award: D.L. Haynes (146*).

17 April at Queen's Park Oval, Port-of-Spain, Trinidad. WEST INDIES won by 10 wickets. Toss: West Indies. New Zealand 116 (42.2 overs) (J. Garner 6-1-10-4). West Indies 117-0 (25.2 overs) (D.L. Haynes 85*). Award: J. Garner (6-1-10-4).

23 April at Kensington Oval, Bridgetown, Barbados. WEST INDIES won by 112 runs. Toss: New Zealand. West Indies 265-3 closed (49 overs). C.D.L. Haynes 116, H.A. Gomes 78). New Zealand 153-8 closed (49 overs). Award: D.L. Haynes (116).

OVERSEAS CRICKET 1984-85 / WEST INDIES v NEW ZEALAND

New Zealand Tour of West Indies 1984-85

First-Class Matches: Played 7; Won 0, Lost 2, Drawn 5
All Matches: Played 12; Won 0, Lost 7, Drawn 5

First-Class Averages

Batting and Fielding	M	I	NO	HS	R	Avge	100	50	Ct/St
J.V. Coney	6	10	2	99	447	55.87	–	4	3
M.D. Crowe	5	9	–	188	396	44.00	2	1	7
J.G. Wright	7	13	–	101	458	35.23	1	3	1
J.J. Crowe	7	13	–	112	354	27.23	1	2	11
R.J. Hadlee	4	7	1	39*	137	22.83	–	–	1
K.R. Rutherford	7	13	1	109*	256	21.33	1	2	3
J.G. Bracewell	4	7	1	50	113	18.83	–	1	3
B.L. Cairns	5	7	1	52*	111	18.50	–	1	–
I.D.S. Smith	4	7	1	53	111	18.50	–	1	7/1
G.P. Howarth	7	13	–	84	186	14.30	–	1	4
E.J. Chatfield	5	7	5	4*	17	8.50	–	–	2
D.A. Stirling	4	7	2	17	42	8.40	–	–	1
R.T. Hart	3	6	–	8	34	5.66	–	–	2
G.B. Troup	3	5	3	8*	11	5.50	–	–	1
S.L. Boock	6	8	–	22	42	5.25	–	–	1

Bowling	O	M	R	W	Avge	Best	5wI	10wM
D.A. Stirling	60.1	7	308	13	23.69	4-66	–	–
R.J. Hadlee	143	33	409	15	27.26	4-53	–	–
J.V. Coney	52	11	143	5	28.60	2-38	–	–
J.G. Bracewell	88	19	223	7	31.85	3-58	–	–
E.J. Chatfield	179	45	493	14	35.21	6-73	1	1
B.L. Cairns	156.5	22	495	14	35.35	3-45	–	–
G.B. Troup	56	8	250	5	50.00	2-41	–	–
S.L. Boock	177.1	42	493	6	82.16	2-63	–	–

Also bowled: M.D. Crowe 20-4-55-3; G.P. Howarth 9-5-17-0; K.R. Rutherford 9.4-1-48-1; I.D.S. Smith 3-1-5-0; J.G. Wright 3-1-2-0.

Benson & Hedges World Series Cup

The West Indies retained the Benson and Hedges World Series Cup with a 2-1 win over Australia in the best-of-three finals. This was the sixth season of the 50-overs-a-side competition and the fourth time the West Indies had won it in four attempts. They strolled through the qualifying round, winning all 10 matches, but met unexpectedly strong opposition from Australia in the finals.

Australia won the first final by 26 runs under lights in Sydney and were well placed to win the second under Melbourne's sun after scoring 271 for three and having the West Indies at 179 for five. But little Gus Logie and wicketkeeper Jeff Dujon underlined the West Indies' batting depth with a rollicking 86-run partnership, which stole victory from the surprised, deflated Australians, who then succumbed by seven wickets in Sydney two days later.

It was another richly rewarding competition for Clive Lloyd's men, who shared $A67,500 – $30,000 for winning their 10 qualifying matches, $A4,500 for taking nine Player of the Match awards, $32,000 for winning the finals, and $A1,000 for Michael Holding's sharing the Player of the Finals award with Australian captain Allan Border. The Australians collected $A40,000, including $A16,000 for losing the finals, and the Sri Lankans received $A17,500.

On their first major assignment in Australia, the Sri Lankans, led by genial skipper Duleep Mendis, were immensely popular tourists, fine ambassadors, and sometimes stern opponents. Their batting, led by the world-class Roy Dias and Mendis, Aravinda de Silva, and wicketkeeper Amal Silva, often was of the highest quality, but their bowling and unathletic fielding usually were below that expected of an international team. The Sri Lankans enjoyed one day of glory when they defeated Australia by four wickets in Melbourne in the eighth of the 15 qualifying matches.

Injuries and more selectorial experimentation than in previous seasons contributed to Australia's using 20 players, compared with 16 by the other two teams. While there were days when the Australians finally appeared to have come to terms with the demands of limited-overs cricket, there still were other days when batsmen panicked themselves into slogging, bowlers were wayward, and fieldsmen missed too many catches.

Spread over 5½ hectic weeks in the five Test-match venues, and, for the first time, Hobart, the competition developed an air of predictability, largely because of the West Indies' superiority. Border complained of being 'sick of the sight of the West Indies', and the more discerning spectators and television viewers were relieved to get off the 'pyjama game's' merry-go-round. Yet the marketing and TV people again could point to high ratings and an aggregate crowd of 459,616 for 18 days (25,534 a day), compared with 339,933 for 23 days of the Test series (14,779 a day).

OVERSEAS CRICKET 1984-85/BENSON & HEDGES WORLD SERIES 71

Qualifying Rounds

6 January at Melbourne Cricket Ground. WEST INDIES beat AUSTRALIA by 7 wickets. Toss: West Indies. Australia 240-6 closed (50 overs) (A.R. Border 73, D.C. Boon 55). West Indies 241-3 (44.5 overs) (D.L. Haynes 123*). Award: D.L. Haynes (123*).

8 January at Sydney Cricket Ground (floodlit). AUSTRALIA beat SRI LANKA by 6 wickets. Toss: Sri Lanka. Sri Lanka 239-7 closed (49 overs) (S.A.R. Silva 68, R.L. Dias 60; R.M. Hogg 10-0-47-4). Australia 240-4 (46.2 overs) (G.M. Wood 52*, A.R. Border 79*). Award: A.R. Border (79* and 1 ct).

10 January at Tasmania C.A. Ground, Hobart. WEST INDIES beat SRI LANKA by 8 wickets. Toss: West Indies. Sri Lanka 197-7 closed (50 overs) (L.R.D. Mendis 56). West Indies 198-2 (40.4 overs) (C.G. Greenidge 61, R.B. Richardson 52*). Award: L.R.D. Mendis (56).

12 January at Woolloongabba, Brisbane. WEST INDIES beat SRI LANKA by 90 runs. Toss: Sri Lanka. West Indies 270-6 closed (50 overs) (I.V.A. Richards 98, C.H. Lloyd 89*). Sri Lanka 180 (48.1 overs) (R.L. Dias 80). Award: I.V.A. Richards (98, 10-0-45-2, and 1 ct).

13 January at Woolloongabba, Brisbane. WEST INDIES beat AUSTRALIA by 5 wickets. Toss: West Indies. Australia 191 (50 overs). West Indies 195-5 (37.4 overs) (C.H. Lloyd 52*). Award: C.H. Lloyd (52*).

15 January at Sydney Cricket Ground (floodlit). WEST INDIES beat AUSTRALIA by 5 wickets. Toss: Australia. Australia 200-5 closed (50 overs) (K.C. Wessels 63). West Indies 201-5 (43.3 overs) (I.V.A. Richards 103*). Award: I.V.A. Richards (103*, 10-0-41-1).

17 January at Sydney Cricket Ground (floodlit). WEST INDIES beat SRI LANKA by 65 runs. Toss: West Indies. West Indies 267-3 closed (50 overs) (C.G. Greenidge 67, D.L. Haynes 54, R.B. Richardson 57*). Sri Lanka 202-5 closed (50 overs) (R.L. Dias 65*). Award: C.G. Greenidge (67 and 1 ct).

19 January at Melbourne Cricket Ground. SRI LANKA beat AUSTRALIA by 4 wickets. Toss: Sri Lanka. Australia 226-9 closed (50 overs) (W.B. Phillips 67; R.J. Ratnayake 10-3-37-4). Sri Lanka 230-6 (49.2 overs). Award: R.J. Ratnayake (5* and 10-3-37-4).

20 January at Melbourne Cricket Ground. WEST INDIES beat AUSTRALIA by 65 runs. Toss: Australia. West Indies 271-7 closed (50 overs) (I.V.A. Richards 74, A.L. Logie 72). Australia 206-9 closed (50 overs) (A.R. Border 61). Award: I.V.A. Richards (74, 10-0-43-2, and 1 ct).

23 January at Sydney Cricket Ground. AUSTRALIA beat SRI LANKA by 3 wickets. Toss: Australia. Sri Lanka 240-6 closed (50 overs) (L.R.D. Mendis 80, P.A. De Silva 81*). Australia 242-7 (47.1 overs) (K.C. Wessels 82, A.R. Border 57, D.M. Jones 62*). Award: K.C. Wessels (82 and 10-0-61-2).

26 January at Adelaide Oval. WEST INDIES beat SRI LANKA by 8 wickets. Toss: West Indies. Sri Lanka 204-6 closed (50 overs) (R.L. Dias 66). West Indies 205-2 (37.2 overs) (C.G. Greenidge 110*, D.L. Haynes 51). Award: C.G. Greenidge (110*).

27 January at Adelaide Oval. WEST INDIES beat AUSTRALIA by 6 wickets. Toss: West Indies. Australia 200-9 closed (50 overs) (G.M. Wood 104*). West Indies 201-4 (43.4 overs) (I.V.A. Richards 51). Award: J. Garner (10-3-17-3).

28 January at Adelaide Oval. AUSTRALIA beat SRI LANKA by 232 runs. Toss: Sri Lanka. Australia 323-2 closed (50 overs) (S.B. Smith 55, D.M. Jones 99*, A.R. Border 118*). Sri Lanka 91 (35.5 overs). Award: A.R. Border (118*).

2 February at W.A.C.A. Ground, Perth. WEST INDIES beat SRI LANKA by 82 runs. Toss: Sri Lanka. West Indies 309-6 closed (50 overs) (H.A. Gomes 101, C.H. Lloyd 54*). Sri Lanka 227-6 closed (50 overs) (S.A.R. Silva 85, A. Ranatunga 63*). Award: H.A. Gomes (101 and 7-0-41-0).

Qualifying Table	P	W	L	Points
WEST INDIES	10	10	0	20
AUSTRALIA	10	4	6	8
SRI LANKA	10	1	9	2

Final Round Results

6 February at Sydney Cricket Ground (floodlit). AUSTRALIA beat WEST INDIES by 26 runs. Toss: West Indies. Australia 247-6 closed (50 overs) (A.R. Border 127*, W.B. Phillips 50). West Indies 221 (47.3 overs) (I.V.A. Richards 68).

10 February at Melbourne Cricket Ground. WEST INDIES beat AUSTRALIA by 4 wickets. Toss: West Indies. Australia 271-3 closed (50 overs) (S.B. Smith 54, G.M. Wood 81, W.B. Phillips 56*). West Indies 273-6 (49.2 overs) (R.B. Richardson 50, A.L. Logie 60).

12 February at Sydney Cricket Ground (floodlit). WEST INDIES beat AUSTRALIA by 7 wickets. Toss: West Indies. Australia 178 (50 overs) (S.P. O'Donnell 69; M.A. Holding 10-1-26-5). West Indies 179-3 (47 overs) (D.L. Haynes 76*, I.V.A. Richards 76).

Finals awards: A.R. Border and M.A. Holding.

World Championship of Cricket

Sunil Gavaskar's on-again, off-again reign as India's captain ended triumphantly when his team won the $135,000 Benson & Hedges World Championship of Cricket. India defeated Pakistan by eight wickets in the final of the 13-match tournament, contested by the seven Test-match countries over three weeks at the end of the 1984-85 Australian season. The competition was staged by the Victorian Cricket Association as part of Victoria's 150th anniversary celebrations and promoted as 'The Greatest Show on Turf'.

The first all-in championship of its type played outside of England was successful enough to suggest the 1991 World Cup could be played in Australia. The 13 matches drew a total of 245,309 spectators, including 82,494 to the first between Australia and England and 35,296 to the final. Those two matches and five others were played under the magnificent new $A4m six-tower lighting system installed at the Melbourne Cricket Ground.

Australia and England, helped by the huge crowd and associated razzamatazz, provided an appropriate, spectacular opening to a script that originally did not contain even a hint that neither of them would qualify for the semi-finals nor that the West Indies would fail to reach the final.

They were not short of excuses. The Australians said they were physically and mentally drained after having been tormented for most of the summer by the West Indies in the Tests and the World Series Cup competition. The Englishmen were said to have been on a rest and recuperative holiday after the rigours of their successful Test and one-day programme in India. And the West Indians, who also were tired in body and mind, actually complained that the championship programme did not give them enough consistent match practice and they could not pick themselves up again after they had enjoyed a week's break before their semi-final against Pakistan.

In the end, Australia and England were not good enough, the West Indies had an off day (and night), New Zealand were outplayed with bat and ball after a quick trip home, and Sri Lanka, the charming new chums, proved to be boys on men's errands.

So that left a 'curry and rice' final between India and Pakistan, the two most enthusiastic and committed sides in the championship. Kapil Dev's lively bowling wrecked the start of Pakistan's innings, Imran Khan and captain Javed Miandad re-established it, until Imran was run out and then slim young leg-spinner Laxman Sivaramakrishnan and left-arm orthodox Ravi Shastri took the next four wickets to restrict Pakistan to 176 for nine off 50 overs. Opening batsmen Shastri and Krishna Srikkanth, the former watchful, the latter aggressive, laid a 103-run foundation on which Shastri, new young champion Mohammed Azharuddin, and experienced Dilip Vengsarkar prospered to give India victory by eight wickets with 2.5 overs to spare. Who said their winning the '83 World Cup was a fluke?

For Australian eyes, the Indians' graceful batting and subtle medium-pace and spin bowling had provided an interesting welcome contrast to the sheer power and speed of the West Indians. And it helped relieve the monotony of a season of over-kill – 31 one-day internationals in nine weeks.

Qualifying Rounds

17 February at Melbourne Cricket Ground (floodlit). AUSTRALIA beat ENGLAND by 7 wickets. Toss: England. England 214-8 closed (49 overs) (A.J. Lamb 53). Australia 215-3 (45.2 overs) (R.B. Kerr 87*, D.M. Jones 78*). Award: R.B. Kerr (87* and 1 ct).

20 February at Melbourne Cricket Ground (floodlit). INDIA beat PAKISTAN by 6 wickets. Toss: Pakistan. Pakistan 183 (49.2 overs) (Qasim Omar 57; R.M.H. Binny 8.2-3-35-4). India 184-4 (45.5 overs) (M. Azharuddin 93*, S.M. Gavaskar 54). Award: M. Azharuddin (93*).

21 February at Sydney Cricket Ground (floodlit). NEW ZEALAND v WEST INDIES: NO RESULT (rain). Toss: New Zealand. New Zealand 57-2 (18.4 overs).

23 February at Melbourne Cricket Ground (floodlit). NEW ZEALAND beat SRI LANKA by 51 runs. Toss: Sri Lanka. New Zealand 223 (49.4 overs) (J.F. Reid 62). Sri Lanka 172 (42.4 overs) (J.V. Coney 10-0-46-4). Award: J.F. Reid (62).

24 February at Melbourne Cricket Ground. PAKISTAN beat AUSTRALIA by 62 runs. Toss: Australia. Pakistan 262-6 closed (50 overs) (Mudassar Nazar 69, Mohsin Khan 81). Australia 200 (42.3 overs) (S.P. O'Donnell 74*; Wasim Akram 8-1-21-5). Award: Wasim Akram (8-1-21-5).

26 February at Sydney Cricket Ground (floodlit). INDIA beat ENGLAND by 86 runs. Toss: England. India 235-9 closed (50 overs) (K. Srikkanth 57). England 149 (41.4 overs). Award: K. Srikkanth (57 and 1 ct).

27 February at Melbourne Cricket Ground (floodlit). WEST INDIES beat SRI LANKA by 8 wickets. Toss: Sri Lanka. Sri Lanka 135-7 closed (47 overs) (J.R. Ratnayeke 50). West Indies 136-2 (23.1 overs). Award: J.R. Ratnayeke (50).

2 March at Melbourne Cricket Ground (floodlit). PAKISTAN beat ENGLAND by 67 runs. Toss: Pakistan. Pakistan 213-8 closed (50 overs) (Mudassar Nazar 77). England 146 (24.2 overs) (A.J. Lamb 81). Award: A.J. Lamb (81).

3 March at Melbourne Cricket Ground. INDIA beat AUSTRALIA by 8 wickets. Toss: India. Australia 163 (49.3 overs) (W.B. Phillips 60). India 165-2 (36.1 overs) (R.J. Shastri 51, K. Srikkanth 93*). Award: R.J. Shastri (51 and 10-1-34-1).

Group 'A'	P	W	L	Points	Group 'B'	P	W	L	NR	Points
INDIA	3	3	0	6	WEST INDIES	2	1	0	1	3
PAKISTAN	3	2	1	4	NEW ZEALAND	2	1	0	1	3
AUSTRALIA	3	1	2	2	SRI LANKA	2	0	2	0	0
ENGLAND	3	0	3	0						

Semi-Finals

5 March at Sydney Cricket Ground (floodlit). INDIA beat NEW ZEALAND by 7 wickets. Toss: India. New Zealand 206 (50 overs) (J.F. Reid 55; Madan Lal 8-1-37-4). India 207-3 (46 overs) (R.J. Shastri 53, D.B. Vengsarkar 63*, Kapil Dev 54*). Award: R.J. Shastri (53 and 10-1-31-3).

6 March at Melbourne Cricket Ground (floodlit). PAKISTAN beat WEST INDIES by 7 wickets. Toss: West Indies. West Indies 159 (44.3 overs) (Mudassar Nazar 7.3-0-28-5). Pakistan 160-3 (46 overs) (Ramiz Raja 60). Award: Ramiz Raja (60).

(contd at bottom of page 75)

Other Overseas Results

Rothmans Four Nations Trophy

In March 1985, four countries sent teams to play in a limited-overs tournament in the United Arab Emirates at Sharjah CA Stadium. India underlined their aptitude for the one-day game by winning the competition, despite a dreadful start in which they were skittled out for 125 by Pakistan thanks to a marvellous piece of bowling from Imran (6-14).

22 March: INDIA beat PAKISTAN by 38 runs. Toss: Pakistan. India 125 (42.4 overs) (Imran Khan 10-2-14-6). Pakistan 87 (32.5 overs). Award: Imram Khan (0 and 10-2-14-6).

24 March: AUSTRALIA beat ENGLAND by 2 wickets. Toss: Australia. England 177-8 closed (50 overs). Australia 178-8 (50 overs). Award: G.R.J. Matthews (24 and 10-3-15-1).

Plate-Winner's Final

26 March: PAKISTAN beat ENGLAND by 43 runs. Toss: England. Pakistan 175-7 closed (50 overs) (Javed Miandad 71; N. Gifford 10-0-23-4). England 132 (48.2 overs). Award: Javed Miandad (71 and 2 ct).

Final

29 March: INDIA beat AUSTRALIA by 3 wickets. Toss: India. Australia 139 (42.3 overs). India 140-7 (39.2 overs). Award: M. Amarnath (24*, 7-1-19-2 and 2 ct).

Sri Lanka v New Zealand

On their way to Pakistan for their three-Test tour, New Zealand stopped off in Sri Lanka to play two one-day internationals. The two countries won one match each.

One-Day Internationals

3 November at Saravanamuttu Stadium, Colombo. SRI LANKA won by 4 wickets. Toss: New Zealand. New Zealand 171-6 closed (45 overs) (J.J. Crowe 57*). Sri Lanka 174-6 (39.4 overs) (P.A. De Silva 50*). Award: P.A. De Silva (50* and 2 ct).

4 November at Tyronne Fernando Stadium, Moratuwa. NEW ZEALAND won by 7 wickets. Toss: New Zealand. Sri Lanka 114-9 closed (41 overs). New Zealand 118-3 (31.4 overs) M.D. Crowe 52*). Award: M.D. Crowe (52* and 9-3-17-2).

World Championship of Cricket (contd)

Plate-Winner's Final

9 March at Sydney Cricket Ground. WEST INDIES beat NEW ZEALAND by 6 wickets. Toss: West Indies. New Zealand 138-9 closed (50 overs). West Indies 139-4 (37.2 overs) (I.V.A. Richards 51). Award: I.V.A. Richards (51).

Final

10 March at Melbourne Cricket Ground (floodlit). INDIA beat PAKISTAN by 8 wickets. Toss: Pakistan. Pakistan 176-9 closed (50 overs). India 177-2 (47.1 overs) (R.J. Shastri 63*, K. Srikkanth 67). Award: K. Srikkanth (67 and 1 ct).

Cricket in Australia

New South Wales and Queensland waged one of the greatest battles in the long history of the Sheffield Shield before New South Wales won by just one wicket late on the fifth day of an epic final in Sydney. It was the 38th time and the second in three seasons that New South Wales had been the Shield champions. And Queensland, poor old Queensland, were the bridesmaids again, much to the horror and disbelief of their tortured followers, who had convinced themselves that this really and finally was their season – for the first time since Queensland joined the competition in 1926-27.

Queensland had led the Shield table for almost the entire 30-match preliminary round, only to be displaced at the end by New South Wales, who beat Victoria by 25 runs in Sydney while Queensland succumbed to South Australia by 12 runs in Adelaide. Queensland thus forfeited the right to stage the final in Brisbane and faced the added pressure of having to win outright rather than draw it to clinch the Shield.

Bill O'Reilly described the final as 'immortal' – high praise from 'Tiger', who, at 79, and still as sharp as a tack, has not been exactly enchanted with the path cricket has followed in the 1970s and 1980s. But no one disputed him this time, for it was *the* match of the season, outstripping the five Tests and the 31 one-day internationals . . . when the Shield competition was supposed to be the destitute relation.

While Test fast bowlers Geoff Lawson (New South Wales) and Craig McDermott (Queensland) could not play in the final because of injuries, both teams boasted powerful line-ups, each with seven players who had represented Australia in Tests or one-day internationals. New South Wales had John Dyson, Steve Smith, Steve Rixon, Dirk Wellham (captain), Greg Matthews, Murray Bennett, and Bob Holland, and Queensland had Robbie Kerr, Kepler Wessels, Allan Border (captain), Greg Ritchie, John Maguire, Carl Rackemann, and Jeff Thomson.

Two others – Queensland wicketkeeper-batsman Ray Phillips and New South Wales opening bowler Dave Gilbert – later were chosen in the Australian team for the England tour, as replacements for Rixon and Rackemann, who had committed themselves to the proposed 'rebel' tour of South Africa.

New South Wales' trump was Pakistan's champion all-rounder Imran Khan, who played seven of the state's 12 first-class matches for the season, including the final in which he was a match-winner with four for 66 and five for 34. Queensland could not complain about Imran's being an import as three of their players – Border, Thomson, and Phillips – had started their careers with New South Wales before heading for the more lucrative northern pastures. South African-born Wessels also had been lured from Sydney to Brisbane after his stint with World Series Cricket.

Wessels' 49 and 22 in the final lifted his first-class aggregate for the season to 1,020 – the only player to reach 1,000. Held together by Trevor Hohns' second first-class century, Queensland mustered 374 after having been 224 for six. New South Wales replied with 318, of which

Dyson made 66 in nearly six hours, Smith a slashing 76, and talented new all-rounder Steve Waugh a mature 71. When Queensland were dismissed a second time for only 163, thanks to Imran and spinners Bennett and Holland, New South Wales required 220 to win, and started the last day at 64 for three. When they had New South Wales at 209 for 9 in a desperately fought, pulsating finish, Queensland were poised to achieve their impossible dream – until Peter Clifford (83 not out in a heroic five-hour vigil) and Gilbert (8 not out) hung on defiantly against everything Rackemann could hurl at them.

Thomson's dismissal of Clifford in New South Wales' first innings gave him his 600th first-class wicket. The other major milestone in the match was Rixon's equalling Doug Walters' record 90 appearances for New South Wales.

Two weeks before the Shield final, Australian cricket's last playing link with the 1960s was severed when John Inverarity, MBE, played his last first-class match at the age of 41. He finished a distinguished 23-season career in style, scoring 55 and 4 and taking nine for 136 off 49 overs of left-arm orthodox spin, as well as completing the catch that gave South Australia their surprise 12-run win over Queensland in Adelaide. In 233 first-class matches for Western Australia, South Australia, and Australia (six Tests from 1968 to 1972 and two internationals against the World XI in 1971-72), Inverarity scored 11,777 runs (avg 35.9), with 26 hundreds, and claimed 221 wickets and 251 catches. In 159 Shield matches for Western Australia (from 1962-63 to 1978-79) and South Australia (from 1979-80 to 1984-85), he made an Australian record of 9,341 runs (avg 38.44), with 23 hundreds and 45 fifties, and took 157 wickets and 188 catches. As West Australian captain and the elder states-man of South Australian cricket, Inverarity's influence on the game and his team-mates was important and considerable – and his scholarly, authoritative manner, allied with his ability, will be missed.

While playing-times for Shield matches were increased by two hours (half-an-hour a day) to 26 hours, the 30 matches produced only 14 out-right results – one more than the previous season. Despite the busy international programme, Sydney still was able to draw 11,782 spectators to the McDonald's Cup (50 overs a side) final, in which New South Wales scored the first leg of their double by defeating South Australia by 88 runs, and 26,842 for the five days of the Shield final a month later.

Tasmanian batsman David Boon won the Benson & Hedges Sheffield Shield Player of the Year award ($A2,000 plus a gold tray and goblet set), with 16 votes – one more than New South Wales all-rounder Greg Matthews and four more than South Australian batsman Michael Haysman, New South Wales leg-spinner Holland, and Queensland batsman Ritchie.

New South Wales v Queensland 1984-85 Sheffield Shield Final
New South Wales won by 1 wicket
Played at Sydney Cricket Ground, 15, 16, 17, 18, 19 March

Queensland

R.B. Kerr	b Imran	9	lbw b Imran		3
B.A. Courtice	b Gilbert	5	b Imran		0
K.C. Wessels	c Dyson b Gilbert	49	c Dyson b Holland		22
A.R. Border*	c Dyson b Bennett	64	(5) c Dyson b Imran		45
G.M. Ritchie	c Waugh b Imran	20	(6) c and b Bennett		12
G.S. Trimble	c Wellham b Bennett	38	(7) c Waugh b Bennett		16
T.V. Hohns	st Rixon b Holland	103	(8) c Clifford b Bennett		2
R.B. Phillips†	c Smith b Waugh	53	(4) c Wellham b Imran		47
J.N. Maguire	b Imran	19	b Imran		4
C.G. Rackemann	b Imran	1	c Imran b Bennett		3
J.R. Thomson	not out	0	not out		1
Extras	(B3, LB5, NB5)	13	(B3, LB2, W1, NB2)		8
		374			**163**

New South Wales

J. Dyson	c Ritchie b Rackemann	66	c Phillips b Thomson		19
S.B. Smith	c Phillips b Maguire	76	hit wicket b Rackemann		7
S.J. Rixon†	c Phillips b Maguire	0	(4) c and b Thomson		2
D.M. Wellham*	lbw b Thomson	31	(3) b Thomson		39
P.S. Clifford	c Phillips b Thomson	13	not out		83
G.R.J. Matthews	lbw b Maguire	16	c Phillips b Rackemann		8
Imran Khan	c Phillips b Rackemann	7	c Border b Rackemann		18
S.R. Waugh	c Maguire b Thomson	71	c Phillips b Rackemann		21
M.J. Bennett	c Phillips b Border	10	c Border b Rackemann		1
R.G. Holland	c Trimble b Border	0	c Kerr b Rackemann		10
D.R. Gilbert	not out	8	not out		8
Extras	(LB1, NB19)	20	(B3, LB2, NB2)		7
		318			**223**

NSW	O	M	R	W	O	M	R	W
Imran	27.3	6	66	4	19	6	34	5
Gilbert	27	6	67	2	15	5	24	0
Matthews	27	10	53	0	2	0	8	0
Waugh	12	6	15	1	6	1	21	0
Bennett	34	16	54	2	20	4	32	4
Holland	43	13	111	1	15	5	39	1

Queensland	O	M	R	W	O	M	R	W
Thomson	27.3	6	83	3	29	4	81	3
Rackemann	30	9	80	2	30.2	8	54	6
Maguire	33	6	90	3	14	2	27	0
Border	7	2	27	2				
Hohns	24	7	37	0	20	4	56	0

Fall of Wickets

Wkt	QLD 1st	NSW 1st	QLD 2nd	NSW 2nd
1st	12	98	0	13
2nd	18	98	3	53
3rd	99	167	41	59
4th	141	185	116	76
5th	159	219	129	100
6th	224	223	143	140
7th	321	226	154	173
8th	370	281	154	175
9th	374	283	160	209
10th	374	318	163	–

Sheffield Shield 1984-85

Final Table	P	W	L	D	1st Innings points	Total points
New South Wales	10	4	0	6	32	80
Queensland	10	4	3	3	28	76
South Australia	10	4	4	2	12	60
Western Australia	10	2	1	7	18	42
Victoria	10	0	4	6	18	18
Tasmania	10	0	2	8	12	12

(12 points for win, 4 points for 1st innings lead)

Leading First-Class Averages

Batting	State	M	I	NO	HS	R	Avge	100	50
G. Shipperd	WA	11	18	6	139	823	68.58	3	3
D.M. Jones	V	7	11	1	243	681	68.10	2	3
S.P. O'Donnell	V	6	8	1	129*	398	56.85	1	2
K.C. Wessels	Q	11	19	0	173	1020	53.68	3	6
T.J. Barsby	Q	5	9	0	137	461	51.22	2	1
R.D. Woolley	T	11	16	2	144	717	51.21	1	5
P.S. Clifford	NSW	12	21	3	143	919	51.05	3	4
A.M.J. Hilditch	SA	11	19	0	184	960	50.52	2	5
M.D. Taylor	V	11	18	2	234*	801	50.06	2	3
D.R. Gilbert	NSW	12	15	13	38*	96	48.00	–	–
R.B. Kerr	Q	10	18	4	201*	623	44.50	2	1
M.D. Haysman	SA	10	19	2	172	744	43.76	2	3

Qualification: 8 innings.

Bowling	State	O	R	W	Avge	Best	5wI	10wM
Imran Khan	NSW	265.5	536	28	19.14	5-34	1	–
M.J. Bennett	NSW	338.4	677	33	20.51	6-32	2	–
G.F. Lawson	NSW	307.2	785	37	21.21	8-112	2	1
C.J. McDermott	Q	243.3	779	35	22.25	6-45	1	–
R.J. Inverarity	SA	405.4	1016	43	23.62	7-86	2	–
R.G. Holland	NSW	620.3	1522	59	25.79	9-83	2	2
J.N. Maguire	Q	461.1	1273	46	27.67	6-48	3	–
K.H. MacLeay	WA	214.3	589	21	28.04	5-54	2	–
T.M. Alderman	WA	421	1247	44	28.34	6-42	3	1
C.G. Rackemann	Q	436	1201	42	28.59	6-54	1	–
J.R. Thomson	V	326	1135	38	29.86	7-27	1	–
R.J. Bright	V	515.3	1218	40	30.45	5-41	3	–

Qualification: 20 wickets.

McDonald's Cup

Semi-Finals
29 December at Melbourne. NEW SOUTH WALES beat VICTORIA by 7 wickets. Toss: Victoria. Victoria 181-7 closed (50 overs). NSW 185-3 (47 overs) (J. Dyson 84*, Imran Khan 73*). Award: Imran Khan (73* and 10-1-28-2).

5 January at Adelaide. SOUTH AUSTRALIA beat WESTERN AUSTRALIA by 123 runs. Toss: South Australia. S. Australia 296-6 closed (50 overs) (D.W. Hookes 101, M.D. Haysman 100*). W. Australia 173 (44.1 overs) (R.J. McCurdy 10-2-23-5). Award: D.W. Hookes (101, 10-2-46-2 and 1 ct).

Final
16 February at Sydney. NEW SOUTH WALES beat SOUTH AUSTRALIA by 88 runs. Toss: NSW. NSW 278-7 closed (50 overs) (J. Dyson 79, D.M. Wellham 51, P.S. Clifford 69). S. Australia 190 (45.5 overs). Award: D.M. Wellham (captain) (51).

New South Wales gained their first trophy in 16 seasons of limited-overs competition.

Cricket in South Africa

Played 24, won 23, drawn 1 – Transvaal's record in all competitions is an accurate commentary of the extent to which they dominated South African domestic cricket in the 1984-85 season. Indeed, they would have had a full house but for the intervention of rain when they had Eastern Province on the carpet at 109 for eight in their second innings at Port Elizabeth.

Their margins of victory in the major finals were most impressive: an innings and five runs against Northern Transvaal in the Currie Cup, with two days to spare; seven wickets against Northerns in the Benson & Hedges, with more than eight overs to spare; and nine wickets against Western Province in the Nissan Shield, with nine overs to spare.

The season amounted to six months of unbroken triumph for Transvaal and particularly for their captain, Clive Rice. Apart from unquestionably proving himself the best leader in the country, he finished top of the Currie Cup batting averages with 629 runs at 48.38, including three hundreds and two fifties. It was his best season domestically with the bat, and the fact that no batsman managed to average more than 50 – the first time this had happened in some 60 seasons – was more a reflection on some of the green pitches prepared to aid the seamers, notably at Pretoria's Berea Park and Johannesburg's Wanderers Stadium, than any indication of a drop in the standard of the leading batsmen.

With no 'rebel' tours included in the summer's itinerary, the Currie Cup format returned to its normal shape of eight round-robin matches (home and away) for the five competing teams, plus a knock-out semi-final and final. Transvaal won seven of their eight round-robin matches plus their semi-final and final. They were equally invincible in the Nissan Shield (55 overs) and the Benson and Hedges night series (45 overs).

Significant features of the season were the drop in standard of Western Province, previously the leading challengers. They badly missed both Graham Gooch and Ken McEwan; Faoud Bacchus failed to make the grade as a replacement. In contrast was the rise of Northern Transvaal, who deservedly reached the Currie Cup Final for the first time.

However, the manner in which they were outplayed in the final indicated the vast difference between Transvaal and the rest. The batting form of Rice, Jimmy Cook, Henry Fotheringham, Graeme Pollock, Kevin McKenzie, and Alan Kourie was so consistently strong that the decision not to extend the contract of Alvin Kalicharran was hardly noticed. Mark Venter and a promising left-handed all-rounder, Craig Norris, shared the vacancy and both had their moments of success.

It was in bowling, however, that Transvaal showed an even greater degree of supremacy. Sylvester Clarke, in his first full season, shrugged off a nagging knee injury to set a provincial record of 58 wickets, and he was well supported by Alan Kourie (50 wickets) and newcomer Hugh Page (41). With Neal Radford also in the top 15 on the national averages. Transvaal could afford to drop Rupert Hanley into retirement, and Rice used himself only when the conditions were favourable.

Page was one of the success stories of the season. He was not in the Transvaal team at the start of the campaign but, by season's end, every amateur selector had the tall Transvaaler in his Springbok team. He impressed with his control of line and he also made full use of his height from a perfect action to obtain disconcerting bounce and movement. Here certainly is a player to watch for the future.

Two other fast-medium prospects to emerge were Eric Simons of Northern Transvaal and Corrie van Zyl of B Section Free State. Simons, who is returning to his native Western Province next season, exploited some lively Berea Park pitches to pick up 52 wickets. Van Zyl, well handled by Kallicharran, took 50 wickets and looked as impressive as any, admittedly against lesser opposition. This coming season will see him fully put to the test with Free State being promoted to cross swords with the best.

Of the senior South Africa bowlers, the western Province pair of Garth le Roux and Stephen Jefferies were again troubled by injury and illness. Of the others used against the 'rebel' West Indians, Hanley lost his Transvaal place and retired and Kenny Watson missed virtually the whole season through injury.

Certainly, had a Springbok team been chosen, the only survivor of the attack from the previous season would probably have been Kourie, who remained in a class of his own among the spinners.

The batting was very much the same as in previous seasons. Kenny McEwan was missing because of commitments to his Essex benefit, but the rest of the Springbok incumbents retained their rankings. In rough batting order, Cook, Fotheringham, Mandy Yachad, Pollock, Peter Kirsten, Rice, and McKenzie were clearly still the best, with little young talent emerging.

Daryll Cullinan, who had displaced Pollock as the country's youngest first-class centurion the previous season, showed touches of class but was sidelined for a critical couple of months with a fractured wrist. He will clearly be an asset to Western Province in the years ahead. Another to catch the eye was Philip Amm, the young Eastern Province opening batsman. His style is slightly unorthodox but he did significantly well against the awesome Transvaal pace attack, both for Eastern Province and SA Universities.

Otherwise, young batting talent was thin on the ground. No country can afford to lose talent of the calibre of Allan Lamb, Kepler Wessels, and Robin Smith, and it is going to take some time for fresh talent to come to light.

Had a South African team been chosen, it would have come roughly from the following squad: Cook, Yachad, Fotheringham, Pollock, Kirsten, Rice, McKenzie, Noel Day (N Transvaal wicketkeeper-batsman), Ray Jennings, Anton Ferreira, Kourie, Page, Le Roux, Van Zyl, Simons.

Northern Transvaal v Transvaal 1984-85 Currie Cup Final
Transvaal won by an innings and 5 runs
Played at Berea Park, Pretoria, 8, 9 March
Umpires: D.H. Bezuidenhout and D.A. Sansom

Transvaal

S.J. Cook	lbw b Ferreira	26
H.R. Fotheringham	c Morris b Weideman	40
M.S. Venter	c Geringer b Simons	23
R.G. Pollock	b Weideman	9
C.E.B. Rice*	b Simons	0
K.A. McKenzie	c Day b Simons	1
A.J. Kourie	lbw b Simons	28
R.V. Jennings†	run out	50
H.A. Page	b Simons	26
S.T. Clarke	c Day b Simons	11
N.V. Radford	not out	1
Extras	(LB7, W3, NB7)	17
		232

Northern Transvaal

M. Yachad	c Page b Clarke	4	lbw b Rice	7
W. Kirsh	b Clarke	24	c Fotheringham b Page	20
L.J. Barnard*	b Page	0	c Jennings b Page	0
N.T. Day†	b Clarke	0	c Pollock b Clarke	30
C.P.L. de Lange	c Jennings b Clarke	10	lbw b Page	0
A. Geringer	b Clarke	1	c Jennings b Kourie	23
A.M. Ferreira	b Rice	8	b Kourie	37
E.O. Simons	c Jennings b Page	0	c Jennings b Kourie	6
W.F. Morris	c Venter b Page	4	c Jennings b Page	0
I.F.N. Weideman	not out	0	lbw b Rice	37
G.L. Ackermann	lbw b Page	0	not out	0
Extras	(LB6, W3, NB1)	10	(B1, LB3, W1, NB1)	6
		61		**166**

N. Transvaal	O	M	R	W				
Simons	24.5	6	57	6				
Weideman	28	8	71	2				
Ferreira	19	6	31	1				
Ackermann	12	2	36	0				
Morris	7	2	20	0				

Transvaal	O	M	R	W	O	M	R	W
Clarke	11	5	8	5	12	3	34	1
Page	7.4	1	14	4	18	4	67	4
Radford	6	0	21	0	8	2	20	0
Rice	3	2	8	1	6.2	4	10	2
Kourie					8	2	29	3

Fall of Wickets

Wkt	T 1st	NT 1st	NT 2nd
1st	55	10	31
2nd	96	16	31
3rd	101	18	31
4th	101	31	31
5th	109	40	79
6th	109	49	118
7th	178	49	127
8th	215	61	128
9th	219	61	130
10th	232	61	166

Currie Cup Semi-Finals

22, 23, 25, 26 February at Berea Park, Pretoria. NORTHERN TRANSVAAL beat WESTERN PROVINCE by 8 wickets. Western Province 325 (S.F.A.F. Bacchus 58, L. Seeff 76, A.P. Kuiper 86, E.O. Simons 4-62) and 160. Northern Transvaal 371 (M. Yachad 120, L.J. Barnard 51, A. Geringer 56, E.O. Simons 58) and 120-2 (M. Yachad 62).

23, 24, 25 February at Wanderers, Johannesburg. TRANSVAAL beat NATAL by an innings and 4 runs. Natal 308-9 dec (B.J. Whitfield 90, M.B. Logan 81, A.J. Kourie 4-115) and 139 (H.A. Page 5-31, A.J. Kourie 4-53). TRANSVAAL 451-6 dec (S.J. Cook 140, H.R. Fotheringham 100, M.S. Venter 53, R.G. Pollock 84).

Leading First-Class Averages

Batting	Province	M	I	NO	HS	R	Avge	100	50
A.I. Kallicharran	OFS	6	11	2	110	623	69.22	1	7
D.J. Cullinan	Bdr	4	8	2	100	354	59.00	1	3
G.S. Cowley	EP	9	14	6	145*	459	57.37	1	2
M.W. Rushmere	EP	8	12	3	119*	498	55.33	2	2
T.B. Reid	EP	5	9	1	120*	399	49.87	2	1
S.J. Cook	T	11	16	0	140	782	48.87	2	5
C.E.B. Rice	T	10	15	2	126	629	48.38	3	3
L. Potter	GW	6	12	2	165*	462	46.20	1	2
M.D. Logan	N	8	13	1	172*	553	46.08	1	2
I. Foulkes	Bdr	6	11	3	132*	342	42.75	1	–
P.L. Selsick	T	5	9	1	183	342	42.75	1	–
P.N. Kirsten	Wp	8	14	2	133	511	42.58	2	2

Qualification: 8 innings.

Bowling	Province	R	W	Avge	Best	5wI	10wM
S.T. Clarke	T	738	58	12.72	5-8	6	1
G.J. Parsons	Bol	515	39	13.20	9-72	2	1
C.J.P.G. van Zyl	OFS	676	50	13.52	8-84	5	2
C.R. Norris	T	288	20	14.40	5-48	1	–
H.A. Page	T	775	50	15.50	5-61	1	–
J.J. Hooper	T	460	28	16.42	5-29	1	–
E.O. Simons	NT	859	51	16.84	6-26	2	–
G.L. Ackermann	NT	482	27	17.85	7-69	3	1
C.D. Mitchley	T	652	35	18.62	5-50	1	–
T.G. Shaw	EP	446	23	19.39	6-42	1	–
E.A. Moseley	EP	665	34	19.55	5-48	1	–
A.J. Kourie	T	1009	50	20.18	7-94	3	–

Nissan Shield Final

2 February at Wanderers, Johannesburg. TRANSVAAL beat WESTERN PROVINCE by 9 wickets. Western Province 200-8 closed (55 overs) (L. Seeff 67, H.A. Page 3-42). Transvaal 202-1 (46 overs) (S.J. Cook 85, H.R. Fotheringham 103*).

Cricket in the West Indies

With the West Indies team again on tour in Australia, the leading players were absent from the Shell Shield tournament, the standard of which was blatantly affected as a result. Trinidad & Tobago, with the best balanced and most consistent of the six teams, comfortably won the Shield outright for the first time since their successive triumphs in 1970 and 1971, but, generally, the cricket played was cause for concern.

Only two batsmen, the opener Carlisle Best of Barbados and Luther Kelly, aggregated more than 400 runs and there were 13 totals under 200 in the 15 matches against only two over 400. Perhaps the most disturbing feature was the inept fielding and outcricket that was the bane of most teams, the former West Indies captain Rohan Kanhai estimating that Jamaica, of which he was coach, dropped no fewer than 50 catches during the season.

In spite of the predominance of fast bowling in the Test team, two spinners with well established Shell Shield records were the highest wicket-takers. Clyde Butts, the slim off-spinner, took 32 wickets at just under 20 runs each for Guyana, raising his tally to 81 in three seasons. Figures of seven for 90 against the touring New Zealanders for the Shell Shield XI gained him Test selection, but he had the misfortune to encounter ideal batting conditions in the high-scoring Georgetown Test.

Ganesh Mahabir, the Trinidad & Tobago leg-spinner, had 30 wickets at 30 and troubled opponents in every match.

However, there were a few new names to watch for the future. Few young players recently have created the impression the 18-year-old Guyanese all-rounder Carl Hooper did in his first season. Summoned from the West Indies youth team during its series against Young England, he started with a commanding 126 in his debut first-class innings and his confident batting and off-spin bowling gained immediate approval from knowledgeable observers.

In his first full Shield season, Anthony Gray, a 21-year-old fast bowler later signed by Surrey, added a new dimension to a Trinidad & Tobago attack previously almost entirely dependent on spin. Using his height to advantage, he took 23 wickets, as did another 21-year-old fast bowler, the powerfully-built Antiguan Anthony Merrick of the Leeward Islands.

There was one particular individual performance during the season that will become part of West Indian cricket folklore. When Trinidad & Tobago, needing 294 to beat the Windward Islands, were struggling at 171 for five, their strong, muscular all-rounder Kelvin Williams proved the man for the occasion. In just over an hour, he hit nine sixes and three fours in scoring an unbeaten 84 from 51 deliveries, completing an unforgettable, and important, victory by four wickets for his team with four consecutive sixes off the bemused opposing captain, Norbert Phillip.

Guyana beat Jamaica by five wickets in the final of the Geddes Grant-Harrison Line Trophy, the 50-overs competition.

Barbados retained the annual youth championships for 1984, as in 1983, with a 100 per cent record, winning all five matches outright.

Performances in that tournament led to the selection of the West Indies youth team for the Agatha Christie Foundation Series of three Tests and three one-day internationals against Young England on their tour early in 1985. The West Indies won the first and third 'Tests', with the second almost totally washed out by rain, and also won the limited-overs series, 2-1.

Shell Shield

Final Table	P	W	L	D	1st innings points in draw	Total points
TRINIDAD & TOBAGO	5	3	1	1	1	56
Leeward Islands	5	2	1	2	1	44
Guyana	5	1	1	3	2	36
Windward Islands	5	1	1	3	0	33*
Barbados	5	1	2	2	1	28
Jamaica	5	1	3	1	0	20

* Includes 5 points for 1st innings lead in match lost. (16 points for win, 4 points for draw, 4 points for 1st innings lead in draw.)

Leading Shell Shield Averages

Batting	Team	M	I	NO	HS	R	Avge	100	50
C.A. Best	B	5	9	1	147	437	54.62	2	1
P.V. Simmons	TT	5	8	0	118	390	48.75	1	3
A.B. Williams	J	5	8	0	102	379	47.37	1	3
A.L. Kelly	LI	5	10	0	88	403	40.30	–	4
E.E. Lewis	LI	5	9	0	103	361	40.11	1	2
T. Mohamed	G	5	9	1	80	310	38.75	–	3
C.L. Hooper	G	5	7	0	126	267	38.14	1	–
W.W. Lewis	J	5	9	0	127	341	37.88	1	1
G. Powell	J	4	7	0	110	261	37.28	1	1
K.C. Williams	TT	5	8	1	84*	255	36.42	–	2
L.D. John	WI	5	8	0	137	266	33.25	1	1

Qualification: 7 innings; 250 runs.

Bowling	Team	O	R	W	Avge	Best	5wI	10wM
G. Mahabir	TT	187.2	462	30	15.40	6-62	1	–
T.Z. Kentish	WI	167	342	20	17.10	5-88	2	–
C.G. Butts	G	299.2	615	32	19.21	7-107	3	1
A.H. Gray	TT	126	458	23	19.91	6-78	2	1
W.W. Daniel	B	148	458	22	20.81	7-33	2	–
A.G. Daley	J	195.4	638	29	22.00	5-64	1	–
T.A. Merrick	LI	146.2	530	23	23.04	5-101	2	–
R.O. Estwick	B	142	495	20	24.75	5-83	2	–

Qualification: 20 wickets.

Cricket in New Zealand

Wellington won the Shell Trophy competition for the third time in four seasons, and finished runner-up in the one-day Shell Cup contest to prove themselves New Zealand's most efficient all-round cricket unit.

When the final round of Trophy play began, only Auckland had a chance of heading off Wellington. To do that, they had to beat the disappointing Central Districts side outright, and Wellington had to gain no more than first innings points from Otago. With the first day's play rained out, Auckland's prospects slumped. Some inspired bowling, however, contrived to leave Auckland 264 to win on the last afternoon, with Wellington's match droning on to a tedious draw, Otago having taken first innings points. But Auckland's hopes of a dramatic finale were dashed by bad light, and in any case, at 190 for nine, they were on course for defeat.

Wellington's batting revolved around the deeds of four players – the captain, Robert Vance, the opening batsmen, Bruce Edgar and Justin Boyle, and a promising youngster, Tim Ritchie. Evan Gray, the former international all-rounder, was the country's leading wicket-taker, with 43. There was also a significant contribution from the wicketkeeper, Ervin McSweeney, easily the most prolific, with 37 dismissals.

Canterbury and Auckland shared second place. Canterbury, the defending champions, actually recorded three outright wins, but another three matches produced no points, highlighting an inconsistent season's work. There were runs from Paul McEwan and Vaughan Brown, and, predictably, Richard Hadlee headed the bowling averages, in limited appearances.

Auckland spent most of the summer near the top of the table. They produced a 19-year-old medium-pacer with potential in Willie Watson, who picked up a hat-trick against Otago.

Six times Otago won first innings points, but only once did they go on to complete the job. In Andrew Jones they had the leading batsman in the competition, while Neil Mallender headed a strong bowling attack, including the left-arm spinner Stephen Boock.

Northern Districts had a forgettable season. Bruce Cooper was the best of the batsmen – 22nd in the national averages – while Brendon Bracewell's 20 wickets was the best haul of an uninspiring bowling attack.

Ron Hart and Tony Blain both passed 650 runs for Central Districts, the Shell Cup winners, but they were let down by poor returns from the bowlers. Only the veteran spinner David O'Sullivan, in his last season, did himself justice, with 36 wickets.

Shell Trophy

Final Table	P	W	L	D	1st innings points	Penalty points	Total points
WELLINGTON	8	2	1	5	24	–	48
Canterbury	8	3	2	3	8	–	44
Auckland	8	2	0	6	20	–	44
Otago	8	1	2	5	24	3	33
Northern Districts	8	1	4	3	16	2	26
Central Districts	8	1	1	6	4	–	16

(12 points for win, 4 points for 1st innings lead.)

Leading First-Class Averages

Batting	Team	M	I	NO	HS	R	Avge	100	50
J.F. Reid	Auckland	6	9	1	158*	465	58.12	2	1
A.H. Jones	Otago	8	15	4	102*	608	55.27	1	4
M.D. Crowe	C. Districts	6	10	0	143	541	54.10	1	3
T.E. Blain	C. Districts	8	15	1	129	678	48.42	2	4
P.E. McEwan	Canterbury	6	11	1	105	482	48.20	1	4
J.G. Wright	Canterbury	7	12	1	151*	495	45.00	2	2
R.T. Hart	C. Districts	8	15	0	111	665	44.33	2	3
K.R. Rutherford	Otago	6	11	1	130	442	44.20	1	2
B.L. Cairns	N. Districts	5	7	1	89	252	42.00	–	2
P.N. Webb	Auckland	6	9	3	76	245	40.83	–	2
T.J. Franklin	Auckland	8	14	1	181	522	40.15	1	3
R.H. Vance	Wellington	9	14	1	99	522	40.15	–	5

Qualification: 7 innings.

Bowling	Team	O	R	W	Avge	Best	5wI	10wM
R.J. Hadlee	Canterbury	287.3	652	38	17.15	6-51	3	–
M.C. Snedden	Auckland	253.3	533	30	17.76	6-63	1	–
N.A. Mallender	Otago	262.5	637	35	18.20	7-27	2	–
G.B. Troup	Auckland	151	432	21	20.57	6-53	1	–
E.J. Gray	Wellington	437	1044	48	21.75	6-89	6	1
G.K. MacDonald	Canterbury	156.4	449	20	22.45	6-62	1	–
W. Watson	Auckland	208	547	24	22.79	5-36	1	–
S.L. Boock	Otago	300	597	26	22.96	6-64	2	–
J.A.J. Cushen	Otago	331.4	748	31	24.12	5-37	1	–
C.H. Thiele	Canterbury	183.5	604	24	25.16	4-35	–	–
E.J. Chatfield	Wellington	297.5	617	24	25.70	4-56	–	–
G.N. Cederwall	Wellington	208.2	618	23	26.86	4-54	–	–

Qualification: 20 wickets.

Shell Cup

Final. 24 February at Wellington. CENTRAL DISTRICTS beat WELLINGTON (153 – E.J. Gray 53) by 8 wickets.

Cricket in India

Domestic cricket was relegated to the background – an unfortunate, worrying, but now almost regular phenomenon – by Test cricket and international limited-overs competition schedules.

An exhausted Sunil Gavaskar arrived at Bombay airport from Bahrain after playing an exhibition game, at 3 a.m. on the opening day of the Ranji Trophy final against Delhi. He managed to grab a couple of hours of sleep and then beat the snarling Bombay traffic to reach the Wankhede Stadium in time. Within half an hour of the start he was in the middle battling it out to make his 20th Championship century and finally, after a hard five days of nerve-racking cricket, led his side to its 30th triumph, in Bombay Cricket Association's golden jubilee year.

With the exception of the Ranji Trophy final, it was a season *sans* almost all the stars. The Duleep Trophy, ultimately won by South Zone, began when the Indian team were in Pakistan. The final, which had to be postponed because of political disturbances in Ahmedabad, was played in New Delhi on the day the Indian team took off for Australia for the Benson & Hedges World Championship of Cricket.

North Zone's national selector, Bishan Singh Bedi, reportedly switched the pitch, preferring one of dubious quality and deliberately prepared, once it was known that South Zone would be without the services of their main fast bowler T.A. Sekhar. The gamble misfired against the obdurate and intelligent batsmanship of Test stumper Syed Kirmani – smarting under the selectorial rebuff of being dropped from the side to Australia – the bowling of stocky Tamil Nadu seamer B. Arun, and a pitch that had become beastly on the final day.

It was a season that did not really throw up many young players of potential. Test reject Sandip Patil powered his way to big scores, but nobody is quite sure whether he is serious about making a comeback; his brief flirtation with films has not quite helped his cricket career. Test failure Ghulam Parkar was Bombay's principal run getter, emphasizing the yawning gap between domestic and international cricket.

Tamil Nadu's ageing but determined left-hander V. Sivaramakrishnan made three centuries in the Ranji Trophy Championship, including two in the knock-out stage, against Bihar and Bombay, respectively. His partner, C.S. Suresh Kumar, surely one the selectors can take a close look at, especially now that Gavaskar is unwilling to open the innings, came back with impressive scores in the knock-out stage, including a first-appearance century against Bombay.

Delhi, the losing finalist, can hope that Maninder Singh will soon be back bowling for India. Their major discovery has been a combative middle-order batsman in Ajay Sharma, who made a fighting century against Bombay when Delhi were in serious trouble.

But it was ultimately Ravi Shastri's season. He signed off with a match-winning career-best haul of eight for 91 in the Ranji Trophy final, beating Delhi almost on his own on the final day. This, coming in the wake of his exploits in Australia, however, was no real surprise.

Bombay v Delhi 1984-85 Ranji Trophy Final
Bombay won by 90 runs
Played at Wankhede Stadium, Bombay, 1, 2, 3, 5, 6 April
Umpires: B. Ganguli and V.K. Ramaswamy

Bombay

L.S. Rajput	c Chauhan b Prabhakar	0	st Khanna b Maninder		63
G.A. Parkar	c Khanna b Madan Lal	23	b Madan Lal		14
S.S. Hattangadi	c Khanna b Valson	7	c Sharma b Madan Lal		5
S.M. Patil	c Pillai b Maninder	54	c Azad b Maninder		57
S.M. Gavaskar*	b Madan Lal	106	b Maninder		64
R.J. Shastri	b Maninder	29	c Prabhakar b Maninder		76
C.S. Pandit†	lbw b Prabhakar	49	c Maninder b Azad		44
A. Sippy	c Sharma b Madan Lal	16			
K.D. Mokashi	b Maninder	14			
R.R. Kulkarni	c Srivastava b Madan Lal	15	not out		17
R.V. Kulkarni	not out	2			
Extras	(LB2, W1, NB7)	10	(B7, LB6, W1, NB2)		16
Penalty runs		8			8
		333	(7 wkts dec)		**364**

Delhi

C.P.S. Chauhan	c Hattangadi b Shastri	98	c Pandit b Shastri	54
S.C. Khanna†	lbw b R.R. Kulkarni	13	st Pandit b Shastri	27
Gursharan Singh	b R.R. Kulkarni	10	lbw b Mokashi	2
K. Azad	c Pandit b R.R. Kulkarni	9	b Shastri	0
Bhaskar Pillai	c Pandit b R.R. Kulkarni	0	c sub b Shastri	60
M. Prabhakar	c R.R. Kulkarni b Shastri	21	c Rajput b Shastri	44
Madan Lal*	c Pandit b Shastri	78	run out	6
A. Sharma	c Hattangadi b Mokashi	131	b Shastri	10
Maninder Singh	lbw b R.R. Kulkarni	3	lbw b Shastri	0
S. Srivastava	c Hattangadi b Shastri	7	b Shastri	3
S. Valson	not out	21	not out	0
Extras	(LB7)	7	(B1, LB2)	3
		398		**209**

Delhi	O	M	R	W	O	M	R	W
Madan Lal	25	8	42	4	19	3	57	2
Prabhakar	17	3	69	2	10	3	39	0
Valson	12	0	50	1	2	0	33	0
Maninder	29.5	7	75	3	34	6	132	4
Srivastava	9	0	37	0	8	1	28	0
Azad	6	0	35	0	18.3	1	54	1
Sharma	4	1	15	0				

Bombay	O	M	R	W	O	M	R	W
R.R. Kulkarni	32	4	106	5	7	0	28	0
R.V. Kulkarni	21	4	55	0	4	0	15	0
Shastri	48	18	91	4	39.5	17	91	8
Sippy	3	0	20	0				
Mokashi	16	3	63	1	32	10	63	1
Rajput	15	2	40	0	3	0	9	0
Patil	2	0	9	0				
Gavaskar	1	0	7	0				

Fall of Wickets

Wkt	B 1st	D 1st	B 2nd	D 2nd
1st	1	27	13	95
2nd	27	41	31	100
3rd	42	52	129	100
4th	142	65	160	122
5th	194	87	275	171
6th	274	191	306	187
7th	276	268	356	198
8th	300	311	–	198
9th	318	330	–	206
10th	325	398	–	209

Leading First-Class Averages

Batting	I	NO	HS	R	Avge	100
M. Azharuddin (Hyderabad)	14	4	151	991	99.10	6
P. Shastri (Rajasthan)	12	2	159	711	71.10	2
R.J. Shastri (Bombay)	14	3	200*	761	69.18	3
M. Amarnath (Baroda)	13	3	95	687	68.70	–
K. Bhaskar Pillai (Delhi)	11	2	149*	576	64.00	2
A. Malhotra (Haryana)	12	2	132	542	54.20	2
G.A. Parkar (Bombay)	15	1	170*	748	53.42	1
V. Sivaramakrishnan (Tamil Nadu)	14	2	117	639	53.25	3
K. Srikkanth (Tamil Nadu)	14	1	101	674	51.84	1
R. Madhavan (Tamil Nadu)	17	3	153*	719	51.35	3
D.B. Vengsarkar (Bombay)	12	2	200*	509	50.90	2
A. Jabbar (Tamil Nadu)	13	1	143	581	48.41	1
S.M.H. Kirmani (Karnataka)	13	2	102	502	45.63	1
C.P.S. Chauhan (Delhi)	16	2	115	629	44.92	1
C.S. Pandit (Bombay)	16	2	126	610	43.57	2
S.M. Patil (Bombay)	18	2	165	682	42.62	1
L.S. Rajput (Bombay)	18	0	136	737	40.94	2
R. Khanvilkar (Karnataka)	14	1	156	526	40.46	2
S.M. Gavaskar (Bombay)	17	3	106	566	40.42	1
S.S. Khandkar (Uttar Pradesh)	15	1	261*	557	39.78	1
Gursharan Singh (Delhi)	19	1	68	501	27.83	–

Qualification: 500 runs.

Bowling	O	M	R	W	Avge
Madan Lal (Delhi)	145	42	318	27	11.77
R.S. Hans (Uttar Pradesh)	320.4	96	617	42	14.69
R. Goel (Haryana)	388	133	652	39	16.71
Maninder Singh (Delhi)	390.3	118	889	46	19.32
A.R. Bhat (Karnataka)	363.2	85	952	47	20.25
R.S. Ghai (Punjab)	151.4	26	534	26	20.53
S. Venkataraghavan (Tamil Nadu)	260.5	54	632	30	21.06
R.P. Singh (Uttar Pradesh)	203	31	735	30	24.50
A. Patel (Saurashtra)	276.5	50	829	32	25.90
R.J. Shastri (Bombay)	347.4	107	746	28	26.64
S. Talwar (Haryana)	256.1	39	776	29	26.75
G. Sharma (Uttar Pradesh)	357	80	906	33	27.45
L. Sivaramakrishnan (Tamil Nadu)	362.3	81	998	34	29.35
K.D. Mokashi (Bombay)	262	52	786	26	30.23
N.S. Yadav (Hyderabad)	293.2	61	882	29	30.41
B.S. Sandhu (Bombay)	224.2	43	771	25	30.84
R.R. Kulkarni (Bombay)	272.3	32	1050	30	35.00

Qualification: 25 wickets.

Irani Trophy
7, 8, 9, 11 September at Delhi. REST OF INDIA beat BOMBAY (1983-84 Ranji Trophy champions) by 4 wickets. Toss: Rest. Bombay 236 (R.J. Shastri 58) and 163 (G.A. Parkar 55, Maninder Singh 4-34). Rest 293 and 107-6 (M. Azharuddin 51*, B.S. Sandhu 4-41).

Duleep Trophy
Final: 9, 10, 11, 12 February at Delhi. SOUTH ZONE beat NORTH ZONE by 73 runs. Toss: North. South 212 (S.M.H. Kirmani 82) and 236 (A. Jabbar 68, S.M.H. Kirmani 50, A. Jha 5-76, Maninder Singh 4-95). North 164 (Gursharan Singh 68, R. Khanwilkar 4-73, A.R. Bhat 4-42) and 211 (R.S. Ghai 54, B. Arun 5-84).

Cricket in Pakistan

In the 1984-85 domestic season, all three first-class tournaments, the Patron's Trophy, the Quaid-e-Azam Trophy, and the PACO Pentangular, were played and completed – despite the visits of the Indian and New Zealand teams. Although the competitions lacked the presence of most of the established Test players, the matches were competitive and well fought.

The first of the contests was the Patron's Trophy, which was played between the Zonal and the association teams. Once again a Karachi team won the championship. In a tournament in which 17 teams participated in four group matches, the Karachi Whites emerged as the final winners. In the semi-finals they beat Karachi Blues by a margin of 204 runs, while Rawalpindi defeated Sargodha by 32 runs. The final was a one-sided affair as the Karachi Whites won the match by 10 wickets in two days.

United Bank regained the Quaid-e-Azam Trophy by virtue of their first-innings lead in the final against Railways. Divided into two groups, the 1984-85 tournament was played between 12 teams instead of 10. The two sides added to the 10 departmental and commercial organization teams, Karachi and Lahore, were included in the championship because they are recognized as breeding grounds for Test cricketers. House Bank Finance Corporation (HBFC) and Allied Bank finished with 60 points each in group A, but HBFC topped the table because of a faster run-rate. In Group B, only one of the 15 matches ended in a draw. United Bank beat HBFC by 244 runs in the first semi-final, while Railways reached the final by gaining a first innings lead over Allied Bank. The tournament, however, was marred by a controversy, when the umpires reported HBFC and Allied Bank for 'fixing' their group match, enabling Allied Bank to reach the semi-finals. The inquiry committee observed that no fewer than 1,176 runs were scored in that game in 886 minutes, both teams reaching the semi-finals by gaining maximum points. The two teams were banned for one year, and thus were barred from playing in the PACO Pentangular. The ban, however, was lifted after the season was over.

The PACO Cup, which was not contested last year, was also won by United Bank, with Habib Bank second, followed by Karachi, Railways, and PACO. United Bank's Ali Zia topped the batting averages in the tournament by scoring 434 runs (avg 62.00), and off-spinner Tauseef Ahmed bagged 41 wickets (avg 12.53). The leading batsman of the season was PIA's Rizwan-uz Zaman, who scored 1,101 runs (avg 78.64) followed by Arshad Pervez of Habib Bank, who made 1,253 runs (avg 56.95). Both of them scored five hundreds during the season. Tauseef Ahmed of United Bank finished with 83 wickets (avg 15.85) and wicketkeeper Zulqarnain of Railways bagged 49 victims. The Wills One-Day Cup was not played.

Leading First-Class Averages

Batting	M	I	NO	HS	R	Avge	100
Rizwan-uz-Zaman	9	17	3	166	1101	78.64	5
Salim Malik	6	8	3	119*	361	72.20	2
Munir-ul-Haq	5	10	3	120*	483	69.00	2
Javed Miandad	6	9	2	104	410	58.57	2
Arshad Pervez	14	27	5	152*	1253	56.95	5
Mohammad Aslam (Sg)	5	9	0	167	483	53.66	1
Shahid Anwar	8	15	1	153*	746	52.28	4
Ijaz Faqih	8	9	2	125*	371	53.00	2
Tariq Alam	6	12	4	89	422	52.75	–
Tahir Mahmood	4	8	0	108	405	50.62	1
Qasim Omar	5	8	0	210	396	49.50	1
Mudassar Nazar	5	8	0	199	395	49.37	2
Mohammad Aslam (K)	9	15	2	164	637	49.00	2
Masood Anwar (Rp)	7	11	0	186	529	48.09	1
Shaukat Mirza	12	22	3	132	894	47.05	2
Ijaz Ahmed (G/PACO)	12	23	2	201*	983	46.80	2
Anwar-ul-Haq	5	8	0	113	368	46.00	1
Salim Anwar	4	8	1	125*	313	44.71	1
Shoaib Habib	6	9	2	84*	313	44.71	–
Ijaz Ahmed (M/HBFC)	9	17	1	117	710	44.37	2
Naved Anjum	10	17	3	159	617	44.07	1
Shafiq Ahmed	11	21	4	118	742	43.64	2
Saadat Ali	11	20	1	169	817	43.00	3

Qualification: 8 innings.

Bowling	O	R	W	Avge	Best
Iqbal Qasim	304.3	606	48	12.62	5-6
Ijaz Faqih	227.2	525	38	13.81	6-35
Mohammad Nazir	546.2	947	66	14.34	7-62
Aziz-ur-Rehman	203.3	522	34	15.35	7-45
Tausif Ahmed	546.2	1316	83	15.85	8-83
Shahid Pervez	196.2	490	28	17.50	5-27
Tanvir Afzal	173	513	29	17.68	6-80
Ali Zia	140.2	359	20	17.95	4-37
Humayun Farkhan	149.3	360	20	18.00	4-25
Abdul Qadir	471.5	1349	72	18.73	9-59
Naeem Ghauri	385.3	956	50	19.12	8-68
Ghulam Abbas	226	518	27	19.18	7-66
Ehteshamuddin	145.3	413	21	19.66	9-124
Zahid Ahmed	178.5	480	23	20.86	7-68
Farrukh Zaman	255.3	731	34	21.50	6-42
Kazim Mehdi	270.3	747	34	21.97	6-97
Azeem Hafeez	243.4	642	29	22.13	6-46
Abdur Raqeeb	339.4	913	41	22.26	5-61
Rashid Khan	153	474	21	22.57	6-110
Jalaluddin	245.2	766	33	23.21	6-66
Mian Fayyaz	296	665	28	23.75	6-101
Iqbal Butt	229.3	701	29	24.17	5-59
Masood Anwar (M/PACO)	413.4	1141	47	24.27	6-94
Tanvir Ali	618.4	1771	72	24.59	8-83

Qualification: 20 wickets.

Teams: G – Gujranwala; HBFC – House Building Finance Corporation; K – Karachi; M – Multan; PACO – Pakistan Automobile Corporation; Rp – Rawalpindi; Sg – Sargodha.

Cricket in Sri Lanka

An unprecedented move by the Executive Committee of the Sri Lanka Cricket Board in overruling a decision of the Tournament Committee, and England's unscheduled visit to Sri Lanka from troubled India, saw the 1984-85 Lakspray Trophy championship unusually prolonged till late May.

The Executive Committee suspended Sebastianites CC from participation in mid-season after finding the club guilty of violating the rule governing watering of the pitch in their match against Moors SC. As a result, the Tournament Committee members resigned *en bloc* and Sebastianites eventually returned to the fray. This meant that the matches during the period of suspension had to be rescheduled.

Unlike previous years, the championship this time was run on a league basis, with the 18 clubs playing each other once. Colombo Cricket Club (CCC), the oldest cricket club in Sri Lanka, won the title by a clear 45 points from last season's champions, Singhalese SC. The youthful CCC side dominated the season to such an extent that they had the championship sewn up well before the scheduled finish. Captained by left-arm spinner Roger Wijesuriya, who toured England with Sri Lanka teams in 1979 and 1981, CCC scored a record 10 outright victories in 17 matches, losing only to Panadura SC and Police SC, both on first innings.

SSC and Nondescripts CC failed to repeat their one-two performance of last year, and finished second and fourth. Panadura SC, a club from the South, showed vast improvement to finish in third place – the highest position attained in their history. During the early stages, Moors SC and Air Force SC gave promise of having a tilt at the title, but their hopes evaporated as CCC steam-rollered past all opposition.

The new league system afforded batsmen and bowlers more opportunities. Ashley de Silva (Tamil Union), Susil Fernando (Air Force), and Sumithra Warnakulasuriya (CCC) each made over 1,000 runs. De Silva and Fernando led the batting with averages of over 50 apiece. Sunil Wettimuny, elder brother of Lord's Test hero Sidath Wettimuny, made a comeback to club cricket after two years and finished fifth in the averages. Sunil had opened the batting for Sri Lanka in the inaugural World Cup competition in England in 1975.

Right-arm medium-pacer Jayananda Warnaweera (Galle CC) and left-arm leg-spinner Jayantha Amerasinghe (Nomads SC) became the first bowlers to reach a century of wickets in one season. Warnaweera finished with a record haul of 121 wickets and Amerasinghe 105 wickets, the previous record for one season being 87 wickets, by Anton Benedict of Burgher RC in 1974-75.

Dhammika Ranatunga, elder brother of Test batsman Arjuna Ranatunga, hit the season's highest score, 231 not out for SSC against Sebastianites. Lalith Wijeratne (Kandy CC) had the best return in an innings, 9 for 29 against NCC.

Lakspray Trophy 1984-85

	P	W	WF	L	LF	NR	Pts
COLOMBO CRICKET CLUB	17	10	5	0	2	0	230.610
Singhalese Sports Club	17	6	5	1	4	1	185.500
Panadura Sports Club	17	4	9	1	2	1	180.100
Nondescripts Cricket Club	17	7	2	2	4	2	170.375
Moors Sports Club	17	5	5	3	2	2	155.210
Bloomfield C & AC	17	5	5	1	2	4	148.920
Air Force Sports Club	17	2	7	5	3	0	141.655
Tamil Union C & AC	17	0	9	1	4	3	128.050
Colombo Colts Cricket Club	17	2	6	0	7	2	125.845
Galle Cricket Club	17	4	3	7	1	2	122.135
Police Sports Club	17	2	7	1	5	2	104.835
Moratuwa Sports Club	17	2	4	4	5	2	100.715
Saracens Sports Club	17	3	0	7	4	3	85.975
Kandy Cricket Club	17	2	3	5	7	0	85.655
Kurunegala Youth Cricket Club	16	2	1	5	6	2	80.660
Sebastianites Cricket Club	17	0	3	5	5	4	63.855
Burgher Recreation Club	17	0	2	6	8	1	60.215
Nomads Sports Club	16	3	1	5	6	1	35.765

WF = won first innings, LF = lost first innings, NR = no result.
Kurunegala Youth CC v Nomads SC match not played owing to lack of time. Nomads SC penalized points for not reporting scores of 11 matches.

Leading Lakspray Trophy Averages
Batting (Minimum qualification: 500 runs)

	M	I	NO	HS	R	Avge	100	50
Ashley de Silva (Tamil Union)	16	25	2	173	1163	50.56	4	5
E.R.N.S. Fernando (Air Force)	17	29	5	191	1204	50.16	2	7
J. Paranathala (Police)	15	23	4	134	848	44.63	1	7
S. Warnakulasuriya (CCC)	16	25	1	181	1044	43.50	3	5
Sunil Wettimuny (SSC)	10	12	0	199	520	43.33	1	3
I. Sahabdeen (Moors SC)	12	17	2	108*	646	43.06	1	3

Bowling (Minimum qualification: 25 wickets)

	O	M	R	W	Avge	5wI	10wM
S. Kamalasuriya (NCC)	138.5	27	267	27	9.88	1	0
D. Sahabandu (NCC)	274.3	97	431	37	11.64	3	0
A.M.J.G. Amerasinghe (Nomads)	645	185	1272	105	12.11	12	5
R.G.C.E. Wijesuriya (CCC)	564	155	1150	94	12.23	7	1
A. Hashim (CCC)	207.1	51	490	40	12.25	3	0
E.A.R. de Silva (NCC)	539.5	143	1096	89	12.31	6	1
K.P.J. Warnaweera (Galle CC)	527.5	89	1522	121	12.57	11	3

Tours to England 1985

THE ASHES

When goes back with the urn, one day
Steel, Read and Tylecote return
The welkin will ring loud,
The great crowd will feel proud,
Barlow and Bates with the urn
The rest coming home with the urn

Australia in England

The Australian touring team of 1985 had its problems even before it set off for England, when adjustments to it were needed because of the ban on several players for their commitment to the projected tour of South Africa. Speculation on how such changes affect a team's performance is usually a waste of time, but it is fair to say that this side certainly missed the bowling of Terry Alderman, who was successful in England in 1981 and since then had had a fine season for Kent.

The Australian selection may have been further confused by the fact that their victory over West Indies in the final Test of 1984-85 was on a pitch highly favourable to spin. Australian spinners in England since the war have seldom had much success, and it was a stirring sight to see Bob Holland in action in the Lord's Test. He played a big part in the Australians' victory on a ground on which they have lost only once since 1896 – and that, in 1934, only after rain had completely transformed the pitch.

But that was the limit of Holland's achievement. He had no well disguised googly, and his accuracy was largely employed in bowling defensively into what rough there was. Nearly 20 years before, he was a teen-age member of an attack savaged by M.J.K. Smith and Fred Titmus at Newcastle, New South Wales. This time, he was reduced to ineffectiveness more soberly by the England batsmen, notably by Gatting who had been mainly responsible for subduing the talented Indian leg-spinner Sivaramakrishnan during the winter.

In Australia at the end of the winter tour, the England batting had looked in some disorder during the one-day tournament, and it must have been an ugly shock for the Australians to find it now consistent, fast-scoring, and, by a feat of selectorial judgement, settled.

Whereas Australia had looked likely to have advantages in depth of batting and in fast bowling, this did not work out in practice. Too much depended on Lawson, whose fitness, especially in the first Test, was suspect despite official denials. His 20-year-old partner McDermott, strong and determined, was one of the successes of the tour, but he and Lawson could not make up for the lack of a class fast-medium bowler to support them. O'Donnell, who made a dashing hundred against MCC at Lord's, could become the all-rounder needed, but was not ready yet. When the England selectors introduced Ellison, who had been out of action earlier in the season, the Australian weakness in medium-paced bowling became even more apparent. Furthermore, Australia could not match the variety and steadiness provided by the spin of Emburey and Edmonds, even when the pitch was of little use to them.

Depth of batting could not cover up deficiencies higher up the order. Hilditch had a tremendous first Test, but did little afterwards. Wood also had only one good match – at Trent Bridge. Boon fell away. Wellham worked his way into the team for the last Test but without success in it. The potential of Phillips as a batsman-wicketkeeper was an encouragement for the future, as was the form of Ritchie. But the one big success of the tour was the captain himself.

Allan Border was throughout far ahead of the other batsmen in technique and application. In the matches against the counties, he reeled off one hundred after another with ease, and his 196 in the Lord's Test was a match-winning innings of high calibre. As the other batsmen looked ever more vulnerable with the England bowlers' growing appreciation of their weaknesses, Border gained in stature. He also played a full part with David Gower in making this an unusually friendly series, and he was one of the most popular visiting captains for many years – with public as well as opponents. He will get a hearty welcome back to English cricket when he returns in 1986 for his two seasons with Essex.

The Australians were not helped by a wet summer, which hindered their preparations more than their actual performance on the field. Indeed rain may well have saved them at Old Trafford. In these days of covered pitches, visiting sides are not as handicapped by bad weather as once they were. The prolonged rain certainly made for a succession of slow pitches. But when one with pace was produced at the Oval for the final Test, Australia suffered their swiftest and most conclusive defeat of all.

When a touring side finds that some of its members are not developing as hoped, team selection becomes difficult and a proper balance hard to achieve. The Australian choice of only four bowlers almost throughout, and of little or no spin, must always have been a source of comfort to English eyes. It emphasized both Australian limitations and the wisdom on the English side of selectors who stuck to the convention of playing a balanced side. But with an all-rounder of Botham's class and spinners of the ability of Emburey and Edmonds, England's choice was much the easier.

First Test, Headingley, 13, 14, 15, 17, 18 June.
England won by 5 wickets.

England won a handsome victory just inside the final hour of a match that in its early stages had suggested a very different result.

On the first day, the Australian vice-captain Andrew Hilditch, who had scored few runs on the tour hitherto, made 116, and the England bowling was so wayward on a pitch on which the ball moved about a lot that they seemed to have lost their chance by letting Australia reach 284 for six. This impression was fortified next morning when Ritchie and the nightwatchman McDermott added 42 with ease. But after the first stoppage for rain on an interrupted day, a strong-looking Australian tail subsided, largely to Botham, who had not previously taken a wicket but now took three of the last four which fell for five runs.

England's reply was even more surprising. Even allowing for the fast outfield, their 134 for two in only 25 overs was positive stuff, the work mainly of Robinson and Gatting, who made 84 together off 15 overs. On the third day, they took their stand to 136, setting the tone for some consistently enterprising England batting, the highlight of which was Botham's 60 in 51 balls, including 10 fours and two sixes. Robinson, given plenty of opportunity to show his strength off the back foot, batted for nearly seven hours in all, playing, as at Delhi six months before, the decisive innings.

England, having made 350 runs on the third day, finished it 153 ahead, with hopes of victory stirring. Several things had become clear. Australia had been unwise to play only four bowlers and no spinner and to include Lawson who had clearly not fully recovered from a virus. England had been lucky to have Robinson dropped at third slip off McDermott when only 22 and to face Lawson below pace, but they had made the right decision in picking Emburey. And they were right again in batting on with nine wickets down on Monday morning. The 49-run last-wicket stand by Downton and Cowans was an unexpected but probably vital bonus.

Australia had bowled little better than England on a pitch still rewarding accuracy, but England's batsmen deserved full credit for maintaining the momentum on a pitch on which they always had to expect the odd ball to deviate sharply.

Australia's second innings began with the early loss of Wood through a mishook, but Hilditch and Wessels added 139 in a second-wicket stand. When Emburey removed both that night and, with a shooter, Ritchie, Australia were still 12 runs behind. But the depth of their batting always threatened England's chances, and a bold seventh-wicket stand of 80 between Phillips and O'Donnell on the last morning increased the lead rapidly.

Just in time, Botham and Emburey, helped by a brilliant running catch by Gooch, finished off the innings, and England needed 123 – not much on paper but quite enough for a side batting last with the shadow of Headingley 1981 (when Australia in the last innings made only 111) hovering over them. Against improved bowling the job was done, not without mishap but without serious moments of doubt.

Cornhill Insurance
When it comes to the Test

Ask your broker about Cornhill's competitive range of insurances — for your car, your house, your life and your business.

Cornhill Insurance Test Series

Cornhill Insurance Group
32 Cornhill, London EC3V 3LJ

100 AUSTRALIA IN ENGLAND 1985

AUSTRALIA 1ST INNINGS v. ENGLAND (1ST TEST) at HEADINGLEY, LEEDS on 13,14,15,17,18 JUNE, 1985.
TOSS: AUSTRALIA.

IN	OUT	MINS	No.	BATSMAN	HOW OUT	BOWLER	RUNS	WKT	TOTAL	6s	4s	BALLS	NOTES ON DISMISSAL
11.00	11.26	26	1	G.M. WOOD	LBW	ALLOTT	14	1	23	-	3	22	Pushed half forward - beaten by break back.
11.00	4.21	249	2	A.M.J. HILDITCH	C'DOWNTON	GOOCH	119	3	201	2	17	182	(2nd HS in Tests. Pushed at outswinger. 80 in boundaries.
11.28	2.38	151	3	K.C. WESSELS	C' BOTHAM	EMBUREY	36	2	155	-	4	103	Edged cut to slip - sharp head-high catch.
2.40	5.10	117	4	A.R. BORDER*	C' BOTHAM	COWANS	32	5	229	-	5	94	Edged low to 2nd slip - in front of his left shin.
4.23	5.05	42	5	D.C. BOON	LBW	GOOCH	14	4	229	-	-	45	Attempted to cut short ball that cut back and kept low.
5.07	2.15	93	6	G.M. RITCHIE	BOWLED	BOTHAM	46	7	326	-	8	64	Under-edged pull at long-hop into leg stump.
5.12	5.56	44	7	W.B. PHILLIPS†	C' GOWER	EMBUREY	30	6	284	-	6	35	Inside edge to silly point via pad - left-handed catch (low).
5.58	2.26	53	8	C.J. McDERMOTT	BOWLED	BOTHAM	18	10	331	-	4	38	HS in Tests. Ball kept low. BOTHAM 3 WKTS in 4 BALLS
2.16	2.17	1	9	S.P. O'DONNELL	LBW	BOTHAM	0	8	326	-	-	1	Out 1st ball in Test cricket. First dismissed late on stroke. (t.j.) on hat trick
2.19	2.22	3	10	G.F. LAWSON	C' DOWNTON	ALLOTT	0	9	327	-	-	3	His first first-class innings of the tour. Edged drive.
2.23	(2.26)	3	11	J.R. THOMSON	NOT OUT		4			-	1	3	
				EXTRAS	b -	1b 13	w 4	nb 1	18				2b 4½ 590 balls (including 1 no-ball).
				TOTAL	(98.1 OVERS - 399 MINUTES)		331		all out at 2.26 on the 2nd day.				

*CAPTAIN †WICKET-KEEPER
UMPIRES:
B.J. MEYER and K.E. PALMER

14 OVERS 4 BALLS/HOUR
3·37 RUNS/OVER
56 RUNS/100 BALLS

© Bill Frindall 1985

BOWLER	O	M	R	W	w/nb	HRS	OVERS	RUNS	RUNS	MINS	OVERS	LAST 50 (in mins)
COWANS	20	4	78	1	-	1	13	48	50	72	16.1	72
ALLOTT	22	3	74	2	-	2	17	48	100	135	32.3	61
BOTHAM	29.1	8	86	3	1/-	3	14	59	150	173	42.1	40
GOOCH	21	4	57	2	2/1	4	15	39	200	247	60.5	74
EMBUREY	6	1	23	2	-	5	16	40	250	318	78.5	71
			13			6	14	55	300	364	90.1	46
	98.1	20	331	10								

2nd NEW BALL taken at 6.00pm 1st day
- AUSTRALIA 284-6 after 86 overs

LUNCH: 96-1 (30 OVERS) HILDITCH 61 (112) (122 MIN.) WESSELS 19 (94)
TEA: 194-2 (58·1 OVERS) HILDITCH 115 (238) BAD LIGHT at 3.37pm (15 LOST) (238 MIN.) BORDER 19 (57)
STUMPS: 284-6 (87 OVERS) RITCHIE 22 (56) (1ST DAY) (351 MIN.) McDERMOTT 0 (6)
RAIN STOPPED PLAY AT 11.25 am - RESUMED at 2.05pm
LUNCH: 307-6 (93·2 OVERS) RITCHIE 36 (81) (376 MIN.) McDERMOTT 8 (30)

FIRST TEST INNINGS IN ENGLAND TO DEBIT WIDES AND NO-BALLS TO BOWLERS' ANALYSES.

WKT	PARTNERSHIP		RUNS	MINS
1st	Wood	Hilditch	23	26
2nd	Hilditch	Wessels	132	151
3rd	Hilditch	Border	46	68
4th	Border	Boon	28	42
5th	Border	Ritchie	0	3
6th	Ritchie	Phillips	55	44
7th	Ritchie	McDermott	42	42
8th	McDermott	O'Donnell	0	1
9th	McDermott	Lawson	1	3
10th	McDermott	Thomson	4	3
			331	

AUSTRALIA IN ENGLAND 1985

ENGLAND 1ST INNINGS (in reply to Australia's 331 all out)

IN	OUT	MINS	No.	BATSMAN	HOW OUT	BOWLER	RUNS	MINS	TOTAL	6s	4s	BALLS	NOTES ON DISMISSAL
2:36	3:15	14	1	G.A. Gooch	LBW	McDermott	5	1	14	·	1	11	Missed backfoot defensive stroke - ball came back.
2:36	4:55	413	2	R.T. Robinson	c' Boon	Lawson	175	6	417	·	27	270	100 on debut v Aus. Edged low to 1st slip. HS in Tests.
3:17	3:45	28	3	D.I. Gower *	c' Phillips	McDermott	17	2	50	·	2	22	Edged firm-footed off-side push.
3:47	12:15	143	4	M.W. Gatting	c' Hilditch	McDermott	53	3	186	·	7	109	Mistimed hook - gentle skier to wide mid-on.
12:17	2:18	83	5	A.J. Lamb	Bowled	O'Donnell	38	4	264	·	8	64	Through 'gate' - ball cut back - faint inside edge.
2:20	3:20	60	6	I.T. Botham	Bowled	Thomson	60	5	344	2	10	51	Played on - edged cut at ball that cut back. 50 off 15 balls
3:21	5:07	88	7	P. Willey	c' Hilditch	Lawson	36	7	422	·	5	67	Deceived by slower ball - flicked simple catch to wide mid-on.
4:57	5:42	128	8	P.R. Downton †	c' Border	McDermott	54	10	533	·	9	98	Miscued offside steer - high catch to cover-point.
5:09	5:42	33	9	J.E. Emburey	Bowled	Lawson	21	8	462	·	4	22	Beaten by low breakback.
5:44	6:19	35	10	P.J.W. Allott	c' Boon	Thomson	12	9	484	·	2	34	Edged to 1st slip - two-handed catch to his left.
6:21	(11:41)	44	11	N.G. Cowans	NOT OUT		22			·	5	28	
				EXTRAS	b 5 lb 16	w 5 nb 14	40		2b 80 4				
				TOTAL	(125 overs - 543 minutes)	(LEAD: 202)	533	all out at 11:41 am on the fourth day.				776 balls (including 26 no balls)	

* CAPTAIN   † WICKET-KEEPER

BOWLER	O	M	R	W	w/nb	HRS	OVERS	RUNS
Lawson	26	4	117	3	½	1	13	70
McDermott	32	2	134	4	⅘	2	13	65
Thomson	34	3	166	2	¹⁄₇	3	14	45
O'Donnell	27	8	77	1	¹/-	4	15	57
Border	3	0	16	0	-	5	13	40
Wessels	3	2	2	0	-	6	14	84
			21			7	13	57
	125	19	533	10		8	13	48
						9	16	65

2nd NEW BALL taken at 4:15pm on 3rd day
- ENGLAND 381·5 after 85 overs.

RUNS	MINS	OVERS	LAST 50 (in mins)
50	43	9.2	43
100	83	18.4	40
150	144	32.1	61
200	210	47.2	66
250	248	56.5	38
300	315	71.5	67
350	348	79.4	33
400	382	87.1	34
450	450	102	68
500	513	118	63

TEA: 81-2 (15 overs) (69 min)

STUMPS: 134-2 (2nd day) (24.4 overs) (114 min) [197 behind] Robinson 66 (IW), Gatting 31 (64) (88 MIN LOST 2ND DAY)

LUNCH: 229-3 (54 overs) (136 min) Robinson 111 (236), Lamb 20 (45)

TEA: 361-5 (82 overs) (359 min) Robinson 144 (359), Willey 10 (22)

STUMPS: 484-9 (3rd day) (LEAD: 153) (115 overs) (502 min) Downton 28 (17), Cowans 0 (3)

ENGLAND'S TOTAL OF 533:-
THEIR TWELFTH-HIGHEST v. AUSTRALIA
THEIR HIGHEST v AUSTRALIA SINCE 1965-66 (558 at Melbourne)
THEIR HIGHEST v. AUSTRALIA at HEADINGLEY.

13 OVERS 5 BALLS/HOUR
4·26 RUNS/OVER
69 RUNS/100 BALLS

WKT	PARTNERSHIP		RUNS	MINS
1st	Gooch	Robinson	14	14
2nd	Robinson	Gower	36	28
3rd	Robinson	Gatting	136	143
4th	Robinson	Lamb	78	83
5th	Robinson	Botham	80	60
6th	Robinson	Willey	73	76
7th	Willey	Downton	5	10
8th	Downton	Emburey	40	33
9th	Downton	Allott	22	35
10th	Downton	Cowans	49	44
			533	

© Bill Frindall 1985

102 AUSTRALIA IN ENGLAND 1985

AUSTRALIA 2ND INNINGS (202 RUNS BEHIND ON FIRST INNINGS)

IN	OUT	MINS	No.	BATSMAN	HOW OUT	BOWLER	RUNS	WKT	TOTAL	6s	4s	BALLS	NOTES ON DISMISSAL
11.52	4.06	196	1	A.M.J. HILDITCH	C' ROBINSON	EMBUREY	80	3	151	1	13	155	Top-edged sweep to backward square-leg.
11.52	12.03	11	2	G.M. WOOD	C' LAMB	BOTHAM	3	1	5	-	-	12	Hooked long-hop to long-leg — running two-handed catch.
12.05	3.18	154	3	K.C. WESSELS	BOWLED	EMBUREY	64	2	144	-	10	128	Bowled via pads by ball that kept low.
3.20	4.16	37	4	A.R. BORDER*	C' DOWNTON	BOTHAM	8	4	159	-	-	35	Failed to avoid ball that lifted and left him.
4.08	11.04	78	5	D.C. BOON	BOWLED	COWANS	22	6	192	-	2	69	Played across line of yorker.
4.18	4.21	3	6	G.M. RITCHIE	BOWLED	EMBUREY	1	5	160	-	-	6	Played back to ball that hit stumps near base.
4.23	1.49	190	7	W.B. PHILLIPS †	C' LAMB	BOTHAM	91	8	307	-	12	171	Mistimed pull — skier to wide mid-on.
11.06	12.43	97	8	S.P. O'DONNELL	C' DOWNTON	BOTHAM	24	7	272	-	3	73	Edged ball that lifted and left him.
12.45	2.01	38	9	G.F. LAWSON	C' DOWNTON	EMBUREY	15	9	318	-	3	20	Skied slog.
1.51	2.10	19	10	C.J. McDERMOTT	C' GOOCH	EMBUREY	6	10	324	-	-	20	Superbly-judged running catch on long-on boundary.
2.03	(2.10)	7	11	J.R. THOMSON	NOT OUT		2			-	-	5	
				EXTRAS	b 4 lb 3	w 1 nb -	8				16 4	694 balls (0 no-balls)	

TOTAL (115.4 OVERS - 424 MINUTES) 324 all out at 2:10 pm on the fifth day.

16 OVERS 2 BALLS/HOUR
2.80 RUNS/OVER
47 RUNS/100 BALLS

* CAPTAIN † WICKET-KEEPER

© BILL FRINDALL

BOWLER	O	M	R	W	HRS	OVERS	RUNS	LAST 50 (in mins)
BOTHAM	33	7	107	4	1	13	43	
ALLOTT	17	1	67	0	2	10	60	
EMBUREY	43.4	14	82	5	3	18	44	
COWANS	13	2	50	1	4	17	31	
GOOCH	9	3	21	0	5	17	21	
			7		6	15	65	
	115.4	30	324	10	7	17	58	

RUNS	MINS	OVERS	
50	69	15.5	69
100	115	30.2	46
150	188	51.3	73
200	302	84	114
250	342	93.4	40
300	401	110.1	59

2ND NEW BALL taken at 11.45 am 5TH day
- AUSTRALIA 211-6 after 88 overs.

LUNCH: 50-1 (16 OVERS) HILDITCH 26 (69)
            (69 MIN.) WESSELS 20 (56)

TEA: 151-2 (52 OVERS) HILDITCH 80 (141)
           (190 MIN.) BORDER 2 (21)

STUMPS: 190-5 (76 OVERS) BOON 20 (74)
(4TH DAY)   (272 MIN.) PHILLIPS 11 (59)
              (2 BEHIND) (31 MIN LOST ON 4TH DAY)

LUNCH: 291-7 (108 OVERS) PHILLIPS 76 (181)
             (394 MIN.) LAWSON 6 (17)
             (89 AHEAD)

WKT	PARTNERSHIP			RUNS	MINS
1st	Hilditch	Wood		5	11
2nd	Hilditch	Wessels		139	154
3rd	Hilditch	Border		7	27
4th	Border	Boon		8	8
5th	Boon	Ritchie		1	3
6th	Boon	Phillips		32	63
7th	Phillips	O'Donnell		80	97
8th	Phillips	Lawson		35	26
9th	Lawson	McDermott		11	10
10th	McDermott	Thomson		6	7
				324	

AUSTRALIA IN ENGLAND 1985

ENGLAND 2ND INNINGS (REQUIRING 123 RUNS TO WIN IN A MINIMUM OF 200 MINUTES)

IN	OUT	MINS	No.	BATSMAN	HOW OUT	BOWLER	RUNS	WKT	TOTAL	6s	4s	BALLS	NOTES ON DISMISSAL
2.20	4.08	88	1	G.A. GOOCH	LBW	O'DONNELL	28	3	71	-	3	65	Beaten by breakback – played back.
2.20	3.08	48	2	R.T. ROBINSON	BOWLED	LAWSON	21	1	44	-	4	30	off stump – through bat/pad gap pushing forward.
3.10	3.32	22	3	D.I. GOWER *	C' BORDER	O'DONNELL	5	2	59	-	1	18	Edged drive low to 2nd slip – two-handed, diving forward
3.34	4.24	30	4	M.W. GATTING	C' PHILLIPS	LAWSON	12	4	83	-	2	20	Edged push at offside ball to keeper's right – two-handed, low
4.10	(5.31)	81	5	A.J. LAMB	NOT OUT		31			-	5	63	Made winning hit.
4.26	5.05	39	6	I.T. BOTHAM	BOWLED	O'DONNELL	12	5	110	-	1	23	Played across ball that kept low and hit off stump.
5.07	(5.31)	24	7	P. WILLEY	NOT OUT		3			-	-	16	
			8	P.R. DOWNTON †									
			9	J.E. EMBUREY									
			10	P.J.W. ALLOTT									
			11	N.G. COWANS									
				EXTRAS	b - lb 7	w 1 nb 3	11			0	6	16⁴	235 balls (including 3 no-balls)
				TOTAL	(38.4 OVERS – 171 MINUTES)		123-5						

* CAPTAIN † WICKET-KEEPER

13 OVERS 3 BALLS/HOUR
3.18 RUNS/OVER
52 RUNS/100 BALLS

BOWLER	O	M	R	W	HB	HRS	OVERS	RUNS	RUNS	MINS	OVERS	LAST 50 (in mins)
McDERMOTT	4	0	20	0	7/1	1	13	44	50	61	14	61
LAWSON	16	4	51	2	2½/1	2	14	56	100	120	27	59
O'DONNELL	15.4	5	37	3	-							
THOMSON	3	0	8	0	-/1							
			7									
	38.4	9	123	5								

© BILL FRINDALL

TEA: 62-2 (18 OVERS) GOOCH 27 (80')
(80 MIN.) GATTING 0 (6')

NEEDING 61 IN 60 MINUTES PLUS 20 OVERS

ENGLAND WON BY 5 WICKETS
WITH 13.2 OVERS TO SPARE

MAN OF THE MATCH: R.T. ROBINSON
(Adjudicator: R.G.D. WILLIS)

ATTENDANCE: 54,018
RECEIPTS: £301,000

WKT	PARTNERSHIP		RUNS	MINS
1st	Gooch	Robinson	44	48
2nd	Gooch	Gower	15	22
3rd	Gooch	Gatting	12	14
4th	Gatting	Lamb	12	14
5th	Lamb	Botham	27	39
6th	Lamb	Willey	13*	24
			123	

Second Test, Lord's, 27, 28, 29, June, 1, 2 July.
Australia won by 4 wickets.

The second Test followed a curiously similar pattern to the first, save that this time it was England who dropped the catches and allowed Australia to gain a first-innings lead of 135. This need not have been decisive, but it proved enough when England's second innings never recovered fully from a troubled start.

Australia caused some surprise by again playing only four bowlers, but here one of the four was the 38-year-old leg-spinner Bob Holland. The heavy rains which, but for many hours of hard work by the MCC staff, would have delayed the start, made the decision to put England in understandable.

In fact, the ball moved only a little, and then very slowly, and England at one time promised to build a healthy score, reaching 179 for three at a brisk pace. But with the end of an elegant innings by Gower, wickets fell, and early on the second morning they were out for 290.

This looked an adequate score when Australia were 24 for two and later that afternoon 101 for four, but hereabouts things began to go wrong for England. Early on Ritchie survived a chance at second slip which Gooch seemed late in sighting. Border, when 87, jumped out and edged a ball from Edmonds hard to a close short-leg, Gatting, who lost the ball in plucking it out of his lap.

By that evening Border and Ritchie had steadied the ship and reached 183 for four. On the Saturday they turned recovery into something like a winning position by extending their fifth-wicket stand to 216. Botham then had Ritchie lbw and in a much livelier spell hurried the innings to an end. Border was eventually caught at second slip after a brilliant innings of seven and a half hours, and Botham for the 25th time finished with five wickets or more in a Test innings.

The Australian innings had ended at an unfortunate time for England, leaving them to bat for 13 overs, which neither Robinson nor Gooch survived. Thus after the week-end it was two nightwatchmen, Emburey and Allott, who resumed – an unsatisfactory position, not only because it gave Australia the chance of early successes on Monday morning but because the two would undoubtedly have been more use further down. Both were soon out, and, when Gower and Lamb followed, England were still 37 runs behind with four wickets standing.

From this bleak position, Botham and Gatting steered them to more sheltered ground with an excellent stand of 131 marked by its calm judgement and effective despatch of the loose ball.

Holland switched to bowling round the wicket into the rough created by McDermott, who had been twice warned. Eventually, just when it seemed that another hour of the partnership might turn the match to England, Botham lost patience and aimed a fatal blow against the spin.

Gatting made 25 of the last 26 runs from the bat, but Holland and the rough were too much for the others and Australia needed only 127. At 22 for three, with Botham bowling with much of his old fire, they were in some trouble, but the continued presence of Border prevented any panic. Though on the final morning they were 65 for five, Border was still there and Australia never seriously looked in danger.

AUSTRALIA IN ENGLAND 1985 105

ENGLAND 1ST INNINGS v. AUSTRALIA (2ND TEST) at LORD'S, LONDON on 27, 28, 29 JUNE, 1, 2 JULY, 1985. TOSS: AUSTRALIA

IN	OUT	MINS	No.	BATSMAN	HOW OUT	BOWLER	RUNS	WKT	TOTAL	6s	4s	BALLS	NOTES ON DISMISSAL
11·00	12·11	71	1	G.A. GOOCH	LBW	McDERMOTT	30	2	51	·	2	46	Breakback beat off drive.
11·00	11·37	37	2	R.T. ROBINSON	LBW	McDERMOTT	6	1	26	·	-	23	Breakback beat defensive push.
11·39	3·36	197	3	D.I. GOWER *	C' BORDER	McDERMOTT	86	4	179	·	12	146	Edged drive to second slip.
12·13	1·50	57	4	M.W. GATTING	LBW	LAWSON	14	3	99	·	2	32	Padded up to breakback (cf 1984 v West Indies at Lord's - twice)
1·52	4·49	156	5	A.J. LAMB	C' PHILLIPS	LAWSON	47	6	211	·	4	119	Driving on the up - two-handed catch towards slip.
3·38	4·04	5	6	I.T. BOTHAM	C' RITCHIE	LAWSON	5	5	184	·	1	8	Skied drive to deep backward point.
4·06	5·35	89	7	P.R. DOWNTON †	C' WESSELS	McDERMOTT	21	7	241	·	1	71	Gentle skier to short cover - leading edge - short ball (legside)
4·51	6·25	94	8	J.E. EMBUREY	LBW	O'DONNELL	33	8	273	·	4	74	Pushed outside breakback.
5·37	12·06	93	9	P.H. EDMONDS	C' BORDER	McDERMOTT	21	10	290	·	2	78	Edged push to second slip.
6·27	11·40	31	10	N.A. FOSTER	C' WESSELS	McDERMOTT	3	9	283	·	·	16	Edged drive to deep gully.
11·42	(2·06)	10	11	P.J.W. ALLOTT	NOT OUT		1			·	·	6	
				EXTRAS	b 1 lb 4	w 1 nb 17	23			0	28	6/4	619 balls (including 23 no balls)

* CAPTAIN † WICKET-KEEPER   TOTAL (99·2 OVERS; 429 MINUTES) 290 all out at 12·06 pm on 2nd day.

UMPIRES:
H.D. BIRD & D.G.L. EVANS

© BILL FRINDALL 1985

BOWLER	O	M	R	W	W/nb	HRS	OVERS	RUNS	RUNS	MINS	OVERS	LAST 50 (in mins)
LAWSON	25	2	91	3	-/5	1	13	43	50	68	15·0	68
McDERMOTT	29·2	5	70	6	-/4	2	13	45	100	135	28·1	67
O'DONNELL	22	3	82	1	1/-	3	10	42	150	207	43·5	72
HOLLAND	23	6	42	0	-	4	16	50	200	274	59·3	67
				5		5	14	35	250	351	79·3	77
	99·2	16	290	10		6	16	48				
						7	15	20				

2ND NEW BALL taken at 11·10 am 2nd day
- ENGLAND 273-8 after 90 overs.

LUNCH: 88-2 [26 OVERS / 121 MIN.] GOWER 38* (82) GATTING 10* (48)

TEA: 180-4 [52 OVERS / 240 MIN] LAMB 28* (108¹) BOTHAM 1* (2¹)

STUMPS: 273-8 [90 OVERS / 387 MIN] EDMONDS 9* (51¹) FOSTER 0* (1¹)
(1ST DAY)

13 OVERS 5 BALLS/HOUR
2·92 RUNS/OVER
47 RUNS/100 BALLS

WKT	PARTNERSHIP		RUNS	MINS
1st	Gooch	Robinson	26	37
2nd	Gooch	Gower	25	32
3rd	Gower	Gatting	48	57
4th	Gower	Lamb	80	104
5th	Lamb	Botham	5	5
6th	Lamb	Downton	27	43
7th	Downton	Emburey	30	44
8th	Emburey	Edmonds	32	48
9th	Edmonds	Foster	10	31
10th	Edmonds	Allott	7	10
			290	

106 AUSTRALIA IN ENGLAND 1985

AUSTRALIA 1ST INNINGS (IN REPLY TO ENGLAND'S 290 ALL OUT)

IN	OUT	MINS	No.	BATSMAN	HOW OUT	BOWLER	RUNS	WKT	TOTAL	6s	4s	BALLS	NOTES ON DISMISSAL
12.18	12.34	16	1	G.M. WOOD	c EMBUREY	ALLOTT	8	1	11	.	1	17	Hooked directly to deep fine leg.
12.18	2.08	41	2	A.M.J. HILDITCH	BOWLED	FOSTER	14	2	24	.	2	25	Off stump out – bowled between bat and pad (driving).
12.36	3.18	93	3	K.C. WESSELS	LBW	BOTHAM	11	3	80	.	1	41	Delayed decision. Leg-stump delivery.
2.10	4.27	450	4	A.R. BORDER *	c GOOCH	BOTHAM	196	7	398	.	22	318	Edged drive to second slip. (13 × HS in Tests. [THIRD-HIGHEST SCORE FOR AUSTRALIA AT HOME])
3.20	3.41	21	5	D.C. BOON	c DOWNTON	BOTHAM	4	4	101	.	1	20	Failed to avoid bouncer (glove) - penultimate ball before tea.
4.05	2.37	269	6	G.M. RITCHIE	LBW	BOTHAM	94	5	317	.	10	212	Played across breakback.
2.39	3.13	34	7	W.B. PHILLIPS †	c EDMONDS	BOTHAM	21	6	347	1	3	22	Sliced drive to gully.
3.15	4.41	66	8	S.P. O'DONNELL	c LAMB	EDMONDS	48	8	414	1	6	69	Edged drive at leg-break to backward-point (driving).
4.29	(4.58)	29	9	G.F. LAWSON	NOT OUT		5	.		.	.	16	
4.43	4.55	12	10	C.J. McDERMOTT	RUN OUT [O'DONNELL/DOWNTON]		9	9	425	.	.	11	Responded slowly to Lawson's call for single to mid-wicket.
4.57	4.58	1	11	R.G. HOLLAND	BOWLED	EDMONDS	0	10	425	.	.	1	Attempted to pull a six off his first ball.
			* CAPTAIN † WICKET-KEEPER	EXTRAS	b - lb 10 w 1 nb 4		15			2b 46⁴		752 balls (including 4 no-balls)	
				TOTAL	(124.4 OVERS; 524 MINUTES)		425	all out at 4.58 pm on 3rd day.				14 OVERS 1 BALLS/HOUR	
					(LEAD: 135)							3.41 RUNS/OVER	
												57 RUNS/100 BALLS	

LUNCH: 16-1
TEA: 101-4 [5.4 OVERS / 28 MINUTES] 81 17.2
STUMPS: 183-4 (2ND DAY) [26 OVERS LOST] [29.5 OVERS / 134 MINUTES]
LUNCH: 261-4 [52 OVERS / 228 MINUTES]
TEA: 371-6 [82.2 OVERS / 343 MIN.]
                [110 OVERS / 466 MIN.]
HILDITCH 7* (28¹) / WESSELS 0* (10¹)
BORDER 58* (91¹)
BORDER 93* (118) / RITCHIE 46* (94)
BORDER 144* (300) / RITCHIE 69* (209)
BORDER 184* (433) / O'DONNELL 20* (25)

BOTHAM'S 25TH INSTANCE OF FIVE OR MORE
WICKETS IN A TEST INNINGS (WORLD RECORD)

© BILL FRINDALL 1985

BOWLER	O	M	R	W	Nb	W	HRS	OVERS	RUNS		RUNS	MINS	OVERS	LAST 50 (in minutes)
FOSTER	23	1	83	1	½	-	1	12	36		50	81	17.2	81
ALLOTT	30	4	10	1	-	-	2	14	52		100	130	28.3	49
BOTHAM	24	2	109	5	4	-	3	14	56		150	184	41.0	54
EDMONDS	25.4	5	85	2	-	-	4	14	44		200	258	58.4	74
GOOCH	3	1	11	0	-	-	5	15	40		250	332	79.4	74
EMBUREY	19	3	57	0	-	-	6	17	55		300	377	89.5	45
			10		1		7	13	41		350	446	104.4	69
	124.4	16	425	10			8	15	57		400	498	118.4	52

2ND NEW BALL TAKEN AT 1.51 pm 3RD day
- AUSTRALIA 281-4 after 85.3 overs.

WKT	PARTNERSHIP		RUNS	MINS
1ST	Wood	Hilditch	11	16
2ND	Hilditch	Wessels	15	23
3RD	Wessels	Border	56	68
4TH	Border	Boon	21	21
5TH	Border	Ritchie	216	269
6TH	Border	Phillips	30	34
7TH	Border	O'Donnell	51	52
8TH	O'Donnell	Lawson	16	12
9TH	Lawson	McDermott	11	12
10TH	Lawson	Holland	0	1
			425	

AUSTRALIA IN ENGLAND 1985

ENGLAND 2ND INNINGS (135 RUNS BEHIND ON FIRST INNINGS)

IN	OUT	MINS	No.	BATSMAN	HOW OUT	BOWLER	RUNS	WKT	TOTAL	6s	4s	BALLS	NOTES ON DISMISSAL
5.11	5.49	38	1	G.A. GOOCH	c Phillips	McDermott	17	1	32	.	1	29	Legside catch - missed leg glance.
5.11	5.55	44	2	R.T. ROBINSON	Bowled	HOLLAND	12	2	34	.	.	29	Misjudged flight - played round straight ball.
5.51	11.22	41	3	J.E. EMBUREY	Bowled	LAWSON	20	4	57	.	2	31	Played on - under edged chop at short ball.
5.57	11.03	16	4	P.J.W. ALLOTT	Bowled	LAWSON	0	3	38	.	.	7	Off stump out - late on ball angled in to him.
11.05	11.37	32	5	D.I. GOWER*	c Phillips	McDermott	22	5	77	.	5	21	Edged firm-footed drive at ball angled across him.
11.24	(4.27)	246	6	M.W. GATTING	NOT OUT		75	.	.	.	6	181	
11.39	12.20	41	7	A.J. LAMB	c Holland	LAWSON	9	6	98	.	1	32	Deceived by slower ball - spooned catch to mid-off.
12.22	3.15	135	8	I.T. BOTHAM	c Border	HOLLAND	85	7	229	1	12	116	Skied drive to cover.
3.17	3.18	1	9	P.R. DOWNTON †	c Boon	HOLLAND	0	8	229	.	.	1	Edged leg-break low to slip - first ball (walked).
3.20	4.24	45	10	P.H. EDMONDS	c Boon	HOLLAND	1	9	261	.	.	34	Edged cut to slip.
4.26	4.27	1	11	N.A. FOSTER	c Border	HOLLAND	0	10	261	.	.	3	Pushed forward to silly point.
				EXTRAS	b 1 lb 12	w 4 nb 3	20			1	6 27	484 balls (including 4 no-balls)	
				TOTAL	(80 OVERS; 329 MINUTES)		261	all out at 4·27 pm on 4th day.

*CAPTAIN   †WICKET-KEEPER

BOWLER	O	M	R	W	N/w	HRS	OVERS	RUNS	RUNS	MINS	OVERS	LAST 50 (in mins)
McDERMOTT	20	2	84	2	4/2	1	13	37	50	79	17.1	79
LAWSON	23	0	86	3	7/1	2	13	56	100	149	33.1	70
HOLLAND	32	12	68	5	-	3	16	39	150	197	46.3	48
O'DONNELL	5	0	10	0	-	4	15	76	200	229	54.2	32
						5	15	35	250	310	75.0	81
		13										
	80	14	261	10								

© BILL FRINDALL 1985

STUMPS: 37-2 (3rd day)   13 OVERS 59 MINUTES   EMBUREY 4* (9') ALLOTT 0* (8')
LUNCH: 132-6   42 OVERS 181 MINUTES   GATTING 20* (98') BOTHAM 23* (46')
TEA: 244-8   73 OVERS 303 MINUTES   GATTING 64* (226') EDMONDS 0* (22')

WKT	PARTNERSHIP		RUNS	MINS
1st	Gooch	Robinson	32	38
2nd	Robinson	Emburey	2	4
3rd	Emburey	Allott	4	16
4th	Emburey	Gower	19	15
5th	Gower	Gatting	20	13
6th	Gatting	Lamb	21	41
7th	Gatting	Botham	131	135
8th	Gatting	Downton	0	1
9th	Gatting	Edmonds	32	45
10th	Gatting	Foster	0	1

14 OVERS 3 BALLS/HOUR
3·26 RUNS/OVER
54 RUNS/100 BALLS

261

AUSTRALIA 2ND INNINGS

REQUIRING 127 TO WIN IN A MINIMUM OF 441 MINUTES

IN	OUT	MINS	No.	BATSMAN	HOW OUT	BOWLER	RUNS	WKT	TOTAL	6s	4s	BALLS	NOTES ON DISMISSAL
4.39	4.41	2	1	A.M.J. HILDITCH	c LAMB	BOTHAM	0	1	0	·	·	4	Hooked short ball to deep backward square-leg
4.39	5.01	22	2	G.M. WOOD	c LAMB	BOTHAM	6	2	9	·	·	17	Fended short ball to gully via bat shoulder
4.43	11.21	109	3	K.C. WESSELS	RUN OUT (GOWER)		28	4	63	·	3	86	Underarm throw from silly point
5.03	5.27	24	4	G.M. RITCHIE	BOWLED	ALLOTT	2	3	22	·	·	16	Off stump out - drove across line off back foot
5.29 (2.32)	134	5	A.R. BORDER*	NOT OUT		41			·	6	89	Completed 5000 runs in Tests
11.23	11.31	8	6	D.C. BOON	BOWLED	EDMONDS	1	5	65	·	·	8	Off stump - beaten by quicker leg-break
11.33	12.13	40	7	W.B. PHILLIPS †	c EDMONDS	EMBUREY	29	6	116	·	4	32	Walk-away cut - point dived to right - superb low catch
12.15 (2.32)	17	8	S.P. O'DONNELL	NOT OUT		9			1	·	24	Made winning hit off Edmonds
			9	G.F. LAWSON									
			10	C.J. McDERMOTT									
			11	R.G. HOLLAND									
				EXTRAS	b - lb 11 w - nb -		11			1b	13"	276 balls (0 no-balls)	
				TOTAL	(46 OVERS; 184 MINUTES)		127-6						

*CAPTAIN †WICKET-KEEPER

15 OVERS 0 BALLS/HOUR
2·76 RUNS/OVER
46 RUNS/100 BALLS

BOWLER	O	M	R	W	N/b	W/d	HRS	OVERS	RUNS		RUNS	MINS	OVERS	LAST 50 (in mins)
BOTHAM	15	0	49	2	-	-	1	12	28		50	93	21.2	93
ALLOTT	7	4	8	1	-	-	2	17	37		100	156	37.5	63
EDMONDS	16	5	35	1	-	-	3	15	54					
EMBUREY	8	4	24	1	-	-								
			11											
	46	13	127	6										

© BILL FRINDALL 1985

STUMPS 46-3 [21 OVERS] [WESSELS 23*(86)]
(4th DAY) (81 REQUIRED) [92 MINUTES] [BORDER 12*(42)]

AUSTRALIA WON BY 4 WICKETS
at 12·32 pm on fifth day.

MATCH AWARD: A.R. BORDER
(Adjudicator: E.R. Dexter)

WKT	PARTNERSHIP		RUNS	MINS
1st	Hilditch	Wood	0	2
2nd	Wood	Wessels	9	18
3rd	Wessels	Ritchie	13	24
4th	Wessels	Border	41	63
5th	Border	Boon	2	8
6th	Border	Phillips	51	40
7th	Border	O'Donnell	11*	17
			127	

Third Test, Trent Bridge, 11, 12, 13, 15, 16 July.
Match drawn.

Though the third Test was drawn, and to that extent was an anticlimax after its two predecessors, its first three days lived up to the entertainment and competitiveness of the series.

England won the toss and batted at a brisk pace on a slow pitch. Robinson, not Gooch, set the tempo, and after he was out Gower came in and played at his best in an innings which, despite subsequent big innings by Wood and Ritchie, earned the Man of the Match award. By the end of the first day England had made 279 for two and had Gower, 107, and Gatting, 53, well established.

Next morning Gower played brilliantly. Gatting, entirely safe, gave him the strike at will; and at 358 for two, England seemed destined for a huge score in front of a 15,000 crowd on whom the gates had already been closed.

At this point Gatting suffered a piece of cruel luck. Gower shaped to play Holland to extra cover but, doubtless because the ball turned rather more than expected from the rough, hit it hard back at the bowler who accidentally deflected it on to the stumps. Gatting, who had not looked like being shifted by normal means, was run out, having seemingly been deceived by Gower's original intention.

Just before lunch, Gower himself was caught at the wicket, and England's last eight wickets fell for 98 runs to a mixture of misplaced confidence, ill luck, and good catching and bowling, notably by Lawson.

It was soon clear that Australia would also make a big score, though on the Saturday afternoon when they declined from 205 for two to 263 for five, a useful England lead was briefly conceivable.

However, Ritchie, almost caught and bowled first ball by Emburey, settled in with Wood in a stand of 161 which was to last into the fourth day, until Australia were almost level. The luck was with the batsmen, but England were not holding the half-chances. Moreover, Allott was unwell and Sidebottom, who had been a late replacement for the injured Foster, split a big toe and took no further part. Australia had been criticized for playing only four bowlers, but it was England who found themselves short-handed.

Edmonds and Emburey bowled away hour after hour – often to close-set fields as Edmonds tried hopefully to exploit the rough – but the pitch was too slow to threaten batsmen taking fewer chances than England's had taken. Wood batted with scarcely an error for over 10 hours.

England had batted for only 130 overs. Australia needed 202 to earn their 83-run lead, by which time there were only 17 overs of the fourth day left, and bad light soon spared England the bulk of those. On so mild a pitch it would have required very bad batting and a panic to have them in trouble, and after a delayed start on the last day they batted comfortably to a draw.

110 AUSTRALIA IN ENGLAND 1985

ENGLAND 1ST INNINGS v. AUSTRALIA (3RD TEST) at TRENT BRIDGE, NOTTINGHAM on 11, 12, 13, 15, 16 JULY, 1985. TOSS: ENGLAND

IN	OUT	MINS	No.	BATSMAN	HOW OUT	BOWLER	RUNS	WKT	TOTAL	6s	4s	BALLS	NOTES ON DISMISSAL
11.00	3.16	170	1	G.A. GOOCH	c† WESSELS	LAWSON	70	2	171	.	12	132	Reflex gully catch off low, firmly hit cut.
11.00	12.31	65	2	R.T. ROBINSON	c† BORDER	LAWSON	38	1	55	.	6	54	Edged low to 2nd slip — two-handed juggled catch.
12.33	12.57	38½	3	D.I. GOWER *	c† PHILLIPS	O'DONNELL	166	4	365	.	17	283	10th (*for 23 mins) Edged steer at lifting ball.
3.18	12.46	245	4	M.W. GATTING	RUN OUT (HOLLAND)		74	3	358	.	9	162	Backing up - bowler deflected Gower drive into stumps.
12.48	2.13	47	5	A.J. LAMB	LBW	LAWSON	17	5	416	.	3	29	Beaten by ball that kept low.
12.59	2.16	39	6	I.T. BOTHAM	c† O'DONNELL	Mc DERMOTT	38	6	416	.	7	35	Leading edge skier to extra-cover - aiming to mid-wicket
2.15	2.21	6	7	P.R. DOWNTON †	c† RITCHIE	Mc DERMOTT	0	7	419	.	.	1	1st ball — driving left-handed catch at square leg
2.18	2.25	7	8	A. SIDEBOTTOM	c† O'DONNELL	LAWSON	2	8	419	.	.	8	Hooked short ball to backward square-leg
2.23	(3.21)	58	9	J.E. EMBUREY	NOT OUT		16			.	2	26	
2.27	3.00	33	10	P.H. EDMONDS	BOWLED	HOLLAND	12	9	443	.	1	31	Bowled behind legs sweeping at full toss.
3.02	3.21	19	11	P.J.W. ALLOTT	c† BORDER	LAWSON	7	10	456	.	.	21	Edged low to 2nd slip.
				EXTRAS	b - lb 12 w 1 nb 3		16			0⁶ 57⁴	782 balls (including 4 no balls)

TOTAL (129.4 OVERS, 554 MINUTES) 456 all out at 3.21 pm on 2nd day.

* CAPTAIN † WICKET-KEEPER
UMPIRES: D.J. CONSTANT
A.G.T. WHITEHEAD

© BILL FRINDALL 1985

BOWLER	O	M	R	W		HRS	OVERS	RUNS
LAWSON	39.4	10	103	5	½	1	13	52
Mc DERMOTT	35	3	147	2	-/1	2	14	51
O'DONNELL	29	4	104	1		3	15	63
HOLLAND	26	3	90	1		4	16	41
			12			5	16	58
	129.4	20	456	10		6	13	23
						7	12	52
						8	14	62
2nd new ball taken at 11.29am 2nd day						9	13	45

- ENGLAND 288-2 after 87.1 overs.

RUNS	MINS	OVERS	LAST 50 (in mins)
50	54	11.5	54
100	114	25.5	60
150	170	39.1	56
200	232	55.5	62
250	280	69.4	48
300	381	91.5	101
350	427	101.0	46
400	469	111.2	42
450	543	127.1	74

LUNCH: 85 - 1 (21 OVERS) 2½ min (6 over) last. (94 MINUTES)
TEA: 182 - 2 (51 OVERS) (215 MINUTES)
STUMPS: 279 - 2 (80.4 OVERS) (1st DAY - 9.2 OVERS LOST) (331 MINUTES)
LUNCH: 369 - 4 (107 OVERS) (453 MINUTES)

ENGLAND reached 416-4 before losing
4 WICKETS for 3 RUNS off 11 BALLS in 12 MINUTES

14 OVERS 0 BALLS/HOUR
3.52 RUNS/OVER
58 RUNS/100 BALLS

WKT	PARTNERSHIP			RUNS	MINS
1ST	Gooch	Robinson		55	65
2ND	Gooch	Gower		116	123
3RD	Gower	Gatting	GOWER 63⁵ (148⁷) GATTING 1⁺ (23¹)	187	245
4TH	Gower	Lamb	GOWER 107³ (264⁶) GATTING 53⁴ (135¹)	7	9
5TH	Lamb	Botham	LAMB 4⁺ (14¹) BOTHAM 4⁺ (3¹)	51	36
6TH	Botham	Downton		0	1
7TH	Downton	Sidebottom		3	3
8TH	Sidebottom	Embury		0	2
9TH	Embury	Edmonds		24	33
10TH	Embury	Allott		13	19

GOOCH 17⁴ (94¹)
GOWER 23⁴ (27¹)

456

AUSTRALIA IN ENGLAND 1985

AUSTRALIA 1ST INNINGS (IN REPLY TO ENGLAND'S 456 ALL OUT)

IN	OUT	MINS	No.	BATSMAN	HOW OUT	BOWLER	RUNS	WKT	TOTAL	6s	4s	BALLS	NOTES ON DISMISSAL
3.42	12.29	599	1	G.M.WOOD	c ROBINSON	BOTHAM	172	6	424	.	21	448	8th HS in Test. 3000 Runs. 1000 v. ENG. Pulled long-hop to mid-wicket
3.42	5.52	130	2	A.M.J. HILDITCH	LBW	ALLOTT	47	1	87	.	5	89	Beaten on forward stroke by breakback.
5.54	11.39	57	3	R.G. HOLLAND	LBW	SIDEBOTTOM	10	2	128	.	2	41	Missed pull. HS in Tests. Sidebottom's 1st wkt in his 12th Test
11.41	1.56	95	4	K.C. WESSELS	c DOWNTON	EMBUREY	33	3	205	.	.	85	Edged forward push at ball that straightened.
1.58	2.15	17	5	A.R. BORDER*	c BOTHAM	EDMONDS	23	4	234	1	2	18	Edged via pad to slip
2.17	3.03	46	6	D.C. BOON	c and BOWLED	EMBUREY	15	5	263	.	3	47	Deceived by slower, flighted ball - waist-high catch.
3.05	3.02	359	7	G.M. RITCHIE	BOWLED	EDMONDS	146	8	491	.	16	308	2nd HS in Tests. Missed drive at leg-break that chipped off stump.
12.31	12.53	22	8	W.B. PHILLIPS †	BOWLED	EMBUREY	2	7	437	.	.	23	Missed sweep and fell over. 'Arm' ball removed leg stump.
12.55	4.30	156	9	S.P. O'DONNELL	c DOWNTON	BOTHAM	46	9	539	.	6	117	Skied hook - running catch taken at fine leg.
3.04	4.32	68	10	G.F. LAWSON	c GOOCH	BOTHAM	18	10	539	.	3	50	Edged to slip - Botham's 2nd wicket in successive balls.
4.31	(4.32)	1	11	C.J. McDERMOTT	NOT OUT		0			.	.	.	
				EXTRAS	b 6 lb 7 w 2 nb 12		27					1 59*	1226 balls (including 18 no balls)
				TOTAL	(201.2 OVERS, 783 MINUTES)		539						all out at 4.32 pm on 4th day

*CAPTAIN †WICKET-KEEPER   LEAD: 83

	RUNS	MINS	OVERS	LAST 50 (in mins)
	50	66	13.5	66
	100	161	37.3	95
	150	222	50.3	61
	200	283	68.2	61
	250	338	84.1	55
	300	413	104.4	75
	350	487	123.2	74
	400	562	147.1	75
	450	644	165.2	82
	500	726	188.0	82

STUMPS: 94-1 (2nd DAY) (362 BEHIND) (35 OVERS / 150 MINUTES) WOOD 38* (156') HOLLAND 4* (18')

LUNCH: 187-2 (64 OVERS / 270 MINUTES) WOOD 85* (270') WESSELS 26* (19')

TEA: 289-5 (100 OVERS / 390 MINUTES) WOOD 125* (396') RITCHIE 21* (35')

STUMPS: 366-5 (3rd DAY) (90 BEHIND) (131 OVERS / 510 MINUTES) WOOD 152* (510') RITCHIE 65* (155')

LUNCH: 440-7 (162 OVERS / 632 MINUTES) RITCHIE 113* (277') O'DONNELL 2* (7')

TEA: 526-8 (195 OVERS / 752 MINUTES) O'DONNELL 35* (127') LAWSON 17* (51')

AUSTRALIA'S HIGHEST TOTAL AT TRENT BRIDGE

15 OVERS 2 BALLS/HOUR
2.68 RUNS/OVER
44 RUNS/100 BALLS

WKT	PARTNERSHIP		RUNS	MINS
1st	Wood	Hilditch	87	130
2nd	Wood	Holland	41	57
3rd	Wood	Wessels	77	95
4th	Wood	Border	29	17
5th	Wood	Boon	29	46
6th	Wood	Ritchie	161	244
7th	Ritchie	Phillips	13	22
8th	Ritchie	O'Donnell	54	89
9th	O'Donnell	Lawson	48	66
10th	Lawson	McDermott	0	1
			539	

© BILL FRINDALL 1985

BOWLER	O	M	R	W	w/	HRS	OVERS	RUNS
BOTHAM	34.2	3	107	3		1	12	42
SIDEBOTTOM	18.4	3	65	1	-1	2	15	36
ALLOTT	18	4	55	1		3	14	38
EDMONDS	66	18	155	2		4	13	48
EMBUREY	55	15	129	3		5	19	62
GOOCH	8.2	2	13	0		6	18	39
GATTING	1	0	2	0		7	15	43
	201.2	45	539	10		8	16	36
						9	19	39
						10	14	41
						11	14	38
						12	17	30
						13	15	47

2nd NEW BALL taken at 4.02 pm 3rd day
- AUSTRALIA 289-5 after 100 overs.
3rd NEW BALL taken at 3.30 pm 4th day
- AUSTRALIA 512-8 after 193 overs.

112 AUSTRALIA IN ENGLAND 1985

ENGLAND 2ND INNINGS   (83 RUNS BEHIND ON FIRST INNINGS)

IN	OUT	MINS	No.	BATSMAN	HOW OUT	BOWLER	RUNS	WKT	TOTAL	6s	4s	BALLS	NOTES ON DISMISSAL
4·42	2·57	117	1	G.A.GOOCH	c RITCHIE	McDERMOTT	48	1	79	·	6	91	Late on hook — skied simple catch to mid-wicket.
4·42	5·32	272	2	R.T.ROBINSON	NOT OUT		77			·	4	198	Completed 1000 f·c runs for season. Hit · Aus by Notts batsman at Trent Bridge.
2·39	3·20	41	3	D.I.GOWER*	c PHILLIPS	McDERMOTT	17	2	107	·	2	33	Edged waft at widish offside ball.
3·22	5·32	110	4	M.W.GATTING	NOT OUT		35			·	5	89	
			5										
			6										
			7										
			8										
			9										
			10										
			11										
				EXTRAS	b 1 lb 16 w — nb 2	19	0⁶ 17⁴ 411 balls (including 3 no balls)
				TOTAL (68 OVERS — 272 MINUTES)	**196-2**

*CAPTAIN †WICKET-KEEPER

15 OVERS 0 BALLS/HOUR
2·88 RUNS/OVER
48 RUNS/100 BALLS

© BILL FRINDALL 1985

BOWLER	O	M	R	W	nb	HRS	OVERS	RUNS	RUNS	MINS	OVERS	LAST 50 (in mins)
LAWSON	13	4	32	0	·	1	13	40	50	84	17.2	84
McDERMOTT	16	2	42	2	·	2	15	39	100	152	26.3	68
HOLLAND	28	9	69	0	·	3	14	33	150	217	53.0	65
O'DONNELL	10	2	26	0	·	4	17	55				
RITCHIE	1	0	10	0	·							
			17									
	68	17	196	2								

BAD LIGHT STOPPED PLAY AT 4·55pm — 17·1 OVERS LOST
STUMPS: 8-0 (2·5 OVERS · 13 MIN) GOOCH 4* ROBINSON 3*
LUNCH: 40-0 (13 OVERS / 60 MINUTES) GOOCH 25* ROBINSON 11
TEA: 112-2 (42 OVERS / 180 MINUTES) ROBINSON 35* (16o) GATTING 4* (18)

WKT	PARTNERSHIP		RUNS	MINS
1st	Gooch	Robinson	79	117
2nd	Robinson	Gower	28	41
3rd	Robinson	Gatting	89*	110
			196	

MATCH DRAWN

MAN OF THE MATCH: D.I. GOWER
(Adjudicator: T.W. GRAVENEY)

Fourth Test, Old Trafford, 1, 2, 3, 5, 6 August.
Match drawn.

Despite the spell of bad weather suffered all over Britain, the fourth Test began with three days of 90, 80, and 53 overs play, at the end of which England were handsomely placed 191 runs ahead with four first innings wickets standing. After a country-wide week-end of floods and gales, Old Trafford still provided a full day's play on the Monday, but the last day was severely interrupted and Australia in the end easily earned a draw.

Having been put in by Gower on a very slow, slightly damp pitch, Australia had started the match well with an opening stand of 71, made with no apparent difficulty by Wessels and Hilditch. But the innings went into decline against the spin of Edmonds and Emburey, Border being stumped while aiming an untypically wild slog at Edmonds. A fifth-wicket stand between Boon and Phillips partially repaired the damage, but Botham, suddenly finding his rhythm, removed both in a spell which brought him four wickets, and, after a last-wicket stand of 33 between O'Donnell and Holland, Australia were all out that day for 257.

England's innings, begun next morning, was remarkable for the fact that, despite the sluggishness of the pitch (or perhaps because that sluggishness blunted the other bowlers) all the eight wickets that fell to a bowler were taken by the youthful McDermott, fast, strong, and persistent.

After Robinson's early departure, Gooch and Gower batted well in a stand of 121. But when both were out in quick succession – Gower superbly caught on the long-leg boundary by Hilditch – the England innings, at 148 for three, needed rebuilding. This was done soundly and sensibly by Gatting and Lamb, and their stand reached 156 next day before Lamb, hesitant over starting for a sharp single, was run out by Matthews' throw from extra cover. Gatting, however, had always been the dominant partner, and he continued through Saturday's foreshortened play to make a splendid and chanceless 160 before he was caught at the wicket in the effort to press on quickly.

England batted on briefly on the fourth morning, bringing their lead up to 225, mainly through Emburey, and then set about the difficult task of prising out Australia on a pitch taking spin only fitfully, and then sometimes too extravagantly, and always too slowly to upset a well organized defence. The ball seldom bounced much, and England can never have been really confident either about their ability to bowl the opposition out or about the weather.

When, soon after tea on that fourth day, Australia were 138 for four, still 87 behind, England certainly did have a good chance on paper, especially as, with the spinners on, they were bowling their overs at 20 an hour. But Border produced the technique and application required. Equally important, he showed his partners – Ritchie that evening and Phillips on the abbreviated last day – what was needed. With their support he took his side slowly but surely out of danger.

114 AUSTRALIA IN ENGLAND 1985

AUSTRALIA 1ST INNINGS v. ENGLAND (4TH TEST) at OLD TRAFFORD, MANCHESTER ON 1, 2, 3, 5, 6 AUGUST, 1985. TOSS: ENGLAND

IN	OUT	MINS	No.	BATSMAN	HOW OUT	BOWLER	RUNS	WKT	TOTAL	6s	4s	BALLS	NOTES ON DISMISSAL
11.00	12.23	83	1	K.C.WESSELS	C' BOTHAM	EMBUREY	34	1	71	-	3	60	Edged drive to slip.
11.00	1.50	131	2	A.M.J.HILDITCH	C' GOWER	EDMONDS	49	2	97	-	4	93	Silly point - juggled catch. Ball rebounded from pad - hit bat.
12.25	4.36	191	3	D.C.BOON	C' LAMB	BOTHAM	61	6	198	-	6	146	HS in TESTS. Cut hard to deep gully - sharp catch.
1.52	2.29	37	4	A.R.BORDER*	S' DOWNTON	EDMONDS	8	3	118	-	1	18	Down wicket - pulled across line. First stumping of rubber.
2.31	2.33	2	5	G.M.RITCHIE	C' AND BOWLED	EDMONDS	4	4	122	-	1	3	Mistimed short ball that held up — simple catch.
2.35	4.21	85	6	W.B.PHILLIPS †	C' DOWNTON	BOTHAM	36	5	193	-	4	71	Top-edged cut.
4.23	5.00	37	7	G.R.J.MATHEWS	BOWLED	BOTHAM	4	7	211	-	.	25	Played no stroke to breakback that removed off stump.
4.38	6.14	96	8	S.P.O'DONNELL	BOWLED	EDMONDS	45	10	257	1	3	78	Beaten by 'arm' ball.
5.02	5.20	18	9	G.F.LAWSON	C' DOWNTON	BOTHAM	4	8	223	.	.	17	Edged push at away seamer.
5.22	5.23	1	10	C.J.McDERMOTT	LBW	EMBUREY	0	9	224	.	.	1	Padded up to 'arm' ball - first ball.
5.25	(6.14)	49	11	R.G.HOLLAND	NOT OUT		5			.	.	27	
				EXTRAS	b - lb 3 w 1 nb 3		7			1 b	4 22	539 balls (including 4 no balls)	
				TOTAL	(89.1 OVERS - 374 MINUTES)		257	ALL OUT AT 6.14pm (30th over of 1st day)					

*CAPTAIN † WICKET-KEEPER

UMPIRES:
H.D. BIRD
D.R. SHEPHERD

LUNCH: 85-1 (27 OVERS / 122 MIN) HILDITCH 43 (156) / BOON 6 (16)

TEA: 168-4 (58 OVERS / 241 MIN) BOON 51* (156) / PHILLIPS 18* (65)

14 OVERS 2 BALLS/HOUR
         2.88 RUNS/OVER
         48 RUNS/100 BALLS

© BILL FRINDALL 1985

BOWLER	O	M	R	W	HRS	OVERS	RUNS
BOTHAM	23	4	79	4	1/-	1	12	51
AGNEW	14	0	65	0	-/3	2	14	34
ALLOTT	13	1	29	0	.	3	15	40
EMBUREY	24	7	41	2	.	4	17	43
EDMONDS	15.1	4	40	4	.	5	14	43
				3		6	14	35
	89.1	16	257	10				

2ND NEW BALL TAKEN at 5.59pm ON 1st day
- AUSTRALIA 246-9 after 86 overs

	RUNS	MINS	OVERS	LAST 50 (in mins)
50	56	11.4	56
100	138	30.4	82
150	210	50.0	72
200	280	66.3	70
250	366	87.4	86

WKT	PARTNERSHIP		RUNS	MINS
1st	Wessels	Hilditch	71	83
2nd	Hilditch	Boon	26	46
3rd	Boon	Border	21	37
4th	Boon	Ritchie	4	2
5th	Boon	Phillips	71	85
6th	Boon	Matthews	5	13
7th	Matthews	O'Donnell	13	22
8th	O'Donnell	Lawson	12	18
9th	O'Donnell	McDermott	1	1
10th	O'Donnell	Holland	33	49

257

AUSTRALIA IN ENGLAND 1985

ENGLAND 1st INNINGS IN REPLY TO AUSTRALIA'S 257 ALL OUT

IN	OUT	MINS	No.	BATSMAN	HOW OUT	BOWLER	RUNS	WKT	TOTAL	6s	4s	BALLS	NOTES ON DISMISSAL
11.00	4.06	209	1	G.A.GOOCH	LBW	McDERMOTT	74	2	142	.	9	144	Late on fast breakback - played back.
11.00	11.18	18	2	R.T.ROBINSON	C' BORDER	McDERMOTT	10	1	21	.	2	12	Edged steer at widish ball waist-high to 2nd slip.
11.21	4.15	197	3	D.I.GOWER *	C' HILDITCH	McDERMOTT	47	3	148	.	5	140	(500 runs when 34) Hooked to long-leg boundary - tumbling catch.
4.08	6.05	357	4	M.W.GATTING	C' PHILLIPS	McDERMOTT	160	6	430	.	21	266	(1st in 40 Test innings in England. Edged cover drive - walked.
4.17	3.13	194	5	A.J.LAMB	Run out (MATTHEWS)		67	4	304	.	8	135	Direct throw from cover-point - Gatting's stroke.
3.15	3.49	34	6	I.T.BOTHAM	C' O'DONNELL	McDERMOTT	20	5	339	.	3	25	Hooked bouncer to deep backward square-leg (running catch).
3.51	11.01	134	7	P.R.DOWNTON†	BOWLED	McDERMOTT	23	7	448	.	1	82	Break back - second ball of fourth day.
6.07	(11.46)	62	8	J.E.EMBUREY	NOT OUT		31			.	3	37	
11.03	11.08	5	9	P.H.EDMONDS	BOWLED	McDERMOTT	1	8	450	.	.	7	Yorked, leg stump - late inswinger.
11.10	11.28	18	10	P.J.W.ALLOTT	BOWLED	McDERMOTT	7	9	470	.	1	11	Middle stump out - attempting slog over long-on.
11.30	(11.46)	16	11	J.P.AGNEW	NOT OUT		2			.	.	8	
				EXTRAS	b 7 lb 16 w - nb 17		40						
				TOTAL	(141 OVERS - 631 MINUTES)		482-9 DECLARED at 11.46am on 4th day			0	53	867	balls (including 21 no balls)

* CAPTAIN † WICKET-KEEPER   (LEAD: 225)

RSP 11.33 TO 12.14 1st DAY (24-1)
LUNCH: 55-1 (15 OVERS) GOOCH 18* (81 min)
                      (81 MINUTES) GOWER 19* (60 min)
TEA: 141-1 (45 OVERS) GOOCH 73* (203 min)
           (203 MINUTES) GOWER 46* (182 min)
STUMPS: 233-3 (80 OVERS) GATTING 45* (130 min)
(2nd DAY)   (341 MIN.) LAMB 38* (121 min)
TEA: 354-5 (107 OVERS) GATTING 103* (261 min)
           (472 MIN.) DOWNTON 7* (20 min)
STUMPS: 448-6 (132.4 OVERS) DOWNTON 23* (135)
(3rd DAY) (LEAD: 191) (585 MIN.) EMBUREY 12* (16')
ENGLAND added 34 RUNS in 46 MINUTES
off 8.2 OVERS for the loss of 3 WICKETS on
the fourth morning (McDERMOTT 3-14 in 4.2 OVERS).

13 OVERS 2 BALLS/HOUR
3.42 RUNS/OVER
56 RUNS/100 BALLS

WKT	PARTNERSHIP		RUNS	MINS
1st	Gooch	Robinson	21	18
2nd	Gooch	Gower	121	188
3rd	Gower	Gatting	6	7
4th	Gatting	Lamb	156	194
5th	Gatting	Botham	35	34
6th	Gatting	Downton	91	115
7th	Downton	Embuery	18	17
8th	Embuery	Edmonds	2	5
9th	Embuery	Allott	20	18
10th	Embuery	Agnew	12*	16
			482	

BOWLER	O	M	R	W	nb	HRS	OVERS	RUNS	RUNS	MINS	OVERS	LAST 50 (in mins)
LAWSON	37	7	114	0	9	1	11	37	50	73	13.2	73
McDERMOTT	36	3	141	8	2	2	13	39	100	146	29.5	73
HOLLAND	38	7	101	0		3	15	42	150	223	49.1	77
O'DONNELL	21	6	82	0		4	15	51	200	283	66.0	60
MATTHEWS	9	2	21	0	1	5	16	39	250	359	84.5	76
			23			6	15	42	300	410	94.3	51
	141	25	482	9		7	11	54	350	466	105.4	56
						8	13	61	400	521	118.3	55
						9	13	45	450	590	133.5	69
						10	13	40				

2nd NEW BALL taken at 2.30pm on 3rd day
- ENGLAND 256-3 after 87 overs.

© BILL FRINDALL 1985

116 AUSTRALIA IN ENGLAND 1985

AUSTRALIA 2ND INNINGS — 225 RUNS BEHIND ON FIRST INNINGS

IN	OUT	MINS	No.	BATSMAN	HOW OUT	BOWLER	RUNS	WKT	TOTAL	6s	4s	BALLS	NOTES ON DISMISSAL
11.57	2.34	118	1	A.M.J. HILDITCH	BOWLED	EMBUREY	40	2	85	.	3	88	Played back to straight ball (bowled through bat-pad gap)
11.57	1.41	65	2	G.R.J. MATTHEWS	C' AND BOWLED	EDMONDS	17	1	38	.	2	42	Held fierce chest-high drive – second post-lunch ball.
1.43	3.38	115	3	K.C. WESSELS	C' AND BOWLED	EMBUREY	50	3	126	.	8	112	Low return catch – beaten in flight.
2.36	(5.32)	346	4	A.R. BORDER *	NOT OUT		146			.	13	334	(1000 F.C. Runs) when 51
4.00	4.28	28	5	D.C. BOON	BOWLED	EMBUREY	7	4	138	.	1	36	Down wicket – drove outside off-break.
4.30	2.13	127	6	G.M. RITCHIE	BOWLED	EMBUREY	31	5	213	1	3	102	Played on – inside edge rolled into stumps.
2.15	(5.32)	125	7	W.B. PHILLIPS †	NOT OUT		39			.	6	130	
			8										
			9										
			10										
			11										

EXTRAS b 1 lb 6 w - nb 3 = 10

TOTAL (140 OVERS – 466 MINUTES) = 340-5

2⁶ 36⁴ 844 balls (including 4 no balls)

18 OVERS 0 BALLS/HOUR
2.43 RUNS/OVER
40 RUNS/100 BALLS

* CAPTAIN † WICKET-KEEPER

BOWLER	O	M	R	W	nb	HRS	OVERS	RUNS
BOTHAM	15	3	50	0	-	1	14	31
ALLOTT	6	2	4	0	-	2	14	54
EDMONDS	54	12	122	1	-	3	21	36
EMBUREY	51	17	99	4	1	4	19	38
AGNEW	9	2	34	0	2	5	20	31
GATTING	4	0	14	0	-	6	18	29
LAMB	1	0	10	0	-	7	20	69
	140	36	340	5				

© BILL FRINDALL 1985

2ND NEW BALL taken at 1.51 pm on 5th day
– AUSTRALIA 200-4 after 94 overs.

	RUNS	MINS	OVERS	LAST 50 (in mins)
	50	82	19.2	82
	100	152	38.5	70
	150	231	65.1	79
	200	315	93.2	84
	250	390	117.5	75
	300	430	130.0	40

LUNCH: 38-0 (15 OVERS / 64 MIN.) HILDITCH 20* MATTHEWS 17*

TEA: 126-3 (49.5 OVERS / 182 MINUTES) BORDER 15* (62 min)

STUMPS: 192-4 (90 OVERS / 304 MIN) BORDER 49* (184¹) RITCHIE 22* (92¹)
(4th DAY) (32 BEHIND)

RAIN DELAYED START UNTIL 12·30pm (23 OVERS LOST)
RSP at 12·40 - 3 OVERS (10 MINUTES) PLAY

LUNCH: 194-4 (95 OVERS / 314 MIN) BORDER 50* (194¹) RITCHIE 28* (102¹)

RESTART at 1.48 pm. RSP (TEA TAKEN) at 3·10pm.

TEA: 253-5 (118.3 OVERS / 394 MINUTES) BORDER 93* (274¹) PHILLIPS 6* (53¹)

MATCH DRAWN

MAN OF THE MATCH: C.J. McDERMOTT
(Adjudicator: R. ILLINGWORTH)

WKT	PARTNERSHIP		RUNS	MINS
1st	Hilditch	Matthews	38	65
2nd	Hilditch	Wessels	47	51
3rd	Wessels	Border	41	62
4th	Border	Boon	12	28
5th	Border	Ritchie	75	127
6th	Border	Phillips	127*	125
7th				
8th				
9th				
10th			340	

Fifth Test, Edgbaston, 15, 16, 17, 19, 20 August.
England won by an innings and 118 runs.

England's win in the fifth Test owed something to luck, a lot to the speed with which they made their runs – they averaged nearly four and a half runs an over – and a lot to the spells in which Ellison took most of his 10 wickets in conditions that defeated other bowlers.

The luck lay mainly in being able to complete the match (with 11.5 overs to spare) in weather that upset cricket throughout the country. Only the third day's play was uninterrupted, and though 90 overs per day were scheduled, the respective days' ration was 64, 50, 88, 68, 43. This works out at about three and a half days' play, and England's ability to win in that time on a slow pitch underlines their superiority.

There was no hint of this on the first two days. On the first, Australia, put in, made 181 for two, England missing the half-chances and leaving Wessels and Border prospering in a stand that reached 97 on the second day before Ellison's swing took four for 12 and reduced Australia to 218 for seven. But Lawson, McDermott, and Thomson batted positively with relatively little difficulty to reach 335 for eight that evening.

From the first ball on Saturday morning the match turned England's way. Lawson was run out off that ball and in four more the innings was over. Then Robinson and Gower batted with such freedom that by the third evening England led by 20 runs at 355 for one, with the weather the main obstacle ahead. The forecast was dismal.

Delays on Monday at the start and after lunch totalled only 90 minutes and, as on the first two days, the extra hour was used. The second wicket stand ended worth 331, but England rocketed on, Gower passing his previous best, Botham making 16 off his first four balls, and Gatting, with useful support from Lamb, playing the ideal innings for the situation. When the Middlesex captain reached his second successive Test 100, off only 125 balls, Gower declared, leaving Australia 95 minutes' batting.

So easy had batting looked and so gloomy was the weather forecast that an England victory still seemed remote. Yet after Ellison had taken four wickets in 15 balls, Australia at 37 for five were left showing signs of demoralization.

Rain and bad light allowed play to begin, after a false start of two balls, at only 2.45 on the last day. Ellison now made no impact, and Gower relied mainly on his spinners, who had the added virtue of providing a brisk over-rate. But Phillips and Ritchie played well until the final hour was only 25 minutes away. Then England, with a field clustered round the bat, had one great piece of luck.

Phillips cut Edmonds hard. Lamb, jumping as he turned away at point, was struck on the left instep and the ball lobbed up to his neighbour, Gower. This was the breakthrough. Edmonds and Emburey quickly took two more wickets and Botham, called up for the *coup de grace*, took the last two in seven balls.

118 AUSTRALIA IN ENGLAND 1985

AUSTRALIA 1st INNINGS v ENGLAND (5th TEST) at EDGBASTON, BIRMINGHAM on 15,16,17,19,20 AUGUST 1985. TOSS: ENGLAND

IN	OUT	MINS	No.	BATSMAN	HOW OUT	BOWLER	RUNS	WKT	TOTAL	6's	4's	BALLS	NOTES ON DISMISSAL
11.00	11.53	53	1	G.M. WOOD	C' EDMONDS	BOTHAM	19	1	44	·	3	45	Edged via thigh pad to short-leg - left-handed diving catch.
11.00	12.52	112	2	A.M.J. HILDITCH	C' DOWNTON	EDMONDS	39	2	92	·	5	71	1000 runs in 16th Test. Legside catch - edged 'arm' ball.
11.55	11.32	228	3	K.C. WESSELS	C' DOWNTON	ELLISON	83	4	191	·	8	204	Edged outswinger.
12.54	11.22	159	4	A.R. BORDER*	C' EDMONDS	ELLISON	45	3	189	·	5	111	Turned inswinger low to backward short leg.
11.24	12.02	38	5	G.M. RITCHIE	C' BOTHAM	ELLISON	8	5	207	·	1	22	Edged outswinger to 2nd slip.
11.34	12.30	56	6	W.B. PHILLIPS†	C' ROBINSON	ELLISON	15	7	218	·	3	42	Cut long hop low and hard to cover-point.
12.04	12.13	9	7	S.P. O'DONNELL	C' DOWNTON	TAYLOR	1	6	208	·	·	3	Edged inswinger that cut away on pitching.
12.15	11.00	140	8	G.F. LAWSON	RUN OUT (GOWER)		53	9	335	·	7	93	First ball of 3rd day. Direct hit from cover - Thomson's call.
12.32	6.07	69	9	C.J. McDERMOTT	C' GOWER	ELLISON	35	8	276	·	4	51	Skied off-drive - superb two-handed running, diving catch.
6.09	(11.03)	55	10	J.R. THOMSON	NOT OUT		28			·	1	2	43	
11.01	11.03	2	11	R.G. HOLLAND	C' EDMONDS	ELLISON	0	10	335	·	·	4	Skim-high catch at backward point. Mistimed drive.
				EXTRAS	b - lb 4	w 1 nb 4	9			1⁶	38⁴	689 balls (including 6 no balls)	
				TOTAL	(113.5 OVERS - 469 MINUTES)		335	ALL OUT at 11.03 am on 3rd day.

* CAPTAIN † WICKET-KEEPER
UMPIRES: D.J. CONSTANT
D.R. SHEPHERD

14 OVERS 3 BALLS/HOUR
2.94 RUNS/OVER
49 RUNS/100 BALLS

© BILL FRINDALL 1985

BOWLER	O	M	R	W	w/nb	HRS	OVERS	RUNS	RUNS	MINS	OVERS	LAST (in mins)
BOTHAM	27	1	108	1	-/1	1	13	44	50	65	15.0	65
TAYLOR	26	5	78	1	-/2	2	14	50	100	131	31.1	66
ELLISON	31.5	9	77	6	1/-	3	18	42	150	206	52.2	75
EDMONDS	20	4	47	1	-/-	4	16	38	200	304	75.5	98
EMBUREY	9	2	21	0	-/1	5	14	24	250	378	91.0	74
			4			6	11	27	300	431	103.4	53
	113.5	21	335	10		7	15	51				

2nd NEW BALL taken at 12.42 pm on 2nd day
- AUSTRALIA 229-7 after 86.2 OVERS.

LUNCH: 96-2 (28 OVERS) (122 MIN.)	WESSELS 33* (67) BORDER 2* (8)
RAIN PREVENTED RESTART UNTIL 4.55pm - 175 MIN (43 OVERS) LOST	
STUMPS: 181-2 (64 OVERS) (251 MIN.)	WESSELS 76* (196)
(1st DAY) NETT LOSS: 26 OVERS	BORDER 43* (137)
LUNCH: 230-7 (87 OVERS) (342 MIN.)	LAWSON 6* (36) McDERMOTT 5* (9)
RSP at 12.51 pm.	
TEA: 248-7 (89.5 OVERS) (378 MIN.)	LAWSON 11* (47) McDERMOTT 18* (36)
(2.5 OVERS IN 11 MIN.)	
STUMPS: 335-8 (113 OVERS) (460 MIN.)	LAWSON 53* (140) THOMSON 28* (52)
(2nd DAY) NETT LOSS: 41 OVERS	

3RD MORNING - AUSTRALIA LOST TWO WICKETS
IN 3 MINUTES OFF 5 BALLS WITHOUT ADDITION

AUSTRALIA'S 8th AND 9th WICKET PARTNERSHIPS WERE RECORDS FOR THIS SERIES AT EDGBASTON.

WKT	PARTNERSHIP		RUNS	MINS
1st	Wood	Hilditch	44	53
2nd	Hilditch	Wessels	48	57
3rd	Wessels	Border	97	159
4th	Wessels	Ritchie	2	8
5th	Ritchie	Phillips	16	24
6th	Phillips	O'Donnell	9	9
7th	Phillips	Lawson	10	15
8th	Lawson	McDermott	58	69
9th	Lawson	Thomson	59	52
10th	Thomson	Holland	0	2

335

ENGLAND 1ST INNINGS
IN REPLY TO AUSTRALIA'S 335 ALL OUT

IN	OUT	MINS	No.	BATSMAN	HOW OUT	BOWLER	RUNS	WKT	TOTAL	6s	4s	BALLS	NOTES ON DISMISSAL
11.13	12.01	48	1	G.A. GOOCH	C' PHILLIPS	THOMSON	19	1	38	·	4	29	Edged outswinger. THOMSON'S 200th WKT (51 TESTS) & 100th v. ENG (21 TESTS)
11.13	12.10	393	2	R.T. ROBINSON	BOWLED	LAWSON	148	2	369	·	18	293	3rd = TESTS. Breakback - Edged backfoot force into leg stump
12.03	3.08	452	3	D.I. GOWER *	C' BORDER	LAWSON	215	3	463	1	25	314	11th = TESTS. HS. Mishined drive - gentle catch to cover-point
12.12	(5.14)	214	4	M.W. GATTING	NOT OUT		100			·	13	127	4th in TESTS. (2nd in successive innings)
3.10	4.55	86	5	A.J. LAMB	C' WOOD	Mc DERMOTT	46	4	572	·	5	62	Clipped half-volley to mid-wicket
4.57	5.08	11	6	I.T. BOTHAM	C' THOMSON	Mc DERMOTT	18	5	592	2	1	7	Skied full toss to deep mid-wicket - failing catch
5.11	(5.14)	3	7	P.R. DOWNTON†	NOT OUT		0			·	·	0	
			8	J.E. EMBUREY									
			9	R.M. ELLISON	did not bat								
			10	P.H. EDMONDS									
			11	L.B. TAYLOR									
			EXTRAS	b 7 lb 20 w - nb 22		49			3^b 66⁴	832 balls (including 28 no balls)

* CAPTAIN † WICKET-KEEPER

TOTAL (134 OVERS - 609 MINUTES) 595-5 DECLARED at 5:14pm on 4th day.

ENGLAND'S HIGHEST TOTAL v. AUSTRALIA AT EDGBASTON

BOWLER	O	M	R	W	NB	HRS	OVERS	RUNS	RUNS	MINS	OVERS	LAST 50 (in mins)
LAWSON	37	1	135	2	11	1	11	43	50	63	12.3	63
McDERMOTT	31	2	155	2	2	2	13	63	100	102	20.4	39
THOMSON	19	1	101	1	9	3	13	38	150	179	37.3	77
HOLLAND	25	4	95	0	·	4	15	58	200	232	49.5	53
O'DONNELL	16	3	69	0	·	5	14	53	250	298	65.4	66
BORDER	6	1	13	0	·	6	16	86	300	326	72.5	28
			27			7	12	46	350	375	86.1	49
	134	12	595	5		8	13	50	400	443	99.2	68
2ND NEW BALL taken at 6.21 pm on 3rd day						9	12	58	450	494	109.4	51
- ENGLAND 342-1 after 85 overs.						10	13	93	500	540	119.3	46
									550	571	126.2	31

LUNCH: 103-1 (22 OVERS / 107 MIN.) ROBINSON 42* (110) / GOWER 30* (57)

TEA: 197-1 (49 OVERS / 228 MIN.) ROBINSON 77* (225) / GOWER 80* (178)
(158 BEHIND)

STUMPS: 355-1 (87 OVERS / 378 MIN.) ROBINSON 140* (378) / GOWER 169* (322)
(3RD DAY) (20 AHEAD)

4TH DAY'S START DELAYED BY 55 MINUTES - RAIN.

LUNCH: 403-2 (100 OVERS / 447 MIN.) GOWER 189* (357) / GATTING 8* (52)
(LEAD 68)

TEA: 545-3 (125 OVERS / 565 MIN.) GATTING 81* (170) / LAMB 35* (61)
(LEAD 210)

331 - ENGLAND'S SECOND-HIGHEST PARTNERSHIP FOR ANY WICKET AGAINST AUSTRALIA.

13 OVERS 1 BALLS/HOUR
4.44 RUNS/OVER
72 RUNS/100 BALLS

WKT	PARTNERSHIP		RUNS	MINS
1st	Gooch	Robinson	38	48
2nd	Robinson	Gower	331	343
3rd	Gower	Gatting	94	107
4th	Gatting	Lamb	109	86
5th	Gatting	Botham	20	11
6th	Gatting	Downton	3*	3
			595	

© BILL FRINDALL 1985

AUSTRALIA 2ND INNINGS (260 RUNS BEHIND ON FIRST INNINGS)

IN	OUT	MINS	No.	BATSMAN	HOW OUT	BOWLER	RUNS	WKT	TOTAL	6s	4s	BALLS	NOTES ON DISMISSAL
5.25	5.37	12	1	A.M.J. HILDITCH	c ELLISON	BOTHAM	10	1	10	·	1	14	Hooked short ball to deep backward square-leg.
5.25	6.46	81	2	G.M. WOOD	c ROBINSON	ELLISON	10	4	35	·	1	51	Skied outside hit - leading edge to short cover.
5.39	6.32	53	3	K.C. WESSELS	c DOWNTON	ELLISON	10	2	32	·	1	36	Edged loose drive at slower ball - low catch to his left.
6.34	6.35	1	4	R.G. HOLLAND	LBW	ELLISON	0	3	32	·	·	1	First ball - pushed across line of straight ball. 'PAIR'.
6.37	6.54	17	5	A.R. BORDER*	BOWLED	ELLISON	2	5	36	·	·	17	Breakback - chipped pad top. ELLISON (10 WKTS IN MATCH) 4 IN 15 b.
6.48	4.54	126	6	G.M. RITCHIE	c LAMB	EMBUREY	20	7	117	·	3	103	Edged off-break via pad to silly point - walked.
6.56	4.40	104	7	W.B. PHILLIPS†	c GOWER	EDMONDS	59	6	113	·	11	90	50 off 78 balls. Cut via silly point's instep to silly mid-off.
4.42	5.23	41	8	S.P. O'DONNELL	BOWLED	BOTHAM	11	9	137	·	1	39	Drove over yorker. BOTHAM'S 129th WKT v AUS (ENGLAND RECORD)
4.56	5.02	6	9	G.F. LAWSON	c GOWER	EDMONDS	3	8	120	·	·	8	Edged push to silly point - held rebound off chest.
5.04	5.28	24	10	C.J. McDERMOTT	c EDMONDS	BOTHAM	8	10	142	·	1	22	Low catch - falling to left at forward short leg.
5.25	5.28	3	11	J.R. THOMSON	NOT OUT		4					5	
*CAPTAIN †WICKET-KEEPER				EXTRAS	b 1 lb 3 w - nb 1		5			0 6 17 4		386 balls (including 1 no-ball)	
				TOTAL	(64.1 OVERS - 242 MINUTES)		142 ALL OUT at 5.28 pm on 5TH day.						

15 OVERS 5 BALLS/HOUR
2·21 RUNS/OVER
37 RUNS/100 BALLS

BOWLER	O	M	R	W		HRS	OVERS	RUNS		RUNS	MINS	OVERS	LAST 50 (in mins)
BOTHAM	14.1	2	52	3		1	14	32		50	106	23.5	106
TAYLOR	13	4	27	0		2	13	26		100	180	44.3	74
ELLISON	9	3	27	4		3	17	41					
EDMONDS	15	9	13	2		4	19	38					
EMBUREY	13	5	19	1									
			4										
	64.1	23	142	10									

© BILL FRINDALL 1985

STUMPS: 37-5 (21 OVERS RITCHIE 0* (1)
(4TH DAY)   (225 BEHIND)   95 MINUTES) PHILLIPS 1* (4)
5TH DAY: START DELAYED UNTIL 2.30 pm. 2 balls - 1 min. (KEY)
TEA: 80-5   (37 OVERS RITCHIE 12* (71 min.)
            154 MINUTES) PHILLIPS 31* (63 min.)

ENGLAND WON BY AN INNINGS
AND 118 RUNS (WITH 11·5 OVERS TO SPARE)

MAN OF THE MATCH: R.M. ELLISON
(10-104)
(Adjudicator: F.S. TRUEMAN)

WKT	PARTNERSHIP		RUNS	MINS
1st	Hilditch	Wood	10	12
2nd	Wood	Wessels	22	53
3rd	Wood	Holland	0	1
4th	Wood	Border	3	9
5th	Border	Ritchie	1	6
6th	Ritchie	Phillips	77	104
7th	Ritchie	O'Donnell	4	12
8th	O'Donnell	Lawson	3	6
9th	O'Donnell	McDermott	17	19
10th	McDermott	Thomson	5	3
			142	

AUSTRALIA IN ENGLAND 1985 **121**

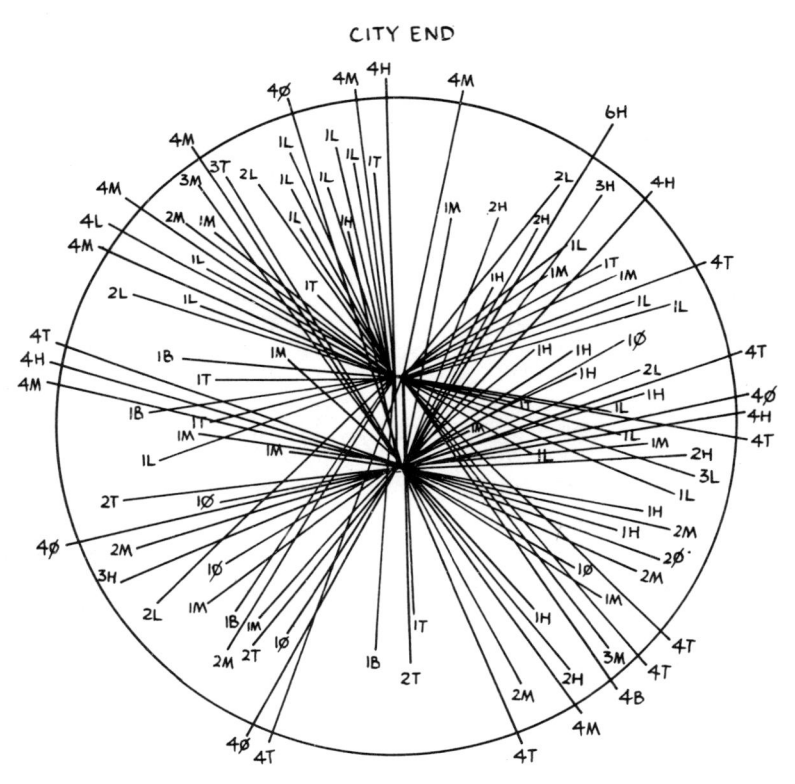

CITY END

PAVILION END

BOWLER	SYMBOL	R U N S					
		1	2	3	4	6	TOTAL
BORDER	B	4	-	-	1	-	8
HOLLAND	H	9	4	2	4	1	45
LAWSON	L	16	5	1	1	-	33
McDERMOTT	M	12	6	2	7	-	58
O'DONNELL	Ø	5	1	-	4	-	23
THOMSON	T	7	3	1	8	-	48
TOTALS		53	19	6	25	1	215

D.I. GOWER at Edgbaston

215 RUNS
314 BALLS
452 MINUTES
(left-handed batsman)

© BILL FRINDALL 1985

Sixth Test, The Oval, 29, 30, 31 August, 2 September.
England won by an innings and 94 runs.

England's victory in the last Test not only recovered the Ashes but established beyond any doubt that they were the stronger and better-equipped side. The match was over after 95 minutes play on the fourth day but, allowing for a long stoppage for rain on the Saturday afternoon, it was completed in less than three normal days' play, this on an excellent pitch which gave a fair chance to the batsmen and to bowlers of all types.

England played the team that had also won by an innings at Edgbaston, but Australia made three changes, leaving out the leg-spinner, Holland, on a pitch that with its full bounce might have been of more use to him than the previous four on which he had played.

Far from sitting cautiously on a 2-1 lead, England rattled through the first day's play at sometimes around five runs an over. A magnificent second-wicket stand of 351 in 76 overs between Gooch and Gower ended when Gower was out well after six o'clock but with six overs left to play. Gatting then suffered almost his only failure of the series, but a significant one. Coming in, as it were, as his own nightwatchman, he was caught at slip while playing quietly forward to the first ball of the last over. The ball had turned, not exactly a depressing sight for England, who were ending the day at 376 for three.

However, next morning, beginning with the end of Gooch's fine innings, England lost their last seven wickets for 61, largely through reckless and overconfident batting. Thus Australia began their innings soon after lunch in some relief.

The fact that the ball would turn a little was soon proved of high importance, for it was Edmonds and Emburey who took the vital wickets of Wessels, Border, and Phillips. Australia finished the second day at 145 for six.

On the Saturday, their last four wickets added 96, failing to avoid the follow-on by 24 runs. Gower had an interesting decision to make. By batting again, he would almost certainly make the match and the Ashes safe, but, in view of the weather forecast, would not necessarily win the match. His decision to send Australia in again while he had them down was in keeping with England's positive cricket and was handsomely rewarded.

Rain fell soon after the second innings started, but 105 minutes' play was still possible on a sunny evening. In that time, Botham, bowling very fast, Ellison, looking a high-class swing bowler, and Taylor took four wickets for 62 aided by some indifferent strokes.

After the week-end, the question was whether England would beat the belt of rain accurately forecast for the afternoon ahead. They did so, before the fourth successive capacity crowd, without recourse to spin. Ellison moved the ball about with life and accuracy; Botham took two splendid catches off him at second slip, as well as a wicket; and Taylor finished the series by taking a return catch. A wet afternoon could be spent in celebration.

AUSTRALIA IN ENGLAND 1985

ENGLAND 1ST INNINGS v AUSTRALIA (6TH TEST) at KENNINGTON OVAL, LONDON on 29, 30, 31 AUGUST, 2 SEPTEMBER 1985. TOSS: ENGLAND

IN	OUT	MINS	No.	BATSMAN	HOW OUT	BOWLER	RUNS	WKT	TOTAL	6s	4s	BALLS	NOTES ON DISMISSAL
11.01	11.18	424	1	G.A.GOOCH	C' and BOWLED	McDERMOTT	196	4	403	·	27	310	(5th (1st AUS) HS in TESTS. Drove full toss - low catch following through
11.01	11.36	35	2	R.T.ROBINSON	BOWLED	McDERMOTT	3	1	20	·	·	21	Yorked off stump by fast late inswinger.
11.38	6.14	357	3	D.I.GOWER *	C' BENNETT	McDERMOTT	157	2	371	·	20	215	2000 R · AUST. Fierce gully catch held at second attempt (2)
6.16	6.41	25	4	M.W.GATTING	C' BORDER	BENNETT	4	3	376	·	·	27	Edged low to slip who dived forward. Leg break.
6.43	11.25	27	5	J.E.EMBUREY	C' WELLHAM	LAWSON	9	5	405	·	1	17	Night-watchman. Cut short ball chest high to cover.
11.20	11.49	29	6	A.J.LAMB	C' McDERMOTT	LAWSON	1	6	418	·	·	15	Top-edged hook at bouncer to deep fine-leg.
11.27	12.00	33	7	I.T.BOTHAM	C' PHILLIPS	LAWSON	12	7	425	·	2	23	Edged firm-footed drive at widish ball.
11.51	1.45	74	8	P.R.DOWNTON †	BOWLED	McDERMOTT	16	9	452	·	1	46	Late inswinger removed middle stump - through gate. *
12.03	12.47	44	9	R.M.ELLISON	C' PHILLIPS	GILBERT	3	8	447	·	·	32	Faint edge - defensive back stroke.
12.48	2.02	34	10	P.H.EDMONDS	LBW	LAWSON	12	10	464	·	2	26	Hit across full length ball.
1.47	(2.02)	15	11	L.B.TAYLOR	NOT OUT		1			·	·	10	First test innings.
				EXTRAS		b 13 1b 11 w - nb 26	50			0	6 53 4	742 balls (including 32 no balls)	
					TOTAL	(118.2 OVERS - 547 MINUTES)	464	all out at 2.02 pm on 2nd day.

* CAPTAIN † WICKET-KEEPER

UMPIRES:
H.D.BIRD
K.E.PALMER
© Bill Frindall 1985

BOWLER	O	M	R	W	NB	HRS	OVERS	RUNS		RUNS	MINS	OVERS	LAST 50 (in mins)
LAWSON	29.2	6	101	4	9	1	11	38		50	72	14.0	72
McDERMOTT	31	2	108	4	7	2	14	62		100	120	25.0	48
GILBERT	21	2	96	1	10	3	14	54		150	174	38.0	54
BENNETT	32	8	111	1	-	4	15	66		200	222	49.0	48
BORDER	2	0	8	0	-	5	13	68		250	266	59.3	44
WESSELS	3	0	16	0	-	6	12	61		300	313	69.5	47
			24			7	14	52		350	361	79.2	48
	118.2	18	464	10		8	10	31		400	420	92.5	59
						9	14	26		450	521	112·1	101

2nd NEW BALL taken at 11·02 am on 2nd day
- ENGLAND 380-3 after 90·3 overs.

12 OVERS   5 BALLS/HOUR
           3·92 RUNS/OVER
           63 RUNS/100 BALLS

WKT	PARTNERSHIP			RUNS	MINS
1st	Gooch	Robinson		20	35
2nd	Gooch	Gower		351	357
3rd	Gooch	Gatting		5	25
4th	Gooch	Embury		27	20
5th	Emburey	Lamb		2	5
6th	Lamb	Botham		13	22
7th	Botham	Downton		7	9
8th	Downton	Ellison		22	44
9th	Downton	Edmonds		5	17
10th	Edmonds	Taylor		12	15
				464	

LUNCH: 100-1 (25 OVERS) GOOCH 35*(20)
              (120 MIN.) / GOWER 44*(83)

TEA: 220-1 (54 OVERS) GOOCH 94*(246)
           (240 MIN.) / GOWER 100*(203)

STUMPS: 376-3 (90 OVERS) GOOCH 179*(465)
(1st DAY)   (405 MIN.) EMBUREY 0* (2·1)

LUNCH: 452-8 (114 OVERS) DOWNTON 16*(65)
             (525 MIN.) / EDMONDS 1* (12)

ENGLAND LOST THEIR LAST 9 WICKETS FOR
93 RUNS - INCLUDING 7 FOR 88 ON SECOND
DAY. McDERMOTT 30 WICKETS IN RUBBER.
LAWSON ACHIEVED A SPELL OF 3 FOR 3.
351 - ENGLAND'S SECOND-HIGHEST PARTNERSHIP
FOR ANY WICKET AGAINST AUSTRALIA.

AUSTRALIA 1st INNINGS IN REPLY TO ENGLAND'S 464 ALL OUT

IN	OUT	MINS	No.	BATSMAN	HOW OUT	BOWLER	RUNS	WKT	TOTAL	6s	4s	BALLS	NOTES ON DISMISSAL
2:14	2:45	31	1	G.M.WOOD	LBW	BOTHAM	22	1	35	.	3	26	Beaten by inswinger - hit on shoulder previous ball.
2:14	3:14	60	2	A.M.J.HILDITCH	c' GOOCH	BOTHAM	17	2	52	.	1	32	Hooked bouncer to long-leg.
2:47	4:02	55	3	K.C.WESSELS	BOWLED	EMBUREY	12	3	56	.	.	51	Missed cut at arm-ball.
3:16	5:21	105	4	A.R.BORDER*	BOWLED	EDMONDS	38	5	109	.	4	67	Played back - off break deflected into wicket by inside edge.
4:04	4:57	53	5	D.M.WELLHAM	c' DOWNTON	ELLISON	13	4	101	.	2	41	Edged outswinger.
5:01	(1:46)	195	6	G.M.RITCHIE	NOT OUT		64			.	5	155	
5:23	6:01	38	7	W.B.PHILLIPS†	BOWLED	EDMONDS	18	6	144	.	2	29	Missed square-cut - off-break turned sharply.
6:03	11:43	50	8	M.J.BENNETT	c' ROBINSON	ELLISON	12	7	171	.	1	46	Head high catch at cover-point - drove at outswinger.
11:45	12:14	29	9	G.F.LAWSON	c' BOTHAM	TAYLOR	14	8	192	.	1	26	Edged drive to 2nd slip - right-handed high leaping catch.
12:16	12:51	35	10	C.J.McDERMOTT	RUN OUT (ROBINSON/EMBUREY)		25	9	235	1	2	23	Hesitated over single to cover who returned to bowler.
12:53	1:46	13	11	D.R.GILBERT	BOWLED	BOTHAM	1	10	241	.	.	9	Fended short-pitched ball into wicket. First Test innings.
				EXTRAS	b - 1b 5	w 2 nb -	5			1 6 21	505 balls (including 1 no ball)
				TOTAL	(84 OVERS - 342 MINUTES)		241		all out at 1.46 pm on 3rd day.

	HRS	OVERS	RUNS	RUNS	MINS	OVERS	LAST 50 (in mins)
	1	13	52	50	58	12.3	58
	2	15	31	100	140	32.3	82
	3	14	33	150	229	55.4	89
	4	16	42	200	300	73.5	71
	5	16	42				

© BILL FRINDALL 1985

BOWLER	O	M	R	W	n/b
BOTHAM	20	3	64	3	2/-
TAYLOR	13	1	39	1	-
ELLISON	18	5	35	2	-
EMBUREY	19	7	48	1	-
EDMONDS	14	2	52	2	-
			3	1	
	84	18	241	10	

* CAPTAIN † WICKET-KEEPER

TEA: 56-2 (19 OVERS / 87 MINUTES) WESSELS 12* (54') BORDER 1* (25')

STUMPS: 145-6 (52 OVERS / 216 MIN.) RITCHIE 26* (69') BENNETT 0* (7')
(2ND DAY) 319 BEHIND

LUNCH: 237-9 (82 OVERS / 336 MIN.) RITCHIE 60* (183) GILBERT 1* (7')
227 BEHIND

AUSTRALIA invited to follow-on
(223 RUNS BEHIND)
(FIRST INSTANCE AGAINST ENGLAND SINCE LEEDS 1977)

WKT	PARTNERSHIP		RUNS	MINS
1st	Wood	Hilditch	35	31
2nd	Hilditch	Wessels	17	27
3rd	Wessels	Border	4	26
4th	Border	Wellham	45	53
5th	Border	Ritchie	8	20
6th	Ritchie	Phillips	35	38
7th	Ritchie	Bennett	27	50
8th	Ritchie	Lawson	21	29
9th	Ritchie	McDermott	43	35
10th	Ritchie	Gilbert	6	13
			241	

14 OVERS 4 BALLS/HOUR
2.87 RUNS/OVER
48 RUNS/100 BALLS

AUSTRALIA IN ENGLAND 1985

AUSTRALIA 2ND INNINGS FOLLOWING-ON 223 RUNS BEHIND

IN	OUT	MINS	No.	BATSMAN	HOW OUT	BOWLER	RUNS	WKT	TOTAL	6s	4s	BALLS	NOTES ON DISMISSAL
1.59	5.31	37	1	A.M.J. HILDITCH	C' GOWER	TAYLOR	9	2	16	.	.	27	Chipped gentle catch to cover.
1.59	5.21	27	2	G.M. WOOD	BOWLED	BOTHAM	6	1	13	.	1	18	Played on – crooked defensive jab at short ball.
5.23	5.57	34	3	K.C. WESSELS	C' DOWNTON	BOTHAM	7	3	37	.	.	21	Edged drive at widish ball – fine catch – diving in front of slip.
5.33	12.08	157	4	A.R. BORDER*	C' BOTHAM	ELLISON	58	7	114	.	7	92	Edged to 2nd slip – driving at ball that bounced generously.
5.59	6.19	20	5	D.M. WELLHAM	LBW	ELLISON	5	4	51	.	.	17	Beaten by late inswing.
6.21	11.18	59	6	G.M. RITCHIE	C' DOWNTON	ELLISON	6	5	71	.	.	42	Edged drive at widish outswinger.
11.20	11.49	29	7	W.B. PHILLIPS†	C' DOWNTON	BOTHAM	10	6	96	.	1	24	Top-edged square-cut.
11.52	12.35	43	8	M.J. BENNETT	C' AND BOWLED	TAYLOR	11	10	129	.	1	29	Slower ball – simple return catch.
12.10	12.26	16	9	G.F. LAWSON	C' DOWNTON	ELLISON	7	8	127	.	.	10	Edged drive at outswinger.
12.28	12.30	2	10	C.J. McDERMOTT	C' BOTHAM	ELLISON	2	9	129	.	.	4	Edged drive at outswinger – high catch at 2nd slip.
12.33	(12.35)	2	11	D.R. GILBERT	NOT OUT		0			.	.	1	Did not face a ball.
				EXTRAS	b 4 lb -	w - nb 4	8			0 6 11 4		284 balls (including 5 no balls)	

TOTAL (46.3 OVERS - 223 MINUTES) 129 ALL OUT at 12.35 pm on 4th day

BOWLER	O	M	R	W	nb	HRS	OVERS	RUNS	MINS	OVERS	LAST 50 (in mins)
BOTHAM	17	3	44	3	1	1	12	33	50	80	16.2	80
TAYLOR	11.3	1	34	2	3	2	13	26	100	183	39.0	103
ELLISON	17	3	46	5	-	3	13	37				
EMBUREY	1	0	1	0	-							
			4									
	46.3	7	129	10								

© BILL FRINDALL 1985

12 OVERS 3 BALLS/HOUR
2.77 RUNS/OVER
45 RUNS/100 BALLS

WKT	PARTNERSHIP			RUNS	MINS
1st	Hilditch	Wood		13	27
2nd	Hilditch	Wessels		3	8
3rd	Wessels	Border		21	24
4th	Border	Wellham		14	20
5th	Border	Ritchie		20	59
6th	Border	Phillips		25	29
7th	Border	Bennett		18	16
8th	Bennett	Lawson		13	16
9th	Bennett	McDermott		2	2
10th	Bennett	Gilbert		0	3
				129	

RSP 2:14 to 2:24 pm and 2:29 to 5:15pm (156 MIN. LOST)
TEA: 12-0 (4.4 OVERS; 20 MIN.) HILDITCH 7′; WOOD 5″
STUMPS: 62-4 (27 OVERS) BORDER 26* (89′)
(3RD DAY)   (128 MIN., RITCHIE 6′ (41′)
             NETT 96 MIN (29 OVERS) LOST
161 BEHIND

ENGLAND WON BY AN INNINGS & 94 RUNS
with a day and 70.3 overs to spare.

ENGLAND WON RUBBER 3-1
AND REGAINED ASHES LOST IN JANUARY 1983

PLAYER OF THE MATCH : G.A. GOOCH
PLAYER OF THE SERIES : D.I. GOWER
(Adjudicator: A.R. LEWIS)

*CAPTAIN †WICKET-KEEPER

126 STATISTICAL SURVEY: ENGLAND v AUSTRALIA 1985

Statistical Survey: England v Australia 1985

England – Batting and Fielding

	M	I	NO	HS	R	Avge	100	50	6s	4s	Min	Balls	r/hb	Ct/St
M.W. Gatting	6	9	3	160	527	87.83	2	3	–	65	1427	1013	52	–
D.I. Gower	6	9	0	215	732	81.33	3	1	1	89	1687	1192	61	6
R.T. Robinson	6	9	1	175	490	61.25	2	1	–	61	1325	930	53	5
G.A. Gooch	6	9	0	196	487	54.11	1	2	–	65	1179	857	57	4
A.J. Lamb	6	8	1	67	256	36.57	–	1	–	34	717	519	49	7
J.E. Emburey	6	6	2	33	130	32.50	–	–	–	16	315	207	63	3
I.T. Botham	6	8	0	85	250	31.25	–	2	5	37	356	288	87	8
P.R. Downton	6	7	1	54	114	19.00	–	1	–	12	435	299	38	19/1
P.H. Edmonds	5	5	0	21	47	9.40	–	–	–	5	210	176	27	8
P.J.W. Allott	4	5	1	12	27	6.75	–	–	–	3	98	79	34	–
Also batted:														
J.P. Agnew	1	1	1	2*	2	–	–	–	–	–	16	8	25	–
N.G. Cowans	1	1	0	22*	22	–	–	–	–	5	44	28	79	1
R.M. Ellison	2	2	0	3	3	3.00	–	–	–	–	44	32	9	–
N.A. Foster	1	1	0	3	3	1.50	–	–	–	–	32	19	16	–
A. Sidebottom	1	1	0	2	2	2.00	–	–	–	–	7	8	25	–
L.B. Taylor	2	1	1	1*	1	–	–	–	–	–	15	10	10	1
P. Willey	1	2	1	36	39	39.00	–	–	–	5	112	83	47	–
Totals	66	84	13	(215)	3132	44.11	8	11	6	397	8019	5748	54	62/1

England – Bowling

	O	M	R	W	Avge	Best	5wI	10wM	b/w	r/hb	NB	wides
R.M. Ellison	75.5	20	185	17	10.88	6-77	2	1	27	41	–	1
I.T. Botham	251.4	36	855	31	27.58	5-109	1	–	49	57	12	7
J.E. Emburey	248.4	75	544	19	28.63	5-82	1	–	79	36	2	–
P.H. Edmonds	225.5	59	549	15	36.60	4-40	–	–	90	41	2	–
P.J.W. Allott	113	22	297	5	59.40	2-74	–	–	136	44	–	–
Also bowled												
J.P. Agnew	23	2	99	0	–	–	–	–	–	72	6	–
N.G. Cowans	33	6	128	2	64.00	1-50	–	–	99	65	–	–
N.A. Foster	23	1	83	1	83.00	1-83	–	–	138	60	–	1
M.W. Gatting	5	0	16	0	–	–	–	–	–	53	–	–
G.A. Gooch	41.2	10	102	2	51.00	2-57	–	–	124	41	1	3
A.J. Lamb	1	0	10	0	–	–	–	–	–	167	–	–
A. Sidebottom	18.4	3	65	1	65.00	1-65	–	–	112	58	11	–
L.B. Taylor	63.3	11	178	4	44.50	2-34	–	–	95	47	9	–
Totals	1123.3	245	3111	97	32.07	(6-77)	4	1	69	46	44	12

Statistical Survey: England v Australia 1985

Australia – Batting and Fielding

	M	I	NO	HS	R	Avge	100	50	6s	4s	Min	Balls	r/hb	Ct/St
A.R. Border	6	11	2	196	597	66.33	2	1	1	65	1576	1193	50	11
G.M. Ritchie	6	11	1	146	422	42.20	1	2	1	44	1295	1033	41	3
A.M.J. Hilditch	6	11	0	119	424	38.54	1	1	4	51	1088	780	54	3
W.B. Phillips	6	11	1	91	350	35.00	—	2	1	52	767	669	52	11
K.C. Wessels	6	11	0	83	368	33.45	—	3	—	39	1170	927	40	3
G.M. Wood	5	9	0	172	260	28.88	1	—	—	33	866	656	40	1
S.P. O'Donnell	5	8	1	48	184	26.28	—	—	3	19	483	404	46	3
D.C. Boon	4	7	0	61	124	17.71	—	1	—	14	414	371	33	4
G.F. Lawson	6	9	1	53	119	14.87	—	1	—	15	347	243	49	—
C.J. McDermott	6	9	1	35	103	12.87	—	—	1	11	216	170	61	2
R.G. Holland	4	5	1	10	15	3.75	—	—	—	2	110	74	20	1
J.R. Thomson	2	4	4	28*	38	—	—	—	1	4	68	56	68	1
Also batted:														
M.J. Bennett	1	2	0	12	23	11.50	—	—	—	2	93	75	31	1
D.R. Gilbert	1	2	1	1	1	1.00	—	—	—	—	15	9	11	—
G.R.J. Matthews	1	2	0	17	21	10.50	—	—	—	2	102	67	31	1
D.M. Wellham	1	2	0	13	18	9.00	—	—	—	2	73	58	31	1
Totals	66	114	13	(196)	3067	30.36	5	11	12	355	8683	6785	45	45/–

Australia – Bowling

	O	M	R	W	Avge	Best	5wI	10wM	b/w	r/hb	NB	wides
C.J. McDermott	234.2	21	901	30	30.03	8-141	2	—	47	64	43	6
G.F. Lawson	246	38	830	22	37.72	5-103	1	—	67	56	67	3
R.G. Holland	172	41	465	6	77.50	5-68	1	—	172	45	—	—
S.P. O'Donnell	145.4	31	487	6	81.16	3-37	—	—	146	56	1	2
Also bowled:												
M.J. Bennett	32	8	111	1	111.00	1-111	—	—	192	58	—	—
A.R. Border	11	1	37	0	—	—	—	—	—	56	—	—
D.R. Gilbert	21	2	96	1·	96.00	1-96	—	—	126	76	13	—
G.R.J. Matthews	9	2	21	0	—	—	—	—	—	39	—	—
G.M. Ritchie	1	0	10	0	—	—	—	—	—	167	—	—
J.R. Thomson	56	4	275	3	91.66	2-166	—	—	112	82	20	1
K.C. Wessels	6	2	18	0	—	—	—	—	—	50	—	—
Totals	934	150	3251	69	47.11	(8-141)	4	—	81	58	144	12

* not out; r/hb = runs per 100 balls; b/w = balls per wicket; 5wI = 5 wickets in an innings; 10wM = 10 wickets in a match.

Statistical Highlights of the Tests

1st Test, Headingley. For the first time Leeds staged the opening Test of an Ashes series. The first test to have a standby umpire (Ray Julian) in attendance, it was also the first in England in which no-balls and wides were debited to the bowlers' analyses. Botham became only the second England bowler after Bill Voce (at Sydney in 1936-37) to take three wickets (Ritchie, O'Donnell, and McDermott) in four balls against Australia. Robinson was the 15th England batsman to score a hundred in his first Test against Australia; only R.E. ('Tip') Foster (287 at Sydney in 1903-04) had made a higher score on such a debut. England's total of 533 was their highest against Australia at Leeds. Lamb scored his 2,000th run in 33 Tests, and Cowans took his 50th wicket in 19 Tests when he dismissed Border. When England completed their victory, with 13.2 overs to spare, it was only the second time since 1930 that they had beaten Australia in the first match of a home rubber.

2nd Test, Lord's. Gower lost the toss for the sixth successive time in Tests. Australia achieved the first victory in an Ashes Test at Lord's since 1972; England have defeated Australia only once (in 1934) in 22 matches there since 1896. Having played in a combined total of 51 Tests, Edmonds and Emburey appeared together for only the second time (also v New Zealand at Lord's in 1978 on Emburey's debut). Border (196) recorded his highest Test score, the highest by an Australian captain at Lord's (beating 155 by Bill Woodfull in 1930), and the third-highest for Australia on that ground (after 254 by Donald Bradman in 1930, and 206 not out by Bill Brown in 1928). Border also completed 5,000 Test runs in the record time of 6 years 186 days. The partnership of 216 between Border and Ritchie was Australia's highest for the fifth wicket at Lord's, whilst that of 131 between Gatting and Botham set a seventh-wicket record for England against Australia there. In taking five or more wickets in an innings for the 25th time, Botham gained the world Test record held by Sydney Barnes since 1914. When Wood became his 326th victim, Botham succeeded Bob Willis as England's leading wicket-taker.

3rd Test, Trent Bridge. Sidebottom became Yorkshire's first England representative since January 1982, when Geoffrey Boycott played in the last of his 108 Tests. England scored 358 before losing their third wicket – their best start against Australia since 1964 at Old Trafford. Gower's 166 was his first Test century for 23 innings, the highest score by an England captain at Trent Bridge (previously Bob Wyatt's 149 against South Africa in 1935), and the third-highest in Nottingham Tests against Australia (after 216 not out by Eddie Paynter in 1938 and 184 by Denis Compton in 1948). Gower's partnership of 187 with Gatting established a third-wicket record against Australia at Trent Bridge, whilst that of 161 between Wood and Ritchie was Australia's highest there for the sixth wicket. Wood completed 1,000 runs against England and 3,000 runs in Tests during the highest of his eight Test hundreds. His 599-minute innings was the second-longest for Australia in England, after Bobby Simpson's 762-minute 311 at Old Trafford in 1964. Australia achieved their highest total at Trent Bridge and their highest against England since 1965-66 (Melbourne). Robinson's 77 not out was the highest score by a Nottinghamshire batsman against Australia on his home ground.

Above: The England team who won the last two Test matches and the Ashes. Standing (l-r): Paul Downton, John Emburey, Richard Ellison, Les Taylor, Phil Edmonds, Tim Robinson, Bernard Thomas (physiotherapist); seated (l-r): Allan Lamb, Mike Gatting, David Gower (captain), Ian Botham, Graham Gooch.

Right: A moment to remember. David Gower holds aloft a conveniently handy replica of the Ashes urn produced by Peter West.

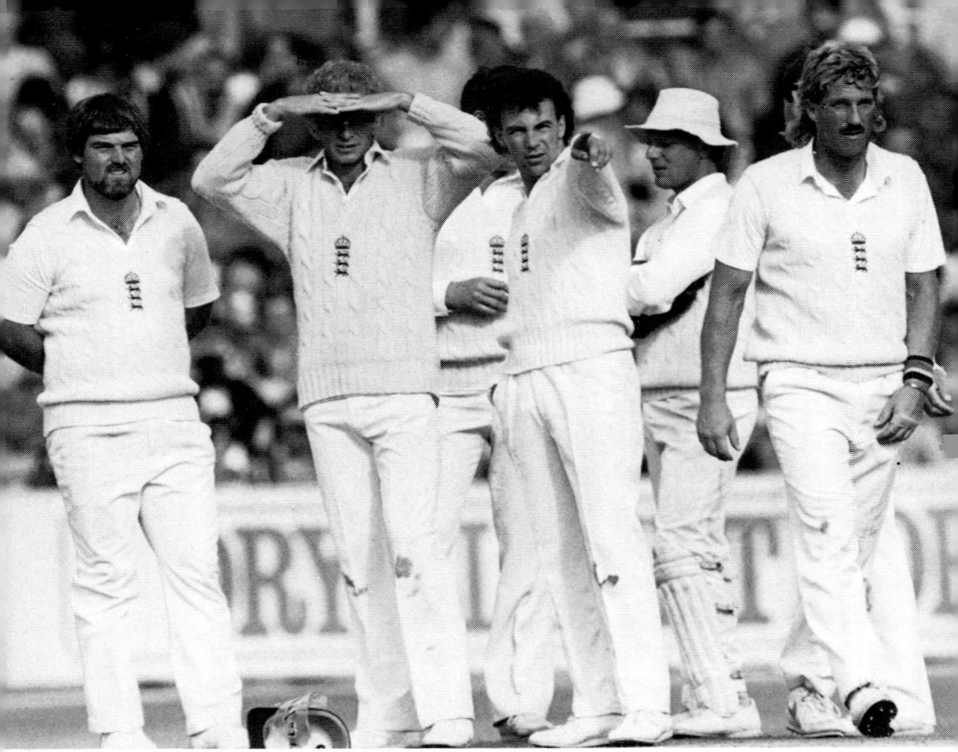

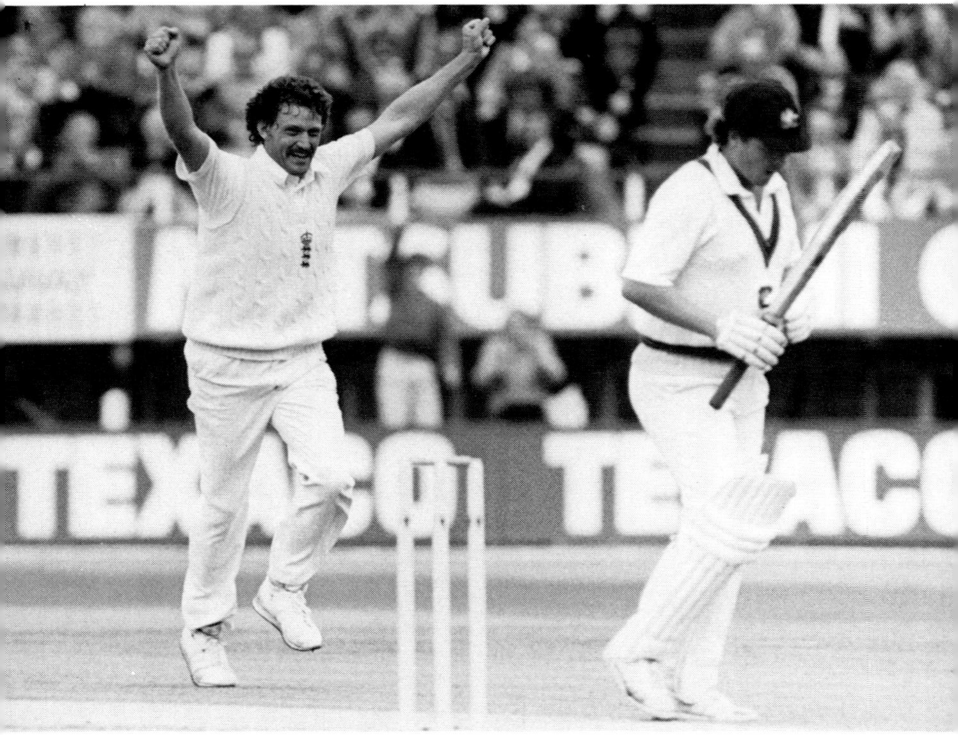

Above: A fast bowler with a future. The 20-year-old Craig McDermott, one of the few successes on the Australian side.

Opposite page top: Old Trafford, fourth Test. Gatting, Gower, and Robinson, England's most successful batsmen in the series, and Botham, the chief wicket-taker, discuss the next move during an Australian collapse.

Opposite page, bottom: Edgbaston, fifth Test. A jubilant Ellison has just had Ritchie caught at second slip by Botham. Ellison finished with a match-winning haul of 10 wickets for 104.

Right: Allan Border at the moment when the loss of the Ashes must suddenly have seemed ominously near. Bowled by Ellison, he walks off as Australia subside to 37 for five on the fourth evening at Edgbaston.

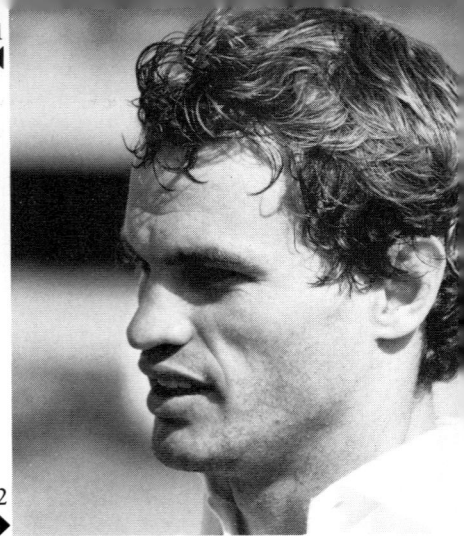

The *Daily Telegraph* Cricketers of the Year (see pages 17-18):
1 Tim Robinson (England)
2 Kepler Wessels (Australia)
3 Malcolm Marshall (West Indies)
4 Ravi Shastri (India)
5 Wasim Akram (Pakistan)
6 John Reid (New Zealand)
7 Clive Rice (South Africa)
8 Aravinda de Silva (Sri Lanka)

5 ◀

6 ▶

7 ◀

8 ▶

Winners of the *Daily Telegraph* 'Twin Hundreds' (see page 16): Ian Botham (above), whose fastest hundred was made off only 50 balls; and Neil Radford (left), who took his 100th wicket on the last day of the season.

Right: Derek Randall had his best season for Notts at the age of 34 and was named as Britannic Assurance Cricketer of the Year.

Below: Jeff Thomson, in a chequered tour, took his 200th Test wicket.

Below right: David Lawrence, Gloucestershire's young fast bowler, more than doubled his previous best season's tally with 85 wickets.

Above: A pre-season picture of the Middlesex staff, including the reserves who were to help win the Championship despite the numerous Test calls on the leading players. Back row (l-r): P. Tufnell, K.R. Brown, N. MacLaurin, A. Harwood, G. Brown, S.P. Hughes, C.P. Metson; middle row: J.E. Miller (physiotherapist), D. Bennett (coach), N.G. Cowans, J.F. Sykes, A.R.C. Fraser, C.D. Rose, W.N. Slack, N.F. Williams, K.P. Tomlins, H.P. Sharp (scorer); seated (l-r): P.R. Downton, W.W. Daniel, G.D. Barlow, J.E. Emburey, M.W. Gatting (captain), C.T. Radley, P.H. Edmonds, R.O. Butcher. Also called on were the Oxford blues, J.D. Carr and A.J.T. Miller.

Below: Phil Edmonds takes the important wicket of Andy Lloyd, caught by Radley, as Middlesex press for the Championship at Edgbaston on the last day of the season.

Peter Willey during his match-winning innings of 86 not out in the B & H Cup final.

Above: Essex celebrating at Chelmsford after adding the John Player title to the NatWest Trophy won eight days before.

Below: Brian Hardie, the Man of the Match, during his innings which had much to do with Essex's narrow victory over Notts in the NatWest final.

Keith Fletcher with the NatWest Trophy, which gave Essex a full set of all four competitions won under his captaincy.

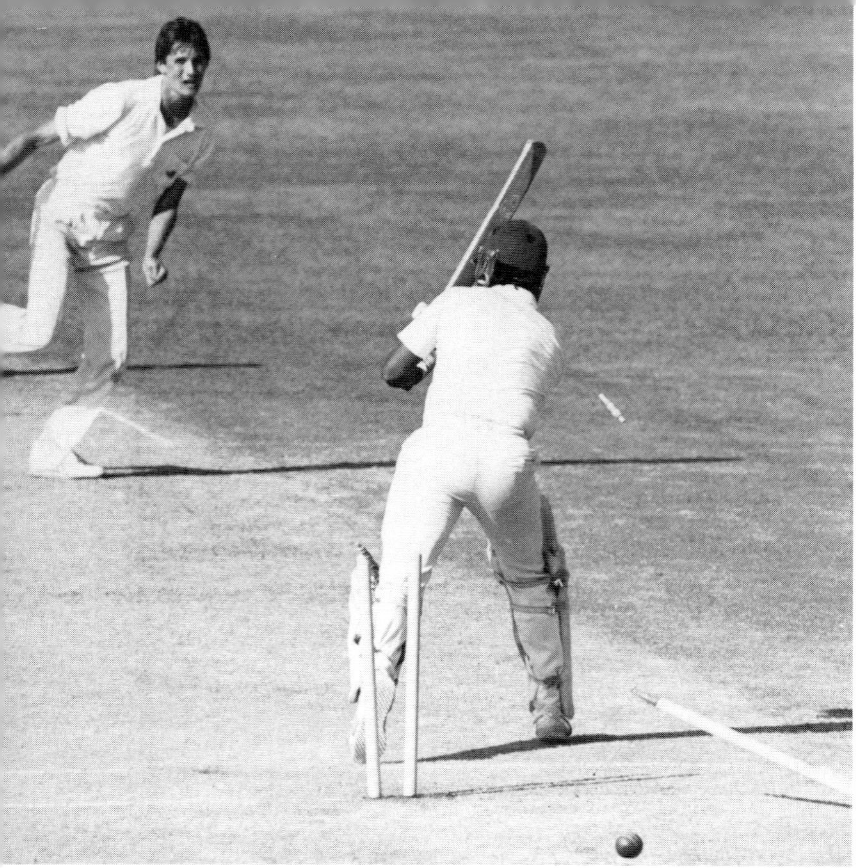

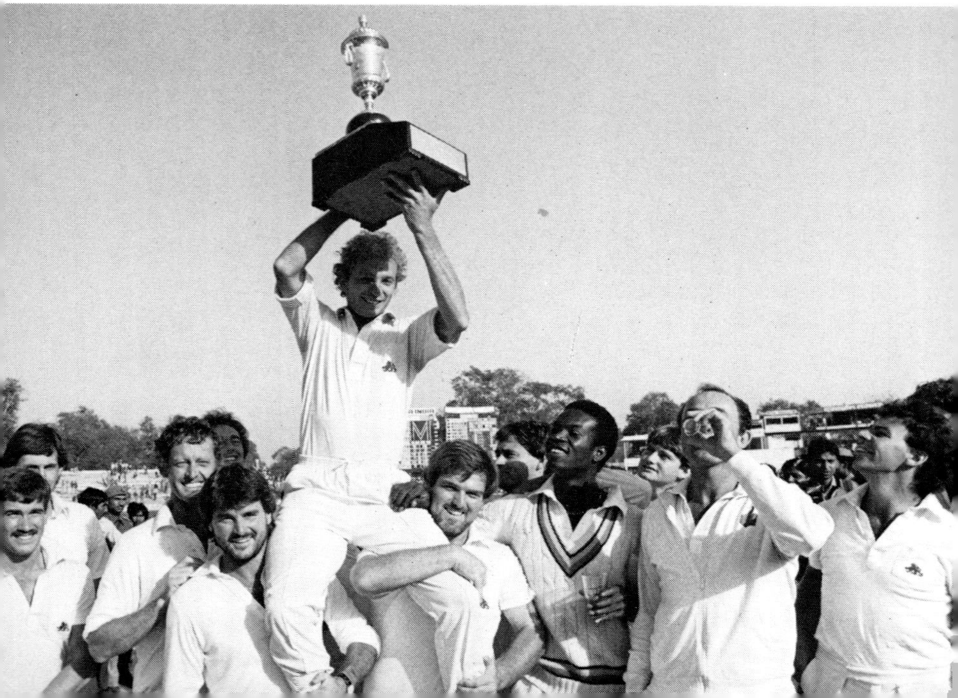

Opposite page, top: Neil Foster bowls Yadav, one of his 11 wickets, a performance that played a big part in England's victory in the fourth Test in Madras.

Left: The Indian series won, David Gower is carried shoulder-high by the first team ever to come from behind to win a series in India.

Above: Graeme Fowler (right) and Mike Gatting on their way to a double hundred apiece against India in Madras.

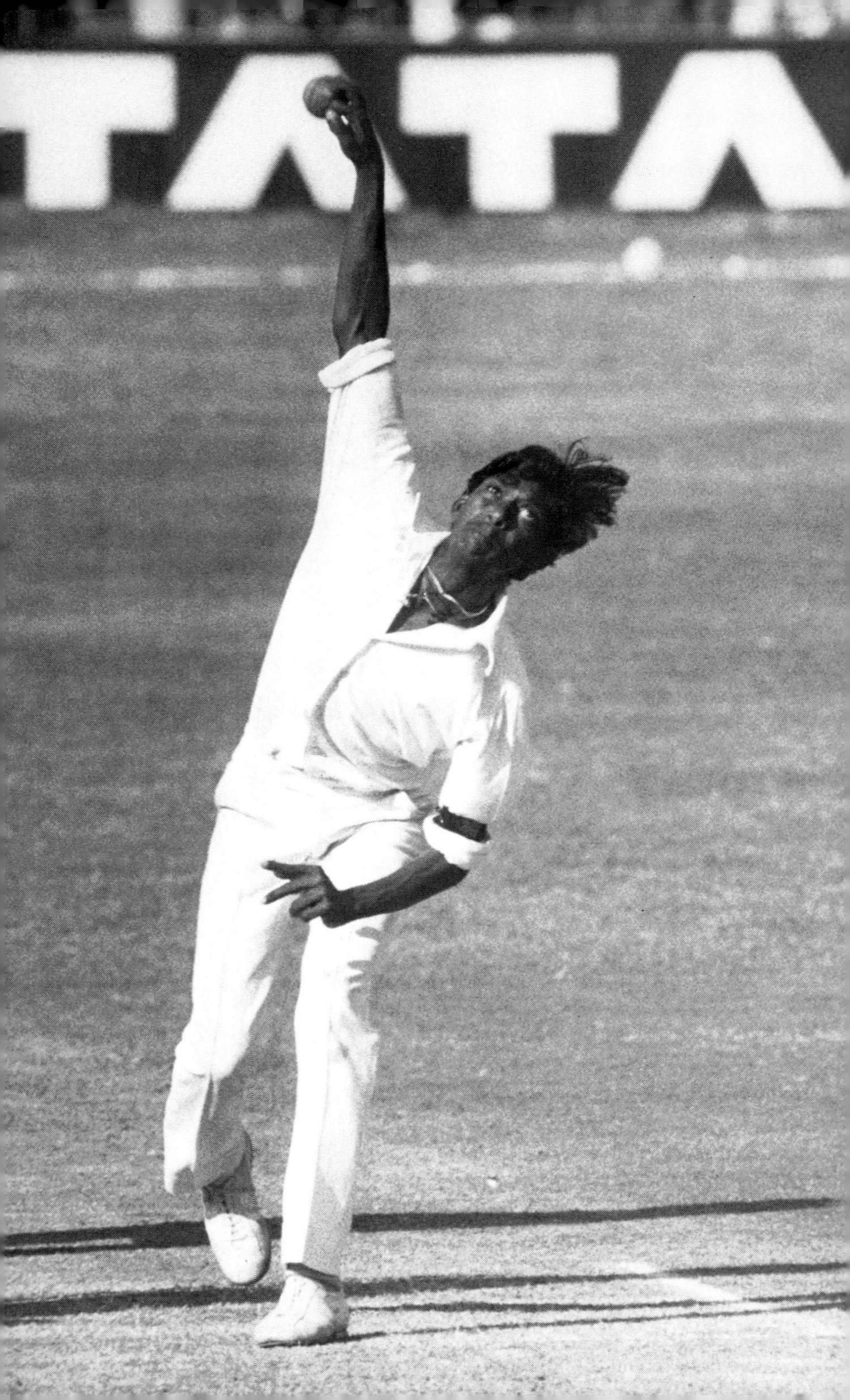
TATA

Left: The 18-year-old leg-spinner Sivaramakrishnan during the first Test against England, in Bombay, in which he took 12 wickets.

Right: Mohammed Azharuddin in Kanpur on his way to a historic third Test hundred – one in each of his first three Tests.

Below: Ravi Shastri, the Man of the Series, plays a lofted on-drive during the 'Mini World Cup' final in Melbourne between India and Pakistan.

Above: Greg Thomas of Glamorgan, one of the uncapped players chosen for England's winter tour of West Indies.

Left: David Smith, late of Surrey, now of Worcestershire, also uncapped but, as an outstanding player of fast bowling, not a surprise choice for a tour of West Indies.

4th Test, Old Trafford. England's first three bowlers provided a unique coincidence – Botham, Agnew, and Allott were all born in Cheshire. Border succumbed to England's first stumping in a home Test since 1980. Gower completed 5,000 runs in 74 Tests in 7 years 62 days – the fastest of England's nine instances. Gatting's first century against Australia was also his first in 40 Test innings in England. At 20 years 113 days, McDermott became the youngest Australian to take eight wickets in a Test innings. Phillips scored his 1,000th run in 16 Tests. During his 14th Test hundred, Border completed 1,000 runs in first-class matches on the tour – the first left-handed Australian captain to achieve this feat since Joe Darling in 1905.

5th Test, Edgbaston. Gower became the first England captain to put Australia in to bat in successive Tests. Hilditch completed 1,000 runs in his 16th Test. Thomson's 200th wicket in 51 Tests was also his 100th in 21 matches against England. Gower's score of 215 was his highest in all first-class cricket, the highest against Australia at Edgbaston (beating 180 by Ted Dexter in 1961), and the second-highest by an England captain against Australia after Walter Hammond's 240 at Lord's in 1938. Gower also passed Denis Compton's record aggregate for a home Ashes series of 562 in 1948. The second-wicket partnership of 331 between Robinson and Gower was England's second-highest for any wicket against Australia – after 382 (also for the second wicket) by Len Hutton and Maurice Leyland at The Oval in 1938; it was England's sixth-highest stand against all countries. Gatting's second century in successive innings took his aggregate in 10 Tests since 28 November 1984 past 1,000 runs. Botham (28 Tests) became the leading wicket-taker against Australia when he bowled O'Donnell and overtook Bob Willis (128 wickets in 35 matches). Ellison captured the wickets of Wessels, Wood, Holland, and Border in a spell of 15 balls to return match figures of 10 for 104 in only his second Test against Australia. England completed their remarkable victory with 11.5 overs in hand.

6th Test, The Oval. After compelling Australia to follow-on for the first time since 1977 (Headingley), England recorded their second victory by an innings in successive Tests – an ignominy last inflicted in 1956. The Ashes lost at Sydney in January 1983 had been regained by a handsome 3-1 margin. On the first day, England (376-3) achieved their highest total in a single day's play against Australia since 1938 (409-5 at Lord's), and their highest such total in all Tests since 1962 (406-2) at The Oval. The highest of Gooch's five Test centuries was his first in 40 innings against Australia. Gower's 12th Test hundred (5th against Australia) took his aggregate for the rubber to 732 (the fourth-highest for England against all countries); it enabled him to become the ninth England batsman to complete 2,000 runs against Australia. For the second consecutive innings Gower shared in a triple-century stand, the 351 he added in 337 minutes with Gooch succeeding the 331 of Edgbaston (with Robinson) as England's second-highest for any wicket against Australia and sixth-highest in all Tests. Physiotherapist Bernard Thomas ended his 17-year association with England teams. Income from the six Cornhill Tests amounted to £2,467,030, the total attendance being 373,000.

Australian Tour of Britain 1985

Results: Played 20; Won 4, Lost 3, Drawn 13

First-Class Averages

Batting and Fielding	M	I	NO	HS	R	Avge	100	50	Ct/St
A.R. Border	14	21	2	196	1355	71.31	8	1	13
D.M. Wellham	10	16	4	125*	669	55.75	2	4	1
D.C. Boon	15	20	5	206*	832	55.46	3	3	13
G.M. Ritchie	16	23	3	155	1097	54.85	4	4	7
W.B. Phillips	14	22	3	128	899	47.31	1	6	20/1
S.P. O'Donnell	11	16	5	100*	448	40.72	1	–	5
K.C. Wessels	16	26	1	156	905	36.20	1	8	9
G.M. Wood	16	25	3	172	691	31.40	2	–	6
A.M.J. Hilditch	17	27	0	119	829	30.70	1	4	7
R.B. Phillips	7	7	2	39	130	26.00	–	–	13
G.R.J. Matthews	10	12	3	51*	216	24.00	–	1	3
C.J. McDermott	16	14	3	53*	183	16.63	–	1	2
J.R. Thomson	11	11	6	28*	82	16.40	–	–	2
M.J. Bennett	11	10	3	23	111	15.85	–	–	6
G.F. Lawson	13	13	2	53	154	14.00	–	1	1
D.R. Gilbert	10	8	3	12	39	7.80	–	–	2
R.G. Holland	13	10	1	35	59	6.55	–	–	5

Bowling	O	M	R	W	Avge	Best	5wI	10wM
C.J. McDermott	421.5	49	1609	51	31.54	8-141	3	–
J.R. Thomson	241.3	33	988	29	34.06	6-44	2	–
R.G. Holland	376	94	1017	29	35.06	5-51	2	–
G.F. Lawson	347	61	1165	31	37.58	5-103	1	–
D.R. Gilbert	253.2	42	885	21	42.14	4-41	–	–
G.R.J. Matthews	159.4	34	521	12	43.41	3-76	–	–
M.J. Bennett	266.4	62	766	16	47.87	4-39	–	–
S.P. O'Donnell	242.4	47	819	12	68.25	3-37	–	–

Also bowled: D.C. Boon 6-0-33-0; A.R. Border 13-2-38-0; A.M.J. Hilditch 7-2-29-0; G.M. Ritchie 6.3-0-33-1; K.C. Wessels 32-9-79-0.

Texaco Trophy

Australia won the first two matches in the Texaco series, at Old Trafford and Edgbaston, so convincingly that England's sweeping eight-wicket victory in the third came as a surprise even allowing for the uncertainties of limited-over cricket.

The ill-founded tendency to regard Australians as unused to this form of cricket – they now play far more than England at international level – was rudely corrected at Old Trafford, where they bowled more effectively than England to better placed fields.

Gooch's form on his reappearance in an England side was encouraging, and his fourth-wicket stand of 116 in 28 overs with Botham, who hit five sixes in his 72, restored a start of 27 for three. But England had too much ground to make up and, with Gatting appearing belatedly at number six, seemed to have their batting order awry. Australia, needing 220, made no great haste, and at 157 for six seemed in some trouble. But, with England persisting in bowling at the legs of left-handers highly proficient in that area, Phillips and Matthews followed by Lawson won the match with three wickets and five balls to spare. Botham, who had given his wicket away through trying an unnecessary reverse sweep, was for some reason named man of the match, though Lawson (four for 26 and some important runs) seemed to have stronger claims.

Two days later at Edgbaston, England's outcricket was little better. Gooch again batted well, this time until the 54th over, and, with the ball moving about, 231 for seven seemed a fair, if not decisive, score.

On this occasion, Cowans and Botham began with a tidy spell in which they had Australia 19 for two, and if Border, then 35, had been caught off Edmonds at short extra cover, Australia might have had to work hard, for they were then behind the required rate.

But Wessels and Border made 116 for the third wicket, and while Border stayed, which he did to the end in the 54th over, there never seemed a chance that he and the strong middle batting would fail to make the runs.

Australia's 2-0 lead did not stop a capacity crowd from gathering at Lord's in the same perfect weather. Here, Australia, put in, did not quite reach their full potential, perhaps because the ball moved just enough to upset timing. But Graeme Wood batted through the 55 overs, well supported by Border and Boon, and they overcame a sluggish start to reach 254 for five.

England's batting on a now staightforward pitch made light of this. Though Robinson was out at 27, Gooch made another hundred and Gower, short of runs previously if not obviously out of form, came into his own again with a rapturously acclaimed 102, full of characteristically charming strokes. Their stand of 202 was a record for international one-day cricket in England, and England won with six overs unused.

England v Australia 1st Texaco Trophy International
Australia won by 3 wickets
Played at Old Trafford, Manchester, 30 May
Toss: England. Umpires: D.G.L. Evans and K.E. Palmer
Man of the Match: I.T. Botham (Adjudicator: J.B. Statham)

England		Runs	Mins	Balls	6s	4s
G.A. Gooch	c O'Donnell b Holland	57	153	123	–	5
G. Fowler	c Phillips b McDermott	10	27	17	–	2
D.I. Gower*	b Lawson	3	12	11	–	–
A.J. Lamb	c Phillips b Lawson	0	1	1	–	–
I.T. Botham	b Matthews	72	119	82	5	2
M.W. Gatting	not out	31	71	54	–	1
P. Willey	b Holland	12	15	18	–	2
P.R. Downton†	c Matthews b Lawson	11	22	18	–	–
P.H. Edmonds	c Border b Lawson	0	1	2	–	–
P.J.W. Allott	b McDermott	2	6	5	–	–
N.G. Cowans	c and b McDermott	1	7	2	–	–
Extras	(B 2, LB 7, W 2, NB 9)	20				
	(54 overs; 226 minutes)	**219**				

Australia		Runs	Mins	Balls	6s	4s
K.C. Wessels	c Botham b Willey	39	102	88	–	5
G.M. Wood	c Downton b Cowans	8	19	12	–	1
D.M. Wellham	c and b Edmonds	12	49	39	–	–
A.R. Border*	c and b Allott	59	96	76	1	4
D.C. Boon	c Botham b Gooch	12	31	24	–	–
W.B. Phillips†	c Gatting b Cowans	28	56	37	–	3
S.P. O'Donnell	b Botham	1	3	3	–	–
G.R.J. Matthews	not out	29	50	31	–	1
G.F. Lawson	not out	14	30	15	–	1
C.J. McDermott	did not bat					
R.G. Holland	"					
Extras	(B 2, LB 12, W 4)	18				
	(54.1 overs; 225 minutes)	**220-7**				

Australia	O	M	R	W
Lawson	10	1	26	4
McDermott	11	0	46	3
O'Donnell	11	0	44	0
Matthews	11	1	45	1
Holland	11	2	49	2

England	O	M	R	W
Cowans	10.1	1	44	2
Botham	11	2	41	1
Allott	11	0	47	1
Edmonds	11	2	33	1
Willey	9	1	31	1
Gooch	2	0	10	1

Fall of Wickets

Wkt	E	A
1st	21	15
2nd	27	52
3rd	27	74
4th	143	118
5th	160	156
6th	181	157
7th	203	186
8th	203	–
9th	213	–
10th	219	–

England v Australia 2nd Texaco Trophy International
Australia won by 4 wickets
Played at Edgbaston, Birmingham, 1 June
Toss: Australia. Umpires: D.J. Constant and D.R. Shepherd
Man of the Match: A.R. Border (Adjudicator: R.G.D. Willis)

England		Runs	Mins	Balls	6s	4s
G.A. Gooch	b McDermott	115	218	159	1	9
R.T. Robinson	c and b O'Donnell	26	66	48	–	4
D.I. Gower*	c Phillips b O'Donnell	0	8	7	–	–
A.J. Lamb	b Thomson	25	70	56	–	1
I.T. Botham	c Wellham b Lawson	29	45	36	–	2
M.W. Gatting	c Lawson b McDermott	6	13	13	–	–
P. Willey	c Phillips b Lawson	0	3	2	–	–
P.R. Downton†	not out	16	12	9	–	1
P.H. Edmonds	not out	6	8	6	–	–
P.J.W. Allott	did not bat					
N.G. Cowans	"					
Extras	(LB 2, W 2, NB 4)	8				
	(55 overs; 227 minutes)	231-7 (closed)				

Australia		Runs	Mins	Balls	6s	4s
K.C. Wessels	c and b Willey	57	125	100	–	6
G.M. Wood	lbw b Cowans	5	13	14	–	1
D.M. Wellham	lbw b Botham	7	17	19	–	1
A.R. Border*	not out	85	193	123	–	5
D.C. Boon	b Allott	13	23	12	1	1
W.B. Phillips†	c Gatting b Cowans	14	15	16	–	2
S.P. O'Donnell	b Botham	28	47	34	–	4
G.R.J. Matthews	not out	8	9	7	–	1
G.F. Lawson	did not bat					
C.J. McDermott	"					
J.R. Thomson	"					
Extras	(LB 13, W 2, NB 1)	16				
	(54 overs; 226 minutes)	233-6				

Australia	O	M	R	W
Lawson	11	0	53	2
McDermott	11	0	56	2
O'Donnell	11	2	32	2
Thomson	11	0	47	1
Matthews	10	0	38	0
Border	1	0	3	0

England	O	M	R	W
Botham	10	2	38	2
Cowans	11	2	42	2
Allott	10	1	40	1
Willey	11	1	38	1
Edmonds	10	0	48	0
Gooch	2	0	14	0

Fall of Wickets

Wkt	E	A
1st	63	10
2nd	69	19
3rd	134	116
4th	193	137
5th	206	157
6th	208	222
7th	216	–
8th	–	–
9th	–	–
10th	–	–

England v Australia 3rd Texaco Trophy International
England won by 8 wickets
Played at Lord's, 3 June
Toss: England. Umpires: H.D. Bird and B.J. Meyer
Man of the Match: D.I. Gower (Adjudicator: E.R. Dexter)

Australia		Runs	Mins	Balls	6s	4s
G.M. Wood	not out	114	234	165	1	10
A.M.J. Hilditch	lbw b Foster	4	7	8	–	1
G.M. Ritchie	c Gooch b Botham	15	66	46	–	2
A.R. Border*	b Gooch	44	83	60	–	5
D.C. Boon	c Gower b Willey	45	57	47	1	3
W.B. Phillips†	run out (Downton/Willey)	10	8	5	–	2
S.P. O'Donnell	not out	0	2	1	–	–
G.R.J. Matthews	did not bat					
G.F. Lawson	"					
C.J. McDermott	"					
J.R. Thomson	"					
Extras	(B 2, LB 13, W 6, NB 1)	22				
	(55 overs; 234 minutes)	254-5 (closed)				

England		Runs	Mins	Balls	6s	4s
G.A. Gooch	not out	117	207	164	1	13
R.T. Robinson	lbw b McDermott	7	28	18	–	1
D.I. Gower*	c Border b McDermott	102	159	118	1	14
A.J. Lamb	not out	9	15	8	–	1
I.T. Botham	did not bat					
M.W. Gatting	"					
P. Willey	"					
P.R. Downton†	"					
N.A. Foster	"					
P.J.W. Allott	"					
N.G. Cowans	"					
Extras	(B 2, LB 9, W 2, NB 9)	22				
	(49 overs; 207 minutes)	257-2				

England	O	M	R	W
Cowans	8	2	22	0
Foster	11	0	55	1
Botham	8	1	27	1
Allott	7	1	45	0
Gooch	11	0	46	1
Willey	10	1	44	1

Australia	O	M	R	W
Lawson	9	0	37	0
McDermott	10	0	51	2
Thomson	8	1	50	0
O'Donnell	11	0	54	0
Matthews	10	0	49	0
Border	1	0	5	0

Fall of Wickets

Wkt	A	E
1st	6	25
2nd	47	227
3rd	143	–
4th	228	–
5th	252	–
6th	–	–
7th	–	–
8th	–	–
9th	–	–
10th	–	–

Zimbabwe in England

In 1983 Zimbabwe defeated Australia by 13 runs in the Prudential World Cup. Their tour to England this summer indicated that similar upsets may well be in store when the 1987 tournament takes place. As for everyone else this season, the rain had a major effect on matches, but the cricket that was fitted in between downpours revealed a side a little lopsided in make-up, yet capable of competing with anyone. The record of five draws and one defeat (in a declaration game against Gloucestershire at Bristol), is no disgrace, and in one-day matches notable victories were gained over both Somerset and Sussex.

Without doubt the greatest success of the tour was the emergence of Zimbabwe's new batting star, Graeme Hick. At 19, Hick's potential is massive, and Worcestershire have been nurturing him for the past two seasons. He finished with a tour average of over 66, his double-century at The Parks against Oxford causing many cricketing eyebrows to rise. By following that up with a superb 192 against Glamorgan at Swansea, he lived up to the claim of ZCU President, Alwyn Pichanick, that Hick is 'perhaps the best young cricketer Zimbabwe has produced'.

Around Hick the side had some other very capable batsmen, as evidenced by the fact that six other players finished the tour averaging over 30 with the bat. The captain, Andrew Pycroft, had an excellent tour, and the talented wicketkeeper-batsman David Houghton achieved his maiden first-class century. These two provide the experience in the middle order and do an effective job.

However, the bowling strength was woefully weak at times. John Traicos is an off-spinner nearing the veteran stage, and though still a fine bowler his best days are behind him. But it was in the seam-bowling department that the most glaring deficiencies were apparent. Ian Butchart toiled away for his 20 wickets at 27, but received precious little support. Unfortunately the two most experienced seam bowlers, Peter Rawson and Kevin Curran, were not available: Rawson for business reasons, while Curran was one of the main reasons why Gloucestershire made such a bold bid for the County Championship. Had these two players been in the side, the constant problem of bowling out the opposition would have been nowhere near as great.

While the side had its limitations in the three-day game, the victories over Sussex and Somerset were proof of its limited-overs capabilities. A brilliant fielding side, Zimbabwe at full strength may just provide another shock in the next World Cup. Test match status is still some way off, but experience gained from tours of this nature can only improve the standard of a team with definite potential.

Zimbabwe Tour of England 1985

Results: Played 6; Lost 1, Drawn 5

First-Class Averages

Batting and Fielding	M	I	NO	HS	R	Avge	100	50	Ct/St
G.A. Hick	6	9	0	230	598	66.44	2	1	6
A.J. Pycroft	4	6	2	110*	245	61.25	1	–	2
D.H. Streak	3	3	1	29	72	36.00	–	–	1
G.A. Paterson	6	9	0	92	320	35.55	–	2	–
A.C. Waller	2	3	1	56*	69	34.50	–	1	2
D.L. Houghton	6	8	1	104	231	33.00	1	–	3
L.L. de Grandhomme	5	6	1	59	157	31.40	–	1	2
I.P. Butchart	6	8	1	82	134	19.14	–	1	1
A.H. Shah	4	6	1	40	95	19.00	–	–	1
A.J. Traicos	6	5	2	27*	57	19.00	–	–	7
K.G. Walton	3	5	1	20*	57	14.25	–	–	2
R.D. Brown	5	8	0	27	113	14.12	–	–	1
E.A. Brandes	3	4	1	19	30	10.00	–	–	–
M.P. Jarvis	4	3	1	6	10	5.00	–	–	1
K.G. Duers	3	2	0	1	1	0.50	–	–	–

Bowling	O	M	R	W	Avge	Best	5wI	10wM
Butchart	167	42	547	20	27.35	5-65	1	–
Jarvis	110	13	392	10	39.20	3-37	–	–
Traicos	167.1	48	439	8	54.87	2-33	–	–

Also bowled: Brandes 47.4-3-190-3; de Grandhomme 46-9-148-4; Duers 66-13-235-4; Hick 71-9-236-3; Shah 28-7-106-0; Streak 20.3-4-69-3.

English season
1985

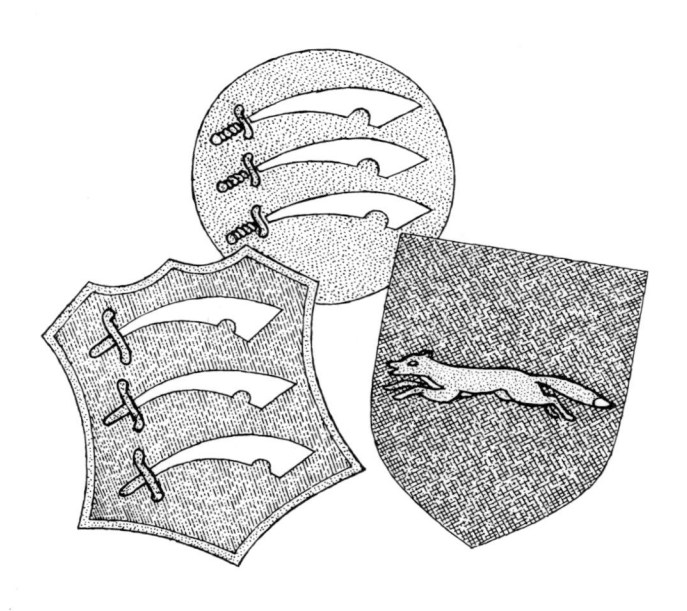

Britannic Assurance Championship

Middlesex's win in the Britannic Assurance County Championship, achieved on the last day of the season, September 17, was one of the most remarkable for some time. It was won by a county who overall contributed five players to England's winning of the Ashes and were short of four outstanding players for 10 out of 24 matches.

If most people thought that this handicap would be too great, they were in good company. The Middlesex captain himself said at the start of the season that he believed Middlesex would do well to finish in the first five and that their main hope lay in one of the knock-out competitions. They had won one of these in each of the previous two years of Mike Gatting's captaincy, but this year they were beaten in each by Essex at an early stage. Yet they found themselves unexpectedly well placed in the Championship.

Three sides had drawn away from the others when the championship table began to take shape in late July. Beside a surprised Middlesex were Hampshire and Gloucestershire, who had finished 15th and 17th (last), respectively, in 1984.

Hampshire had always promised to make a serious challenge this year, with the return of Greenidge and Marshall and the qualification of Robin Smith. Gloucestershire, who last won in 1877, had revived themselves by shrewd signings to boost a nucleus of improving young players of previous years.

Gloucestershire dropped away a little in the last week of August with defeats by Hampshire and Essex. Hampshire's two wins at Bournemouth over Gloucestershire and Leicestershire sent them surging to the front. But by that time Middlesex were back at full strength for their last four matches. They were to win two of them. They began the penultimate series of matches with a lead of two points over Hampshire. Having failed to capitalize on a highly successful first day against Essex, they began the last series with the lead down to just one point.

Here they had one of three healthy slices of luck, for whereas all three contenders – Gloucestershire were still only 16 points behind – were playing away, Middlesex for this crucial three days had easily the weakest opponents on current form in Warwickshire. By soon after three o'clock on the third afternoon they had swept them aside by an innings, their main concern having been the unsettled weather.

Middlesex's two other pieces of luck were relative freedom from injuries and, probably most significant, the favours conferred on them by the rain of July and August. During a period when their weakened side seldom looked in a winning position, they lost very little ground because the weather prevented their rivals from winning. Indeed, when Hampshire beat Gloucestershire on August 27, it was their first win since July 9, though they were still looking the likely champions. Another sign of the weather's influence was that Middlesex ultimately became champions with eight victories, compared with Essex's 13 in 1984.

When at half-strength, Middlesex did bring off two coups that must have affected the final result. In the last days of June, they won an extraordinary victory at Worcester – with Daniel absent as well as four Test players – despite having the first day's play completely washed out. A fortnight earlier, their young ninth-wicket pair of Sykes and Hughes had held out for the last 29 overs when Hampshire looked certain to win.

This was one of several exasperating near-misses for Hampshire, the last a defeat in the penultimate match by Northants by one wicket off the last ball. The fact that they introduced young local talent to augment their overseas-born players was a good omen for the future, as was the ebullient leadership of the new captain, Mark Nicholas. His gracious acknowledgement in the hour of defeat that Middlesex were deserving winners was greatly to his and Hampshire's credit.

Middlesex's strength lay in the quality and variety of their bowling, and this year in less dependence on Gatting. He still seldom failed them, but it was not until the last match but one that he made his first championship 100 of the season. His runs were less vital because of the consistently prolific start provided by Barlow and Slack and the contributions usually forthcoming in the middle order from Radley, Emburey, and Downton. It is hard to think of a county side with comparable reserve strength and all-round qualities since Surrey in the 1950s.

Their success could be applauded for numerous reasons, not only for their reliance on a balanced side and the spin of Edmonds and Emburey, but for the fact that they had only one player, Daniel, not available for England. They did not win one of their eight victories on a declaration. Worcestershire declared in the first innings of their first match of the season; otherwise they bowled all their victims out twice. Moreover, as tenants of MCC, they have no say in the type of pitches produced at Lord's. In fact, they won only twice there.

Of the other counties, Essex still looked as formidable as any, and came into fourth place at the end. But, like Notts, whom they so narrowly beat in 1984 and who lost only twice – once to Middlesex – they fell too far behind early on to be a serious threat. At times, so much depended on the weather. Sussex lost only once – to Middlesex in May. Kent promised to come with a run in early July, but it faded away. Somerset will no doubt be working out how, after finishing seventh in 1984 without Richards and Garner, they now finished bottom – despite having earned more batting points than any of the other 16 sides.

Britannic Assurance County Championship 1985 – Final Table

	P	W	L	D	1st Innings Points Batting	1st Innings Points Bowling	Total Points
1 MIDDLESEX (3)	24	8	4	12	61	85	274
2 Hampshire (15)	24	7	2	15	66	78	256
3 Gloucestershire (17)	23	7	3	13	51	78	241
4 Essex (1)	23	7	2	14	42	70	224
5 Worcestershire (10)	24	5	6	13	65	68	221
6 Surrey (8)	24	5	5	14	62	76	218
7 Sussex (6)	23	6	1	16	52	57	205
8 Nottinghamshire (2)	24	4	2	18	66	69	199
9 Kent (5)	24	4	5	15	51	71	186
10 Northamptonshire (11)	24	5	4	15	52	51	183
11 Yorkshire (14)	23	3	4	16	58	59	165
12 Glamorgan (13)	24	4	4	16	41	50	163
13 Derbyshire (12)	24	3	9	12	46	69	163
14 Lancashire (16)	24	3	7	14	44	67	159
15 Warwickshire (9)	24	2	8	14	47	74	153
16 Leicestershire (4)	24	2	3	19	48	65	145
17 Somerset (7)	24	1	7	16	70	45	131

1984 final positions are shown in brackets. The totals for Worcestershire and Glamorgan include eight points for levelling the scores in drawn matches. Where sides are equal on points, the one with the most wins has priority. The Yorkshire v Essex and Gloucestershire v Sussex matches were abandoned and are not included in the table.

Points

For a win: 16 points, plus any first innings points. For winning a match reduced to a single innings because it started with less than eight hours of playing time remaining: 12 points. First innings points (awarded during the first 100 overs of each first innings):

Batting		Bowling	
150 to 199 runs	1	3 or 4 wickets	1
200 to 249 runs	2	5 or 6 wickets	2
250 to 299 runs	3	7 or 8 wickets	3
300 runs and over	4	9 or 10 wickets	4

Final Positions 1890-1985

	D	E	Gm	Gs	H	K	La	Le	M	Nh	Nt	Sm	Sy	Sx	Wa	Wo	Y
1890	—	—	—	6	—	3	2	—	7	—	5	—	1	8	—	—	3
1891	—	—	—	9	—	5	2	—	3	—	4	5	1	7	—	—	8
1892	—	—	—	7	—	7	4	—	5	—	2	3	1	9	—	—	6
1893	—	—	—	9	—	4	2	—	3	—	6	8	5	7	—	—	1
1894	—	—	—	9	—	4	4	—	3	—	7	6	1	8	—	—	2
1895	5	9	—	4	10	14	2	12	6	—	12	8	1	11	6	—	3
1896	7	5	—	10	8	9	2	13	3	—	6	11	4	14	12	—	1
1897	14	3	—	5	9	12	1	13	8	—	10	11	2	6	7	—	4
1898	9	5	—	3	12	7	6	13	2	—	8	13	4	9	9	—	1
1899	15	6	—	9	10	8	4	13	2	—	10	13	1	5	7	12	3
1900	13	10	—	7	15	3	2	14	7	—	5	11	7	3	6	12	1
1901	15	10	—	14	7	7	3	12	2	—	9	12	6	4	5	11	1
1902	10	13	—	14	15	7	5	11	12	—	3	7	4	2	6	9	1
1903	12	8	—	13	14	8	4	14	1	—	5	10	11	2	7	6	3
1904	10	14	—	9	15	3	1	7	4	—	5	12	11	6	7	13	2
1905	14	12	—	8	16	6	2	5	11	13	10	15	4	3	7	8	1
1906	16	7	—	9	8	1	4	15	11	11	5	11	3	10	6	14	2
1907	16	7	—	10	12	8	6	11	5	15	1	14	4	13	9	2	2
1908	14	11	—	10	9	2	7	13	4	15	8	16	3	5	12	6	1

ENGLISH SEASON 1985/BRITANNIC ASSURANCE CHAMPIONSHIP 141

	D	E	Gm	Gs	H	K	La	Le	M	Nh	Nt	Sm	Sy	Sx	Wa	Wo	Y
1909	15	14	—	16	8	1	2	13	6	7	10	11	5	4	12	8	3
1910	15	11	—	12	6	1	4	10	3	9	5	16	2	7	14	13	8
1911	14	6	—	12	11	2	4	15	3	10	8	16	5	13	1	9	7
1912	12	15	—	11	6	3	4	13	5	2	8	14	7	10	9	16	1
1913	13	15	—	9	10	1	8	14	6	4	5	16	3	7	11	12	2
1914	12	8	—	16	5	3	11	13	2	9	10	15	1	6	7	14	4
1919	9	14	—	8	7	2	5	9	13	12	3	5	4	11	15	—	1
1920	16	9	—	8	11	5	2	13	1	14	7	10	3	6	12	15	4
1921	12	15	17	7	6	4	5	11	1	13	8	10	2	9	16	14	3
1922	11	8	16	13	6	4	5	14	7	15	2	10	3	9	12	17	1
1923	10	13	16	11	7	5	3	14	8	17	2	9	4	6	12	15	1
1924	17	15	13	6	12	5	4	11	2	16	6	8	3	10	9	14	1
1925	14	7	17	10	9	5	3	12	6	11	4	15	2	13	8	16	1
1926	11	9	8	15	7	3	1	13	6	16	4	14	5	10	12	17	2
1927	5	8	15	12	13	4	1	7	9	16	2	14	6	10	11	17	3
1928	10	16	15	5	12	2	1	9	8	13	3	14	6	7	11	17	4
1929	7	12	17	4	11	8	2	9	6	13	1	15	10	4	14	16	2
1930	9	6	11	2	13	5	1	12	16	17	4	13	8	7	15	10	3
1931	7	10	15	2	12	3	6	16	11	17	5	13	8	4	9	14	1
1932	10	14	15	13	8	3	6	12	10	16	4	7	5	2	9	17	1
1933	6	4	16	10	14	3	5	17	12	13	8	11	9	2	7	15	1
1934	3	8	13	7	14	5	1	12	10	17	9	15	11	2	4	16	5
1935	2	9	13	15	16	10	4	6	3	17	5	14	11	7	8	12	1
1936	1	9	16	4	10	8	11	15	2	17	5	7	6	14	13	12	3
1937	3	6	7	4	14	12	9	16	2	17	10	13	8	5	11	15	1
1938	5	6	16	10	14	9	4	15	2	17	12	7	3	8	13	11	1
1939	9	4	13	3	15	5	6	17	2	16	12	14	8	10	11	7	1
1946	15	8	6	5	10	6	3	11	2	16	13	4	11	17	14	8	1
1947	5	11	9	2	16	4	3	14	1	17	11	11	6	9	15	7	7
1948	6	13	1	8	9	15	5	11	3	17	14	12	2	16	7	10	4
1949	15	9	8	7	16	13	11	17	1	6	11	9	5	13	4	3	1
1950	5	17	11	7	12	9	1	16	14	10	15	7	1	13	4	6	3
1951	11	8	5	12	9	16	3	15	7	13	17	14	6	10	1	4	2
1952	4	10	7	9	12	15	3	6	5	8	16	17	1	13	10	14	2
1953	6	12	10	6	14	16	3	3	5	11	8	17	1	2	9	15	12
1954	3	15	4	13	14	11	10	16	7	7	5	17	1	9	6	11	2
1955	8	14	16	12	3	13	9	6	5	7	11	17	1	4	9	15	2
1956	12	11	13	3	6	16	2	17	5	4	8	15	1	9	14	9	7
1957	4	5	9	12	13	14	6	17	7	2	15	8	1	9	11	16	3
1958	5	6	15	14	2	8	7	12	10	4	17	3	1	13	16	9	11
1959	7	9	6	2	8	13	5	16	10	11	17	12	3	15	4	14	1
1960	5	6	11	8	12	10	2	17	3	9	16	14	7	4	15	13	1
1961	7	6	14	5	1	11	13	9	3	16	17	10	15	8	12	4	2
1962	7	9	14	4	10	11	16	17	13	8	15	6	5	12	3	2	1
1963	17	12	2	8	10	13	15	16	6	7	9	3	11	4	4	14	1
1964	12	10	11	17	12	7	14	16	6	3	15	8	4	9	2	1	5
1965	9	15	3	10	12	5	13	14	6	2	17	7	8	16	11	1	4
1966	9	16	14	15	11	4	12	8	12	5	17	3	7	10	6	2	1
1967	6	15	14	17	12	2	11	3	7	9	16	8	4	13	10	5	1
1968	8	14	3	16	5	2	6	9	10	13	4	12	15	17	11	7	1
1969	16	6	1	2	5	10	15	14	11	9	8	17	3	7	4	12	13
1970	7	12	2	17	10	1	3	15	16	14	11	13	5	9	7	6	4
1971	17	10	16	8	9	4	3	5	6	14	12	7	1	11	2	15	13
1972	17	5	13	3	9	2	15	6	8	4	14	11	12	16	1	7	10
1973	16	8	11	5	1	4	12	9	13	3	17	10	2	15	7	6	14
1974	17	12	16	14	2	10	8	4	6	3	15	5	7	13	9	1	11
1975	15	7	9	16	3	5	4	1	11	8	13	12	6	17	14	10	2
1976	15	6	17	3	12	14	16	4	1	2	13	7	9	10	5	11	8
1977	7	6	14	3	11	1	16	5	1	9	17	4	14	8	10	13	12
1978	14	2	13	10	8	1	12	6	3	17	7	5	16	9	11	15	4
1979	16	1	17	10	12	5	13	6	14	11	9	8	3	4	15	2	7
1980	9	8	13	7	17	16	15	9	1	12	3	5	2	4	14	11	6
1981	12	5	14	13	7	9	16	8	4	15	1	3	6	2	17	11	10
1982	11	7	16	15	3	13	12	2	1	9	4	6	5	8	17	14	10
1983	9	1	15	12	3	7	12	4	2	6	14	10	8	11	5	16	17
1984	12	1	13	17	15	5	16	4	3	11	2	7	8	6	9	10	14
1985	13	4	12	3	2	9	14	16	1	10	7	17	6	7	15	5	11

Derbyshire

Victory in their last Championship game of the season and a final run of four consecutive John Player League victories revived Derbyshire during the closing stages of the season, but the summer was already cast as one of disappointment and underachievement. Barnett, the captain, predicted 'eight or nine Championship' wins before the campaign began, but they ended with only three and lost nine times, more than any other county. Fourth place in the Sunday competition was overshadowed by the jarring memory of defeat by Durham in the NatWest Trophy and Barnett's final assessment of the causes of failure was 'too many batsmen averaging under 30 and too many bowlers averaging over 30!'

Until Barnett moved down the order to give Roberts the chance to open, the captain's form was the only consistent source of pleasure for Derbyshire supporters. He frequently had to shore up the innings, with negligible support, and the defensive technique and self-denial he demonstrated in such situations did much to erase suspicions of recklessness voiced in the past. With Wright limited by Holding's presence to only 16 innings, the improving Roberts was the only other batsman to pass 1,000 runs, and the solid qualities of Hill were badly missed when his prosperous start was undermined by injuries.

Anderson's willingness to graft earned him his cap, but Morris's career went into sharp decline and there were doubts about both technique and temperament until a late return to better form again revealed his massive potential. The middle order frequently capsized, and the tailenders often had to carry the innings to respectability, Newman in particular rising to the responsibility with more than 600 runs and a maiden century to emerge as a genuine all-rounder.

Barnett's initial optimism was based on the presence of Holding, the return to fitness of Mortensen, and the arrival of Warner from Worcestershire to support Finney and Newman in the seam-bowling department. But none was consistently successful.

Holding's pace and penetration was too often blunted by overwork as the other seamers wilted, though he was still able to make good batsmen contort on the more helpful pitches.

Finney, though less consistent than the previous season, was the only other bowler to average under 30. And though Warner fell well short of expectations, it was the spinners who proved the most disappointing. Miller's rich form of 1984 did not survive the cares of a testimonial, and though he batted with modest success, his off-spin was rarely an affordable weapon. Moir, mysteriously capped early on, again appeared a diffident and enigmatic figure, and his failure to exploit helpful conditions at Old Trafford and Bradford, when victory chances were turned to defeat, explained the decision not to re-engage him.

Maher, who had the burdensome task of replacing Taylor as wicketkeeper, suffered a gradual disintegration of technique and confidence. So it was Marples who ended the season with the gloves, expiating some early sloppiness with an encouraging improvement in the last month.

ENGLISH SEASON 1985/DERBYSHIRE

Britannic Assurance County Championship: 13th; Won 3, Lost 9, Drawn 12
All First-Class Matches: Won 3, Lost 9, Drawn 13
NatWest Bank Trophy: Lost to Durham in 1st round
Benson & Hedges Cup: Lost to Essex in quarter-final
John Player League: 4th; Won 8, Lost 5, No result 3

Championship Averages

Batting and Fielding	M	I	NO	HS	R	Avge	100	50	Ct/St
J.G. Wright	10	16	2	177*	797	56.92	2	4	5
K.J. Barnett	24	41	1	134*	1568	40.20	4	7	13
A. Hill	9	14	3	120	333	30.27	1	1	3
B. Roberts	24	42	4	100*	1128	29.68	2	2	21
G. Miller	20	31	5	105	744	28.61	1	4	27
J.E. Morris	17	27	1	109*	722	27.76	1	3	5
I.S. Anderson	19	35	3	95	876	27.37	–	7	16
P.G. Newman	19	29	3	115	604	23.23	1	3	2
M.A. Holding	12	19	1	80	413	22.94	–	3	6
R. Sharma	7	12	2	41*	209	20.90	–	–	6
W.P. Fowler	9	14	1	79	266	20.46	–	2	3
D.G. Moir	7	9	0	46	178	19.77	–	–	7
A.E. Warner	15	20	2	60	314	17.44	–	2	2
R.J. Finney	24	37	10	82	381	14.11	–	1	3
B.J.M. Maher	13	18	6	46	150	12.50	–	–	17/2
M.A. Fell	5	8	0	27	98	12.25	–	–	–
C. Marples	11	15	5	34	114	11.40	–	–	23/1
O.H. Mortensen	13	15	7	16*	39	4.87	–	–	4

Also batted: A.M. Brown (2 matches) 3, 16, 74 (3 ct); D.E. Malcolm (1 match) 0; P.E. Russell (3 matches) 3*, 2, 0*.

Hundreds (12)

4 **K.J. Barnett:** 134* v Leics, Leicester; 103 v Lancs, Chesterfield; 109 v Sussex, Derby; 125 v Yorkshire, Chesterfield.
2 **B. Roberts:** 100* v Glos, Derby; 100 v Notts, Derby.
  J.G. Wright: 117 v Worcs, Worcester; 177* v Warwicks, Birmingham.
1 **A. Hill:** 120 v Hampshire, Basingstoke.
  G. Miller: 105 v Essex, Colchester.
  J.E. Morris: 109* v Warwicks, Chesterfield.
  P.G. Newman: 115 v Leics, Chesterfield.

Bowling	O	M	R	W	Avge	Best	5wI	10wM
M.A. Holding	354.5	68	1124	50	22.48	6-65	3	1
R.J. Finney	435.3	80	1401	53	26.43	7-61	4	–
K.J. Barnett	173.4	33	514	17	30.23	6-115	1	–
P.G. Newman	393.5	74	1288	42	30.66	4-29	–	–
O.H. Mortensen	340	75	1026	33	31.09	5-87	1	–
A.E. Warner	267.3	40	1013	24	42.20	5-51	1	–
G. Miller	346.2	72	1085	25	43.40	6-110	1	–
D.G. Moir	159	41	450	10	45.00	3-102	–	–

Also bowled: I.S. Anderson 3-1-9-0; D.E. Malcolm 17-2-82-3; J.E. Morris 5.1-0-55-0; B. Roberts 20-1-106-0; P.E. Russell 89.5-22-243-4; J.G. Wright 6-0-42-0.

Essex

Essex dropped to fourth place, after two years as champions, but their final position in the table itself was a great improvement on all prospects and form shown at one stage of the season. They won their first match in April, when defeating Warwickshire, but it was not until victory over the bottom county Somerset, at Southend on 12 July, that Essex gained their next success. Indeed, at the beginning of June, they even suffered the indignity themselves of being at the bottom of the table.

Until that win over Somerset, the batting had generally been disappointing – apart, that is, from one Graham Gooch. England duties, of course, often kept Gooch away from the Essex team, but he reached his 1,000 runs in only 9 matches, to finish with a championship aggregate of 1,368 and the telling average of 91.20. In first-class games, Gooch scored more runs than any other batsman – 2,208. It even looked that Gooch would be the only Essex batsman to reach 1,000 runs in the championship before finally Hardie and McEwan obliged.

It was particularly rewarding that McEwan ended in top form, after a moderate start, for he retired and returns to South Africa as a dairy farmer. The batting of McEwan was an invaluable help for Essex. He scored 1,000 runs in each of his 12 years with the county – including 2,176 in 1983. In 1977 he hit 4 consecutive hundreds and that same year played his highest innings of 218 against Sussex at Chelmsford. McEwan's consistency will be sadly missed by the county, but they have, at least, made the most significant of 'signings' to replace him next season in Australia's captain, Alan Border.

Essex scored only 42 bonus batting points – fewer than any other county except Glamorgan – and significant losses of form were suffered by Prichard, 20, who had shown such promise the previous season, and the newly capped Gladwin. Unfortunately, they both sustained injuries, with Prichard having a seven weeks' absence with a broken thumb and Gladwin cracking his ribs. One marked batting advance, though, came from wicket-keeper East, who, with some most aggressive batting at No. 7, hit 754 runs, which included two championship hundreds, to finish second in the Essex averages.

Lever was the leading bowler, with 75 wickets, while all-rounder Pringle, in taking 45 wickets, not only effectively cut down his run-up by five yards, but also cured his previous no-ball problems. Even more encouraging for the Essex attack was the introduction of two medium-paced recruits – Ian Pont, younger brother of Keith Pont, and Topley, from the Lord's ground staff.

The captain, Fletcher, has now handed over the leadership to Gooch, but he will continue to play for the county. He continued to prove his worth with the bat when lowering himself down the order to No. 6 and scoring 623 runs in 1985. Fletcher had 12 triumphant years as captain of Essex, which included the county's first ever Championship in 1979, and how fitting that he should end with the glory of winning both the NatWest Bank Trophy and the John Player League.

ENGLISH SEASON 1985/ESSEX

Britannic Assurance County Championship: 4th; Won 7, Lost 2, Drawn 14, Abandoned 1
All First-Class Matches: Won 7, Lost 2, Drawn 17, Abandoned 1
NatWest Bank Trophy: Winners
Benson & Hedges Cup: Lost to Leicestershire in final
John Player League: 1st; Won 9, Lost 3, Tied 1, No result 3

Championship Averages

Batting and Fielding	M	I	NO	HS	R	Avge	100	50	Ct/St
G.A. Gooch	11	17	2	202	1368	91.20	6	4	17
D.E. East	23	26	3	131	754	32.78	2	4	63/4
K.S. McEwan	23	36	4	121	1035	32.34	2	5	14
B.R. Hardie	23	39	5	162	1074	31.58	2	4	22
K.W.R. Fletcher	21	26	6	78*	631	31.55	–	6	11
P.J. Prichard	18	28	4	95	694	28.91	–	5	13
C. Gladwin	12	20	2	92*	468	26.00	–	2	4
D.R. Pringle	21	27	4	121*	573	24.91	1	1	15
A.W. Lilley	14	23	2	68*	474	22.57	–	4	6
N.A. Foster	13	10	1	63	164	18.22	–	1	8
K.R. Pont	8	12	2	38	177	17.70	–	–	3
I.L. Pont	6	5	2	12	48	16.00	–	–	–
J.K. Lever	22	23	9	24*	193	13.78	–	–	8
S. Turner	4	6	0	35	75	12.50	–	–	–
N. Phillip	3	5	0	21	57	11.40	–	–	2
D.L. Acfield	22	19	10	10*	65	7.22	–	–	5

Also batted: J.H. Childs (4 matches) 5, 3, 3* (1 ct); J.P. Stephenson (1 match) 10, 4 (1 ct); T.D. Topley (4 matches) 0, 0, 9* (1 ct).

Hundreds (13)

6 G.A. Gooch: 202 v Notts, Nottingham; 125 v Kent, Dartford; 173* v Somerset, Taunton; 132* v Surrey, Chelmsford; 145 v Middlesex, Lord's; 142 v Yorkshire, Chelmsford.
2 D.E. East: 131 v Northants, Southend; 100 v Middlesex, Lord's.
  B.R. Hardie: 131 v Northants, Ilford; 162 v Somerset, Southend.
  K.S. McEwan: 121 v Middlesex, Chelmsford; 106 v Glos, Bristol.
1 D.R. Pringle: 121* v Surrey, Oval.

Bowling	O	M	R	W	Avge	Best	5wI	10wM
G.A. Gooch	155.3	35	432	18	24.00	5-46	1	–
N.A. Foster	366.5	77	1163	47	24.74	5-40	4	–
I.L. Pont	115.5	15	485	19	25.52	5-103	1	–
J.K. Lever	700.3	178	1963	75	26.17	6-47	6	–
T.D. Topley	134.1	31	400	15	26.66	4-57	–	–
D.R. Pringle	518.1	124	1374	45	30.53	6-42	1	–
D.L. Acfield	498.4	107	1462	38	38.47	6-81	1	–

Also bowled: J.H. Childs 130-38-377-3; K.W.R. Fletcher 4-0-35-1; C. Gladwin 3-0-12-0; B.R. Hardie 6-1-35-1; A.W. Lilley 28.4-0-179-3; N. Phillip 50-10-148-2; K.R. Pont 76-10-278-7; S. Turner 86.5-15-224-8.

Glamorgan

After a heady start to the season which saw them leading both the County Championship and the John Player League at the end of May, Glamorgan fell away, but they still have cause for satisfaction with their progress. Early exits from the Benson & Hedges and NatWest competitions gave evidence of the fragility of their challenge at the top level, but it must be said that Glamorgan, as severely hit as anyone by the weather, also had dreadful luck with injuries.

Their fast bowling spearhead Greg Thomas, whose early form brought him close to Test match recognition, suffered a series of minor injuries, but though taking only 39 first-class wickets he was impressive enough in between to be selected for the West Indies tour. More regular availability would have greatly benefited his county. John Steele, who made such an important contribution in 1984, broke a finger in June and did not play thereafter. Javed Miandad, as befits a world-class batsman, was a major force when fit, but missed several games through back trouble. A.L. Jones, after an excellent season in 1985, dislocated a shoulder in May and struggled for fitness and form, and Steve Barwick did not fulfil his promise of the previous season. Despite this dismal catechism, there were things to enthuse about.

Rodney Ontong, maturing as a captain, had a fine season personally, making 1,121 first-class runs at an average of nearly 49 and taking 64 wickets at 27 apiece. At Trent Bridge in August he beat Notts almost single-handed, scoring a century and taking 13 wickets in the match.

Younis Ahmed, at 37 now something of a veteran, showed no sign of diminishing skills. He batted brilliantly and consistently throughout the season, his highest points probably a magnificent 177 against Middlesex in May and his century against the Australians at Neath.

Geoff Holmes, having reached 1,000 runs for the first time in 1984, repeated the feat without developing perceptibly, but his whippy seamers proved extremely effective at times in all types of cricket. John Hopkins, normally a most reliable player, suffered vagaries of form and was left out of some matches. He is, however, a tough competitor and at 32 has much cricket left in him. He takes a deserved benefit in 1986.

The mixed fortunes of Hopkins and Jones meant increased opportunities for Morris. Though as yet displaying no great variety of stroke, he batted maturely and is a player with a future. He should develop rapidly during the coming season when he will be available full-time.

The performances of other young players were encouraging. Matthew Maynard, a 19-year-old batsman from Menai Bridge, made a brilliant hundred against Yorkshire in his first match and played several other innings of quality. Price and North both showed promise as slow left-armers, the former being the more accurate and the latter having the greater power of spin. Both have genuine claims to succeed Steele as the foil to Ontong's off-spin.

ENGLISH SEASON 1985/GLAMORGAN

Britannic Assurance County Championship: 12th; Won 4, Lost 4, Drawn 16
All First-Class Matches: Won 4, Lost 4, Drawn 19
NatWest Bank Trophy: Lost to Worcestershire in quarter-final
Benson & Hedges Cup: Failed to qualify for Q-F (3rd in Group D)
John Player League: 14th; Won 4, Lost 7, Tied 1, No result 4

Championship Averages

Batting and Fielding	M	I	NO	HS	R	Avge	100	50	Ct/St
Younis Ahmed	20	28	7	177	1190	56.66	3	4	3
Javed Miandad	18	27	5	164*	1194	54.27	3	8	13
R.C. Ontong	24	29	7	130	1105	50.22	2	8	10
G.C. Holmes	24	36	3	112	1062	32.18	2	7	9
T. Davies	24	24	7	75	457	26.88	–	2	42/5
S.P. Henderson	6	10	2	111	207	25.87	1	–	3
H. Morris	13	16	4	62	305	25.41	–	1	4
A.L. Jones	16	23	2	75	521	24.80	–	3	8
J.F. Steele	10	11	3	48	183	22.87	–	–	9
J.A. Hopkins	20	30	2	114*	626	22.35	1	3	8
J.G. Thomas	14	15	2	60*	266	20.46	–	1	6
M.R. Price	12	9	3	36	98	16.33	–	–	2
J. Derrick	13	14	2	52	156	13.00	–	1	2
L.L. McFarlane	11	4	2	8	12	6.00	–	–	4
S.R. Barwick	21	15	5	29	57	5.70	–	–	4

Also batted: S.J. Malone (7 matches) 0, 0, 0*, 0 (2 ct); M.P. Maynard (4 matches) 102, 58, 38 (1 ct); P.D. North (1 match) 0*; I. Smith (5 matches) 0, 12, 11, 4. S.P. James (1 match) did not bat.

Hundreds (13)

3 **Javed Miandad:** 125 v Surrey, Oval; 107 v Somerset, Cardiff; 164* v Lancs, Manchester
   Younis Ahmed: 177 v Middlesex, Cardiff; 100* v Worcs, Worcester; 143* v Hampshire, Cardiff.
2 **G.C. Holmes:** 106* v Worcs, Abergavenny; 112* v Leics, Leicester.
   R.C. Ontong: 122 v Sussex, Hove; 130 v Notts, Nottingham.
1 **S.P. Henderson:** 111 v Sussex, Hove.
   J.A. Hopkins: 114* v Worcs, Abergavenny.
   M.P. Maynard: 102 v Yorkshire, Swansea.

Bowling	O	M	R	W	Avge	Best	5wI	10wM
R.C. Ontong	563.5	137	1726	62	27.83	8-67	4	1
J.G. Thomas	298.3	43	1104	34	32.47	4-61	–	–
S.R. Barwick	464	95	1345	36	37.36	7-43	1	–
M.R. Price	239.4	59	616	16	38.50	4-97	–	–
J. Derrick	211.1	37	650	14	46.42	4-60	–	–
G.C. Holmes	313.3	73	962	20	48.10	3-25	–	–
J.F. Steele	180.1	45	498	10	49.80	3-6	–	–
L.L. McFarlane	219	35	886	14	63.28	4-100	–	–

Also bowled: S.P. Henderson 8-2-31-0; J.A. Hopkins 6-1-22-0; Javed Miandad 27.3-2-120-3; A.L. Jones 1-0-24-0; S.J. Malone 129-12-517-9; M.P. Maynard 0.1-0-4-0; H. Morris 3-0-32-0; P.D. North 27-7-60-1; I. Smith 38.4-10-117-1; Younis Ahmed 67.4-19-158-2

Gloucestershire

The 1985 season witnessed a remarkable and most welcome change of fortune for Gloucestershire, who climbed from bottom position to 3rd in the County Championship and from 15th to 6th in the John Player League. In the Benson & Hedges Cup they won their first three zonal matches, only to be unluckily eliminated when rain washed out play in their final match at a point when Derbyshire were marginally ahead on scoring rate though Gloucestershire looked likely winners. They also reached the quarter-finals of the NatWest competition, but were narrowly defeated by Notts.

Gloucestershire maintained their Championship challenge virtually to the end, and could have won even after suffering successive defeats at the hands of Hampshire and Essex in August. Unfortunately, their next two games, against Glamorgan and Northants, were so severely curtailed by rain that only three points could be secured from them. Even so, the season gave much cause for satisfaction, particularly after the events of the previous winter, during which a group of disaffected members called for the head of skipper David Graveney on a platter and, when he was supported by the cricket committee, demanded their decapitation also.

The reasons for the county's resurgence are not hard to find. Since the retirement of Brain and Procter, Gloucestershire's crucial weakness had been the absence of high quality pace bowling, a deficiency rectified with a vengeance by the availability for the whole season of West Indian Test bowler Courtney Walsh and the emergence of David Lawrence as a fast bowler with real claims to Test status. The powerful Lawrence showed improved control without sacrificing pace and took 85 wickets. Walsh, lean and lithe, commanded a subtle change of pace in capturing the same number at lower cost and finished 5th in the first-class averages. In 1986 Lawrence will be 22 and Walsh 23, so the pair have plenty of mileage in them.

The other main bowlers were the Irish-Zimbabwean Kevin Curran, who supported the opening pair most effectively at a hostile if sometimes erratic fast-medium, and Graveney himself, who bowled steadily and took important wickets.

The batting was more problematical, despite the excellence of Phil Bainbridge, who had the best season of his career, and of Bill Athey, who was called up for the final Test at the Oval but omitted when Botham was declared fit. Important contributions also came from Brian Davison, formerly with Leicestershire, and Jeremy Lloyds, shrewdly signed from Somerset, while Curran played a number of vauable forcing innings. But their sterling efforts could not camouflage the fact that the side rarely got a satisfactory start from their openers. Paul Romaines, though scoring heavily in the one-day competitions, could not get going in the Championship. The same was true of Andrew Stovold, and though various permutations were tried involving these two, Tony Wright, and Lloyds, the solution could not be found.

On a brighter note, Jack Russell, after a sketchy year in 1985, confirmed his position among the best wicketkeepers in the country. His form, together with the admirable close catching of Athey, Lloyds, and Stovold, was a feature of the season.

Britannic Assurance County Championship: 3rd; Won 7, Lost 3, Drawn 13, Abandoned 1
All First-Class Matches: Won 8, Lost 4, Drawn 14, Abandoned 1
NatWest Bank Trophy: Lost to Nottinghamshire in quarter-final
Benson & Hedges Cup: failed to qualify for Q-F (4th in Group A)
John Player League: 6th; Won 8, Lost 8

Championship Averages

Batting and Fielding	M	I	NO	HS	R	Avge	100	50	Ct/St
P. Bainbridge	21	33	7	151*	1456	56.00	4	10	9
C.W.J. Athey	21	33	6	170	1190	44.07	4	6	24
B.F. Davison	22	33	6	111	902	33.40	1	4	8
J.W. Lloyds	22	30	5	101	734	29.36	1	4	23
K.M. Curran	23	31	3	83	677	24.17	–	4	7
I.R. Payne	6	6	1	37	106	21.20	–	–	2
A.W. Stovold	20	33	2	112	656	21.16	2	2	18
D.A. Graveney	22	23	10	53*	237	18.23	–	1	17
A.J. Wright	7	12	2	47*	173	17.30	–	–	2
C.A. Walsh	20	16	5	37	183	16.63	–	–	4
P.W. Romaines	17	28	2	64	423	16.26	–	2	9
D.V. Lawrence	23	24	5	41	258	13.57	–	–	10
R.C. Russell	21	23	4	34	253	13.31	–	–	55/5
G.E. Sainsbury	4	5	3	8*	11	5.50	–	–	2

Also batted: A.J. Brassington (2 matches) 3* (4 ct); R.G.P. Ellis (1 match) 3, 20 (2 ct). J.N. Shepherd (1 match) did not bat.

Hundreds (12)

4 **C.W.J. Athey:** 170 v Derbys, Derby; 101 v Yorkshire, Gloucester; 139* v Worcs, Gloucester; 115 v Glamorgan, Bristol.
P. Bainbridge: 151* v Derbys, Derby; 119 v Yorkshire, Gloucester; 143* v Glamorgan, Bristol; 102 v Surrey, Oval.
2 **A.W. Stovold:** 104 v Sussex, Hove; 112 v Derbys, Derby.
1 **B.F. Davison:** 111 v Middlesex, Lord's.
J.W. Lloyds: 101 v Essex, Southend.

Bowling	O	M	R	W	Avge	Best	5wI	10wM
G.E. Sainsbury	138	45	380	21	18.09	7-38	2	–
C.A. Walsh	540.3	122	1636	82	19.95	7-51	4	1
D.A. Graveney	360.5	116	887	38	23.34	4-91	–	–
K.M. Curran	414.2	87	1233	52	23.71	5-42	1	–
D.V. Lawrence	500.5	59	1923	79	24.34	7-48	5	–
P. Bainbridge	182	45	492	18	27.33	5-60	1	–
J.W. Lloyds	131.1	25	450	15	30.00	5-37	1	–

Also bowled: C.W.J. Athey 41.1-6-189-8; R.G.P. Ellis 3-1-7-1; I.R. Payne 39-9-112-3; P.W. Romaines 10-0-42-3; J.N. Shepherd 14-3-41-0.

Hampshire

For Hampshire, with their new captain, Mark Nicholas, 1985 was a season of vast improvement in fortunes and yet disappointing for narrow misses. In the County Championship, they were pipped at the post by Middlesex. They lost by the narrowest margin to Essex in the NatWest semi-finals, and so were again denied a first appearance in a Lord's final. They qualified for the Benson & Hedges quarter-finals and finished third in the John Player League, and overall were third in the prize-money table.

In the Championship, it was inevitable that Hampshire would place a long way higher than their lowly 15th in 1984. Firstly, the captaincy issue had been resolved, and thus tension and uncertainty in the dressing-room eliminated. Apart from the strengthening effect of the return of Greenidge and Marshall, who were away touring with the West Indies in 1984, they had Terry available for the full season, as also Robin Smith, now domiciled for cricket purposes.

For depth, dependability, and firepower, Hampshire's batting was as strong, if not more formidable, than that of their rivals. Chris Smith was one of only three batsmen to score 2,000 runs, and four other batsmen, Greenidge, Terry, Nicholas, and Robin Smith, overtook the thousand mark. Chris Smith was not only prolific (seven 100's, eleven 50's), but more positive than in past seasons. Second in the aggregates was his brother. There was, of course, previous evidence of Robin's skill and power. But even in his first full season he displayed judgement and maturity by adapting to pitches not conducive to his natural style.

Seemingly jaded, Greenidge, by his own lofty standards, had a moderate season. More than a quarter of his runs came in two big innings (204 and 143). But such other good scores as he made were got in adversity or in testing conditions.

Nicholas started the season with a flourish and then slipped into a trough, only to lift his game during the final effort to catch up with Middlesex and ward off Gloucestershire's dogged challenge. As captain, Nicholas was confident, positive, and decisive. A measure of Hampshire's batting strength was that they were not beaten from being bowled out twice. And their tally of batting points was second only to Somerset's.

However, while their bowling was not without quality, it lacked depth. Marshall, as his figures make plain, was outstanding. Undeterred by slow pitches, he bowled more overs than any of his team-mates except Maru, the left-arm spinner, and five times captured five wickets or more in an innings. Tremlett won rewards for perseverance and control. Maru, playing his first full season, was, in aggregate, only three wickets behind Edmonds (76), the season's most successful spinner. However, Maru was more steady than penetrative, his value being highest when the opposition was chasing runs or targets.

Falling only 18 points short of the champions, Hampshire could curse the rain for having deprived them of at least two wins. But then the weather spared no county in the truant summer of 1985. Instead, Hampshire needed to blame their catching, which let them down most conspicuously in their crucial tie with Middlesex in June.

Britannic Assurance County Championship: 2nd; Won 7, Lost 2, Drawn 15
All First-Class Matches: Won 7, Lost 2, Drawn 17
NatWest Bank Trophy: Lost to Essex in semi-final
Benson & Hedges Cup: Lost to Leicestershire in quarter-final
John Player League: 3rd; Won 8, Lost 4, No result 4

Championship Averages

Batting and Fielding	M	I	NO	HS	R	Avge	100	50	Ct/St
C.L. Smith	21	35	3	143*	1720	53.75	5	11	10
C.G. Greenidge	19	32	2	204	1236	41.20	2	8	16
R.A. Smith	24	40	6	140*	1351	39.73	2	7	13
K.D. James	6	9	3	124	217	36.16	1	–	5
J.J.E. Hardy	14	22	4	107*	624	34.66	1	3	4
M.C.J. Nicholas	22	35	3	146	1109	34.65	1	7	18
V.P. Terry	24	40	2	148*	1224	32.21	2	9	34
T.M. Tremlett	24	29	15	102*	450	32.14	1	–	5
M.D. Marshall	22	33	2	66*	768	24.77	–	5	10
R.J. Parks	24	23	9	53*	344	24.57	–	2	54/4
N.G. Cowley	12	13	4	51	202	22.44	–	1	3
R.J. Maru	21	18	8	62	223	22.30	–	1	15
D.R. Turner	6	8	1	44	153	.21.85	–	–	2
C.A. Connor	15	8	3	36*	61	12.20	–	–	6
S.J.W. Andrew	10	4	3	6*	8	8.00	–	–	5

Hundreds (15)

5 C.L. Smith: 121 v Somerset, Taunton; 143* v Yorkshire, Middlesbrough; 121 v Lancs, Liverpool; 102 v Somerset, Bournemouth; 121 v Kent, Folkestone.
2 C.G. Greenidge: 204 v Warwicks, Birmingham; 143 v Northants, Southampton.
R.A. Smith: 140* v Derbys, Basingstoke; 134* v Leics, Bournemouth.
V.P. Terry: 148* v Somerset, Bournemouth; 128* v Notts, Nottingham.
1 J.J.E. Hardy: 107* v Essex, Southampton.
K.D. James: 124 v Somerset, Taunton.
M.C.J. Nicholas: 146 v Leics, Bournemouth.
T.M. Tremlett: 102* v Somerset, Taunton.

Bowling	O	M	R	W	Avge	Best	5wI	10wM
M.D. Marshall	688.1	193	1680	95	17.68	7-59	5	–
T.M. Tremlett	665.5	180	1620	75	21.60	5-42	2	–
N.G. Cowley	234.5	56	650	24	27.08	3-17	–	–
R.J. Maru	652	178	1809	64	28.26	5-16	3	–
S.J.W. Andrew	258	46	915	28	32.67	6-43	1	–
C.A. Connor	417.5	83	1310	29	45.17	4-62	–	–

Also bowled: C.G. Greenidge 4-1-16-0; K.D. James 126-17-549-7; M.C.J. Nicholas 119-21-436-6; C.L. Smith 61-6-269-4; R.A. Smith 26.4-8-72-4.

Kent

Kent's decline in the County Championship, though not drastic, was disappointing in its implication that a youth policy, the envy of many counties, had either failed to mature or had been misdirected.

Tapping the barometer of national batting and bowling averages throughout the season revealed an acute shortage of individual consistency as one source of depression. Of the bowlers, only Richard Ellison featured significantly – from late June to the end of the season. Apart from Graham Dilley, fleetingly, no other Kent bowler appeared among the top 25.

Similarly, the batting seldom rose above mediocrity. Mark Benson, for a couple of weeks in May, Chris Cowdrey, in June, and Neil Taylor, at the end of July, were the only Kent batsmen to creep into the charts. However, the overall blandness of individual achievement was not generally reflected in team performances that soared and dived in a manner that suggested those on the flight deck were not totally in control.

Cowdrey's dilemmas arose from a variety of sources. Dilley, apart from achieving a hat-trick at the Oval in July, only rarely suggested he had fully regained the fire and fitness of his heyday. Baptiste and Jarvis, likewise, blew hot and cold, and even the admirable Underwood could not bowl at both ends.

The captain's personal frustration was exacerbated by a mid-term period in which loss of fitness and form so affected his batting that he scored only one half-century in almost six weeks. Batting, indeed, was central to Kent's Jekyll and Hyde performances, as exemplified by two NatWest matches. In the first round, Benson, Hinks, and Tavare swept them to 296 for four and a majestic victory over Surrey. But in a one-sided quarter-final, they mustered only 172 for nine against Essex and were beaten by six wickets.

Another example of inexplicable frailty unfolded at Chelmsford on July 21, at which time they were heading the John Player League. With eight overs remaining and six wickets in hand, Kent required only 26 to win. They lost those six wickets for 12 runs.

The one positive aspect of that match was provided by Laurie Potter who, making only his fourth appearance of the season, scored a gritty half-century which helped install him in the senior side. Another factor was Potter's reluctant persuasion as a spin bowler which, as things transpired, was not unconnected with an all too familar Kentish trauma. This concerned the 'release' and subsequent dismissal of batsman/spinner Graham Johnson, who thereby joined Alan Ealham and John Shepherd among the ranks of long-serving players who, in recent years, have departed the county in less than amicable circumstances.

It was with muted pleasure, then, that many Kent supporters, at Folkestone, watched Underwood and Potter, his new slow-bowling partner, share 67 overs and six wickets in a marathon, but vain, attempt to dislodge Derbyshire. Setting aside such frustrations, Kent's season was not entirely without satisfaction. Ellison – as England gratefully acknowledged – established himself as a highly valuable asset, Hinks emerged as a positive and potentially prolific opening bat, and young Cowdrey G.R. hinted at the class of Cowdrey M.C.

Britannic Assurance County Championship: 9th; Won 4, Lost 5, Drawn 15
All First-Class Matches: Won 4, Lost 6, Drawn 16
NatWest Bank Trophy: Lost to Essex in quarter-final
Benson & Hedges Cup: Lost to Leicestershire in semi-final
John Player League: 10th; Won 6, Lost 7, No result 3

Championship Averages

Batting and Fielding	M	I	NO	HS	R	Avge	100	50	Ct/St
N.R. Taylor	14	22	6	102*	715	44.68	2	3	6
G.R. Cowdrey	5	7	2	53	187	37.40	–	1	5
M.R. Benson	23	42	2	162	1446	36.15	3	9	14
C.J. Tavare	23	40	6	150*	1225	36.02	3	4	20
S.G. Hinks	24	44	3	117	1423	34.70	1	9	20
C.S. Cowdrey	19	34	3	159	1035	31.36	2	4	19
E.A.E. Baptiste	21	33	4	82	897	30.93	–	6	12
D.G. Aslett	11	20	1	111	521	27.42	1	1	4
R.M. Ellison	14	22	5	98	457	26.88	–	3	3
C. Penn	8	7	2	50	102	20.40	–	1	9
A.P.E. Knott	19	24	5	87*	379	19.94	–	2	53/1
G.W. Johnson	10	14	3	30*	198	18.00	–	–	5
L. Potter	11	13	2	55	159	14.45	–	1	6
G.R. Dilley	16	19	5	31	153	10.92	–	–	1
D.L. Underwood	23	23	9	16*	121	8.64	–	–	7
K.B.S. Jarvis	18	18	5	7	41	3.15	–	–	5

Also batted: S.A. Marsh (2 matches) 25, 3 (3 ct, 3 st); S.N.V. Waterton 16*, 6* (5 ct, 2 st).

Hundreds (12)

3 M.R. Benson: 162 v Hampshire, Southampton; 102 v Lancs, Manchester; 107 v Yorkshire, Maidstone
   C.J. Tavare: 102* v Hampshire, Southampton; 123 v Yorkshire, Maidstone; 150* v Essex, Dartford.
2 C.S. Cowdrey: 159 v Surrey, Canterbury; 131 v Hampshire, Folkestone.
   N.R. Taylor: 102* v Yorkshire, Scarborough; 100 v Worcs, Worcester.
1 D.G. Aslett: 111 v Surrey, Canterbury.
   S.G. Hinks: 117 v Surrey, Oval.

Bowling	O	M	R	W	Avge	Best	5wI	10wM
R.M. Ellison	318.2	78	863	44	19.61	7-87	3	1
D.L. Underwood	745	277	1635	64	25.54	6-56	1	1
E.A.E. Baptiste	518	106	1521	52	29.25	6-42	2	–
L. Potter	203.3	57	554	18	30.77	4-87	–	–
K.B.S. Jarvis	513.4	111	1636	51	32.93	5-43	2	–
C. Penn	124.4	17	466	14	33.28	4-63	–	–
G.R. Dilley	323.1	62	1031	27	38.18	5-53	2	–
C.S. Cowdrey	200.1	27	721	14	51.50	3-5	–	–

Also bowled: D.G. Aslett 6-0-25-0; M.R. Benson 20.2-0-138-1; S.G. Hinks 21-0-72-1; G.W. Johnson 115.3-16-409-9; N.R. Taylor 52-8-168-5.

Lancashire

For the tenth successive season, Lancashire finished in the bottom six of the Championship table and there were, inevitably, rumbles from all parts as another summer closed so disappointingly.

The principal disappointment was the batting. Of the four players who passed 1,000 runs in 1984, O'Shaughnessy, Ormrod, Abrahams, and Fairbrother, only the last named was able to repeat the feat. O'Shaughnessy was capped and them dropped, while Fowler, triumphant after his winter tour, had a disastrous summer and was also dropped. The England left-hander was handicapped by a neck injury, and Ormrod was unable to return after suffering a fractured cheekbone. By August, Chadwick, Varey, and Hayes were all making runs in sufficient numbers to suggest that any batting crisis would be only temporary, but never at any time was there an aura of confidence and authority about the order.

Allott was one of four Englishmen to finish in the top ten of the national bowling averages and with consistent support would have made a bigger impact on the opposition. Patterson could be as fast and hostile as any bowler in England, but was erratic, unpredictable, and prone to injury. Watkinson is developing into a valuable all-rounder, while Makinson, left-arm fast-medium and a big hitter, had a highly promising first season.

Under Abrahams's cheerful leadership, Lancashire did fulfil their promise to go for a victory whenever possible, but the end result brought seven defeats to three wins. A high-class spinner would be a godsend, but those once fecund nurseries, the Lancashire leagues, are limited in overs and barren.

While Old Trafford continues to expand and shine as a Test match ground, the club must give some thought to the pitch. Complaints, from home and opposing players, of its slow and sluggish nature abound, with neither batsmen nor bowlers having a good word for the surface. A Lancashire revival seems unlikely unless a faster pitch appears at Old Trafford.

The summer had one success, in unlikely circumstances. Rain allowed little cricket at Lytham, but local effort and sponsorship were so impressive that Lancashire soon confirmed a Championship fixture there for the next two years. The Church Road pitch, it is said, will guarantee a result in three days.

Not surprisingly, the season ended with rumours of sweeping changes, but in the event the Committee resolved only on a different captain, John Abrahams standing down to allow Clive Lloyd to resume the office he occupied in 1981-83. As Clive is now relieved of his West Indies' responsibilities, and as 1986 will be the year of his second benefit, all Lancashire will be hoping for the spectacular Indian summer to a great career.

ENGLISH SEASON 1985/LANCASHIRE

Britannic Assurance County Championship: 14th; Won 3, Lost 7, Drawn 14
All First-Class Matches: Won 4, Lost 7, Drawn 14
NatWest Bank Trophy: Lost to Worcestershire in 2nd round
Benson & Hedges Cup: Failed to qualify for Q-F (5th in Group B)
John Player League: 14th; Won 3, Lost 6, Tied 2, No result 5

Championship Averages

Batting and Fielding	M	I	NO	HS	R	Avge	100	50	Ct/St
C.H. Lloyd	4	7	1	131	288	48.00	1	1	4
K.A. Hayes	5	7	0	117	310	44.28	1	2	2
S.T. Jefferies	4	7	0	93	274	39.14	–	3	–
N.H. Fairbrother	24	38	3	164*	1327	37.91	3	6	10
D.J. Makinson	14	21	9	58*	372	31.00	–	1	2
D.W. Varey	20	33	3	87	848	28.26	–	2	5
P.J.W. Allott	14	15	5	78	242	24.20	–	1	4
D.P. Hughes	9	15	1	68	336	24.00	–	2	9
J. Abrahams	24	38	3	77*	831	23.74	–	4	14
M. Watkinson	18	28	1	106	633	23.44	1	3	6
M.R. Chadwick	11	16	1	132	347	23.13	1	–	5
J. Simmons	21	30	4	101	485	18.65	1	2	18
G. Fowler	15	24	0	88	404	16.83	–	1	4
I. Folley	20	27	8	69	262	13.78	–	1	8
S.J.O'Shaughnessy	13	23	2	63	275	13.09	–	1	10
C. Maynard	18	26	4	43	240	10.90	–	–	36/7
J. Stanworth	6	10	2	50*	70	8.75	–	1	6/3
J.A. Ormrod	4	7	0	23	54	7.71	–	–	3
B.P. Patterson	15	15	5	22	38	3.80	–	–	4

Also batted: I.C. Davidson (1 match) 13, 0 (2 ct); A.N. Hayhurst (1 match) 17; S. Henriksen (1 match) 10*, 0* (1 ct); A.J. Murphy (2 matches) 2*, 1, 0.

Hundreds (8)

3 **N.H. Fairbrother:** 128 v Yorkshire, Manchester; 164* v Hampshire, Liverpool; 147 v Yorkshire, Leeds.
1 **M.R. Chadwick:** 132 v Somerset, Manchester.
  K.A. Hayes: 117 v Somerset, Manchester.
  C.H. Lloyd: 131 v Leics, Leicester.
  J. Simmons: 101 v Sussex, Hastings.
  M. Watkinson: 106 v Surrey, Southport.

Bowling	O	M	R	W	Avge	Best	5wI	10wM
P.J.W. Allott	403.2	128	927	49	18.91	6-71	3	–
S.T. Jefferies	116.1	13	379	12	31.58	4-64	–	–
B.P. Patterson	341.5	54	1085	34	31.91	6-45	2	1
D.J. Makinson	346	62	1029	31	33.19	5-60	1	–
S.J.O'Shaughnessy	142	21	521	15	34.73	4-68	–	–
M. Watkinson	391.5	83	1182	34	34.76	5-109	1	–
I. Folley	436.3	100	1271	35	36.31	4-39	–	–
J. Simmons	543.1	155	1427	37	38.56	4-55	–	–

Also bowled: J. Abrahams 25.2-7-93-3; M.R. Chadwick 5-0-20-0; I.C. Davidson 10-3-24-2; N.H. Fairbrother 26-7-75-1; A.N. Hayhurst 13-4-37-3; S. Henriksen 12-1-44-1; D.P. Hughes 21-12-26-1; A.J. Murphy 56.2-15-207-6.

Leicestershire

After finishing in the top ten in each of the previous 15 seasons and in the top four in the last three, Leicestershire's headlong plummet to 16th in the Championship was probably the summer's most startling decline. The departure 'by mutual consent' of left-arm-spinner Nick Cook and seamer Gordon Parsons and the retirement at 25 of wicket-keeper Mike Garnham inevitably fuelled rumours of dressing-room disharmony. But victory in the Benson & Hedges Cup final and a modest rise of four places in the John Player League argued against such speculation. In any case, more obvious causes were available.

Leicestershire lost more than 110 hours of playing time to rain and bad light, more than all but three other counties, and were for much of the summer depleted by the calls of the England selectors. Captain David Gower was limited to only 19 innings for his county. Leicestershire had also, on various occasions, to manage without the all-round talent and bristling professionalism of Peter Willey and the penetration of their two most successful seamers, Les Taylor and Jon Agnew.

With Gordon Ferris, absent through injury in 1984, fit again but all too often luridly inaccurate, and Parsons unable to recapture the zest that earned him 67 first-class victims in that year, Leicestershire's limitations in the spin-bowling department were cast into harsher relief. Willey's off-spin was reliable as a weapon of containment, but with Cook an apparently disaffected figure, his 30 wickets costing more than 44 runs each, the side were starved of alternatives when, as was often the case, pitches offered nothing to encourage seam.

Clift shouldered more than 600 overs, many when conditions did not encourage either of his modes, and claimed his first hat-trick in ten seasons, against Derbyshire on one of those rare occasions when there was some life and bounce. Taylor, enjoying more reliable fitness after two seasons of injury problems, and Agnew, proving that 1984 was no flash in the pan, shared the top two places in the bowling averages with 104 Championship wickets between them. When England called them, there was much to impress in the form of Philip De Freitas. The 19-year-old Dominican took 27 wickets in only 235 overs, and his ability to make the best batsmen play and miss no doubt influenced the decision to allow Parsons to leave.

Willey's match-winning innings in the Benson & Hedges Cup final was the focus of another season of consistent success with the bat. But the season ended with suggestions that his unsparing brand of man-management in Gower's absences was bruising some of the more sensitive natures.

Balderstone, Whitaker, and Butcher topped 1,000 runs and Cobb hinted at maturing technique, but with Boon missing the whole season following a car crash and Briers a diminished force, Leicestershire occasionally seemed short of experienced batting cover.

Garnham curbed anarchic tendencies to stay clear of disciplinary trouble and claim 60 victims, while Whitticase, his young deputy, added a maiden half-century to some secure performances behind the wicket to stimulate hopes that this particular change in first-team personnel will be achieved without a stutter.

Britannic Assurance County Championship: 16th; Won 2, Lost 3, Drawn 19
All First-Class Matches: Won 3, Lost 3, Drawn 20
NatWest Bank Trophy: Lost to Hampshire in second round
Benson & Hedges Cup: Winners
John Player League: 6th; Won 5, Lost 5, Tied 1, No result 5

Championship Averages

Batting and Fielding	M	I	NO	HS	R	Avge	100	50	Ct/St
P. Willey	19	28	3	147	1194	47.76	3	5	10
D.I. Gower	12	17	2	128	575	38.33	2	2	1
J.J. Whitaker	23	32	3	109	1085	37.41	3	5	4
P. Whitticase	3	5	1	55*	149	37.25	–	1	9
J.C. Balderstone	23	37	4	101	1130	34.24	1	6	9
R.A. Cobb	16	23	4	78	601	31.63	–	4	11
I.P. Butcher	23	36	2	120	1043	30.67	1	7	18
N.E. Briers	21	27	4	129	561	24.39	1	1	7
P.B. Clift	21	25	5	106	472	23.60	1	1	9
M. Blackett	2	4	2	28*	41	20.50	–	–	–
M.A. Garnham	21	24	3	51	415	19.76	–	1	46/7
P.A.J. De Freitas	8	11	3	30*	117	14.62	–	–	2
G.J. Parsons	14	14	4	32	139	13.90	–	–	–
N.G.B. Cook	17	15	4	45	151	13.72	–	–	7
G.J.F. Ferris	10	9	6	22*	29	9.66	–	–	–
L.B. Taylor	16	15	7	20*	77	9.62	–	–	5
J.P. Agnew	14	13	2	36	100	9.09	–	–	3

Also batted: D.J. Billington (1 match) 19 (1 ct).
Hundreds (12)

3 J.J. Whitaker: 109 v Surrey, Leicester; 105 v Somerset, Taunton; 103 v Glamorgan, Swansea.
 P. Willey: 133 v Derbys, Leicester; 101 v Derbys, Chesterfield; 147 v Northants, Northampton.
2 D.I. Gower: 100* v Glamorgan, Leicester; 128 v Sussex, Hove.
1 J.C. Balderstone: 101 v Glamorgan, Swansea.
 N.E. Briers: 129 v Essex, Chelmsford.
 I.P. Butcher: 120 v Notts, Nottingham.
 P.B. Clift: 106 v Essex, Chelmsford.

Bowling	O	M	R	W	Avge	Best	5wI	10wM
L.B. Taylor	472.2	120	1102	52	21.19	5-45	3	–
J.P. Agnew	396.4	85	1269	52	24.40	9-70	3	1
P. Willey	343.5	102	834	31	26.90	6-43	3	–
P.A.J. De Freitas	208.4	34	619	21	29.47	5-39	1	–
P.B. Clift	577.3	165	1407	45	31.26	5-38	1	–
N.G.B. Cook	529.1	177	1245	29	42.93	4-59	–	–
G.J.F. Ferris	231.3	32	826	15	55.06	3-84	–	–
G.J. Parsons	306.2	61	869	14	62.07	3-31	–	–

Also bowled: J.C. Balderstone 15-3-68-1; N.E. Briers 88-18-303-8; I.P. Butcher 2-1-5-0; D.I. Gower 2.1-0-16-0.

Middlesex

In winning the County Championship at the end of a Test summer that removed Mike Gatting, John Emburey, Phil Edmonds, and Paul Downton for 10 matches and Norman Cowans for four, Middlesex clearly demonstrated the virtues of depth and dependability in the traditional campaign. That they again failed to come to terms with the Sunday style of cricket and could not reach the final of either knock-out competition was, perhaps, an acceptable side-effect.

Another, more positive, factor arose in the necessary introduction of youthful replacements for the absent Test players. Long-term aspirants such as Carr and Sykes, both spinner/batsmen, Rose and Fraser, strongly built pace bowlers, and wicketkeeper Metson all gained valuable experience – not least in the gratifying disciplines of winning.

From the onset of the Championship, Middlesex were always among the front runners, and there was little comfort for opponents in the absence of those senior players. Indeed, several of the more stirring performances were achieved by the 'B-team'. At Bournemouth, for example, with only Edmonds spared by the England selectors, it was Sykes (52) and Hughes (30) whose unbroken ninth-wicket partnership of 84 earned Middlesex a fighting draw. Again, at Worcester in June, lacking all five Test men, they were magnificently served by Rose who, on his Championship debut, claimed six for 41 to set up a Middlesex victory, by three wickets, which sent them to the top of the table.

It must be emphasized, however, that the 'old guard' were also in splendid form, notably Slack and Barlow who, in that same encounter, produced their third three-figure opening stand in consecutive Championship matches: 203 against Leicester, at Lord's, 171 against Notts, at Trent Bridge, and exactly 100 against Worcestershire.

The remarkable Radley, unruffled – inspired, even – by his frequent calls to the helm, seemed determined to match the batting as well as the leadership of Gatting. The club captain hit 90 against Kent at Lord's and an undefeated 143 in the Benson & Hedges fixture at Hove. Radley promptly produced 127 not out at Cardiff and, eight days later, 105 not out at the Oval.

Butcher, too, conjured several spectacular innings, two of which, coincidentally, were instrumental in the double success against Worcestershire. At Lord's he sped Middlesex to victory with an undefeated 80 in little over an hour, and at Worcester he emerged unbeaten with a dazzling 120.

Daniel, Cowans, Williams, and the two spinners – as available – bowled with great application throughout the campaign. So, too, did the newcomers. It was almost inevitable, therefore, and thoroughly deserved, that Middlesex should win the Championship.

Occasional shortcomings were best epitomized, perhaps, in their performances against sides whose general approach contained elements of audacity – a quality particularly valuable in the limited-overs context. Essex, whom they failed to beat in any competition all season, provided a notable example with two victories over them in the Benson & Hedges series, one in the NatWest, and one in the Championship.

Britannic Assurance County Championship: 1st; Won 8, Lost 4, Drawn 12
All First-Class Matches: Won 8, Lost 4, Drawn 14
NatWest Bank Trophy: Lost to Essex in second round
Benson & Hedges Cup: Lost to Essex in semi-final
John Player League: 12th; Won 5, Lost 7, No result 4

Championship Averages

Batting and Fielding	M	I	NO	HS	R	Avge	100	50	Ct/St
C.T. Radley	24	32	8	200	1260	52.50	3	7	10
M.W. Gatting	14	21	2	114	936	49.26	1	8	18
G.D. Barlow	20	32	4	141	1343	47.96	6	2	6
W.N. Slack	24	41	7	112	1618	47.58	3	10	27
P.R. Downton	14	20	5	104	687	45.80	1	5	34/4
R.O. Butcher	24	36	6	120	1154	38.46	1	8	24
J.E. Emburey	15	16	1	68	432	28.80	–	4	14
K.R. Brown	7	10	2	67	196	24.50	–	1	8
K.P. Tomlins	8	13	0	58	306	23.53	–	1	6
N.F. Williams	19	20	4	46	311	19.43	–	–	3
J.F. Sykes	10	12	3	52*	149	16.55	–	1	9
S.P. Hughes	11	11	5	30*	94	15.66	–	–	6
P.H. Edmonds	15	16	5	29*	155	14.09	–	–	11
C.P. Metson	8	9	3	14*	59	9.83	–	–	18
J.D. Carr	5	7	0	29	59	8.42	–	–	3
N.G. Cowans	19	14	2	15*	99	8.25	–	–	5
W.W. Daniel	22	15	5	19*	48	4.80	–	–	7

Also batted: A.J.T. Miller (2 matches) 16, 15, 13*; G.D. Rose (2 matches) 4, 15.
A.R.C. Fraser (1 match) did not bat.

Hundreds (15)

6 G.D. Barlow: 115 v Surrey, Oval; 102 v Leics, Lord's; 103* v Worcs, Worcester; 141 v Northants, Northampton; 112 v Notts, Lord's; 132 v Somerset, Lord's.
3 C.T. Radley: 127 v Glamorgan, Cardiff; 105* v Surrey, Oval; 200 v Northants, Uxbridge.
W.N. Slack: 105 v Kent, Lord's; 109 v Leics, Lord's; 112 v Notts, Nottingham.
1 R.O. Butcher: 120 v Worcs, Worcester.
P.R. Downton: 104 v Northants, Uxbridge.
M.W. Gatting: 114 v Essex, Lords.

Bowling	O	M	R	W	Avge	Best	5wI	10wM
N.G. Cowans	372.4	65	1286	60	21.43	6-31	4	–
P.H. Edmonds	542	158	1206	51	23.64	6-87	2	–
W.W. Daniel	575.1	89	2111	79	26.72	7-62	2	–
N.F. Williams	434.2	65	1542	54	28.55	5-15	2	–
J.E. Emburey	451	106	976	30	32.53	6-35	1	–
S.P. Hughes	246.2	42	871	23	37.86	5-64	1	–
J.F. Sykes	175.5	41	540	13	41.53	3-58	–	–

Also bowled: G.D. Barlow 3-0-14-0; R.O. Butcher 18-5-39-2; J.D. Carr 65.1-17-154-9; P.R. Downton 8-6-5-0; A.R.C. Fraser 19.5-3-71-4; M.W. Gatting 73.5-15-222-8; C.T. Radley 13-3-43-2; G.D. Rose 45.1-8-142-9; W.N. Slack 9-1-29-0; K.P. Tomlins 2-0-9-0.

Northamptonshire

Northants improved only one place in the Championship table to finish 10th, but at least in the last fortnight of the season they did play a prominent part in the outcome of the Championship. At Bristol, their last-wicket pair of Mallender and Griffiths surprised the third county Gloucestershire by holding on for 8 overs for a draw, and then in the next match, at Southampton, their last-wicket pair – this time Harper and Griffiths – were again involved in an exciting finish. In a memorable match, Northants won by one wicket to thwart the runners-up Hampshire. Off the last ball, Hampshire had required one wicket and Northants 6 runs to win. Harper duly struck the winning blow with a straight drive for 6, and it was indeed appropriate that the triumphant batsman here was the 22-year-old West Indian all-rounder.

This was Harper's first season for the county, and what a successful recruit he proved, with aggressive batting and off-spin bowling. He was, arguably, the best No. 8 in the country, with innings of 127 against Kent and 97 not out against the champions Middlesex. He was Northants' leading bowler, with 58 wickets, while his brilliant slip fielding distinctly added to his invaluable all-round contributions.

Northants gained little reward with the ball, and only the bottom team, Somerset, and Glamorgan scored fewer bowling points. Mallender had some success with the new ball, but the averages were, remarkably, headed by Griffiths. At 36, in his 11th season, Griffiths won his place in the team in the second half of the season only because Walker was injured. But in the last 12 matches he bowled with vintage economy to take 31 wickets at 27 runs apiece.

In batting, Northants were fortunate to have the two most experienced of all opening partners in Larkins and, in his benefit year, Cook. Once again they were the leading run scorers. There was much expected from the bat of Bailey, 21, who had shown such potential the previous season. However, he struggled at first, before finding his timing to hit 107 against the Australians and becoming the third Northants batsman to complete 1,000 runs for the season.

One new batsman who certainly made his mark was Storie. This Glaswegian-born, South-African-raised, and now English-qualified 19-year-old made his debut against Hampshire at the beginning of May when Cook was injured. He opened the innings and scored 106, and, although dropping down the order on his captain's return, went on to head the batting averages. Storie played only 12 innings, from 4 May until the end of June, before returning to the 2nd XI, but in that time his dedication and temperament marked him down as a prospective opener.

The wicket-keeper and vice-captain Sharp retired after breaking a finger against Warwickshire, at Edgbaston, in late June. In 305 matches for the county he captured 654 victims (564 caught, 90 stumped), a haul surpassed only by Keith Andrew.

ENGLISH SEASON 1985/NORTHAMPTONSHIRE 161

Britannic Assurance County Championship: 10th; Won 5, Lost 4, Drawn 15
All First-Class Matches: Won 5, Lost 4, Drawn 16
NatWest Bank Trophy: Lost to Gloucestershire in second round
Benson & Hedges Cup: Lost to Kent in quarter-final
John Player League: 5th; Won 7, Lost 4, Tied 1, No result 4

Championship Averages

Batting and Fielding	M	I	NO	HS	R	Avge	100	50	Ct/St
A.C. Storie	7	12	2	106	407	40.70	1	3	3
R.A. Harper	22	26	7	127	734	38.63	1	3	20
G. Cook	23	37	4	126	1271	38.51	1	9	19
W. Larkins	24	39	0	163	1490	38.20	3	4	18
R.J. Bailey	24	36	6	101	1054	35.13	1	7	5
A.J. Lamb	11	17	2	111	525	35.00	1	4	6
R.G. Williams	20	30	2	118	845	30.17	2	4	2
D.J. Wild	18	22	4	80	525	29.16	–	2	4
R.J. Boyd-Moss	19	30	3	121	748	27.70	2	2	6
D.J. Capel	22	30	6	81	599	24.95	–	5	5
N.A. Mallender	23	25	8	52*	267	15.70	–	1	5
A. Walker	12	14	8	18*	83	13.83	–	–	6
G. Sharp	11	13	1	25	111	9.25	–	–	16/3
D. Ripley	13	14	4	27	83	8.30	–	–	21/4
B.J. Griffiths	12	9	4	12	17	3.40	–	–	2

Also batted: R.F. Joseph (2 matches) 26*. M.B.H. Wheeler (1 match) did not bat.

Hundreds (12)

3 W. Larkins: 117 v Surrey, Northampton; 140 v Notts, Northampton; 163 v Worcs, Worcester.
2 R.J. Boyd-Moss: 121 v Glamorgan, Wellingborough; 121 v Worcs, Worcester.
  R.G. Williams: 118 v Warwicks, Northampton; 103 v Derbys, Northampton.
1 R.J. Bailey: 101 v Hampshire, Northampton
  G. Cook: 126 v Warwicks, Northampton.
  R.A. Harper: 127 v Kent, Maidstone.
  A.J. Lamb: 111 v Essex, Northampton.
  A.C. Storie: 106 v Hampshire, Northampton.

Bowling	O	M	R	W	Avge	Best	5wI	10wM
B.J. Griffiths	288.4	71	846	31	27.29	6-76	1	–
D.J. Capel	362.3	63	1192	40	29.80	7-62	1	–
N.A. Mallender	521.4	98	1533	49	31.28	5-83	1	–
A. Walker	251.4	51	786	23	34.17	4-38	–	–
R.A. Harper	764.3	185	2080	58	35.86	5-94	1	–
R.J. Boyd-Moss	125.4	30	380	10	38.00	3-48	–	–
R.G. Williams	291.2	70	913	23	39.69	5-34	1	–

Also bowled: R.J. Bailey 3-0-16-0; G Cook 1-0-6-0; R.F. Joseph 38-5-143-4; A.J. Lamb 1-1-0-0; W. Larkins 77-16-258-1; G. Sharp 1-0-2-0; A.C. Storie 18-6-51-0; M.B.H. Wheeler 14-3-30-0; D.J. Wild 82.5-7-368-2.

Nottinghamshire

The consolidation of Tim Robinson's reputation as a player of international quality, a flood of runs from Derek Randall, and a marvellously sustained if unsuccessful bid for the NatWest Trophy all provided Nottinghamshire supporters with cause to remember 1985. But, judged overall, the final report could say no more than 'satisfactory'.

Nottinghamshire slid to eighth in the Championship, after finishing second the previous year, and their record of only four wins compared to 12 in 1984 was all the more disappointing since only one of them was at home. In the John Player League, in which they were runners-up the previous summer, Notts dipped to 12th place, and in the Benson & Hedges Cup they failed to reach the quarter-final stage after miserable treatment from the weather.

Dwindling returns from both seam- and spin-bowling departments provided the most obvious cause of this regression, though Hadlee could be excused for bowling 300 overs fewer than in his prodigious 'double' season, and he still finished second in the national averages with 59 victims. Cooper again thrived on hard work, unsettling the best batsmen when there was some sap in the conditions, but Saxelby suffered fluctuations of form and fitness, and Pick, though brisk and keen, lacked the necessary command of line and length. Rice, sparingly employed and at a sedate pace these days, helped to share the seamers' work-load. But Notts were often compelled to lean heavily on the spinners even in unhelpful conditions. Hemmings, though not the most streamlined cricketer, again reeled off more than 700 overs, but only latterly discovered his best form, improving his best-of-season figures three times in consecutive matches. Such also had problems in achieving consistency.

The declining standards of the bowling assumed greater significance with the knowledge that Hadlee would miss much of the following season on international duty.

That no more startling a fall-off in results was occasioned was to the credit of the batsmen, with Robinson, Rice, and Randall all averaging better that 50 and Broad admirably consistent with more than 1,700 runs.

Randall, whose previous highest aggregate was 1,546 in 1976, made six centuries and nineteen times scored 50 or more to earn selection as Britannia Assurance's 'Championship Player of the Year'. Hadlee, though also less prolific with the bat, often made his runs at a significant gallop, and there was rich promise in the development of Johnson, cruelly denied a place at Lord's by appendicitis. His exceptional fielding was missed as much as his ability to score quickly. Birch's struggles provided a chance in mid-season for another member of Nottinghamshire's 2nd XI Championship winning side, Duncan Martindale, and his maiden century was followed by several more innings of high potential.

French had fewer opportunities to build an innings, but his wicket-keeping, efficient and unobtrusive, claimed 73 victims.

ENGLISH SEASON 1985/NOTTINGHAMSHIRE 163

Britannic Assurance County Championship: 8th; Won 4, Lost 2, Drawn 18
All First-Class Matches: Won 4, Lost 2, Drawn 19
NatWest Bank Trophy: Lost to Essex in final
Benson & Hedges Cup: Failed to qualify for Q-F (3rd in Group A)
John Player League: 12th; Won 6, Lost 8, No result 2

Championship Averages

Batting and Fielding	M	I	NO	HS	R	Avge	100	50	Ct/St
R.T. Robinson	11	21	3	130*	1107	61.50	4	8	8
C.E.B. Rice	20	33	8	171*	1394	55.76	4	6	21
D.W. Randall	24	45	6	117	1977	50.69	4	13	24
B.C. Broad	24	45	3	171	1706	40.61	2	13	15
R.J. Hadlee	19	29	11	73*	592	32.88	–	5	17
P. Johnson	20	32	4	118	890	31.78	1	6	13
D.J.R. Martindale	9	14	3	104*	317	28.81	1	1	6
B. Hassan	3	5	1	34	109	27.25	–	–	4
J.D. Birch	13	21	6	68*	392	26.13	–	2	4
R.A. Pick	12	14	4	63	240	24.00	–	1	3
E.E. Hemmings	21	22	5	56*	297	17.47	–	1	7
B.N. French	23	33	8	52*	432	17.28	–	1	61/7
M. Newell	6	11	0	59	177	16.09	–	1	2
K.E. Cooper	21	16	4	46	139	11.58	–	–	4
C.D. Fraser-Darling	2	4	1	23*	33	11.00	–	–	4
K. Saxelby	17	13	4	29*	78	8.66	–	–	1
P.M. Such	14	12	5	8	18	2.57	–	–	7

Also batted: J.A. Afford (2 matches) 2 (2ct); K.P. Evans (2 matches) 11, 0. C.W. Scott (1 match) did not bat.

Hundreds (16)

4 **D.W. Randall**: 117 v Essex, Nottingham; 108* v Leics, Nottingham; 106 v Surrey, Oval; 115 v Middlesex, Lord's.
C.E.B. Rice: 108* v Essex, Nottingham; 171* v Leics, Nottingham; 156* v Warwicks, Nuneaton; 101 v Hampshire, Nottingham.
R.T. Robinson: 105 v Somerset, Taunton; 103 and 130* v Glamorgan, Swansea. 118 v Yorkshire, Scarborough.
2 **B.C. Broad**: 171 v Derbys, Derby; 131 v Yorkshire, Worksop.
1 **P. Johnson**: 118 v Leics, Nottingham.
D.J.R. Martindale: 104* v Lancs, Manchester.

Bowling	O	M	R	W	Avge	Best	5wI	10wM
R.J. Hadlee	473.5	136	1026	59	17.38	8-41	2	–
K.E. Cooper	576.3	168	1552	53	29.28	6-53	1	–
C.E.B. Rice	284	82	779	25	31.16	4-24	–	–
P.M. Such	405.1	105	1152	32	36.00	5-73	1	–
K. Saxelby	404	95	1333	35	38.08	6-64	2	1
E.E. Hemmings	716.3	171	2103	55	38.23	6-51	2	–
R.A. Pick	267	44	1021	25	40.84	4-51	–	–

Also bowled: J.A. Afford 22-3-76-2; J.D. Birch 5-0-14-0; B.C. Broad 9.3-2-40-2; K.P. Evans 9-1-38-0; C.D. Fraser-Darling 19-3-88-0; P. Johnson 23-3-129-1; D.J.R. Martindale 2-0-8-0; M. Newell 9-2-38-1; D.W. Randall 28-2-174-5.

Somerset

If proof were ever needed of the old adage that bowlers win matches, Somerset provided it last season. Their batting, which varied from the proficient to the explosively prolific, provided them with more Championship bonus points than any other county, while their bowling earned the least. They finished bottom in the Championship, marked time in the lower reaches of the John Player League, and made no impression in the NatWest or Benson & Hedges competitions. Had they bowled only half as well as they batted, they must have been contenders in all types of cricket.

Vivian Richards, frequently at his most masterful, headed the first-class averages, as he had in 1983. He hit nine centuries, more than any other player in the country, and his 322 against Warwickshire at Taunton in June is the highest score ever by a Somerset player, eclipsing Harold Gimblett's 310 at Eastbourne in 1948. Ian Botham averaged 100 for the county and hit the ball as far and as often as anyone in the game's history. He hit the fastest century at Edgbaston in July, reaching three figures off only 50 balls.

Roebuck, as reliable as ever, had a most satisfactory season, and Popplewell, who towards the end of the campaign announced his retirement, batted adventurously and effectively. Marks, while not scoring as heavily as in 1984, still made nearly 900 runs. Of the younger batsmen, Felton and Wyatt both made significant progress and Harden made a good first impression.

The bowlers by contrast had the leanest of times. Garner, suffering increasingly from problems with his knees, was frequently unavailable. When fit, he proved as hard to get away as ever, but seemed to have lost some of his destructive power. Davis, who had taken 66 wickets in 1984 and had regularly made inroads into opponents' early batting, fell right away. He struggled throughout to find his rhythm, and his tally of wickets dropped to 24 at over 50 runs apiece.

Botham's ability to take Test wickets was not reflected in his county performances, and the slow-left armer Booth, though steady enough, did not possess the power of spin to disturb good batsmen. A small item on the credit side was Dredge's good recovery from a knee operation. Though his overall figures were not impressive, he was bowling with much of his old vigour and tenacity by the end of the season.

Marks must also be excluded from the general strictures. He bowled well over twice as many overs as anyone else and took 72 wickets, though it must be said that these cost him over 7 runs each more than had his victims in 1984. Coombs, a 26-year-old slow left-armer who has just finished a course at Exeter University, appeared in four matches in August. He bowled steadily and intelligently, taking 16 wickets at low cost, and his development will be watched with interest.

Botham resigned the captaincy in early October on the grounds that Test and other commitments prevented him giving the job 100 per cent. Peter Roebuck was appointed in his place.

ENGLISH SEASON 1985/SOMERSET

Britannic Assurance County Championship: 17th; Won 1, Lost 7, Drawn 16
All First-Class Matches: Won 1, Lost 8, Drawn 18
NatWest Bank Trophy: Lost to Hampshire in quarter-final
Benson & Hedges Cup: Failed to qualify for Q-F (4th in Group D)
John Player League: 10th; Won 5, Lost 6, No result 5

Championship Averages

Batting and Fielding	M	I	NO	HS	R	Avge	100	50	Ct/St
I.T. Botham	11	17	5	152	1211	100.91	5	6	5
I.V.A. Richards	19	24	0	322	1836	76.50	9	6	9
J.C.M. Atkinson	6	5	1	79	167	41.75	–	1	–
P.M. Roebuck	19	29	3	132*	1058	40.69	1	7	9
N.F.M. Popplewell	16	27	1	172	972	37.38	1	6	9
M.S. Turner	7	10	6	24*	134	33.50	–	–	1
N.A. Felton	17	25	0	112	794	31.76	1	5	3
V.J. Marks	24	32	5	82	787	29.14	–	6	8
J.G. Wyatt	15	23	0	100	620	26.95	1	2	6
R.J. Harden	10	13	4	52*	240	26.66	–	1	7
M.R. Davis	15	17	6	40*	274	24.90	–	–	4
G.V. Palmer	7	11	3	45*	164	20.50	–	–	2
C.H. Dredge	14	12	6	31	119	19.83	–	–	6
R.E. Hayward	8	11	2	57*	178	19.77	–	1	3
P.A.C. Bail	5	9	2	78*	127	18.14	–	1	–
R.L. Ollis	12	16	1	55	271	18.06	–	1	4
S.C. Booth	8	6	2	28	69	17.25	–	–	10
B.C. Rose	4	8	0	43	115	14.37	–	–	2
J. Garner	15	11	3	22	92	11.50	–	–	4
T. Gard	23	23	3	47	230	11.50	–	–	30/7
A.P. Jones	3	4	2	1*	3	1.50	–	–	1

Also batted: R.V.J. Coombs (4 matches) 0, 0, 1; S.A.R. Ferguson (1 match) 8; S.J. Turner (1 match) 9* (2ct, 2st).

Hundreds (18)

9 **I.V.A. Richards:** 186 v Hampshire, Taunton; 105 v Yorkshire, Leeds; 322 v Warwicks, Taunton; 100 v Glamorgan, Cardiff; 135 v Middlesex, Lord's; 120 v Lancs, Manchester; 123 v Derbys, Derby; 112 v Sussex, Taunton; 125 v Worcs, Taunton.
5 **I.T. Botham:** 112 v Glamorgan, Taunton; 149 v Hampshire, Taunton; 138* v Warwicks, Birmingham; 152 v Essex, Taunton; 134 v Northants, Weston-super-Mare.
1 **N.A. Felton:** 112 v Leics, Taunton.
N.F.M. Popplewell: 172 v Essex, Southend.
P.M. Roebuck: 132* v Worcs, Taunton.
J.G. Wyatt: 100 v Hampshire, Bournemouth.

Bowling	O	M	R	W	Avge	Best	5wI	10wM
R.V.J. Coombs	93	27	268	16	16.75	5-58	1	–
J. Garner	295.4	75	739	31	23.83	5-46	1	–
V.J. Marks	745.4	180	2208	67	32.95	8-17	4	2
C.H. Dredge	286	61	863	21	41.09	5-95	1	–
I.T. Botham	130.4	25	464	11	42.18	4-63	–	–
S.C. Booth	275.2	73	819	19	43.10	4-88	–	–
M.R. Davis	298	45	1029	19	54.15	4-83	–	–

Also bowled: J.C.M. Atkinson 65-9-250-2; P.A.C. Bail 4-2-4-0; R.J. Harden 8.3-2-29-1; A.P. Jones 37-4-142-3; G.V. Palmer 147-13-627-7; N.F.M. Popplewell 18-1-95-0; I.V.A. Richards 183-48-494-7; P.M. Roebuck 7-0-28-0; B.C. Rose 1-0-8-0; M.S. Turner 121.4-22-403-8; J.G. Wyatt 9-0-58-1.

Surrey

It was symptomatic of Surrey's status over the past five years that they ended the 1985 season much as they began – slightly better than average at the traditional game but with little to celebrate – sixth in the Championship, bottom of the John Player League, and nowhere in the Benson & Hedges or NatWest competitions.

Their season began with personnel problems that reflected a lack of depth and experience already hinted by the appointment of 36-year-old Trevor Jesty to replace 39-year-old Roger Knight. The absence of Clarke and the illness of Monkhouse were sorely felt at the Oval, when Glamorgan scored 218 in 145 minutes to win the opening match. That Clarke would miss the entire season was confirmed at Canterbury, where Stewart (158) and Lynch (115) suggested, in a high-scoring draw, that Surrey's batsmen could be relied upon to keep the county afloat. And so it proved throughout a Championship campaign in which Clinton, Butcher, Lynch, Stewart, Needham, and Jesty all prospered.

The scramble for a new pace bowler produced Gray, whose importation from Trinidad posed an embarrassing registration problem that led to the standing down of Howarth, Surrey's New Zealand captain, in favour of Pocock, reluctantly, then Jesty – whose unrequited ambitions in this direction had precipitated his move from Hampshire.

Gray made his debut at Edgbaston on May 22 – a match in which Jesty, coincidentally, recorded his first century for the county. Gray took time to settle to English conditions but, by mid-June, was proving an inspired replacement for Clarke. He ended the season with 79 wickets at an average of 22.98 compared with Clarke's 78 at 21.62 in 1984.

What Surrey clearly lacked, however, was a bowler of similar consistency to share the opening attack. Sickness and injury, which plagued the ranks throughout the season, affected – among others – Thomas, Monkhouse, and Taylor, and, again in some desperation, Surrey found relief in the introduction of Doughty, whose six for 33 at the Oval played a significant part in the two-day rout of Warwickshire at the beginning of August.

For the most part, however, Surrey's steady Championship progress relied heavily on their batsmen and all-rounders, not least Needham, whose five for 42 against Lancashire complemented a successful summer in which, for the first time, he scored 1,000 runs. He, Stewart, and Gray were duly rewarded with county caps as the season closed.

Equally as remarkable as Doughty's emergence was the recruitment of Ward, a Banstead Club cricketer who, on August 3, was rushed to Derby as a replacement for virus victim Jesty. Arriving during the lunch interval, Ward, batting at number seven, scored a maiden century in 135 minutes with seventeen fours.

In view of Surrey's apparent wealth of articulate batsmen – not least the dashing Lynch – their abject failure in the Sunday League was difficult to comprehend – except, perhaps, that they were not the most energetic fielding side. Having said that, it is interesting to note that

Lynch not only continued to catch the eye among Surrey's somewhat sober personalities, but caught the ball more frequently than anyone in the country. At the end of the season he led the national list with 36.

Britannic Assurance County Championship: 6th; Won 5, Lost 5, Drawn 14
All First-Class Matches: Won 5, Lost 5, Drawn 16
NatWest Bank Trophy: Lost to Kent in first round
Benson & Hedges Cup: Failed to qualify for Q-F (3rd in Group C).
John Player League: 17th; Won 4, Lost 9, No result 3

Championship Averages

Batting and Fielding	M	I	NO	HS	R	Avge	100	50	Ct/St
M.A. Lynch	24	37	7	145	1672	55.73	7	6	36
D.M. Ward	5	8	3	143	256	51.20	1	–	2
G.S. Clinton	18	32	6	123	1225	47.11	3	7	13
C.J. Richards	22	27	12	75*	665	44.33	–	3	41/7
T.E. Jesty	23	34	7	141*	1072	39.70	3	4	19
A. Needham	23	33	4	138	1032	35.58	2	5	10
G. Monkhouse	15	14	8	47	203	33.83	–	–	8
A.R. Butcher	24	42	3	126	1233	33.32	2	5	10
A.J. Stewart	21	32	3	158	886	30.55	1	4	27/1
D.B. Pauline	12	16	2	77	374	26.71	–	3	4
R.J. Doughty	10	12	2	65	239	23.90	–	2	8
N.S. Taylor	6	7	3	21*	51	17.00	–	–	–
P.I. Pocock	23	18	6	41	183	15.25	–	–	2
C.K. Bullen	2	4	0	19	53	13.25	–	–	2
D.J. Thomas	11	12	3	25*	116	12.88	–	–	2
A.H. Gray	19	10	1	20	48	5.33	–	–	3

Also batted: M.A. Feltham (1 match) 8, 27; K.T. Medlycott (1 match) 5; P.A. Waterman (4 matches) 0, 1* (2ct).

Hundreds (19)

7 **M.A. Lynch:** 115 v Kent, Canterbury; 144* v Middlesex, Oval; 133 v Yorkshire, Sheffield; 145 v Warwicks, Oval; 121 v Yorkshire, Oval; 108 v Middlesex, Lord's; 110 v Glos, Oval.
3 **G.S. Clinton:** 106 v Essex, Oval; 117 v Worcs, Worcester; 123 v Sussex, Oval.
  T.E. Jesty: 126 v Warwicks, Birmingham; 112* v Essex, Oval; 141* v Yorkshire, Oval.
2 **A.R. Butcher:** 121 v Glamorgan, Oval; 126 v Notts, Oval.
  A. Needham: 132 v Notts, Oval; 138 v Warwicks, Oval.
1 **A.J. Stewart:** 158 v Kent, Canterbury.
  D.M. Ward: 143 v Derbys, Derby.

Bowling	O	M	R	W	Avge	Best	5wI	10wM
A.H. Gray	524	99	1816	79	22.98	8-40	6	1
R.J. Doughty	207.5	35	806	31	26.00	6-33	1	–
G. Monkhouse	370.5	76	1020	37	27.56	5-61	1	–
D.J. Thomas	328.2	54	1055	32	32.96	5-51	1	–
P.I. Pocock	564.2	127	1608	47	34.21	7-42	1	–
T.E. Jesty	144.2	28	517	14	36.92	2-32	–	–
D.B. Pauline	158.4	31	560	15	37.33	5-52	1	–
A.R. Butcher	150	32	439	10	43.90	3-43	–	–
A. Needham	326.4	67	978	22	44.45	5-42	1	–

Also bowled: C.K. Bullen 7-1-39-0; G.S. Clinton 6-0-46-0; M.A. Feltham 11-1-74-0; M.A. Lynch 6-1-46-0; C.J. Richards 27-2-120-4; A.J. Stewart 6-0-43-0; N.S. Taylor 120.2-16-516-9; P.A. Waterman 69-11-284-5.

Sussex

With Imran Khan fit to bowl at speed again after three years, Sussex would have started the season optimistically. But their only major achievement was second prize in the John Player League. In the County Championship, they dropped a rung. They failed to qualify for the Benson & Hedges quarter-finals, and had only a brief career in the NatWest Trophy.

By previous arrangement, Imran played in only 13 Championship matches. Club and Imran were mutually agreed that he would be most effective if he staggered his appearances. Indeed, Imran did not spare himself. He often bowled long spells, and with full effort. With the bat too, Imran achieved a remarkable consistency. By some distance, he topped the averages in both departments, his figures befitting an outstanding all-rounder.

Another area of strength was the opening partnership of Mendis and Green. Mendis made six hundreds and as many 50s, while Green scored three hundreds and ten 50s, among them three scores above 90. In the Championship, they staged six century partnerships. But apart from them, no batsman reached a thousand. Likewise, among the bowlers, only Imran touched the 50-wickets mark.

Undeniably, there was an element of ill-luck in Sussex's plight. The bareness of their fixture list in the early part of the season made it difficult for them to settle down, and they were among the counties that were hit harder by the inclement summer. Not unusual for them, Sussex were impeded by injuries, the most crucial being Le Roux's, early in the season. The South African's back began to play up when he was bowling with a lot of fire, and he was sidelined until mid-June.

Until the end of June, Sussex had won only one match from nine. Then, at Hastings, Mendis hit form with centuries in each innings against Lancashire, whom they beat. Their luck now turned for the better.

Sussex's pace and seam bowlers, however, reaped a smaller harvest than usual, because the wet weather often slowed down pitches at Hove, which are traditionally fast. As for their spinners, Waller was invariably used in a containing role. Barclay, the captain, who takes a benefit in 1986, grossly underbowled himself, particularly in the early part of the season.

Happily, Sussex finished the season on a high note, winning three of their last six matches. Among their victims were Middlesex and Surrey, both front-runners. They would have been encouraged also by the advance of two young members of the staff. Stepping in to replace the injured Parker at number three, Neil Lenham, 19, orthodox and relaxed in style, acquitted himself creditably. Given his head towards the end of the season, Adrian Jones, who has a smooth, high action, bowled with impressive speed and hostility, particularly against Surrey, at the Oval.

Even as their fortunes began to rise, half-way through the season, Sussex announced that Ian Greig was not retained for 1986 – ostensibly for reasons of economy. Out of the side at the time, Greig was later reinstated and, to his credit, remained totally committed. He contributed significantly to Sussex's challenge for the Sunday title, which just eluded them, and also played his part in the winning of the Championship match against Surrey.

Britannic Assurance County Championship: 7th; Won 6, Lost 1, Drawn 16, Abandoned 1
All First-Class Matches: Won 7, Lost 1, Drawn 17, Abandoned 1
NatWest Bank Trophy: Lost to Glamorgan in 2nd round
Benson & Hedges Cup: Failed to qualify for Q-F (4th in Group C)
John Player League: 2nd; Won 10, Lost 5, No result 1

Championship Averages

Batting and Fielding	M	I	NO	HS	R	Avge	100	50	Ct/St
Imran Khan	13	19	7	117*	846	70.50	1	6	–
G.D. Mendis	23	39	5	143*	1604	47.17	6	5	8
A.M. Green	23	39	4	133	1547	44.20	3	10	14
I.J. Gould	22	23	7	101	614	40.93	1	4	33/4
G.S. Le Roux	17	14	3	61	401	36.45	–	2	1
P.W.G. Parker	14	24	4	105	680	34.00	1	4	12
N.J. Lenham	11	16	2	89	473	33.78	–	3	4
C.M. Wells	23	33	6	100*	891	33.00	1	5	6
I.A. Greig	13	14	4	43	241	24.10	–	–	11
A.N. Jones	11	9	5	26	83	20.75	–	–	1
A.P. Wells	21	29	5	102	481	20.04	1	–	11
J.R.T. Barclay	20	14	3	37*	192	17.45	–	–	10
D.A. Reeve	16	15	5	56	170	17.00	–	1	6
C.E. Waller	15	7	2	8	27	5.40	–	–	1

Also batted: A.C.S. Pigott (8 matches) 10*, 0*, 0 (6 ct); D.K. Standing (1 match) 7, 3; P. Moores (1 match) (1 ct). I.C. Waring (1 match) did not bat.

Hundreds (14)

6 **G.D. Mendis:** 103 and 100* v Lancs, Hastings; 111* v Warwicks, Hove; 109 v Hampshire, Portsmouth; 143* v Essex, Colchester; 123 v Yorkshire, Hove.
3 **A.M. Green:** 100* v Glamorgan, Hove; 106 v Surrey, Horsham; 133 v Surrey, Oval.
1 **I.J. Gould:** 101 v Leics, Hove.
  Imran Khan: 117* v Warwicks, Hove.
  P.W.G. Parker: 105 v Surrey, Horsham.
  A.P. Wells: 102 v Glamorgan, Hove.
  C.M. Wells: 100* v Warwicks, Hove.

Bowling	O	M	R	W	Avge	Best	5wI	10wM
Imran Khan	388.5	99	952	48	19.83	5-49	2	–
G.S. Le Roux	392.2	70	1113	39	28.53	6-46	2	–
D.A. Reeve	451.1	101	1377	45	30.06	5-24	2	–
J.R.T. Barclay	252.4	39	804	24	33.50	6-78	2	–
A.C.S. Pigott	166.4	31	612	17	36.00	3-22	–	–
C.M. Wells	470.4	126	1275	34	37.50	4-76	–	–
I.A. Greig	233	41	794	20	39.70	4-37	–	–
A.N. Jones	231	33	814	20	40.70	5-39	1	–
C.E. Waller	318.5	99	755	17	44.41	7-61	1	–

Also bowled: I.J. Gould 4-0-75-0; A.M. Green 32-6-77-2; G.D. Mendis 4-0-65-1.

Warwickshire

Warwickshire's campaign turned out to be more testing than either Norman Gifford, inheriting the captaincy at 45, or the club's sternest critis could have imagined. They were dismissed from the two cup competitions at an early stage, surrendered a promising start to finish seventh in the John Player League, and crumbled to 15th place in the County Championship.

Their long-standing weakness in bowling became so damaging that their own batting strength suffered under the pressure that was passed on to them. All too often, the bowlers would be hammered on helpful pitches which were then exploited by the opposition attack. This was especially evident in the closing weeks of a traumatic season. The batsmen's confidence drained noticeably after batterings on bad pitches at the Oval and Cheltenham, resulting in the side losing four of the last five Championship matches. In that period, Warwickshire took only one batting point, and, for the first time in the memory of most Edgbaston regulars, there was not one batsman in the higher reaches of the national averages.

In case it seems churlish to blame bowlers for the failures of batsmen, it should be stressed that Kallicharran had a poor season by his standards, partly because of a persistent shoulder injury, and there was not the consistency normally associated with Amiss and Humpage. Lloyd made a good start on his return from that dreadful injury sustained on his Test debut in 1984, but broke a thumb in July and was not as effective later on. Likewise, Dyer suffered from a downward trend as morale seemed to collapse in the closing weeks.

During Lloyd's absence, Lord, an attractive left-hander who has promised much in the Second XI, came in to score a John Player century and then made 199 against Yorkshire. He should be one for the future, and, happily, there was a revival in Asif Din's fortunes when Warwickshire tried to stiffen the side with an extra batsman in August.

Paul Smith, an all-rounder of whom much was expected, did not develop as Warwickshire had hoped, especially with his fast bowling, and while Ferreira took 71 Championship wickets, the cost was far too high for him to be regarded as a match-winner.

It is true Warwickshire were unlucky that Old missed the majority of the season because of a shoulder injury, but the failure of younger bowlers to stake a claim is very worrying to the Edgbaston administration. Small bowled well in the first half of the season, but, understandably, he was weighed down by having to carry the pace attack, which explained why Warwickshire were one of the first counties to approach Parsons when it was known that he would be leaving Leicestershire. Gifford, as ever, was a model performer, bowling an enormous number of overs (no fewer than 48 in Middlesex's only innings in the final match), but there were times when he could not rest himself because the seamers were incapable of accepting a containing role.

One saving grace was the continued improvement by Humpage as a wicketkeeper. He has worked hard on this part of his game, and considering the bare nature of the bowling, it was indeed remarkable that he should set a county record of 80 first-class dismissals in the season.

Britannic Assurance County Championship: 15th; Won 2, Lost 8, Drawn 14
All First-Class Matches: Won 3, Lost 8, Drawn 15
NatWest Bank Trophy: Lost to Nottinghamshire in second round
Benson & Hedges Cup: Failed to qualify for Q-F (4th in Group B)
John Player League: 6th; Won 7, Lost 7, No result 2

Championship Averages

Batting and Fielding	M	I	NO	HS	R	Avge	100	50	Ct/St
D.L. Amiss	24	40	4	140	1326	36.83	4	6	23
Asif Din	6	11	2	89	325	36.11	–	2	2
T.A. Lloyd	16	30	2	160	989	35.32	1	6	4
G.W. Humpage	23	38	4	159	1197	35.20	2	5	70/3
A.I. Kallicharran	21	35	2	152*	1052	31.87	2	6	6
G.J. Lord	7	10	1	199	263	29.22	1	–	–
R.I.H.B. Dyer	24	42	2	106	1112	27.80	1	8	17
P.A. Smith	23	35	3	93	783	24.46	–	5	9
A.M. Ferreira	23	35	7	101*	693	24.75	1	1	12
C.M. Old	7	7	2	41	122	24.40	–	–	1
G.C. Small	21	27	8	31*	285	15.00	–	–	7
K.D. Smith	4	7	0	42	99	14.14	–	–	1
S. Wall	10	15	5	28	125	12.50	–	–	4
A.R.K. Pierson	10	12	5	17*	85	12.14	–	–	2
N. Gifford	24	25	8	26	132	7.76	–	–	9
D.S. Hoffman	15	15	4	13*	39	3.54	–	–	3

Also batted: C. Lethbridge (3 matches) 15, 22*, 47; S. Monkhouse (1 match) 2*, 5; G.A. Tedstone (1 match) 22 (1ct, 1st); D.A. Thorne (1 match) 0, 0.

Hundreds (12)

4 D.L. Amiss: 100* v Worcs, Worcester; 140 v Northants, Northampton; 117 v Notts, Nuneaton; 103* v Yorkshire, Birmingham.
2 G.W. Humpage: 123* v Northants, Northampton; 159 v Sussex, Hove.
  A.I. Kallicharran: 152* v Northants, Northampton; 108 v Kent, Canterbury.
1 R.I.H.B. Dyer: 106 v Somerset, Birmingham.
  A.M. Ferreira: 101* Somerset, Taunton.
  T.A. Lloyd: 160 v Glamorgan, Birmingham.
  G.J. Lord: 199 v Yorkshire, Birmingham.

Bowling	O	M	R	W	Avge	Best	5wI	10wM
G.C. Small	592.3	114	1850	69	26.81	5-24	5	–
A.M. Ferreira	624.3	118	2039	71	28.71	5-41	2	1
N. Gifford	611.5	188	1541	46	33.50	5-128	1	–
C.M. Old	153.2	38	466	13	35.84	6-68	1	–
D.S. Hoffman	287.1	41	1081	26	41.57	4-100	–	–
P.A. Smith	234.2	24	1130	26	43.46	4-25	–	–
S. Wall	243.1	36	790	18	43.88	4-59	–	–

Also bowled: Asif Din 5.2-2-7-1; A.I. Kallicharran 11.4-0-56-0; C. Lethbridge 65-7-263-5; T.A. Lloyd 33-1-127-4; S. Monkhouse 17-2-61-1; A.R.K. Pierson 89-19-340-1.

Worcestershire

Phil Neale, the Worcestershire captain, previewed 1985 as a season in which he expected his developing side to be in a position to challenge for honours for the first time in his three years in charge. Confirmation was not long in coming. In June, Worcestershire lost a Benson & Hedges Cup quarter-final to Middlesex only on wicket-taking rates from earlier zonal matches.

By the end of the summer, the county surveyed a satisfactory state of affairs in two other competitions – fifth place in the County Championship and a semi-final appearance in the NatWest Trophy when, again, they were unlucky with the weather. Even Nottinghamshire, the eventual winners of that tie, agreed that the result might have been different but for an interruption that enabled them to revise their tactics.

Their batting did not always fulfil its potential, though six players, including Hick (who scored 598 runs on Zimbabwe's short tour), totalled more than 1,000 runs in first-class matches. Patel had a disappointing season, failing to score a century, and Weston's loss of form meant promotion for d'Oliveira, who opened from mid-June onwards and was awarded a county cap. Curtis was less prolific than in 1984 but, nevertheless, a steady opening batsman; Neale maintained the consistency he has shown for a number of years; and Smith, who missed seven Championship matches through injury, was outstanding, particularly in the longer one-day competitions.

Kapil Dev scored a century off 78 balls against the eventual champions, Middlesex, on the opening day of the season, but played in only half of the Championship programme before flying out to Sri Lanka to captain India in August. He took only 37 wickets, but so economically that he finished in eighth place in the national averages. Even so, Worcestershire will have to reconsider the overseas role as Kapil will miss much of 1986 because of India's tour to England.

Hick, only 19, is already a candidate, and certainly in the longer term. The gifted Zimbabwean right-hander scored a century in only his twelfth Championship innings and has made 746 runs in only 16 innings in that competition.

But, like most counties, Worcestershire may feel tempted to import a genuine fast bowler. Had they possessed a Marshall or a Hadlee, their potential last summer would have been limitless, because they had, in Radford, the only bowler in the country to take 100 first-class wickets. In his first year after being released by Lancashire, the English-qualified paceman from Zambia was a revelation, setting the highest standards of hostility and accuracy while bowling nearly 800 overs. He took his 100th wicket, to win the Swanton Trophy on the last afternoon of the season.

The supporting bowlers had mixed results, though there were impressive patches of form by Newport and Inchmore. The spinners, Patel and Illingworth, were less effective than normal, but, second only to Radford, the other highspot of the season was the form of Rhodes, the young wicketkeeper recruited from Yorkshire.

ENGLISH SEASON 1985/WORCESTERSHIRE 173

Britannic Assurance County Championship: 5th; Won 5, Lost 6, Drawn 13
All First-Class Matches: Won 6, Lost 6, Drawn 15
NatWest Bank Trophy: Lost to Nottinghamshire in semi-final
Benson & Hedges Cup: Lost to Middlesex in quarter-final
John Player League: 16th; Won 5, Lost 9, No result 2

Championship Averages

Batting and Fielding	M	I	NO	HS	R	Avge	100	50	Ct/St
D.M. Smith	18	27	4	112	1113	48.39	3	7	11
G.A. Hick	10	15	1	174*	664	47.42	2	2	5
Kapil Dev	12	21	2	100	816	42.94	1	5	11
T.S. Curtis	24	42	2	126*	1279	31.97	1	11	9
P.A. Neale	24	40	9	152*	1290	31.46	2	7	5
D.B. D'Oliveira	24	41	2	139	1200	30.76	2	7	17
D.N. Patel	24	39	3	88	1006	27.94	–	5	15
M.J. Weston	17	27	1	132	706	27.15	1	2	4
S.J. Rhodes	24	32	12	58*	518	25.90	–	1	53/2
P.J. Newport	16	23	8	36	277	18.46	–	–	2
D.A. Banks	4	5	1	30	70	17.50	–	–	1
N.V. Radford	23	25	7	57*	306	17.00	–	1	3
J.D. Inchmore	16	9	2	24	100	14.28	–	–	4
R.K. Illingworth	18	19	8	39*	129	11.72	–	–	6
S.M. McEwan	9	7	4	7*	12	4.00	–	–	1

Also batted: R.M. Ellcock (1 match) 3.

Hundreds (12)

3 **D.M. Smith:** 112 v Hampshire, Portsmouth; 102 v Glamorgan, Worcester; 104* v Northants, Worcester.
2 **D.B. D'Oliveira:** 139 v Sussex, Eastbourne; 113 v Somerset, Taunton.
  G.A. Hick: 174* v Somerset, Worcester; 128 v Northants, Worcester.
  P.A. Neale: 152* v Surrey, Worcester; 102 v Derbys, Worcester.
1 **T.S. Curtis:** 126* v Surrey, Worcester.
  Kapil Dev: 100 v Middlesex, Lord's.
  M.J. Weston: 132 v Surrey, Worcester.

Bowling	O	M	R	W	Avge	Best	5wI	10wM
Kapil Dev	304.5	83	805	37	21.75	4-56	–	–
P.J. Newport	334.2	57	1089	46	23.67	5-18	3	–
N.V. Radford	764.4	130	2416	100	24.16	6-45	4	–
J.D. Inchmore	320.5	66	806	30	26.86	4-42	–	–
S.M. McEwan	169	28	611	16	38.18	3-47	–	–
D.N. Patel	381	101	1084	28	38.71	3-33	–	–
R.K. Illingworth	344.4	92	940	24	39.16	4-76	–	–
M.J. Weston	259.5	66	746	17	43.88	3-37	–	–

Also bowled: D.B. D'Oliveira 9-0-30-1; R.M. Ellcock 28-0-91-0; G.A. Hick 74-17-265-5.

Yorkshire

From mid-July, Yorkshire were without their only three capped seam bowlers, Sidebottom, Stevenson, and Dennis. That, in a sentence, sums up a frustratingly damp summer in which there was, in the end, more reason for hope than despondency. Even at full strength Yorkshire did not have the resources to bowl out many teams twice, so that any improvement in the County Championship could only be marginal. But the one-day competitions were approached with both optimism and confidence.

The Benson & Hedges quarter-finals were missed by the margin of inches, the difference between a four and a six off the last ball at Old Trafford. The NatWest semi-finals could have been achieved but for Viv Richards's being given the benefit of the doubt in a highly contentious moment, of many repercussions, at Headingley.

Yorkshire were challenging for the John Player League until the final fortnight, allowing three matches to slip from their grasp at times when victories would have put them ahead of the field. It was on those occasions that one more experienced bowler would have been decisive.

There were times when, as one observer who had not seen the team for three seasons put it, 'Yorkshire looked like a school first XI'. Blakey, Swallow, Fletcher, Shaw, and Pickles are all at the undergraduate stage of development; had they been allowed, when joined by Booth and Andrew, the Cambridge captain, another year at Colts' level, Yorkshire's future could be said to be bright. The danger of overexposure remains. The promising Fletcher again broke down for a spell, while Jarvis, fast and penetrative, missed the last month through injury.

The batting was mercurial, although the captain, Bairstow, had his best summer, passing 1,000 for the third time, the first Yorkshire wicket-keeper to do so. Boycott finished second in the national averages and equalled Sutcliffe's 149 centuries, but aroused fierce criticism for his scoring rate at Harrogate and Scarborough. Moxon confirmed his class, while Blakey attracted praise from distinguished judges; Neil Hartley would not be left out, but too many other capped players were inconsistent. Yorkshire are in the process of great change.

The once heretical subject of an overseas professional was widely debated, a large majority of the 11,000 members being still in favour of the traditional birth qualification. However, a reversion to two imports per county could bring the matter to a critical vote, with all its implications for English cricket. E.W. Swanton's call for the uncovering of Championship pitches would receive overwhelming support in the Ridings.

Bairstow will again lead Yorkshire in 1986, a decision of rare unanimity by the General Committee, and with eight seam bowlers on the staff, not including Oldham, there will at least be competition for places. The decision to release Colin Johnson, a year after his team had won the 2nd XI Championship, was regarded by many as churlish.

Britannic Assurance County Championship: 11th; Won 3, Lost 4, Drawn 16, Abandoned 1
All First-Class Matches: Won 3, Lost 4, Drawn 18, Abandoned 1
NatWest Bank Trophy: Lost to Somerset in 2nd round
Benson & Hedges Cup: Failed to qualify for Q-F (3rd in Group B)
John Player League: 6th; Won 6, Lost 6, No result 4

Championship Averages

Batting and Fielding	M	I	NO	HS	R	Avge	100	50	Ct/St
G. Boycott	19	31	11	184	1545	77.25	6	8	9
D.L. Bairstow	23	31	9	122*	1148	52.18	3	3	44/12
M.D. Moxon	20	31	1	168	1224	40.80	3	5	8
J.D. Love	19	26	4	93	830	37.72	–	6	7
P.E. Robinson	13	16	1	79	450	30.00	–	3	2
A. Sidebottom	8	9	2	55	191	27.28	–	1	1
R.J. Blakey	13	21	2	90	487	25.63	–	2	11
S.N. Hartley	15	19	1	60	446	24.77	–	3	7
G.B. Stevenson	4	6	2	35*	99	24.75	–	–	1
K. Sharp	17	29	3	96	613	23.57	–	2	14
P. Carrick	23	25	2	92	540	23.47	–	3	15
P.J. Hartley	12	11	3	35	159	19.87	–	–	1
A.A. Metcalfe	5	10	0	77	125	12.50	–	1	–
S.D. Fletcher	12	10	7	15*	36	12.00	–	–	2
I.G. Swallow	10	11	2	25*	101	11.22	–	–	4
P.W. Jarvis	14	16	2	28	151	10.78	–	–	6
C. Shaw	16	13	5	12	57	7.12	–	–	5

Also batted: P.A. Booth (2 matches) 0 (1 ct); S. Oldham (2 matches) 6, 2* (1 ct); C.S. Pickles (5 matches) 31*, 12, 9 (3 ct). S.J. Dennis (1 match) (1 ct) did not bat.

Hundreds (12)

6 G. Boycott: 114* v Somerset, Leeds; 115 v Hampshire, Middlesbrough; 105* v Worcs, Harrogate; 184 v Worcs, Worcester; 103* v Warwicks, Birmingham; 125* v Notts, Scarborough.
3 D.L. Bairstow: 100* v Leics, Bradford; 113* v Derbys, Chesterfield; 122* v Derbys, Bradford.
M.D. Moxon: 153 v Somerset, Leeds; 168 v Worcs, Worcester; 127 v Lancs, Leeds.

Bowling	O	M	R	W	Avge	Best	5wI	10wM
P. Carrick	709.3	183	1914	65	29.44	7-99	2	1
P.W. Jarvis	371.5	53	1330	44	30.22	7-105	3	–
A. Sidebottom	203.2	28	667	22	30.31	4-70	–	–
P.J. Hartley	315.5	40	1175	31	37.90	5-75	2	–
C. Shaw	398	90	1230	32	38.43	5-76	1	–
S.D. Fletcher	323.5	44	1185	24	49.37	4-91	–	–
I.G. Swallow	225	46	670	12	55.83	4-53	–	–

Also bowled: P.A. Booth 80.1-29-189-3; G. Boycott 10-2-29-0; S.J. Dennis 20.2-2-50-2; S.N. Hartley 74.4-10-272-9; J.D. Love 1-0-8-1; M.D. Moxon 27-1-131-4; S. Oldham 39-10-102-4; C.S. Pickles 112.3-24-345-5; K. Sharp 26-8-60-1; G.B. Stevenson 72.4-10-252-6.

University Cricket

The 141st University Match, at Lord's, was spoilt by a thunderstorm, which waterlogged the ground soon after lunch on the third day, with Cambridge (141 for three) still requiring another 89 runs to make Oxford bat again. However, the 1985 match was already marked by the unexpected and extraordinary all-round success of Giles Toogood, the Oxford captain of 1983.

Cambridge, having been put in to bat, had scored 41 for the first wicket when Toogood bowled Andrew and started a collapse to 134 all out. He finished with eight for 52 off 24 overs. Here was a bowler who had previously taken just 11 first-class wickets in his career – but now became only the second bowler this century to have captured eight wickets in an innings in the University Match. Having changed from off-spin to medium pace at the start of the season, Toogood followed another Oxonian, P.R. Le Couteur, in achieving this feat. By the end of the second day's play, Toogood again joined that Australian Le Couteur in the record books as the only other player to have taken 10 wickets and scored a hundred in the same University Match.

Oxford had a strong batting order and, after a slow start, their captain Miller and Toogood asserted authority in a second wicket partnership of 150. Toogood, principally an on-side player, and Carr, who used his feet nimbly and his bat with much aggression, then added 146 runs for the third wicket before Toogood finally skied a catch for 149. Thus, after his 109 in 1984, Toogood joined the former England captain M.J.K. Smith as the only Oxford batsman to have scored University Match hundreds in consecutive years.

When Oxford declared, with a first innings lead of 230, Cambridge had 50 minutes' batting on the second evening, but in successive overs Toogood had Andrew caught down the leg-side and Fell lbw without scoring. So Cambridge started the last day in the sad state of 35 for two – still 195 runs behind. In that morning's play, Cambridge at least looked in some control for the first time. Lea, who was their top scorer in both innings, and left-hander Roebuck were together in an undefeated partnership of 45 runs, and it looked as though Oxford would pay dearly for dropping Roebuck, behind the wicket, when he had scored only nine.

The unlucky bowler here was Rutnagur, but earlier he had gained a long-awaited wicket for Oxford, in dismissing the nightwatchman Gorman at 96 for three. Gorman had frustrated Oxford for 85 minutes when playing an excellent innings of 43. Toogood put his name in the scorebook yet again, as Gorman hooked a simple catch to him at square leg.

Quite apart from Toogood's celebrated deeds at Lord's, an outstanding University feat was the consistent batting of Oxford's all-rounder Thorne against the counties and Zimbabwe. Thorne scored his maiden hundred against the tourists, and, in all first-class matches for Oxford, he had an aggregate of 849 runs.

Cambridge University v Oxford University
Match Drawn
Played at Lords 3, 4, 5 July
Toss: Oxford. Umpires: B. Leadbeater and K. E. Palmer

Cambridge

A.E. Lea	c Carr b Toogood	41	not out	47
C.R. Andrew*	b Toogood	12	c Franks b Toogood	12
D.J. Fell	b Lawrence	8	lbw b Toogood	0
P.G.P. Roebuck	c Thorne b Toogood	2	(5) not out	34
D.G. Price	lbw b Toogood	12		
A.G. Davies†	lbw b Toogood	11		
T.A. Cotterell	lbw b Toogood	24		
S.R. Gorman	b Toogood	6	(4) c Toogood b Rutnagur	43
C.C. Ellison	c Franks b Toogood	4		
A.M.G. Scott	c Franks b Thorne	5		
J.E. Davidson	not out	1		
Extras	(B3, LB1, W3, NB1)	8	(B2, LB3)	5
		134	(3 wickets)	**141**

Oxford

A.J.T. Miller*	b Andrew	78
W.R. Bristowe	c Lea b Ellison	16
G.J. Toogood	c Andrew b Ellison	149
J.D. Carr	not out	84
D.A. Thorne	c Davies b Ellison	17
J.G. Franks†	c Gorman b Andrew	0
P.C. MacLarnon	b Andrew	2
C.D.M. Tooley	did not bat	
R.S. Rutnagur	"	
J.D. Quinlan	"	
M.P. Lawrence	"	
Extras	(B3, LB8, W5, NB2)	18
	(6 wickets declared)	**364**

Oxford	O	M	R	W	O	M	R	W
Thorne	9.3	1	23	1	9	3	14	0
Quinlan	13	5	18	0	7	3	21	0
MacLarnon	4	1	13	0				
Toogood	24	7	52	8	13	3	41	2
Lawrence	13	8	81					
Carr	11	4	16	0	11	5	25	0
Rutnagur					13	2	35	1

Cambridge	O	M	R	W
Davidson	10	1	40	0
Ellison	27	6	76	3
Scott	11	1	43	0
Cotterell	25	8	78	0
Gorman	4	0	14	0
Lea	1	0	1	0
Andrew	25.4	5	101	3

Fall of Wickets

Wkt	CU 1st	OU 1st	CU 2nd
1st	41	22	20
2nd	62	172	24
3rd	65	318	96
4th	74	351	–
5th	87	352	–
6th	92	364	–
7th	100	–	–
8th	104	–	–
9th	132	–	–
10th	134	–	–

Cambridge University

Results: Played 9; Won 0, Lost 1, Drawn 8

First-Class Averages

Batting	M	I	NO	HS	R	Avge
T.A. Cotterell†	9	12	4	69*	289	36.12
P.G.P. Roebuck†	9	15	3	82	343	28.58
A.E. Lea†	8	15	2	47*	298	22.92
D.J. Fell†	9	16	1	109*	332	22.13
A.D.H. Grimes	6	3	1	22*	43	21.50
C.C. Ellison†	7	6	0	51	109	18.16
C.R. Andrew†	8	15	1	66	253	18.07
S.R. Gorman†	9	15	5	43	177	17.70
J.E. Davidson†	4	4	2	22	25	12.50
A.G. Davies†	9	13	2	43*	124	11.27
M.S. Ahluwalia	4	7	1	31	55	9.16
D.G. Price†	6	9	1	29	60	7.50
A.M.G. Scott†	9	7	4	5*	12	4.00

Also batted: D.W. Browne (1 match) 10; S.N. Siddiqi (1 match) 0.

Hundreds (1)

1 D.J. Fell: 109* v Notts, Cambridge

Bowling	O	M	R	W	Avge	Best
Scott	243.3	34	879	25	35.16	5-68
Ellison	223.5	58	591	13	45.46	3-76
Andrew	80.2	10	279	6	46.50	3-101
Grimes	130	28	480	9	53.33	3-99
Cotterell	232.4	54	742	11	67.45	3-53

Also bowled: Davidson 80-12-254-4; Gorman 117.4-17-465-3; Lea 2-0-9-0; Price 1-0-7-0; Siddiqi 2-0-12-0.

Fielding

13 Davies (11 ct, 2 st); 4 Andrew, Fell, Roebuck; 3 Ahluwalia, Gorman, Lea; 2 Davidson, Scott; 1 Browne, Cotterell, Ellison, Grimes, Price.

Oxford University

Results: Played 11; Won 0, Lost 4, Drawn 7

First-Class Averages

Batting	M	I	NO	HS	R	Avge
D.A. Thorne†	11	18	3	124	849	56.60
J.D. Carr†	6	9	1	115	415	51.87
G.J. Toogood†	9	15	1	149	507	36.21
A.J.T. Miller†	10	17	3	78	462	33.00
J.G. Franks†	3	4	1	35	71	23.66
W.R. Bristowe†	5	8	1	42*	156	22.28
R.S. Rutnagur†	11	15	2	66	246	18.92
P.C. MacLarnon†	7	10	1	56	168	18.66
D.A. Hagan	5	10	1	46	148	16.44
C.D.M. Tooley†	11	16	0	66	257	16.06
T. Patel	9	17	4	47	159	12.23
J.D. Quinlan†	7	6	2	22*	34	8.50
C.M. Denny	4	6	1	19	28	5.60
D.S. Harrison	4	5	2	6	12	4.00
M.P. Lawrence†	11	9	3	9*	20	3.33
D.P. Taylor	4	6	2	5*	5	1.25

Also batted: J.G. Brettell (4 matches) 0,0*.

Hundreds (4)

2 J.D. Carr: 115 v Somerset, Oxford; 101 v Yorks, Oxford.
1 D.A. Thorne: 124 v Zimbabwe, Oxford.
G.J. Toogood: 149 v Cambridge University, Lord's.

Bowling	O	M	R	W	Avge	Best
Toogood	209.2	44	691	18	38.38	8-52
Rutnagur	189	25	728	15	48.53	5-112
Thorne	196.1	34	664	13	51.07	4-64
Lawrence	341.5	65	1154	20	57.70	3-99
Carr	184	48	462	8	57.75	4-65
Quinlan	189	37	635	10	63.50	4-76

Also bowled: Brettell 62.4-14-266-4; Bristowe 1-0-5-0; Hagan 1-0-6-0; MacLarnon 60.3-10-229-1.

Fielding

8 Thorne; 6 Harrison (4 ct, 2 st); 5 Franks (4 ct, 1 st); Patel; 4 Hagan, Toogood; 3 Bristowe, Carr, Denny, MacLarnon, Miller, Rutnagur, Taylor (1 ct, 2 st); 2 Lawrence, Tooley; 1 Brettell, Quinlan.

* not out † Blue 1985

First-Class Averages

Batting
(Qual: 8 innings, avge 10; * not out)

	M	I	NO	HS	Runs	Avge	100s	50s
I.V.A. Richards	19	24	0	322	1836	76.50	9	6
G. Boycott	21	34	12	184	1657	75.31	6	9
G.A. Gooch	21	33	2	202	2208	71.22	7	9
I.T. Botham	19	27	5	152	1530	69.54	5	9
Imran Khan	14	21	8	117*	890	68.46	1	6
Younis Ahmed	22	30	8	177	1421	64.59	5	4
Jarved Miandad	20	29	6	200*	1441	62.65	4	8
R.T. Robinson	18	31	4	175	1619	59.96	6	9
C.L. Smith	23	39	4	143*	2000	57.14	7	11
J.G. Wright	11	16	2	177*	797	56.92	2	4
M.W. Gatting	23	34	5	160	1650	56.89	3	13
P. Bainbridge	24	38	9	151*	1644	56.68	4	11
C.E.B. Rice	20	33	8	171*	1394	55.76	4	6
D.I. Gower	21	29	2	215	1477	54.70	5	3
W.N. Slack	26	43	8	201*	1900	54.28	4	11
D.W. Randall	25	47	7	117	2151	53.77	5	14
M.A. Lynch	25	39	7	145	1714	53.56	7	6
C.T. Radley	27	38	12	200	1375	52.88	3	8
G.A. Hick	17	25	1	230	1265	52.70	4	3
D.A. Thorne	12	20	3	124	849	49.94	1	8
R.C. Ontong	26	30	7	130	1121	48.73	2	8
G.D. Barlow	20	32	4	141	1343	47.96	6	2
G.D. Mendis	25	43	6	143*	1756	47.45	6	6
D.L. Bairstow	26	35	10	122*	1181	47.24	3	3
G.S. Clinton	18	32	6	123	1225	47.11	3	7
N.R. Taylor	16	25	7	120*	843	46.83	3	3
C.W.J. Athey	24	38	7	170	1442	46.51	5	7
D.M. Smith	19	28	4	112	1113	46.37	3	7
P. Willey	23	32	4	147	1292	46.14	3	6
P.M. Roebuck	22	33	5	132*	1255	44.82	2	7
C.J. Richards	22	27	12	75*	665	44.33	0	3
P.A. Neale	25	42	10	152*	1411	44.09	3	7
T.E. Jesty	24	36	8	141*	1216	43.42	4	5
Kapil Dev	12	21	2	100	816	42.94	1	5
R.A. Smith	26	44	8	140*	1533	42.58	3	7
A.M. Green	25	43	4	133	1646	42.20	3	10
M.D. Moxon	23	36	1	168	1447	41.34	4	6
C.G. Greenidge	19	32	2	204	1236	41.20	2	8
A.J. Lamb	19	26	4	122*	903	41.04	2	5
J.D. Love	21	28	5	106	937	40.73	1	6
A.C. Storie	7	12	2	106	407	40.70	1	3
B.C. Broad	25	47	3	171	1786	40.59	2	14
K.J. Barnett	25	41	2	134*	1568	40.20	4	7
D.L. Amiss	26	44	5	140	1555	39.87	5	7
N.H. Fairbrother	25	39	4	164*	1395	39.85	3	7
D.M. Ward	6	10	3	143	279	39.85	1	0
M.C.J. Nicholas	26	41	5	146	1419	39.41	3	8
P.R. Downton	22	29	7	104	856	38.90	1	7
P. Whitticase	3	8	2	79	263	43.83	0	2
R.J. Bailey	26	38	7	107*	1194	38.51	2	7
T.A. Lloyd	18	34	2	160	1230	38.43	2	8

ENGLISH SEASON 1985 / FIRST-CLASS AVERAGES

Batting (Contd)	M	I	NO	HS	Runs	Avge	100s	50s
K.D. James	8	11	4	124	268	38.28	1	0
S.P. Henderson	7	12	4	111	306	38.25	1	1
A. Needham	25	37	5	138	1223	38.21	3	5
G. Cook	24	38	4	126	1295	38.08	1	9
N.F.M. Popplewell	18	30	2	172	1064	38.00	1	7
R.O. Butcher	26	38	6	120	1210	37.81	1	8
G.W. Humpage	25	42	6	159	1360	37.77	2	6
M.R. Benson	24	43	3	162	1501	37.52	3	11
W. Larkins	26	42	0	163	1549	36.88	3	4
R.A. Harper	24	28	7	127	763	36.33	1	3
J.C. Balderstone	25	40	5	134	1271	36.31	2	6
I.J. Gould	24	25	8	101	616	36.23	1	4
G.J. Toogood	9	15	1	149	507	36.21	1	2
B.R. Hardie	26	45	7	162	1374	36.15	4	4
T.A. Cotterell	9	12	4	69*	289	36.12	0	1
Asif Din	6	11	2	89	325	36.11	0	2
C.J. Tavare	23	40	6	150*	1225	36.02	3	4
J.J. Whitaker	25	34	3	109	1103	35.58	3	5
J.J.E. Hardy	16	25	4	107*	742	35.33	1	3
B.F. Davison	24	35	7	111	984	35.14	1	5
G.S. Le Roux	18	16	4	61	421	35.08	0	2
G.R. Cowdrey	6	9	2	53	242	34.57	0	2
D.E. East	26	32	6	131	889	34.19	2	4
N.A. Felton	18	27	0	112	922	34.14	1	7
S.G. Hinks	26	48	3	117	1536	34.13	1	10
P.W.G. Parker	16	28	4	105	818	34.08	1	5
K.S. McEwan	26	42	4	121	1293	34.02	3	6
G. Monkhouse	16	14	8	47	203	33.83	0	0
N.J. Lenham	11	16	2	89	473	33.78	0	3
D.G. Aslett	13	23	1	174	732	33.27	2	1
I.P. Butcher	25	39	3	120	1192	33.11	1	8
K.R. Brown	8	11	2	102	298	33.11	1	1
V.P. Terry	25	41	2	148*	1284	32.92	2	10
R.J. Hadlee	19	29	11	73*	592	32.88	0	5
K.W.R. Fletcher	23	28	7	78*	688	32.76	0	7
A.R. Butcher	26	46	3	126	1407	32.72	2	5
C.S. Cowdrey	20	36	3	159	1079	32.69	2	4
A.I. Kallicharran	21	35	2	152*	1052	31.87	2	6
T.S. Curtis	26	45	2	126*	1365	31.74	1	12
R.A. Cobb	16	23	4	78	601	31.63	0	4
A.J.T. Miller	12	20	4	78	506	31.62	0	3
J.D. Carr	11	16	1	115	474	31.60	2	2
A.J. Stewart	23	36	4	158	1009	31.53	1	5
J.F. Steele	11	12	3	100	283	31.44	1	0
R.G. Williams	21	31	3	118	880	31.42	2	4
J.G. Wyatt	17	26	0	145	816	31.38	2	2
E.A.E. Baptiste	23	36	5	82	972	31.35	0	6
P. Johnson	21	34	4	118	933	31.10	1	6
D.J. Makinson	15	21	9	58*	372	31.00	0	1
D.W. Varey	21	34	3	112	960	30.96	1	2
C.M. Wells	26	37	6	100*	960	30.96	1	4
R.E. Hayward	9	12	3	100*	278	30.88	1	1
S.N. Hartley	17	20	2	108*	554	30.77	1	3

ENGLISH SEASON 1985/FIRST-CLASS AVERAGES

Batting (Contd)	M	I	NO	HS	Runs	Avge	100s	50s
V.J. Marks	26	34	5	82	885	30.51	0	7
G.C. Holmes	27	40	3	112	1129	30.51	2	7
R.J. Harden	12	17	5	107	366	30.50	1	1
J.W. Lloyds	25	6	33	101	818	30.29	1	5
A. Hill	10	14	3	120	333	30.27	1	1
T.M. Tremlett	24	29	14	102*	450	30.00	1	0
P.E. Robinson	13	16	1	79	450	30.00	0	3
B. Roberts	25	42	4	100*	1128	29.68	2	2
D.B. D'Oliveira	26	44	2	139	1244	29.61	2	7
T. Davies	26	25	8	75	503	29.58	0	2
D.P. Hughes	10	16	2	75*	411	29.35	0	3
D.J. Wild	18	22	4	80	525	29.16	0	2
M.J. Weston	19	30	1	132	845	29.13	1	3
R.I.H.B. Dyer	26	46	3	109*	1242	28.88	2	8
D.R. Turner	7	9	2	49*	202	28.85	0	0
D.J.R. Martindale	9	14	3	104*	317	28.81	1	1
A.M. Ferreira	25	38	10	101*	805	28.75	1	2
G. Miller	21	31	5	105	744	28.61	1	4
P.G.P. Roebuck	9	15	3	82	343	28.58	0	1
J.E. Morris	18	27	1	109*	722	27.76	1	3
J.E. Emburey	25	25	4	68	581	27.66	0	4
J.F. Sykes	10	13	3	126	275	27.50	1	1
I.S. Anderson	19	35	3	95	876	27.37	0	7
R.J. Boyd-Moss	20	31	3	121	766	27.35	2	2
G.J. Lord	8	11	1	199	271	27.10	1	0
R.M. Ellison	18	26	6	98	539	26.95	0	3
H. Morris	15	18	4	62	375	26.78	0	1
D.N. Patel	26	42	3	88	1042	26.71	0	5
J. Abrahams	25	39	4	101*	932	26.62	1	4
P.J. Prichard	21	34	4	95	779	25.96	0	5
R.J. Blakey	14	22	2	90	518	25.90	0	2
R.B. Phillips	8	9	2	39	180	25.71	0	0
M.R. Chadwick	12	17	1	132	410	25.62	1	1
S.J. Rhodes	26	34	13	58*	538	25.61	0	1
J.D. Birch	14	23	7	68*	409	25.56	0	2
A.L. Jones	19	27	2	80	636	25.44	0	4
K.P. Tomlins	9	15	1	58	354	25.28	0	1
R.J. Parks	25	24	9	53*	377	25.13	0	0
C. Gladwin	13	22	2	92*	500	25.00	0	2
R.A. Pick	13	15	5	63	250	25.00	0	1
K. Sharp	20	34	4	96	750	25.00	0	3
D.J. Capel	23	30	6	81	599	24.95	0	5
J.A. Hopkins	23	34	2	114*	794	24.81	1	4
M.D. Marshall	22	33	2	66*	768	24.77	0	5
M. Watkinson	19	29	1	106	692	24.71	1	4
M.A. Garnham	23	26	4	100	542	24.63	1	1
K.M. Curran	26	34	3	83	762	24.58	0	5
K.R. Pont	10	15	3	62*	294	24.50	0	2
B.C. Rose	5	10	2	81*	196	24.50	0	1
D.B. Pauline	13	18	2	77	392	24.50	0	3
A. Sidebottom	11	11	3	55	196	24.50	0	1
D.R. Pringle	23	31	4	121*	654	24.22	1	1
P.A. Smith	24	37	3	93	815	23.97	0	5

Batting (Contd)	M	I	NO	HS	Runs	Avge	100s	50s
R.J. Doughty	11	12	2	65	239	23.90	0	2
M.S. Turner	10	12	6	24*	143	23.83	–	–
M. Newell	7	13	0	74	309	23.76	0	3
P.B. Clift	22	26	5	106	495	23.57	1	1
P. Carrick	24	25	2	92	540	23.47	0	3
J.R.T. Barclay	22	17	6	37*	257	23.36	0	0
P.G. Newman	20	29	3	115	604	23.23	1	3
A.P. Wells	23	33	7	102	600	23.07	1	1
N.E. Briers	23	29	4	129	576	23.04	1	1
M.A. Holding	12	19	1	80	413	22.94	0	3
A.E. Lea	8	15	2	47*	298	22.92	0	0
R.J. Maru	23	19	9	62	227	22.70	0	1
M.R. Davis	18	20	6	40*	315	22.50	0	0
W.R. Bristowe	5	8	1	42*	156	22.28	0	0
P.W. Romaines	20	34	4	114*	667	22.23	1	4
N.F. Williams	22	21	4	67	378	22.33	0	1
D.J. Fell	9	16	1	109*	332	22.13	1	1
I.A. Greig	16	16	4	43	264	22.00	0	0
A.W. Lilley	16	26	2	68*	516	21.50	0	4
A.A. Metcalfe	6	12	0	109	257	21.41	1	1
N.G. Cowley	13	14	4	51	213	21.30	0	1
P.J. Newport	18	26	10	36	338	21.12	0	0
R. Sharma	7	12	2	41*	209	20.90	0	0
A.N. Jones	12	9	5	26	83	20.75	0	0
C.H. Dredge	15	13	7	31	124	20.66	0	0
G.V. Palmer	8	11	3	45*	164	20.50	0	0
W.P. Fowler	10	14	1	79	266	20.46	0	2
A.P.E. Knott	19	24	5	87*	379	19.94	0	2
P.J. Hartley	12	11	3	35	159	19.87	0	0
A.W. Stovold	22	37	2	112	694	19.82	2	2
D.G. Moir	8	9	0	46	178	19.77	0	0
G.W. Johnson	11	16	4	30*	237	19.75	0	0
M.R. Price	14	11	4	36	136	19.42	0	0
A.J. Wright	9	16	3	47*	249	19.15	0	0
J.G. Thomas	16	16	2	60*	268	19.14	0	1
D.A. Graveney	24	25	11	53*	266	19.00	0	1
R.S. Rutnagur	11	15	2	66	246	18.92	0	2
L. Potter	13	15	2	58	245	18.84	0	2
S.P. Hughes	11	11	6	30*	94	18.80	0	0
P.C. MacLarnon	7	10	1	56	168	18.66	0	1
J. Simmons	21	30	4	101	485	18.65	1	2
P.A.C. Bail	5	9	2	78*	127	18.14	0	1
P.J.W. Allott	19	21	6	78	272	18.13	0	1
C.R. Andrew	8	15	1	66	253	18.07	0	2
S.R. Gorman	9	15	5	43	177	17.70	0	0
E.E. Hemmings	21	22	5	56*	297	17.47	0	1
A.E. Warner	15	20	2	60	314	17.44	0	2
G. Fowler	16	25	0	88	428	17.12	0	1
R.L. Ollis	15	20	1	55	325	17.10	0	1
N.V. Radford	24	25	7	57*	306	17.00	0	1
D.A. Reeve	17	15	5	56	170	17.00	0	1
B.N. French	24	34	8	52*	439	16.88	0	1

ENGLISH SEASON 1985/FIRST-CLASS AVERAGES

Batting (Contd)	M	I	NO	HS	Runs	Avge	100s	50s
D.A. Hagan	5	10	1	46	148	16.44	0	0
N.A. Foster	15	14	2	63	196	16.33	0	1
C.D.M. Tooley	11	16	0	66	257	16.06	0	1
C.A. Walsh	21	18	6	37	189	15.75	0	0
N.A. Mallender	24	25	8	52*	267	15.70	0	1
S.C. Booth	11	8	3	28	78	15.60	0	0
P.I. Pocock	24	18	6	41	183	15.25	0	0
K.D. Smith	5	9	1	42	120	15.00	0	0
G.C. Small	21	27	8	31*	285	15.00	0	0
J.D. Inchmore	16	9	2	24	100	14.28	0	0
G.J. Parsons	16	16	4	32	170	14.16	0	0
R.J. Finney	25	37	10	82	381	14.11	0	1
A. Walker	12	14	8	18*	83	13.83	0	0
J.K. Lever	23	23	9	24*	193	13.78	0	0
I. Folley	21	27	8	69	262	13.78	0	1
R.K. Illingworth	20	20	8	39*	165	13.75	0	0
R.C. Russell	23	23	4	34	253	13.31	0	0
T. Gard	26	28	6	47	293	13.31	0	0
S.J. O'Shaughnessy	13	23	2	63	275	13.09	0	1
P.H. Edmonds	23	23	6	29*	221	13.00	0	0
C.A. Connor	17	9	4	36	65	13.00	0	0
P.A.J. De Freitas	9	12	3	30*	117	13.00	0	0
D.J. Thomas	12	12	3	25*	116	12.88	0	0
A.R.K. Pierson	12	14	7	17*	90	12.85	0	0
N.G.B. Cook	18	16	4	45	152	12.66	0	0
B.J.M. Maher	14	18	6	46	150	12.50	0	0
D.V. Lawrence	25	26	5	41	259	12.33	0	0
J. Derrick	14	15	2	52	160	12.30	0	1
M.A. Fell	5	8	0	27	98	12.25	0	0
T. Patel	9	17	4	47	159	12.23	0	0
C. Maynard	19	27	5	43	266	12.09	0	0
S.D. Fletcher	14	10	7	15*	36	12.00	0	0
S. Wall	12	16	5	28	128	11.63	0	0
K.E. Cooper	22	16	4	46	139	11.58	0	0
J. Garner	15	11	3	22	92	11.50	0	0
N.S. Taylor	7	8	3	21*	57	11.40	0	0
C. Marples	11	15	5	34	114	11.40	0	0
Andrew G. Davies	9	13	2	43*	124	11.27	0	0
I.G. Swallow	10	11	2	25*	101	11.22	0	0
G.R. Dilley	17	19	5	31	153	10.92	0	0
P.W. Jarvis	14	16	2	28	151	10.78	0	0
J.P. Agnew	16	15	3	36	121	10.08	0	0
N.G. Cowans	23	17	4	22*	130	10.00	0	0

Bowling (Qual: 10 wickets in 10 innings)	O	M	R	W	Avge	Best	5wI
R.M. Ellison	432.1	113	1118	65	17.20	7-87	5
R.J. Hadlee	473.5	136	1026	59	17.38	8-41	2
M.D. Marshall	688.1	193	1680	95	17.68	7-59	5
G.E. Sainsbury	178.0	59	481	27	17.81	7-38	2
C.A. Walsh	560.3	124	1706	85	20.07	7-51	4
Imran Khan	422.1	114	1040	51	20.39	5-49	2
T.M. Tremlett	665.5	181	1620	75	21.60	5-42	2

184 ENGLISH SEASON 1985/FIRST-CLASS AVERAGES

Bowling (Contd)	O	M	R	W	Avge	Best	5wI
Kapil Dev	304.5	83	805	37	21.75	4-56	0
M.A. Holding	354.5	67	1124	50	22.48	6-65	3
P.J.W. Allott	560.2	167	1328	58	22.89	6-71	3
L.B. Taylor	566.5	141	1376	60	22.93	5-45	3
N.G. Cowans	474.2	85	1676	73	22.95	6-31	6
A.H. Gray	524.0	99	1816	79	22.98	8-40	6
K.M. Curran	469.5	104	1419	61	23.26	5-35	2
J. Garner	295.4	75	739	31	23.83	5-46	1
D.V. Lawrence	544.5	66	2093	85	24.62	7-48	5
N.V. Radford	779.4	130	2493	101	24.68	6-45	4
D.A. Graveney	410.1	133	1013	41	24.70	4-91	0
R.J. Doughty	223.5	36	867	34	25.50	6-33	1
P.H. Edmonds	850.1	243	1942	76	25.55	6-87	2
J.D. Inchmore	338.5	72	844	33	25.57	4-42	0
K.E. Cooper	604.3	187	1566	61	25.67	7-10	2
J.K. Lever	720.3	188	1995	77	25.90	6-47	6
P.A.J. De Freitas	234.2	43	703	27	26.03	5-39	1
R.J. Maru	704.5	197	1923	73	26.34	5-16	3
P.J. Newport	362.2	57	1214	46	26.39	5-18	3
M.W. Gatting	92.5	17	293	11	26.63	3-55	0
G.A. Gooch	284.2	66	773	29	26.65	5-46	1
G. Monkhouse	383.4	78	1068	40	26.70	5-61	1
W.W. Daniel	575.1	90	2111	79	26.72	7-62	2
G.C. Small	592.3	114	1850	69	26.81	5-24	5
D.L. Underwood	807.0	290	1802	67	26.89	6-56	1
J.W. Lloyds	180.1	42	575	21	27.38	5-37	1
R.J. Finney	449.3	81	1453	53	27.41	7-61	4
J.P. Agnew	445.4	89	1512	55	27.49	9-70	3
N.A. Foster	436.5	87	1434	52	27.57	5-40	4
R.C. Ontong	586.5	145	1777	64	27.76	8-67	4
B.P. Patterson	364.3	59	1144	41	27.90	7-49	3
N.G. Cowley	247.5	60	699	25	27.96	3-17	0
A.M. Ferreira	673.3	129	2167	77	28.14	5-41	2
P. Willey	399.3	115	1017	36	28.25	6-43	3
R.K. Illingworth	406.5	116	1046	37	28.27	7-50	2
G.S. Le Roux	402.2	72	1132	40	28.30	6-46	2
E.A.E. Baptiste	562.0	116	1661	58	28.63	6-42	2
B.J. Griffiths	313.4	76	918	32	28.68	6-76	1
D.R. Pringle	604.1	146	1556	53	29.35	6-42	1
J.E. Emburey	797.1	230	1737	59	29.44	6-35	2
J.R.T. Barclay	300.4	55	913	31	29.45	6-78	2
P. Carrick	712.3	184	1923	65	29.58	7-99	2
D.A. Reeve	475.5	107	1424	48	29.66	5-24	2
P. Bainbridge	200.0	46	570	19	30.00	5-60	1
P.W. Jarvis	371.5	53	1330	44	30.22	7-105	3
K.J. Barnett	173.4	33	514	17	30.23	6-115	1
N.F. Williams	490.2	69	1784	58	30.75	5-15	2
P.B. Clift	595.3	169	1446	47	30.76	5-38	1
O.H. Mortensen	340.0	75	1026	33	31.09	5-87	1
C.E.B. Rice	284.0	82	779	25	31.16	4-24	0
I.T. Botham	406.2	67	1376	44	31.27	5-109	1
N.A. Mallender	521.4	98	1533	49	31.28	5-83	1
P.G. Newman	400.5	76	1315	42	31.30	4-29	0

Bowling (Contd)	O	M	R	W	Avge	Best	5wI
I. Folley	453.3	113	1286	41	31.36	6-8	1
M. Watkinson	420.1	94	1228	39	31.48	5-109	1
J.G. Thomas	340.3	51	1232	39	31.58	4-47	0
D.J. Capel	384.3	63	1299	41	31.68	7-62	1
P.A. Waterman	115.0	25	382	12	31.83	3-22	0
N.S. Taylor	149.0	22	579	18	32.16	7-44	1
K.B.S. Jarvis	530.4	115	1674	51	32.82	5-43	2
S.J.W. Andrew	284.0	53	992	30	33.06	6-43	1
C. Penn	124.4	17	466	14	33.28	4-63	0
A.C.S. Pigott	184.4	39	633	19	33.31	3-22	0
N. Gifford	611.5	188	1541	46	33.50	5-128	1
G.R. Dilley	350.2	71	1075	32	33.59	5-53	2
V.J. Marks	812.4	197	2421	72	33.62	8-17	4
D.J. Makinson	366.0	68	1079	32	33.71	5-60	1
P.I. Pocock	576.2	131	1632	48	34.00	7-42	1
A. Walker	251.4	51	786	23	34.17	4-38	0
S.J. O'Shaughnessy	142.0	21	521	15	34.73	4-68	0
S. Wall	301.1	44	973	28	34.75	4-59	0
A.M.G. Scott	243.3	34	879	25	35.16	5-68	1
A. Sidebottom	268.4	37	916	26	35.23	4-70	0
D.B. Pauline	161.4	32	567	16	35.43	5-52	1
C.M. Old	153.2	38	466	13	35.84	6-68	1
P.M. Such	405.1	105	1152	32	36.00	5-73	1
J.D. Carr	249.1	65	616	17	36.23	6-61	1
R.A. Harper	775.3	192	2107	58	36.32	5-94	1
D.N. Patel	442.0	117	1244	34	36.58	3-33	0
L. Potter	258.3	66	772	21	36.76	4-87	0
T.E. Jesty	144.2	28	517	14	36.92	2-32	0
D.J. Thomas	361.4	62	1186	32	37.06	5-51	1
C.H. Dredge	317.4	73	929	25	37.16	5-95	1
I.A. Greig	283.0	58	931	25	37.24	5-80	1
R.J. Boyd-Moss	121.4	29	373	10	37.30	3-48	0
P.J. Hartley	315.5	40	1175	31	37.90	5-75	2
S.R. Barwick	473.4	96	1376	36	38.22	7-43	1
E.E. Hemmings	716.3	171	2103	55	38.23	6-51	2
C.M. Wells	537.4	144	1457	38	38.34	4-76	0
G.J. Toogood	209.2	44	691	18	38.38	8-52	1
K. Saxelby	429.0	103	1385	36	38.47	6-64	2
G.C. Holmes	347.3	86	1041	27	38.55	4-49	0
J. Simmons	543.1	155	1427	37	38.56	4-55	0
S.P. Hughes	266.2	43	932	24	38.83	5-64	1
S.M. McEwan	178.0	29	635	16	39.68	3-47	0
C. Shaw	417.0	95	1286	32	40.18	5-76	1
S.C. Booth	390.2	112	1138	28	40.64	4-88	0
R.G. Williams	312.2	75	979	24	40.79	5-34	1
D.L. Acfield	588.4	130	1674	41	40.82	6-81	1
M.J. Weston	273.5	72	777	19	40.89	3-37	0
M.R. Price	258.4	63	697	17	41.00	4-97	0
D.S. Hoffman	326.4	55	1160	28	41.42	4-100	0
C.A. Connor	467.5	91	1467	35	41.91	4-62	0
R.A. Pick	290.0	52	1096	26	42.15	4-51	0
A.E. Warner	267.3	40	1013	24	42.20	5-51	1
K.D. James	177.4	43	635	15	42.33	6-22	1

Bowling (Contd)

	O	M	R	W	Avge	Best	5wI
A.N. Jones	246.0	37	848	20	42.40	5-39	1
G. Miller	385.2	77	1204	28	43.00	6-110	1
G.J. Parsons	356.2	75	1010	23	43.91	6-11	1
P.A. Smith	237.2	24	1143	26	43.96	4-25	0
C.E. Waller	381.5	117	882	20	44.10	7-61	1
A. Needham	351.4	76	1017	23	44.21	5-42	1
J.F. Sykes	191.5	42	575	13	44.23	3-58	0
N.G.B. Cook	558.1	186	1332	30	44.40	4-59	0
A.R. Butcher	158	34	449	10	44.90	3-43	0
C.C. Ellison	223.5	58	591	13	45.46	3-76	0
G.W. Johnson	156.3	24	501	11	45.54	5-78	1
S.D. Fletcher	345.5	47	1253	26	48.19	4-91	0
R.S. Rutnagur	189.0	25	728	15	48.53	5-112	1
M.S. Turner	185.5	30	648	13	49.84	4-74	0
S.J. Malone	174.1	23	654	13	50.30	5-38	1
C.S. Cowdrey	210.1	29	756	15	50.40	3-5	0
J. Derrick	226.1	39	706	14	50.42	4-60	0
D.A. Thorne	196.1	34	664	13	51.07	4-64	0
M.R. Davis	366.0	60	1249	24	52.04	4-83	0
J.F. Steele	215.1	60	581	11	52.81	3-6	0
G.J.F. Ferris	231.3	32	826	15	55.06	3-84	0
I.G. Swallow	225.0	46	670	12	55.83	4-53	0
M.P. Lawrence	341.5	65	1154	20	57.70	3-99	0
L.L. McFarlane	259.0	42	1008	16	63.00	4-100	0
J.D. Quinlan	189.0	37	635	10	63.50	4-76	0
T.A. Cotterell	232.4	54	742	11	67.45	3-53	0

The following bowlers took 10 wickets but bowled in fewer than 10 innings:

R.V.J. Coombs	93	27	268	16	16.75	5-58	
I.L. Pont	115.5	15	485	19	25.52	5-103	
T.D. Topley	161.1	37	464	17	27.29	4-57	
S. Turner	121.5	25	321	11	29.18	4-36	
S.T. Jefferies	116.1	13	379	12	31.58	4-64	
D.G. Moir	186	48	517	12	43.08	3-102	

Fielding Statistics (Qualification: 20 dismissals)

80 G.W. Humpage (76c, 4s)
76 D.E. East (72c, 4s)
72 B.N. French (65c, 7s)
65 R.C. Russell (59c, 6s)
62 R.J. Parks (58c, 4s)
62 P.R. Downton (57c, 5s)
60 M.A. Garnham (53c, 7s)
58 D.L. Bairstow (45c, 13s)
57 S.J. Rhodes (54c, 3s)
54 A.P.E. Knott (53c, 1s)
50 C. Maynard (42c, 8s)
49 T. Davies (44c, 5s)
48 C.J. Richards (41c, 7s)
39 I.J. Gould (35c, 4s)

38 T. Gard (31c, 7s)
36 M.A. Lynch
34 V.P. Terry
29 A.J. Stewart (28c, 1s)
27 G. Miller
27 W.N. Slack
26 C.W.J. Athey
25 G.A. Gooch
25 J.W. Lloyds
25 D. Ripley (21c, 4s)
24 D.L. Amiss
24 R.O. Butcher
24 C. Marples (23c, 1s)
24 D.W. Randall

23 S.G. Hinks
22 P.H. Edmonds
22 J.E. Emburey
22 B.R. Hardie
22 R.A. Harper
22 B. Roberts
21 D.B. D'Oliveira
21 B.J.M. Maher (19c, 2s)
21 C.E.B. Rice
20 I.P. Butcher
20 C.S. Cowdrey
20 M.W. Gatting
20 A.W. Stovold
20 C.J. Tavare

Benson & Hedges Cup

Leicestershire won the Benson and Hedges Cup for the first time since 1975, beating the undoubted favourites Essex by eight wickets in the final.

Played on a slow pitch on a fine day set in merciful isolation amid a wet spell, this was, until around seven o'clock, a dour match in a slow and predictable limited-overs mould. Essex, having been put in, were at one time 147 for two, but even Gooch had been pinned down by the steadiness of the bowling, notably of Taylor and Willey, and it never appeared likely that they would muster much over 200 once Willey had bowled Gooch. They reached 213 for eight.

At 37 for two, Leicestershire were having difficulties on the sluggish pitch, but Gower made 43 so well that Willey had ample time to establish himself. When Gower was brilliantly caught by Lilley at cover point at 120, Willey took over and, after the loss of two more wickets had left the score at 135 for five, found an enterprising but staunch partner in Garnham.

They needed 76 off the last 14 overs, and 58 off the last 10, a high rate in the context of the match. But strokes came from both ends, with bold running between the wickets, and even Lever, for so long a subduing influence on Essex's opponents, could not stem the flow of runs. Until near the end there was always the chance that Essex might surge back with the capture of a wicket, but neither Willey nor Garnham faltered, and their stand was worth 80 in 12 overs when they finished the match with three overs to spare.

Essex had swept through the earlier rounds unbeaten, and Leicestershire's only defeat, in a strong group of five first-class counties, had been by one run against Yorkshire. At that stage the unbeaten Hampshire looked a real threat. Kent were improving and Middlesex, perhaps unlucky to have the worst of a bad pitch at Lord's against Essex, had to be respected, though they qualified only on their bowlers' better striking rate.

The striking rate also saw Middlesex through a washed-out quarter-final at Worcester. Kent went through at Northampton similarly. Essex won a 20-over match on the third available day against Derbyshire. Leicestershire, luckier with the weather at Southampton, caused a surprise by beating Hampshire by four runs, Peter Willey taking the gold award as he was to do in the final.

The semi-finals were poor contests. Middlesex batted feebly against Essex at Chelmsford, and Kent, with the worst of the pitch, lost to Leicestershire by eight wickets.

A week before the final, Leicestershire were still bottom of the Britannic Assurance championship table. Three days before it, they lost to Hampshire in the NatWest second round, while Essex were again routing Middlesex. But at Lord's Leicestershire produced the virtures, often decisive in limited-over cricket, of accurate bowling and strong middle-order batting.

ENGLISH SEASON 1985 / BENSON & HEDGES CUP

Zonal Results

Group A	P	W	L	NR	Pts	Group C	P	W	L	NR	Pts
NORTHAMPTONSHIRE	4	2	0	2	6	ESSEX	4	4	0	–	8
DERBYSHIRRRRRE	4	2	1	1	5	MIDDLESEX	4	2	2	–	4
Nottinghamshire	4	2	1	1	5	Surrey	4	2	2	–	4
Gloucestershire	4	2	2	–	4	Sussex	4	2	2	–	4
Scotland	4	0	4	–	0	Combined Universities	4	0	4	–	0

Group B	P	W	L	NR	Pts	Group D	P	W	L	NR	Pts
WORCESTERSHIRE	4	3	1	–	6	HAMPSHIRE	4	4	0	–	8
LEICESTERSHIRE	4	3	1	–	6	KENT	4	3	1	–	6
Yorkshire	4	2	2	–	4	Glamorgan	4	2	2	–	4
Warwickshire	4	1	3	–	2	Somerset	4	1	3	–	2
Lancashire	4	1	3	–	2	Minor Counties	4	0	4	–	0

Note: Where two or more teams in a group have equal points, their positions are determined by the faster rate of taking wickets in all zonal matches (total balls bowled divided by wickets taken).

Final Rounds

Quarter-Finals 5, 6, 7 June	Semi-Finals 19, 20 June	Final 20 July
Essex† Derbyshire (£2,125)	Essex†	Essex (£8,500)
Middlesex Worcestershire† (£2,125)	Middlesex (£4,250)	
Kent Northamptonshire† (£2,125)	Kent (£4,250)	Leicestershire
Hampshire† (£2,125) Leicestershire	Leicestershire†	

Winner: **LEICESTERSHIRE** (£17,000)

† Home team.
Prize-money in brackets.

Benson & Hedges Cup Winners

1972	Leicestershire	1977	Gloucestershire	1982	Somerset
1973	Kent	1978	Kent	1983	Middlesex
1974	Surrey	1979	Essex	1984	Lancashire
1975	Leicestershire	1980	Northamptonshire	1985	Leicestershire
1976	Kent	1981	Somerset		

Essex v Leicestershire 1985 Benson & Hedges Cup Final
Leicestershire won by 5 wickets
Played at Lord's, 20 July
Toss: Leicestershire. Umpires: H.D. Bird and K.E. Palmer
Man of the Match: P. Willey (Adjudicator: D.C.S. Compton)

Essex		Runs	Mins	Balls	6s	4s
G.A. Gooch*	b Willey	57	122	105	–	3
B.R. Hardie	c and b Clift	25	98	76	–	1
P.J. Prichard	b Taylor	32	55	46	–	4
K.S. McEwan	c Garnham b Taylor	29	50	38	–	2
D.R. Pringle	c Agnew b Taylor	10	13	15	–	1
C. Gladwin	b Clift	14	23	17	–	2
A.W. Lilley	b Agnew	12	27	17	–	1
D.E. East†	not out	7	17	10	–	1
S. Turner	run out (Balderstone)	3	2	4	–	–
N.A. Foster	not out	6	7	4	–	1
J.K. Lever	did not bat					
Extras	(B 1, LB 15, W 1, NB 1)	18				
	(55 overs; 214 minutes)	213-8 (closed)				

Leicestershire		Runs	Mins	Balls	6s	4s
I.P. Butcher	c Prichard b Turner	19	63	49	–	2
J.C. Balderstone	c Prichard b Pringle	12	49	38	–	–
D.I. Gower*	c Lilley b Foster	43	77	61	–	5
P. Willey	not out	86	144	96	–	12
J.J. Whitaker	b Gooch	1	8	9	–	–
N.E. Briers	lbw b Gooch	6	16	16	–	1
M.A. Garnham†	not out	34	54	45	–	4
P.B. Clift	did not bat					
G.J. Parsons	″					
J.P. Agnew	″					
L.B. Taylor	″					
Extras	(B 2, LB 9, W 2, NB 1)	14				
	(52 overs; 209 minutes)	215-5				

Leicestershire	O	M	R	W
Agnew	11	1	51	1
Taylor	11	3	26	3
Parsons	11	0	39	0
Clift	11	1	40	2
Willey	11	0	41	1

Essex	O	M	R	W
Lever	11	0	50	0
Foster	11	2	32	1
Pringle	10	0	42	1
Turner	10	1	40	1
Gooch	10	1	40	2

Fall of Wickets

Wkt	E	L
1st	71	33
2nd	101	37
3rd	147	120
4th	163	123
5th	164	135
6th	191	–
7th	195	–
8th	198	–
9th	–	–
10th	–	–

NatWest Bank Trophy

It was settled at the quarter-finals stage that the 60-overs competition would have new champions for, of the four survivors, Essex, Nottinghamshire, and Hampshire had not even reached Lord's before, while Worcestershire had been twice runners-ups, way back in the 1960s.

Essex, who had won every other title at least once, claimed the NatWest Trophy in a finish as excruciatingly thrilling as the previous year's. Again, the issue rested on the last ball, with Notts, needing two runs to win. They had started the final over requiring 18! Chasing a total of 280, which no county had ever done in a Lord's final, Notts, from the last 25 overs, needed 157. Much nearer the winning post, the asking rate had risen to almost eight an over and even a close finish seemed beyond them. No wonder that at the end, the faces on the balcony of the Notts dressing room, far from being shaded in disappointment, beamed with joyful pride. However, Derek Randall, who was caught off the decisive ball after having pillaged 16 from the five previous deliveries to climax a memorable innings of 66, was in tears as he came off the field.

For Essex, the absence from their attack of Neil Foster – ill with glandular fever – was a handicap that would have crushed them but for the start they were given by Gooch and Hardie after Notts had won the toss and put them in. They conjured up a stand of 202, which McEwan followed with a buccaneering 46. Initially, Gooch and Hardie were restrained by Hadlee and Cooper. They made a strong enough impression on Gooch for him to blend into his innings of 91 a large measure of responsible caution. Instead, Hardie took the initiative and scored a century that was worth the Man of the Match Award.

Fully exploiting home conditions, Essex had disposed of Middlesex and Kent – 1984 champions and runners-up, respectively – in earlier rounds, but survived a tense and close-fought semi-final against Hampshire, at Southampton. They were so hard pressed that rather than go for the winning run from the whole of the last over, curiously delivered by a part-timer in Greenidge, Essex opted to block it out and go through by virtue of having lost fewer wickets in a tied match. Furthermore, they were fortunate in that Gooch, 93 not out, had got the benefit of the doubt in a run-out decision when 53.

Like the Essex v Hampshire semi-final, the contest at New Road between Worcestershire and Notts was also stretched to two days by the weather and produced another photo finish. Notts, indebted to Tim Robinson, who made 139 to follow scores of 98 and 90 in the previous rounds, overtook Worcestershire's 232 with only four balls remaining.

Of the quarter-finals, which were all rain affected, only Gloucestershire v Notts, at Bristol, was close. In the second round, Worcestershire, despite accumulating a massive 312, were stretched by Clive Lloyd, coming into the match cold, making 91 for Lancashire. Durham struck a blow for Minor Counties pride by eliminating the 1981 champions, Derbyshire, in the first round.

FIELDING POSITIONS Nº 2

EXTRA COVER

Since 1980, we've taken up a few interesting positions ourselves.

In 326 years of banking, we've achieved quite a bit and after only five years' major involvement in cricket, our record is already impressive.

In 1981 we introduced the NatWest Trophy; one of the country's most sought after limited overs trophies.

Each season the competition attracts over 100,000 spectators to cricket grounds.

And we're active off the field, too. Together with the National Cricket Association we've produced a first-class series of coaching films.

We lend our support to the Under 13's Ken Barrington Cup.

And the National Cricket Association Proficiency Award Scheme also gets our backing.

Right now our relationship with cricket couldn't be sunnier. Nor our position clearer.

NatWest
The Action Bank

Gillette Cup Winners

1963	Sussex	1969	Yorkshire	1975	Lancashire
1964	Sussex	1970	Lancashire	1976	Northamptonshire
1965	Yorkshire	1971	Lancashire	1977	Middlesex
1966	Warwickshire	1972	Lancashire	1978	Sussex
1967	Kent	1973	Gloucestershire	1979	Somerset
1968	Warwickshire	1974	Kent	1980	Middlesex

NatWest Bank Trophy Winners
1981 Derbyshire 1982 Surrey 1983 Somerset 1984 Middlesex 1985 Essex

1985 Tournament

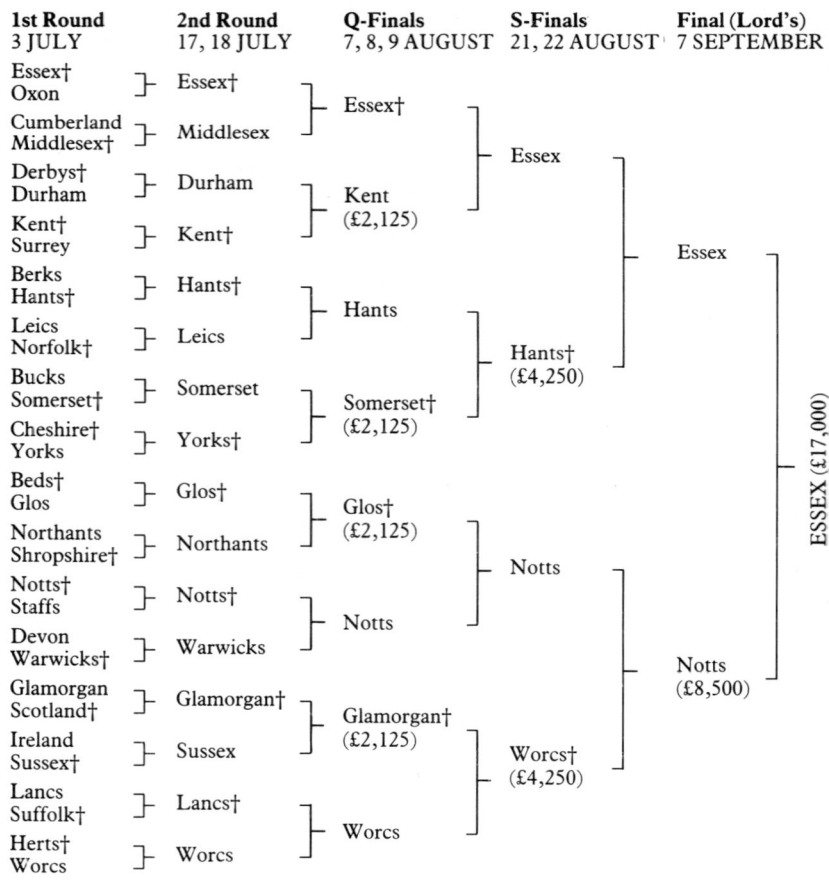

1st Round 3 JULY	2nd Round 17, 18 JULY	Q-Finals 7, 8, 9 AUGUST	S-Finals 21, 22 AUGUST	Final (Lord's) 7 SEPTEMBER
Essex† / Oxon	Essex†	Essex†	Essex	Essex
Cumberland / Middlesex†	Middlesex			
Derbys† / Durham	Durham	Kent (£2,125)		
Kent† / Surrey	Kent†			
Berks / Hants†	Hants†	Hants	Hants† (£4,250)	
Leics / Norfolk†	Leics			
Bucks / Somerset†	Somerset	Somerset† (£2,125)		ESSEX (£17,000)
Cheshire† / Yorks	Yorks†			
Beds† / Glos	Glos†	Glos† (£2,125)	Notts	Notts (£8,500)
Northants / Shropshire†	Northants			
Notts† / Staffs	Notts†	Notts		
Devon / Warwicks†	Warwicks			
Glamorgan / Scotland†	Glamorgan†	Glamorgan† (£2,125)	Worcs† (£4,250)	
Ireland / Sussex†	Sussex			
Lancs / Suffolk†	Lancs†	Worcs		
Herts† / Worcs	Worcs			

†Home team.
Amounts in brackets show prize-money won by that county.

ENGLISH SEASON 1985/NATWEST BANK TROPHY

Essex v Nottinghamshire 1985 NatWest Trophy Final
Essex won by 1 run
Played at Lord's, 7 September
Toss: Nottinghamshire. Umpires: D.J. Constant and B.J. Meyer
Man of the Match: B.R. Hardie (Adjudicator: P.B.H. May)

Essex		Runs	Mins	Balls	6s	4s
G.A. Gooch	b Pick	91	169	142	1	8
B.R. Hardie	run out (Hemmings)	110	176	149	–	15
K.S. McEwan	not out	46	47	39	1	4
D.R. Pringle	not out	29	40	30	–	2
P.J. Prichard	did not bat					
K.W.R. Fletcher*	"					
A.W. Lilley	"					
D.E. East†	"					
S. Turner	"					
I.L. Pont	"					
J.K. Lever	"					
Extras	(B 1, LB 3)	4				
	(60 overs; 217 minutes)	280-2				

Nottinghamshire		Runs	Mins	Balls	6s	4s
R.T. Robinson	c Hardie b Turner	80	149	142	1	4
B.C. Broad	run out (Pont/East)	64	137	107	–	6
C.E.B. Rice*	c Hardie b Turner	12	26	19	–	1
D.W. Randall	c Prichard b Pringle	66	72	54	–	6
R.J. Hadlee	b Pont	22	20	17	1	2
D.J.R. Martindale	not out	20	33	22	–	–
B.N. French†	did not bat					
E.E. Hemmings	"					
R.A. Pick	"					
K. Saxelby	"					
K.E. Cooper	"					
Extras	(LB 14, NB 1)	15				
	(60 overs; 222 minutes)	279-5				

Nottinghamshire	O	M	R	W
Hadlee	12	4	48	0
Cooper	9	3	27	0
Saxelby	12	0	73	0
Rice	7	0	38	0
Pick	8	0	36	1
Hemmings	12	1	54	0

Essex	O	M	R	W
Lever	12	2	53	0
Pont	12	0	54	1
Turner	12	1	43	2
Gooch	12	0	47	0
Pringle	12	1	68	1

Fall of Wickets

Wkt	E	N
1st	202	143
2nd	203	153
3rd	–	173
4th	–	214
5th	–	279
6th	–	–
7th	–	–
8th	–	–
9th	–	–
10th	–	–

John Player League

The Sunday competition has seldom offered such tantalizing prospects or produced a more nerve-racking finish than that of September 15, in which Essex, by a quivering whisker, retained the John Player Trophy.

At the start of this final day, four sides – Essex, Sussex, Northants, and Hampshire – were in various degrees of contention. Essex, the favourites, had 40 points, Sussex and Northants 38 each, and Hampshire 36. Northants, beaten by a faster-scoring Worcestershire, fell further from grace when Hampshire beat Notts to secure a certain place in the first three. Sussex then took up the gauntlet by winning at Cardiff and joining the nation's televiewing fans to watch the final overs at Chelmsford, where Essex were engaged in a frantic struggle with Yorkshire.

Already resolved to offer Kevin Sharp the Freedom of Hove for his brilliant contribution of 114 to Yorkshire's 231, the Sussex players were ready to bestow similar honours on Yorkshire's bowlers as Essex, despite splendid innings by McEwan (62) and Pringle (60), needed 81 from the last ten overs. However, in the wake of falling wickets, Prichard's cultured 25 steadied the Essex schooner and, off the penultimate ball, Foster struck the winning run.

So ended a campaign of many vicissitudes – not least for Kent who, having shared or held outright the lead for eleven consecutive weeks, slumped to tenth position in the final reckoning. Conversely, for most of the season Essex looked rank outsiders. Soundly beaten by nine wickets at Hove in their opening match, they gained only ten points from their first seven fixtures and, at the beginning of August, were still third from the bottom of the league table.

At this stage Kent, though having surrendered a clear lead of six points established on July 7, were still at the top, in company with Sussex. Northants, too, were making their presence felt, notably in the person of Larkins. On July 14 the former England opener partnered Bailey in a stand of 139 which beat Kent by ten wickets, at Maidstone. Later, at Guildford, he and Lamb (134 not out) brought Northants a 93-run victory over Surrey, and the joint leadership with Sussex, when they put on 176 for the second wicket.

Yorkshire also had their moments but, having moved into second place at the end of June, missed a golden opportunity to consolidate when, the following week – with Kent on the sidelines – they lost to lowly placed Gloucestershire.

Thus, as the leaders fell victim to the atrocious weather or their own inconsistency, Essex began to move up the table – most dramatically on July 21 when, at Chelmsford, they harried Kent to a remarkable defeat. A typically ebullient 86 from Gooch, backed by 45 from Pringle, helped Essex to 193 for five off 40 overs – a target which appeared totally vulnerable as Kent reached 168 for four with eight overs in hand. Unbelievably, however, the last six wickets fell for 12 runs and Essex, equally astonished, were elevated from 14th to ninth in the table.

That proved to be the beginning of a remorseless Essex surge that brought them eight wins in their last nine matches. None was more spectacular than the 44-run defeat of Notts, at Trent Bridge, which – on September 8 – took them to the top. Gooch and Hardie blazed the trail with a record John Player opening stand of 239, and Gooch's 171, which fell only five short of his own, individual record, came off only 135 balls.

Sussex, meanwhile – two points clear when they beat Derby at Hove on August 18 – stumbled at the run-in. Four crucial points were lost on September 1, at Taunton, where Somerset, with Popplewell and Richards riding high, defeated them by eight wickets and, as it transpired, denied them the title.

Final Table	P	W	L	T	NR	Pts	6s	4w
1 ESSEX (1)	16	9	3	1	3	44	21	4
2 Sussex (3)	16	10	5	–	1	42	41	6
3 Hampshire (9)	16	8	4	–	4	40	27	2
4 Derbyshire (17)	16	8	5	–	3	38	39	3
5 Northamptonshire (12)	16	7	4	1	4	38	33	2
6 Gloucestershire (13)	16	8	8	–	0	32	39	3
Warwickshire (7)	16	7	7	–	2	32	30	2
Yorkshire (13)	16	6	6	–	4	32	26	–
Leicestershire (13)	16	5	5	1	5	32	11	–
10 Kent (9)	16	6	7	–	3	30	16	2
Somerset (13)	16	5	6	–	5	30	32	3
12 Nottinghamshire (2)	16	6	8	–	2	28	24	–
Middlesex (5)	16	5	7	–	4	28	20	–
14 Glamorgan (9)	16	4	7	1	4	26	14	2
Lancashire (4)	16	3	6	2	5	26	22	2
16 Worcestershire (5)	16	5	9	–	2	24	28	1
17 Surrey (8)	16	4	9	–	3	22	37	1

For the first four places only, the final positions for teams finishing with equal points are decided by the most wins.
1984 final positions are shown in brackets.

Winners

1969	Lancashire	1975	Hampshire	1981	Essex
1970	Lancashire	1976	Kent	1982	Sussex
1971	Worcestershire	1977	Leicestershire	1983	Yorkshire
1972	Kent	1978	Hampshire	1984	Essex
1973	Kent	1979	Somerset	1985	Essex
1974	Leicestershire	1980	Warwickshire		

1985 Awards and Distribution of Prize Money

£17,000 and League Trophy to champions ESSEX
£8,500 to runners-up Sussex
£3,750 to third-placing Hampshire
£2,250 to fourth-placing Derbyshire
£275 to winner of each match (shared in event of 'no results' and ties)
£400 to the batsman hitting most sixes in the season: M.A. Lynch (Surrey) – 16
£400 to the bowler taking four or more wickets most times in the season: J.K. Lever (Essex) – 3
£250 to the batsman scoring the fastest 50 in a match televised on BB2: G.S. Le Roux (Sussex) – 23 balls v Glamorgan at Sophia Gardens, Cardiff, on September 15

Second XI Championship and Under-25s

This was one of the most competitive Second XI competitions for years, with Middlesex, Nottinghamshire, Surrey and Sussex hotly contesting the top places. Nottinghamshire were the final victors by the narrowest of margins, and only after Surrey had 24 points deducted for playing an ineligible cricketer.

Once again there were some outstanding individual performances with both bat and ball. Three double centuries were scored, by G. Cowdrey (255), A. Lilley (224), and K. Smith (207), and over eighty individual hundreds. On over thirty occasions bowlers took five wickets, on twenty occasions six, and on ten occasions seven wickets in an innings. The best performances came from South African Steven Jeffries (7-21) and West Indian George Ferris (7-39). The best match performance came from P. North, playing for Glamorgan against Nottinghamshire, when he took twelve wickets in the match for a cost of only 91 runs (7-48 and 5-43). Ian Pont of Essex performed a hat-trick in his 6-15 against Gloucestershire.

Second XI Championship Final Table

		P	W	L	D	Batting	Bowling	Total points	Avge
1	Nottinghamshire (9)	15	7	2	6	21	46	171†	11.40
2	Surrey (2)	13	6	2	5	33	42	147‡	11.30
3	Middlesex (5)	14	5	2	7	33	44	157	11.21
4	Sussex (17)	12	4	4	4	22	39	125	10.41
5	Lancashire (8)	16	4	3	9	35	50	149	9.31
6	Essex (7)	13	3	5	5	23	43	114	8.76
7	Warwickshire (4)	18	4	3	11	39	46	149	8.27
8	Kent (6)	15	2	3	10	38	44	114	7.60
9	Glamorgan (13)	14	3	2	9	22	35	105	7.50
10	Worcestershire (3)	11	2	1	8	20	29	81	7.36
11	Leicestershire (14)	14	2	2	10	29	40	101	7.21
12	Yorkshire (1)	14	3	3	8	25	26	95*	6.87
13	Hampshire (11)	12	1	4	7	24	41	81	6.75
14	Somerset (10)	11	1	2	8	27	24	63*	5.72
15	Derbyshire (16)	12	1	3	8	24	25	61*	5.08
16	Northamptonshire (12)	13	0	3	10	23	35	58	4.46
17	Gloucestershire (16)	9	0	4	5	6	23	29	3.22

1984 final positions are shown in brackets. * includes 12 points for 1 win in 1-innings match. † includes 24 points for 2 wins in 1-innings match. ‡ 24 points deducted (16 for win/4 bat/4 bowl) from Surrey by TCCB Discipline Committee for playing an ineligible cricketer.

For the first time in several years, the final of the Warwick Under-25 Competition did not go the full distance. A weaker than normal Kent side were unable to contain a strong Warwickshire batting side, led by a magnificent 75 from Asif Din, who raced to 233-8 in their allotted 40 overs. Despite a spirited 65 by T. Ward and 58 by S. Waterton, Kent were unable to attack the accurate Warwickshire bowling with any consistency, and were well beaten in the end by 45 runs. In the semi-finals, Kent had beaten Nottinghamshire and Warwickshire had beaten Middlesex.

Warwickshire v Kent, Warwick Under-25 Final
Warwickshire won by 45 runs

Played at Edgbaston, 25 August (40 overs)
Toss: Kent. Umpires: D.R. Shepherd and K.J. Lyons

Warwickshire

W. Matthews	c Stienhober b Wood	39
A. Moles	b Sabine	19
Asif Din*	c Pepper b Davis	75
G. Charlesworth	c Pepper b Kelleher	16
G. Tedstone†	c Masters b Sabine	38
B. McMillan	run out	11
W. Morton	c Goldsmith b Masters	2
E. Milburn	not out	7
A. Pierson	b Masters	4
T. Munton	not out	4
T. Stancombe	did not bat	
Extras		18
		233-8

Kent

R. Pepper	c Matthews b Morton	34
T. Ward	c Tedstone b Stancombe	68
S. Waterton*†	not out	58
P. Stienhober	b Morton	8
J. Goldsmith	run out	1
D. Sabine	run out	1
V. Wells	b McMillan	4
D. Kelleher	c Tedstone b McMillan	5
R. Davis	c Asif Din b McMillan	1
L. Wood	not out	2
K. Masters	did not bat	
Extras		6
		188-8

Kent	O	M	R	W
Masters	8	0	37	2
Kelleher	8	0	38	1
Sabine	8	0	51	2
Wood	8	0	37	1
Davis	8	0	54	1

Warwicks	O	M	R	W
Munton	8	1	35	0
McMillan	7	2	25	3
Stancombe	8	0	45	1
Pierson	8	1	34	0
Morton	8	0	35	2
Asif Din	1	0	9	0

Fall of Wickets

Wkt	W	K
1st	34	86
2nd	118	118
3rd	168	135
4th	194	138
5th	206	141
6th	213	157
7th	219	171
8th	228	173
9th	–	–
10th	–	–

Minor Counties

In defeating Derbyshire most comprehensively in the NatWest Trophy, Durham became the first Minor County to have achieved victories over first-class opposition in both this competition and its predecessor, the Gillette Cup. Fresh from their triumph, they arrived at Fenner's to beat Dorset in the final of the English Estates Trophy.

In a wet season it was pleasing to find that only one match in the competition had to be played on a reduced overs basis, and that as many as six individual hundreds were scored, Buckinghamshire leading a high scoring first round with a 55-over total of 306 for 2 against Staffordshire.

The United Friendly Insurance Championship was less fortunate in its weather, and the season saw a sorry tally of uncompleted matches. Cheshire repeated their 1984 total domination of the Western Division, achieving, despite the elements, five outright victories from only eight that occurred in their section. The East was, again, much more evenly contested, Suffolk emerging only on the penultimate day of the season, at the expense of Staffordshire. The final, played once again at Worcester, saw Cheshire run out comfortable winners, their retiring captain, Arthur Sutton, deservedly winning the Man of the Match award.

Parvez Mir (Norfolk), last year's winner of the bowling award, showed his versatility by winning, instead, the Wilfred Rhodes Trophy for batting, while Gary Black of Bucks took the Frank Edwards Trophy for bowling back to its native county.

United Friendly Insurance County Championship Final Tables

Drawn

E. Division	P	W	L	W	T	B	NR	Pts
1 Suffolk†	9	3	1¹	1	1	3	0	41
2 Staffs†	9	3	3¹	1	0	1	1	39
3 C'berland†	9	2	1¹	1	0	3	2	33
4 Durham†	9	2	1	3	1	2	0	33
5 Herts†	9	2	0	1	0	4	2	31
6 N'berland†	9	1	1*	4	2	0	1	30
7 Cambs†	9	2	2	2	0	3	0	29
8 Norfolk	9	1	1¹	2	2	1	2	28
9 Lincs	9	0	3¹	3	0	1	2	17
10 Beds	9	0	3	2	2	2	0	12

Drawn

W. Division	P	W	L	W	T	B	NR	Pts
1 Cheshire†	9	5	0	2	0	2	0	58
2 Devon†	9	1	0	3	1	4	0	25
3 Berks†	9	1	2¹	1	1	2	2	24
4 Cornwall†	9	1	1	2	1	2	2	24
5 Dorset†	9	0	1¹	5	0	3	0	21
6 Oxon†	9	0	0	4	2	2	1	20
7 Somerset II	9	0	0	3	1	3	2	18
8 Bucks	9	0	2¹	3	1	3	0	17
9 Shrops	9	0	2¹	2	0	2	3	17
10 Wilts	9	0	2	1	4	2	6	

Points: 10 for win; in matches drawn, U = up on 1st innings (3 pts), T = tied (2), B = behind (1); NR = no result (2); 3 for 1st innings lead in match lost (L), the superior figure in the L column indicating the number of times 1st innings points were gained in matches lost. *1st innings tie in match lost (2 pts). †Qualified for 1986 NatWest Bank Trophy.

Leading UFI Averages

Batting	I	NO	HS	Runs	Avge
Parvez Mir	9	4	126*	332	66.40
A. Fordham	8	0	123	454	56.75
G.S. Warner	9	4	82*	272	54.40
Mudassar Nazar	12	3	112*	488	54.22
S.J. Halliday	13	3	96*	526	52.60
N.J. Archer	12	7	63*	260	52.00
N. Priestley	15	4	126*	551	50.09

Bowling	O	M	R	W	Avge
G.R. Black	105.4	26	252	22	11.45
M. Woods	85.4	28	236	20	11.80
S. Burrow	141.2	54	284	21	13.52
D.R. Parry	329	84	753	53	14.21
J.A. Sutton	203	70	555	38	14.61
H.A. Page	144	36	369	25	14.76
Mudassar Nazar	129	32	305	20	15.25

English Estates Knock-out Competition

Final: At Fenner's, Cambridge, 14 July. DURHAM beat DORSET by 100 runs (55 overs). Durham 229-9 (S.R. Atkinson 85; I.E.W. Sanders 4-47); Dorset 129 (47.2 overs). Man of the Match: S.R. Atkinson.

Cheshire v Suffolk, UFI Championship Play-off
Cheshire won by 58 runs
Played at Worcester, September 7 (55 overs)
Toss: Suffolk. Man of the match: J.A. Sutton
(Adjudicator: D. Humphries)

Chesire

I. Tansley	c McEvoy b Wright	0
J.J. Hitchmough	c Brown b Hayes	32
I. Cockbain	b Hayes	45
N.T. O'Brien	c McEvoy b Bailey	21
S.C. Yates	c Green b Wright	21
S.T. Crawley	lbw b Herbert	1
J.A. Sutton	run out	24
K. Teasdale	not out	17
K.B.K. Ibadulla	b Green	2
J.K. Pickup	lbw b Green	0
A.J. Murphy	run out	1
Extras		30
	(53.2 overs)	**194**

Suffolk

P.D. Barker	c Teasdale b Murphy	1
M.S.A. McEvoy	run out	5
R. Herbert	c Teasdale b Murphy	16
G. Morgan	b Sutton	31
P.J. Caley	b O'Brien	27
R. Bond	lbw b Sutton	14
P.J. Hayes	c Yates b Sutton	2
H. Wright	b O'Brien	2
R. Green	b Murphy	9
M.D. Bailey	not out	8
A.D. Brown	not out	4
Extras		17
	(9 wickets)	**136-9**

Cheshire	O	M	R	W
Murphy	11	1	29	3
Crawley	11	2	22	0
Sutton	11	1	27	3
Teasdale	11	1	33	0
O'Brien	11	4	15	2

Suffolk	O	M	R	W
Green	10	1	43	2
Wright	10.2	2	44	2
Hayes	11	3	16	2
Bailey	11	3	35	1
Herbert	11	0	33	1

Fall of Wickets

Wkt	C	S
1st	1	3
2nd	85	26
3rd	94	28
4th	131	79
5th	140	102
6th	145	107
7th	183	110
8th	189	110
9th	189	122
10th	194	—

Village and Club Cricket

The Bicentenary year of Scottish cricket saw a special milestone reached at Lord's in the traditional 'grassroots' weekend at the end of August with the victory of Freuchie, the first Scottish team to win the Village competition. The club event also broke new ground – for high scoring. In each final, the side that won the toss batted first – and lost.

William Younger Cup (45 overs). Lord's August 31; Reading won toss.
Reading 227-5 (A.D. Walder 75, D.B. Gorman 74 not, M.L. Simmons 32; P.R. Bagley 3-37); Old Hill 228-1 (F.P. Watson 65 not, P.R. Oliver 137 not). **Old Hill won by 9 wickets.**

Reading lost an early wicket, but Walder and Simmons restored order and added 62. Gorman, the vice-captain, and Walder put on 102 for the third wicket, interrupted by rain for 90 minutes. Reading's 227 for five was a record for the final of this competition, albeit short-lived. Mushtaq Mohammed's leg-spin was unrewarded, but Bagley, from the Pavilion end, took three for 49. Old Hill, the holders, were always ahead of the required run-rate. Watson, the wicketkeeper, and Oliver, formerly of Warwickshire, raced to victory with seven and a half overs to spare in near-darkness. Oliver reached his hundred with successive sixes in the 25th over, having received 81 balls. His 137 not out, another record, included 10 sixes. Old Hill received the Cup and £1,000 from Mr George Mann, MCC President, and Reading received £600. The club championship is organized by The National Cricket Association.

National Village Club Championship (40 overs). Lord's September 1; Rowledge won toss. Rowledge 134 (39.3 overs). (N.S. Dunbar 33, A.P. Hook 28, T. Trewartha 4-24, D. Cowan 2-25); Freuchie 134-8 (G. Crichton 24 not, S. Irvine 24; A.B. Field 2-15, B.A. Silver 2-18). **Freuchie won by 2 wickets.**

Rowledge proceeded slowly against determined Scottish out-cricket, Andy Crichton claiming two run-outs and Irvine taking a gallant catch on the leg-side. Dunbar was run out at 56 for two, and Rowledge, Surrey group champions, were all out in the final over. Trewartha, a Cornish-Scot, bowled accurately for his four wickets for 24. Freuchie's feat in getting to the final in this special year was widely acclaimed and the team had marched kilted to Lord's behind their piper. Having fielded like tigers, they batted with less certainty of aim, but their crowd cheered every single until, in the 39th over, George Crichton, admirably composed, and David Christie saw the scores level, when the captain was run out. Brian, his son, and Crichton played out the final maiden over, and Freuchie won the title by virtue of fewer wickets lost. Had Rowledge fielded as well as Freuchie, the championship must have gone to Surrey. The President of MCC presented £500 to Freuchie and £250 to the runners-up. *The Cricketer*, who founded the village competition, ran it from their own resources in 1985; for 1986, the sponsors will be Norsk Hydro Fertilizers of Suffolk.

Schools Cricket

Although fixtures in the early part of the season suffered in many cases from rain, the weather did not prevent some schools from establishing new records in terms of matches won. Bradford GS's total of 13 victories from 26 games set new figures for the school, and Lancing's 12 wins equalled their previous highest. One of the most remarkable performances was achieved by Barnard Castle, who won 16 and drew 5 of their 21 matches. Among those who went through unbeaten were Tonbridge, Manchester GS, Abingdon, RGS Worcester, Durham, and Warwick. When Eton met Harrow at Lord's in their last game of the season, both were undefeated by schools, and the result could not have been much closer – a win for Eton by three runs.

Outstanding individual achievements by batsmen included N. Stanley of Bedford Modern (1,042 runs), N. Hussain of Forest (978), M. Boobyer of Abingdon (965), T. O'Gorman of St George's, Weybridge (910), N. Willetts of King Edward's, Birmingham (889), and J. Robinson of Lancing (868). The young Manchester GS captain, M. Atherton, hit 748 at an average of 187. M.A. Roseberry of Durham (after leading MCC Schools to victory over NAYC (with personal innings of 51 and 105), then led a combined side against Combined Services in a drawn one-day match the next day, and contributed 125.

Among the bowlers, a leg-spinner, S. Heath (King Edward's, Birmingham), captured 63 wickets, and three left-arm spinners, P. Owen (Bedford Modern), D. Panto (Brighton), and M. Cox (Abingdon), had 69, 62, and 53 victims, respectively. Opening bowler J. Pethers set a new Harrow record with 59 wickets; Pocklington's opening pair, P. Balderson and J. Nuttall, took 66 and 60; and M. Taylor (Enfield GS) 73 (10.6).

The English Schools' Cricket Association (ESCA) carried out a full coaching and playing programme despite the weather. Millfield retained the Barclays Bank Cup (Under 17s), beating Bishops Stortford in the final by six wickets. Malvern won the Lord's Taverners Cricketer Colts Trophy from some 1,600 entries who began the two-year competition in 1984, beating RGS High Wycombe in the final at Edgbaston by six wickets.

The MCC Schools XI selected after the trials to play the National Association of Young Cricketers (NAYC) in a two-day match at Lord's was: M.A. Roseberry (Durham), capt, M.A. Atherton (Manchester GS), P.D. Atkins (Aylesbury GS), J.C.M. Atkinson (Millfield), R.J. Bartlett (Taunton), J.D.R. Benson (Cambridge College of Art & Tech), P. Berry (Longlands, Redcar), A.G.J. Fraser (Harrow Weald Sixth Form), G.D. Hodgson (Nelson Thomlinson, Wigton), W.K. Hegg (Stand, Manchester), M.A. Robinson (Hull GS).

Result: MCC Schools won by six wickets. NAYC 224 and 196 (Fraser 4-35, Atherton 4-38); MCC Schools 158-2 dec (Roseberry 51, Atkins 53*) and 263-4 (Roseberry 105, Bartlett 73).

At Under-15 level, England caps were gained by G. Wells (Birkdale HS), J. Goldthorpe (Leeds GS), R. Dawson (Millfield), I. Houseman (Harrogate GS), P. Nixon (Ullswater HS), C. Adams (Chesterfield), P. Rendell (Broad Oak, Weston-super-Mare), J. Porter (Dauntsey's), M. Ramprakash (Gayton HS), A. Penberthy (Camborne), G. Haynes (High Park, Stourbridge), A. Court (Royds), and D. Barr (Bablake).

Women's Cricket

Women's cricket in the 1985 English season took second place to England's winter tour of Australia, which celebrated 50 years of Test cricket between the two countries. Many records were created and broken, but this was inevitable because the Test series was extended from three to five matches and play was over four instead of three days.

England lost a Test match for the first time since 1951 when they were defeated at Gosford NSW in the fourth Test by 117 runs. England's only Test success came in the second, at Adelaide, by just five runs as Australia failed dramatically to score 126 for victory. The series went to Australia 2-1, however, after their seven-wicket win at Bendigo in the fifth Test. This is only the fourth series in the nine between the two countries to have produced an overall series win. The tally now stands at two series to each country.

Australia created most records, but Surrey's Janette Brittin's 112 in the first Test, at Perth, was the highest Test score at the WACA Ground by a woman. Brittin continued her run of good form, which hit the headlines in England in the 1984 series against New Zealand, and on the Australian tour she won the WD & HO Wills Player of the Series award with a total of 429 runs at 42.90, plus four wickets and five catches, in the Tests.

Avril Starling, who teaches physical education in Milton Keynes, took 21 wickets in the series (20.38) to beat totals of 20 by Myrtle Maclagan (1934 v Australia) and Mary Duggan (1951 v Australia). Starling's tally equals the world's highest series total – Betty Wilson 21 for Australia v England in 1957-58.

Denise Emerson, sister of Australian Test star Terry Alderman, was Australia's most consistent scorer, and her series aggregate of 453 (50.33) was a new Australian record. Her 121 at Adelaide Oval just failed to beat the highest women's Test score on that famous ground, 127 by Betty Wilson in 1957. Emerson's run-getting feats really attracted media attention, so much so that Terry Alderman became known as the brother of the very successful woman Test cricketer Denise Emerson!

Batting star of the whole series was South Australia's Jill Kennare, also a lacrosse international. She scored four centuries – two in the Tests and two successively in the one-day internationals, as England crashed to a 3-0 defeat.

No major tour was staged in England during the 1985 season, but short tours were made to this country by Denmark, Holland, and Ireland. All three of these countries are experiencing a tremendous interest in cricket for women, and both Denmark and Ireland have been admitted to the International Women's Cricket Council (Holland are already members). At the IWCC meeting in Melbourne in January, it was agreed that players should be referred to as 'batsmen' – not 'batswomen' or even, as one agency despatch from the Brisbane Test read, 'nightwatchbatsperson'!

India will tour England in the summer of 1986 and play three Tests and three one-day internationals. In 1987, Australia will visit England to mark 50 years of Test cricket between the two countries in England. This is the first time that the English Women's Cricket Association will have hosted tours in two successive summers. Middlesex won the National County Championship in a thrilling final at Hastings, beating Kent by one run off the last ball. The National Club Championship at Lewes was won by Somerset Wanderers for the first time, after five appearances in the final. They beat Nottingham by 62 runs.

Test series: Australia beat England 2-1
First Test, at Perth, 13-16 December. MATCH DRAWN. England 290 (J. Court 90, L. Fullston 4 for 61) and 242 for 9 dec (J. Brittin 112; R. Thompson 4 for 44); Australia 251 (D. Emerson 84, P. Verco 56) and 209 for 8 (J. Kennare 103).

Second Test, at Adelaide, 21-24 December. ENGLAND won by 5 runs. England 91 (K. Price 4 for 22) and 296 (C. Watmough 70, J. Edney 50); Australia 262 (D. Emerson 121; J. McConway 4 for 32) and 120 (A. Starling 5 for 36. J. McConway 3 for 35).

Third Test, at Brisbane, 1-4 January. MATCH DRAWN. England 275 (J. Southgate 74) and 204 for 7 (C. Hodges 95); Australia 326 for 9 dec (D. Emerson 84).

Fourth Test, at Gosford, NSW, 12-15 January. AUSTRALIA won by 117 runs. Australia 232 for 8 dec (D. Emerson 58; J. McConway 3 for 39) and 153 for 9 dec (A. Starling 4 for 57); England 140 (D. Martin 4 for 24) and 128 (J. Brittin 65; L. Fullston 4 for 53).

Fifth Test, at Bendigo, 25-28 January. AUSTRALIA won by 7 wickets. England 196 (J. Southgate 59, R. Thompson 5 for 33) and 204 (Wilson 3 for 40, P. Verco 3 for 30); Australia 285 for 8 dec, (J. Kennare 104) and 116 for 3.

Denmark tour of England
22 July, at Hitchin CC, 45-overs match (reduced from 50 by rain). Denmark 68 (30.2 overs; S. Hillman 3-18, K. Hicken 2-7); Junior England 69-0 (J. Hague 40*). Junior England won by 10 wickets.

23 July, at Chiswick, 50 overs. Middlesex 171-8 (C. Nolder 48); Denmark 129-5 (J. Jonsson 42*). Middlesex won by 42 runs.

24 July, at Tring, 50 overs. East Anglia XI 49 (30.1 overs; B. Langerhuus 2-3); Denmark 50-3 (27 overs). Denmark won by 7 wickets.

25 July, at King's Langley, 50 overs. Denmark 106 (40 overs; J. Jonsson 57; J. Wainwright 5-33); E. Anglia 107-2 (J. Abbott 44). E. Anglia won by 8 wickets.

26 July, at Farningham, 50 overs. Denmark 162-3 (U. Weng 47, C. Bjerregaard 41); Kent 102 (40 overs; T. Preece 30). Denmark won by 60 runs.

Holland and Ireland tournament (Malvern College)
8 August. Young England 146-6 dec (W. Watson 63*); Ireland 66-6 (S. Metcalfe 3-14). Match drawn.

9 August. WCA XI 139-6 dec (C. Hodges 41); Ireland 115-4 (S. Reamsbottom 51). Match drawn.

10 August. Holland 64 (G. McConway 5-8). WCA XI 65-0 (C. Hodges 45*). WCA XI won by 10 wickets.

THE CLUB CRICKETER Magazine

YOU DON'T HAVE TO PLAY FOR ENGLAND TO BE ....

...IN OUR COVERS

Club Cricketer is *the* monthly magazine for the grass roots of our game. Full coverage of leagues, KOs, indoor, womens, university and schools cricket. Plus, all aspects of club management, from secretary to groundsman and not forgetting umpires and scorers.

Regular editorial features include, letters and news, Player Profiles, Umpires Corner, Hall of Fame, Grounds for Pleasure and Tales from the Clubhouse. In addition we have regular updates on coaching, league management, sponsorship, equipment, booklist, accounts, travel and clothing. In other words — something the complete club cricket scene cannot be without.

Order your subscription now. Yearly rates for UK, Eire and BFPO are £12.00, overseas, £21.00, and special club subscription (5 copies per issue with entry into Club Cricketer's national awards scheme) is £50.00

Make your cheque/PO payable to:

**The Club Cricketer (Subscriptions),
3 Bloemfontein Avenue,
LONDON W12 7BH**

Extras

Test Career Records

The following individual career averages and records include all official Test matches to the end of the 1985 English season. The Sri Lanka v India series, which began on 30 August 1985, is not included. A dagger (†) indicates a left-handed batsman. Key to bowling categories:

RF = right-arm fast
RFM = right-arm fast-medium
RMF = right-arm medium-fast
RM = right-arm medium
LF = left-arm fast

LFM = left-arm fast-medium
LM = left-arm medium
OB = right-arm slow off-breaks
LB = right-arm slow leg-breaks
SLA = left-arm slow leg-breaks

England

Batting/Fielding	M	I	NO	HS	R	Avge	100	50	Ct/St
J.P. Agnew	3	4	3	5	10	10.00	–	–	–
P.J.W. Allott	13	18	3	52*	213	14.20	–	1	4
I.T. Botham	79	125	3	208	4409	36.13	13	20	92
N.G. Cowans	19	29	7	36	175	7.95	–	–	9
C.S. Cowdrey	5	6	1	38	96	19.20	–	–	5
P.R. Downton	21	31	6	74	576	23.04	–	4	54/3
P.H. Edmonds	33	39	6	64	652	19.75	–	2	31
R.M. Ellison†	7	8	1	41	89	12.71	–	–	2
J.E. Emburey	28	39	8	57	456	14.70	–	1	18
N.A. Foster	9	12	2	18	78	7.80	–	–	3
G. Fowler†	21	37	0	201	1307	35.32	3	8	10
M.W. Gatting	41	70	10	207	2246	37.43	4	13	35
G.A. Gooch	48	84	4	196	3027	37.83	5	17	40
D.I. Gower†	76	129	11	215	5385	45.63	12	25	55
A.J. Lamb	38	64	6	137*	2211	38.12	7	9	41
P.I. Pocock	25	37	4	33	206	6.24	–	–	15
R.T. Robinson	11	18	3	175	934	62.26	3	3	5
A. Sidebottom	1	1	0	2	2	2.00	–	–	–
L.B. Taylor	2	1	1	1*	1	–	–	–	1
P. Willey	21	40	6	102*	962	28.29	2	4	3

Bowling	Type	Balls	R	W	Avge	Best	5wI	10wM
J.P. Agnew	RFM	552	373	4	93.25	2-51	–	–
P.J.W. Allott	RFM	2223	1084	26	41.69	6-61	1	–
I.T. Botham	RFM	18391	9046	343	26.37	8-34	25	4
N.G. Cowans	RF	3452	2003	51	39.27	6-77	2	–
C.S. Cowdrey	RM	366	288	4	72.00	2-65	–	–
P.H. Edmonds	SLA	8232	2866	88	32.56	7-66	2	–
R.M. Ellison	RFM	1559	674	27	24.96	6-77	2	1
J.E. Emburey	OB	6473	2240	75	29.86	6-33	3	–
N.A. Foster	RFM	1974	985	27	36.48	6-104	3	1
G. Fowler	RM	18	11	0	–	–	–	–
M.W. Gatting	RM	332	167	2	83.50	1-14	–	–
G.A. Gooch	RM	1185	450	10	45.00	2-12	–	–
D.I. Gower	OB	30	15	1	15.00	1-1	–	–
A.J. Lamb	RM	24	22	1	22.00	1-6	–	–
P.I. Pocock	OB	6650	2976	67	44.41	6-79	3	–
R.T. Robinson	RM	6	0	0	–	–	–	–
A. Sidebottom	RMF	112	65	1	65.00	1-65	–	–
L.B. Taylor	RFM	381	178	4	44.50	2-34	–	–
P. Willey	OB	1067	441	6	73.50	2-73	–	–

Australia

Batting/Fielding	M	I	NO	HS	R	Avge	100	50	Ct/St
T.M. Alderman	22	33	15	23*	113	6.27	–	–	17
M.J. Bennett	3	5	2	23	71	23.66	–	–	5
D.C. Boon	7	12	0	61	256	21.33	–	2	6
A.R. Border†	72	127	22	196	5332	50.78	14	29	81
J. Dyson	30	58	7	127*	1359	26.64	2	5	10
D.R. Gilbert	1	2	1	1	1	1.00	–	–	–
A.M.J. Hilditch	17	32	0	119	1061	33.15	2	6	13
R.M. Hogg	38	58	13	52	439	9.75	–	1	7
R.G. Holland	7	9	2	10	30	4.28	–	–	2
K.J. Hughes	70	124	6	213	4415	37.41	9	22	50
G.F. Lawson	34	55	10	57*	696	15.46	–	3	7
C.J. McDermott	8	11	1	35	107	10.70	–	–	3
G.R.J. Matthews†	5	8	1	75	139	19.85	–	1	1
S.P. O'Donnell	5	8	1	48	184	26.28	–	–	3
W.B. Phillips†	18	32	2	159	1106	36.86	2	5	35
C.G. Rackemann	5	5	0	12	16	3.20	–	–	2
G.M. Ritchie	15	28	2	146	871	33.50	2	4	8
S.J. Rixon	13	24	3	54	394	18.76	–	2	42/5
J.R. Thomson	51	73	20	49	679	12.81	–	–	20
D.M. Wellham	5	9	0	103	239	26.55	1	–	2
K.C. Wessels†	23	40	1	179	1688	43.28	4	8	18
G.M. Wood†	53	101	5	172	3109	32.38	8	13	38
G.N. Yallop†	39	70	3	268	2756	41.13	8	9	23

Bowling	Type	Balls	R	W	Avge	Best	5wI	10wM
T.M. Alderman	RFM	5373	2597	79	32.87	6-128	5	–
M.J. Bennett	SLA	665	325	6	54.16	3-79	–	–
A.R. Border	SLA	1582	625	15	41.66	3-20	–	–
D.R. Gilbert	RFM	126	96	1	96.00	1-96	–	–
R.M. Hogg	RF	7633	3499	123	28.44	6-74	6	2
R.G. Holland	LB	1815	869	20	43.45	6-54	2	1
K.J. Hughes	LB	85	28	0	–	–	–	–
G.F. Lawson	RF	7776	4040	140	28.85	8-112	10	2
C.J. McDermott	RF	1820	1174	40	29.35	8-141	2	–
G.R.J. Matthews	OB	601	317	7	45.28	2-48	–	–
S.P. O'Donnell	RMF	874	487	6	81.16	3-37	–	–
C.G. Rackemann	RFM	936	539	23	23.43	6-86	3	1
G.M. Ritchie	RM	6	10	0	–	–	–	–
J.R. Thomson	RF	10535	5601	200	28.00	6-46	8	–
K.C. Wessels	RM/OB	84	35	0	–	–	–	–
G.N. Yallop	LM	192	116	1	116.00	1-21	–	–

West Indies

Batting/Fielding	M	I	NO	HS	R	Avge	100	50	Ct/St
C.G. Butts	1	1	0	9	9	9.00	–	–	–
W.W. Davis	11	12	4	77	157	19.62	–	1	7
P.J.L. Dujon	33	44	4	139	1764	44.10	4	8	108/2
J. Garner	51	60	13	60	609	12.95	–	1	37
H.A. Gomes†	49	75	10	143	2841	43.70	9	12	15
C.G. Greenidge	66	111	13	223	4816	49.14	12	26	62
R.A. Harper	14	17	2	39*	203	13.53	–	–	19
D.L. Haynes	54	88	7	184	3234	39.92	7	20	33
M.A. Holding	55	71	10	69	786	12.88	–	5	18
C.H. Lloyd†	110	175	14	242*	7515	46.67	19	39	90
A.L. Logie	13	17	1	130	493	30.81	1	3	7
M.D. Marshall	40	48	3	92	800	17.77	–	5	19
I.V.A. Richards	77	116	7	291	5889	54.02	19	25	77
R.B. Richardson	15	22	1	185	967	46.04	4	3	19
C.A. Walsh	6	7	4	18*	44	14.66	–	–	2

Bowling	Type	Balls	R	W	Avge	Best	5wI	10wM
C.G. Butts	OB	282	113	0	–	–	–	–
W.W. Davis	RF	2100	1082	32	33.81	4-19	–	–
J. Garner	RFM	11769	4792	220	21.78	6-56	6	–
H.A. Gomes	RM	2215	867	13	66.69	2-20	–	–
C.G. Greenidge	RM	26	4	0	–	–	–	–
R.A. Harper	OB	2548	966	34	28.41	6-57	1	–
D.L. Haynes	RM	18	8	1	8.00	1-2	–	–
M.A. Holding	RF	11842	5414	233	23.23	8-92	13	2
C.H. Lloyd	RM	1716	622	10	62.20	2-13	–	–
A.L. Logie	RM/OB	7	4	0	–	–	–	–
M.D. Marshall	RF	8864	4157	188	22.11	7-53	13	2
I.V.A. Richards	RM/OB	2812	1023	19	53.84	2-20	–	–
R.B. Richardson	OB	12	0	0	–	–	–	–
C.A. Walsh	RF	1028	507	16	31.68	3-55	–	–

County caps awarded in 1985

Derbyshire: I.S. Anderson, R.J. Finney, D.G. Moir
Glamorgan: T. Davies, G.C. Holmes, Younis Ahmed
Gloucestershire: C.W.J. Athey, K.M. Curran, B.F. Davison, D.V. Lawrence, J.W. Lloyds, R.C. Russell, C.A. Walsh
Hampshire: R.A. Smith
Kent: S.G. Hinks
Lancashire: N.H. Fairbrother, S.J. O'Shaughnessy
Northamptonshire: R.J. Bailey
Surrey: A.H. Gray, A. Needham, A.J. Stewart
Sussex: A.M. Green
Worcestershire: D.B. D'Oliveira, N.V. Radford

New Zealand

Batting/Fielding	M	I	NO	HS	R	Avge	100	50	Ct/St
S.L. Boock	25	35	8	35	152	5.62	–	–	13
B.P. Bracewell	6	12	2	8	24	2.40	–	–	1
J.G. Bracewell	13	21	3	30	190	10.55	–	–	12
B.L. Cairns	42	64	8	64*	928	16.57	–	2	30
E.J. Chatfield	23	32	21	21*	126	11.45	–	–	3
J.V. Coney	40	67	12	174*	2094	38.07	2	13	46
J.J. Crowe	20	33	1	128	936	29.25	2	5	27
M.D. Crowe	23	38	1	188	1113	30.08	2	4	27
B.A. Edgar†	30	53	3	161	1577	31.54	3	8	13
E.J. Gray	4	8	0	25	86	10.75	–	–	2
R.J. Hadlee†	57	96	12	103	2088	24.85	1	10	29
G.P. Howarth	47	83	5	147	2531	32.44	6	11	29
P.E. McEwan	4	7	1	40*	96	16.00	–	–	5
J.F. Reid†	13	22	2	180	1077	53.85	5	2	7
K.R. Rutherford	4	7	0	5	12	1.71	–	–	1
I.D.S. Smith	25	37	8	113*	709	24.44	1	2	67/3
D.A. Stirling	4	7	1	16	64	10.66	–	–	–
G.B. Troup	13	17	6	13*	45	4.09	–	–	2
J.G. Wright	41	71	2	141	2133	30.91	4	9	22

Bowling	Type	Balls	R	W	Avge	Best	5wI	10wM
S.L. Boock	SLA	5282	2000	62	32.25	7-87	4	–
B.P. Bracewell	RFM	1036	585	14	41.78	3-110	–	–
J.G. Bracewell	OB	2470	1095	30	36.50	5-75	1	–
B.L. Cairns	RMF	10388	4170	130	32.07	7-74	6	1
E.J. Chatfield	RFM	5317	2208	70	31.54	6-73	3	1
J.V. Coney	RM	2151	706	21	33.61	3-28	–	–
J.J. Crowe	RM	18	9	0	–	–	–	–
M.D. Crowe	RMF	885	445	12	37.08	2-25	–	–
B.A. Edgar	RM	18	3	0	–	–	–	–
E.J. Gray	SLA	642	311	8	38.87	3-73	–	–
R.J. Hadlee	RFM	14292	6341	266	23.83	7-23	19	4
G.P. Howarth	OB	614	271	3	90.33	1-13	–	–
P.E. McEwan	RM	36	13	0	–	–	–	–
J.F. Reid	LB	12	7	0	–	–	–	–
K.R. Rutherford	RM	58	48	1	48.00	1-38	–	–
I.D.S. Smith		18	5	0	–	–	–	–
D.A. Stirling	RFM	638	420	10	42.00	4-88	–	–
G.B. Troup	LFM	2721	1214	36	33.72	6-95	1	1
J.G. Wright	RM	30	5	0	–	–	–	–

India

Batting/Fielding	M	I	NO	HS	R	Avge	100	50	Ct/St
M. Amarnath	49	83	7	120	3241	42.64	8	19	37
M. Azharuddin	3	5	1	122	439	109.75	3	1	1
R.M.H. Binny	18	30	3	83*	618	22.88	–	4	7
A.D. Gaekwad	40	70	4	201	1985	30.07	2	10	15
S.M. Gavaskar	106	185	14	236*	8654	50.60	30	37	92
Kapil Dev	68	101	9	126*	2788	30.30	3	15	26
S.M.H. Kirmani	85	122	22	102	2717	27.17	2	12	157/36
Madan Lal	38	60	16	74	1000	22.75	–	5	15
A. Malhotra	7	10	1	72*	226	25.11	–	1	2
Maninder Singh	13	15	5	15	58	5.80	–	–	3
S.M. Patil	29	47	4	174	1588	36.93	4	7	12
M. Prabhakar	2	4	1	35*	86	28.66	–	–	–
C. Sharma	5	6	4	18*	62	31.00	–	–	1
G. Sharma	1	–	–	–	–	–	–	–	1
R.J. Shastri	34	53	8	142	1676	37.24	5	7	15
L. Sivaramakrishnan	6	6	1	25	76	15.20	–	–	2
K. Srikkanth	8	13	1	84	288	24.00	–	2	3
D.B. Vengsarkar	76	124	11	159	4328	38.30	9	22	52
N.S. Yadav	23	30	9	43	308	14.66	–	–	7

Bowling	Type	Balls	R	W	Avge	Best	5wI	10wM
M. Amarnath	RM	3275	1629	29	56.17	4-63	–	–
M. Azharuddin	LB	6	8	0	–	–	–	–
R.M.H. Binny	RM	1817	1041	24	43.37	3-18	–	–
A.D. Gaekwad	OB	334	187	2	93.50	1-4	–	–
S.M. Gavaskar	RM	350	187	1	187.00	1-34	–	–
Kapil Dev	RFM	14522	7406	258	28.70	9-83	18	2
S.M.H. Kirmani	OB	18	13	1	13.00	1-9	–	–
Madan Lal	RMF	5872	2798	68	41.14	5-23	4	–
A. Malhotra	RM	18	3	0	–	–	–	–
Maninder Singh	SLA	2568	1060	16	66.25	4-85	–	–
S.M. Patil	RM	645	240	9	26.66	2-26	–	–
M. Prabhakar	RM	174	102	1	102.00	1-68	–	–
C. Sharma	RFM	669	433	8	54.12	4-38	–	–
G. Sharma	OB	426	132	3	44.00	3-115	–	–
R.J. Shastri	SLA	7683	2947	73	40.36	5-75	2	–
L. Sivaramakrishnan	LB	1797	818	23	35.56	6-64	3	1
K. Srikkanth	RM	48	21	0	–	–	–	–
D.B. Vengsarkar	RM	47	36	0	–	–	–	–
N.S. Yadav	OB	5052	2336	60	38.93	5-131	1	–

Pakistan

Batting/Fielding	M	I	NO	HS	R	Avge	100	50	Ct/St
Abdul Qadir	33	40	4	54	550	15.27	–	2	10
Anil Dalpat	9	12	1	52	167	15.18	–	1	23/3
Ashraf Ali	4	5	3	65	206	103.00	–	2	7/2
Azeem Hafeez†	18	21	5	24	134	8.37	–	–	1
Iqbal Qasim†	41	46	14	56	380	11.87	–	1	31
Jalaluddin	5	3	2	2	3	3.00	–	–	–
Javed Miandad	68	108	16	280*	5044	54.92	13	27	59/1
Manzoor Elahi	2	3	1	26	49	24.50	–	–	2
Mohsin Khan	40	65	5	200	2468	41.13	7	8	31
Mudassar Nazar	52	81	5	231	3099	40.77	8	12	37
Qasim Omar	17	29	1	210	1128	40.28	2	4	11
Rashid Khan	4	6	3	59	155	51.66	–	1	2
Salim Malik	24	34	6	119*	1242	44.35	5	6	27
Shoaib Mohammad	5	8	1	80	180	25.71	–	1	2
Tahir Naqqash	15	19	5	57	300	21.42	–	1	3
Tausif Ahmed	10	7	4	18	51	17.00	–	–	4
Wasim Akram†	2	4	3	8*	9	9.00	–	–	–
Wasim Raja†	57	92	14	125	2821	36.16	4	18	20
Zaheer Abbas	76	123	11	274	5058	45.16	12	20	34

Bowling	Type	Balls	R	W	Avge	Best	5wI	10wM
Abdul Qadir	LB	8777	4003	114	35.11	7-142	8	2
Azeem Hafeez	LFM	4351	2203	63	34.96	6-46	4	–
Iqbal Qasim	SLA	10787	3995	137	29.16	7-49	5	2
Jalaluddin	RMF	966	449	10	44.90	3-77	–	–
Javed Miandad	LB	1446	672	17	39.52	3-74	–	–
Manzoor Elahi	RM	162	76	1	76.00	1-74	–	–
Mohsin Khan	LB	86	30	0	–	–	–	–
Mudassar Nazar	RM	4120	1794	45	39.86	6-32	1	–
Qasim Omar	RM	6	0	0	–	–	–	–
Rashid Khan	RMF	738	360	8	45.00	3-129	–	–
Salim Malik	RM	122	61	3	20.33	1-3	–	–
Shoaib Mohammad	OB	6	4	0	–	–	–	–
Tahir Naqqash	RFM	2800	1398	34	41.11	5-40	2	–
Tausif Ahmed	OB	2310	924	29	31.86	4-58	–	–
Wasim Akram	LFM	562	233	12	19.41	5-56	2	1
Wasim Raja	LB	4092	1826	51	35.80	4-50	–	–
Zaheer Abbas	OB	370	132	3	44.00	2-21	–	–

Sri Lanka

Batting/Fielding	M	I	NO	HS	R	Avge	100	50	Ct/St
M.J.G. Amerasinghe	2	4	1	34	54	18.00	–	–	3
R.G. de Alwis	5	10	0	28	102	10.20	–	–	9/1
A.L.F. De Mel	7	14	3	34	188	17.09	–	–	5
D.S. De Silva	12	22	3	61	406	21.36	–	2	5
P.A. De Silva	1	2	0	16	19	9.50	–	–	–
R.L. Dias	9	17	0	109	747	43.94	2	5	6
E.R.N.S. Fernando	5	10	0	46	112	11.20	–	–	–
V.B. John	6	10	5	27*	53	10.60	–	–	2
S.M.S. Kaluperuma	3	6	0	23	82	13.66	–	–	6
R.S. Madugalle	12	24	3	91*	681	32.42	–	4	7
L.R.D. Mendis	10	20	0	111	726	36.30	3	3	4
A. Ranatunga†	9	18	0	90	521	28.94	–	5	3
R.J. (Rumesh) Ratnayake	4	8	0	30	76	9.50	–	–	3
J.R. (Ravi) Ratnayeke†	8	16	4	29*	150	12.50	–	–	1
S.A.R. Silva†	2	4	1	102*	118	39.33	1	–	5
S. Wettimuny	11	22	1	190	819	39.00	2	4	4

Bowling	Type	Balls	R	W	Avge	Best	5wI	10wM
M.J.G. Amerasinghe	SLA	300	150	3	50.00	2-73	–	–
A.L.F. De Mel	RFM	1515	1015	29	35.00	5-68	1	–
D.S. De Silva	LB	3031	1347	37	36.40	5-59	1	–
V.B. John	RMF	1281	614	28	21.92	5-60	2	–
S.M.S. Kaluperuma	OB	162	62	2	31.00	2-17	–	–
R.S. Madugalle	OB	24	4	0	–	–	–	–
A. Ranatunga	RM	432	173	5	34.60	2-17	–	–
R.J. (Rumesh) Ratnayake	RFM	678	405	8	50.62	4-81	–	–
J.R. (Ravi) Ratnayeke	RMF	1385	687	17	40.41	5-42	1	–
S. Wettimuny	RM	12	21	0	–	–	–	–

County Leavers 1985

Derbyshire: I. Broome, W.P. Fowler, D.G. Moir
Essex: K.S. McEwan, N. Phillip
Glamorgan: S.P. Henderson, L.L. McFarlane, S.J. Malone
Gloucestershire: Zaheer Abbas
Hampshire: D.J. Hacker, R.C.W. Mason
Kent: G.W. Johnson, A.P.E. Knott, K.D. Masters, L. Potter*, L.J. Wood
Lancashire: S.T. Jeffries, J.A. Ormrod, H. Pilling, G.J. Speak, R.G. Watson
Leicestershire: J.P. Addison, N.G.B. Cook*, M.A. Garnham, G.J. Parsons*
Middlesex: K.P. Tomlins
Northamptonshire: M.G. Beeby, R.F. Joseph, G. Sharp, M.B.H. Wheeler
Nottinghamshire: B. Hassan
Somerset: R.L. Ollis, N.F.M. Popplewell, M.S. Turner
Surrey: G.P. Howarth, N.S. Taylor, P.A. Waterman
Sussex: I.A. Greig, M.S. Scott
Warwickshire: C. Lethbridge, K.D. Smith
Worcestershire: D.A. Banks, D.J. Humphries, S.J.S. Kimber, H.V. Patel

* Expected to join a new county, N.G.B. Cook has joined Northamptonshire on a two-year contract.

THE MAGAZINE THE PLAYERS READ TOO

A probe into the past, present and future
The best in words and pictures

MONTHLY THROUGHOUT THE YEAR

Take out a subscription from:
WISDEN CRICKET MONTHLY
313 KILBURN LANE, LONDON W9 3EQ

Guide to Newcomers

Register of New Players 1985

The following players made their first appearance in English first-class county cricket during the 1985 season. Two of them, G.D. Rose for Middlesex in 1983 and 1984, and D.M. Ward for Surrey in 1984, had appeared previously in limited-overs matches. T.D. Topley made his debut for Surrey v Cambridge University before appearing in four Championship matches for Essex. Players indicated with a dagger (†) had already made their debuts in first-class cricket overseas.

Key to categories:

RH	Right-handed batsman	LFM	Left-arm fast-medium
LH	Left-handed batsman	LM	Left-arm medium
RF	Right-arm fast	OB	Right-arm slow off-breaks
RFM	Right-arm fast-medium	LB	Right-arm slow leg-breaks
RMF	Right-arm medium-fast	SLA	Left-arm slow leg-breaks
RM	Right-arm medium	WK	Wicket-keeper
LF	Left-arm fast		

Surname	Given Names	Birthdate	Place of Birth	Bat	Ball
Derbyshire					
Brown	Andrew Mark	6 Nov 64	Heanor, Derbyshire	LH	OB
Marples	Christopher	3 Aug 64	Chesterfield, Derbyshire	RH	(WK)
Sharma	Rajeshwar	27 Jun 62	Nairobi, Kenya	RH	RM
Essex					
Stephenson	John Patrick	14 Mar 65	Stebbing, Essex	RH	RM
Glamorgan					
James	Stephen Peter	7 Sep 67	Lydney, Gloucestershire	RH	—
Maynard	Matthew Peter	21 Mar 66	Oldham, Lancashire	RH	RM
North	Philip David	16 May 65	Newport, Monmouthshire	RH	RM
Roberts	Martin Leonard	12 Apr 66	Mullion, Cornwall	RH	(WK)
Smith	Ian	11 Mar 67	Chopwell, Co Durham	RH	RM
Gloucestershire					
Curran†	Kevin Malcolm	7 Sep 59	Rusape, S. Rhodesia	RH	RFM
Twizell	Peter Henry	18 Jun 59	Rothbury, Northumberland	RH	RFM
Hampshire					
Chivers	Ian James	5 Nov 64	Southampton, Hampshire	RH	OB
Lancashire					
Davidson	Ian Charles	21 Dec 64	Roe Green, Worsley, Lancs	RH	OB
Hayhurst	Andrew Neil	23 Nov 62	Davyhulme, Manchester	RH	RM
Henriksen	Soren	1 Dec 64	Rodoure, C'hagen, Denmark	RH	RFM
Murphy	Anthony John	6 Aug 62	Manchester	RH	RMF
Leicestershire					
Billington	David James	6 Dec 65	Leyland, Lancashire	RH	—
Blackett	Mark	3 Feb 64	Edmonton, London N18	RH	—
De Freitas	Phillip Anthony Jason	18 Feb 66	Scotts Head, Dominica	RH	RFM
Middlesex					
Rose	Graham David	12 Apr 64	Tottenham, London N17	RH	RM
Northamptonshire					
Harper†	Roger Andrew	17 Mar 63	Georgetown, Br. Guiana	RH	OB
Joseph†	Ray Fitzpatrick	12 Feb 61	Belladrum, British Guiana	RH	RFM
Storie	Alastair Caleb	25 Jul 65	Bishopbriggs, Glasgow	RH	RM
Wheeler	Matthew Benjamin Harold	14 Aug 62	Windlesham, Surrey	RH	RMF
Nottinghamshire					
Martindale	Duncan John Richardson	13 Dec 63	Harrogate, Yorkshire	RH	OB
Somerset					
Atkinson	Jonathon Colin Mark	10 Jul 68	Butleigh, Somerset	RH	RMF
Bail	Paul Andrew Clayden	23 Jun 65	Burnham-on-Sea, Somerset	RH	—
Coombs	Robert Vincent Jerome	20 Jul 59	Barnet, Herts	RH	SLA
Ferguson	Simon Alexander Ross	13 May 61	Lagos, Nigeria	RH	RM
Harden	Richard John	16 Aug 65	Bridgwater, Somerset	RH	LM
Jones	Andrew Paul	22 Sep 64	Southampton, Hants	RH	RMF

Register of New Players (contd)

Surname	Given Names	Birthdate	Place of Birth	Bat	Ball
Surrey					
Davies	Alec George	14 Aug 62	Rawalpindi, Pakistan	RH	(WK)
Gray†	Anthony Hollis	23 May 63	Port-of-Spain, Trinidad	RH	RF
Topley	Thomas Donald	25 Feb 64	Canterbury, Kent	RH	RMF
Ward	David Mark	10 Feb 61	Croydon, Surrey	RH	OB
Sussex					
Waring	Ian Charles	6 Dec 63	Chesterfield, Derbyshire	LH	RFM
Warwickshire					
Hoffman	Dean Stuart	13 Jan 66	Erdington, Birmingham	RH	RMF
Monkhouse	Steven	24 Nov 62	Bury, Lancashire	RH	LFM
Munton	Timothy Alan	30 Jul 65	Melton Mowbray, Leics	RH	RFM
Pierson	Adrian Roger Kirshaw	21 Jul 63	Enfield, Middlesex	RH	OB
Worcestershire					
Barrett	Brian Joseph	16 Nov 66	Auckland, New Zealand	RH	RFM
Bent	Paul	1 May 65	Worcester	RH	OB
Hussain	Mehriyat ('Mel')	17 Oct 63	South Shields, Co Durham	RH	OB
Kimber	Simon Julian Spencer	6 Oct 63	Ormskirk, Lancashire	RH	RMF
Lampitt	Stuart Richard	29 Jul 66	Wolverhampton, Staffs	RH	RM
McEwan	Steven Michael	5 May 62	Worcester	RH	RFM
Patel	Harshad Vallabh	29 Jan 64	Nairobi, Kenya	RH	—
Scothern	Mark	9 Mar 61	Shipton, Yorkshire	RH	RFM
Smith	Lawrence Kilner	6 Jan 64	Mirfield, Yorkshire	RH	—
Yorkshire					
Blakey	Richard John	15 Jan 67	Huddersfield, Yorkshire	RH	(WK)
Pickles	Christopher Stephen	30 Jan 66	Mirfield, Yorkshire	RH	RM
Cambridge University					
Ahluwalia	Manraj Singh	27 Dec 65	Isleworth, Middlesex	RH	OB
Browne	David William	4 Apr 64	Stamford, Lincolnshire	RH	—
Davidson	John Edward	23 Oct 64	Aberystwyth, Cardiganshire	RH	RFM
Fell	David John	27 Oct 64	Stafford	RH	LB
Gorman	Shaun Rodney	28 Apr 65	Middlesbrough, Yorkshire	RH	OB
Scott	Alastair Martin Gordon	31 Mar 66	Guildford, Surrey	RH	LM
Oxford University					
Denny	Christopher Mark	22 Apr 64	Farnborough, Kent	RH	SLA
Hagan	David Andrew	25 Jun 66	Wide Open, Northumberland	RH	OB
MacLarnon	Patrick Craig	24 Sep 63	Nottingham	RH	RM
Patel	Tikendra	9 Oct 65	Ahmedabad, India	RH	OB
Quinlan	Jeremy David	18 Apr 65	Watford, Herts	RH	RM
Rutnagur	Richard Sohrab	9 Aug 64	Bombay, India	RH	RM
Taylor	Darren Philip	15 Feb 65	Burnley, Lancashire	RH	(WK)
Tooley	Christopher Donald Michael	19 Apr 64	Farnborough, Kent	RH	RM

The following players made their first appearance in county cricket during 1985 but in limited-overs matches only. They have yet to make their debuts in first-class cricket:

Surname	Given Names	Birthdate	Place of Birth	Bat	Ball
Middlesex					
Roseberry	Michael Anthony	28 Nov 66	Houghton-le-Spring, Co Durham	RH	RM
Nottinghamshire					
Evans	Russell John	1 Oct 65	Calverton, Notts	RH	RM
Somerset					
Sully	Royston Cyril John	10 Apr 51	Taunton, Somerset	RH	RM
Yorkshire					
Byas	David	26 Aug 63	Kilham, Yorkshire	LH	—

Newcomers Record in English First-Class Cricket

Batting/Fielding		M	I	NO	HS	R	Avge	100	50	Ct/St
Derbyshire	A.M. Brown	2	3	0	74	93	31.00	–	1	3
	C. Marples	11	15	5	34	114	11.40	–	–	23/1
	R. Sharma	7	12	2	41*	209	20.90	–	–	6
Essex	J.P. Stephenson	1	2	0	10	14	7.00	–	–	1
Glamorgan	S.P. James	1	–	–	–	–	–	–	–	–
	M.P. Maynard	4	3	0	102	198	66.00	1	1	1
	P.D. North	1	1	1	0*	0	–	–	–	–
	M.L. Roberts	1	1	0	0	0	0.00	–	–	–
	I. Smith	6	5	0	12	27	5.40	–	–	1
Gloucestershire	K.M. Curran	26	34	3	83	762	24.58	–	5	8
	P.H. Twizell	1	–	–	–	–	–	–	–	–
Hampshire	I.J. Chivers	1	–	–	–	–	–	–	–	–
Lancashire	I.C. Davidson	1	2	0	13	13	6.50	–	–	2
	A.N. Hayhurst	1	1	0	17	17	17.00	–	–	–
	S. Henriksen	1	2	2	10*	10	–	–	–	1
	A.J. Murphy	2	3	1	2*	3	1.50	–	–	–
Leicestershire	D.J. Billington	1	1	0	19	19	19.00	–	–	1
	M. Blackett	2	4	2	28*	41	20.50	–	–	–
	P.A.J. De Freitas	9	12	3	30*	117	13.00	–	–	2
Middlesex	G.D. Rose	2	2	0	15	19	9.50	–	–	–
Northamptonshire	R.A. Harper	24	28	7	127	763	36.33	1	2	22
	R.F. Joseph	2	1	1	26*	26	–	–	–	–
	A.C. Storie	7	12	2	106	407	40.70	1	3	3
	M.B.H. Wheeler	2	–	–	–	–	–	–	–	–
Nottinghamshire	D.J.R. Martindale	9	14	3	104*	317	28.81	1	1	6
Somerset	J.C.M. Atkinson	6	5	1	79	167	41.75	–	1	–
	P.A.C. Bail	5	9	2	78*	127	18.14	–	1	–
	R.V.J. Coombs	4	3	0	1	1	0.33	–	–	–
	S.A.R. Ferguson	1	1	0	8	8	8.00	–	–	–
	R.J. Harden	12	17	5	107	366	30.50	1	1	9
	A.P. Jones	3	4	2	1*	3	1.50	–	–	1
Surrey	A.G. Davies	1	1	1	26*	26	–	–	–	3
	A.H. Gray	19	10	1	20	48	5.33	–	–	3
	T.D. Topley †	5	4	2	9*	15	7.50	–	–	2
	D.M. Ward	6	10	3	143	279	39.85	1	–	2
Sussex	I.C. Waring	1	–	–	–	–	–	–	–	–
Warwickshire	D.S. Hoffman	17	15	3	13*	39	3.25	–	–	3
	S. Monkhouse	1	2	1	5	7	7.00	–	–	–
	T.A. Munton	1	–	–	–	–	–	–	–	–
	A.R.K. Pierson	12	14	7	17*	90	12.85	–	–	3
Worcestershire	B.J. Barrett	1	–	–	–	–	–	–	–	–
	P. Bent	1	1	0	14	14	14.00	–	–	–
	M. Hussain	1	1	0	4	4	4.00	–	–	–
	S.J.S. Kimber	2	1	1	14*	14	–	–	–	1
	S.R. Lampitt	1	1	0	0	0	0.00	–	–	–
	S.M. McEwan	10	8	5	13*	25	8.33	–	–	1
	H.V. Patel	1	1	0	39	39	39.00	–	–	–
	M. Scothern	1	–	–	–	–	–	–	–	–
	L.K. Smith	1	1	0	28	28	28.00	–	–	–
Yorkshire	R.J. Blakey	14	22	2	90	518	25.90	–	2	12
	C.S. Pickles	6	3	1	31*	52	26.00	–	–	3
Cambridge U	M.S. Ahluwalia	4	7	1	31	55	9.16	–	–	3
	D.W. Brown	1	1	0	10	10	10.00	–	–	1
	J.E. Davidson	4	4	2	22	25	12.50	–	–	2
	D.J. Fell	9	16	1	109*	332	22.13	1	1	4
	S.R. Gorman	9	15	5	43	177	17.70	–	–	3
	A.M.G. Scott	9	7	4	5*	12	4.00	–	–	2

† Includes 4 matches for Essex

EXTRAS/GUIDE TO NEWCOMERS 217

Batting/Fielding (contd)		M	I	NO	HS	R	Avge	100	50	Ct/St
Oxford U	C.M. Denny	4	6	1	19	28	5.60	–	–	3
	D.A. Hagan	5	10	1	46	148	16.44	–	–	4
	P.C. MacLarnon	7	10	1	56	168	18.66	–	1	3
	T. Patel	9	17	4	47	159	12.23	–	–	5
	J.D. Quinlan	7	6	2	22*	34	8.50	–	–	1
	R.S. Rutnagur	11	15	2	66	246	18.92	–	2	3
	D.P. Taylor	4	6	2	5*	5	1.25	–	–	1/2
	C.D.M. Tooley	11	16	0	66	257	16.06	–	1	2

Bowling		O	M	R	W	Avge	Best	5wI	10wM
Glamorgan	M.P. Maynard	0.1	0	4	0	–	–	–	–
	P.D. North	27	7	60	1	60.00	1-60	–	–
	I. Smith	44.4	11	154	1	154.00	1-39	–	–
Gloucestershire	K.M. Curran	469.5	104	1419	61	23.26	5-35	2	–
	P.H. Twizell	28	6	98	2	49.00	2-65	–	–
Hampshire	I.J. Chivers	22	5	72	1	72.00	1-5	–	–
Lancashire	I.C. Davidson	10	3	24	2	12.00	2-24	–	–
	A.N. Hayhurst	13	4	37	3	12.33	3-37	–	–
	S. Henriksen	12	1	44	1	44.00	1-44	–	–
	A.J. Murphy	56.2	15	207	6	34.50	3-84	–	–
Leicestershire	P.A.J. De Freitas	234.2	43	703	27	26.03	5-39	1	–
Middlesex	G.D. Rose	45.1	8	142	9	15.77	6-41	1	–
Northamptonshire	R.A. Harper	775.3	187	2107	58	36.32	5-94	1	–
	R.F. Joseph	38	5	143	4	35.75	3-73	–	–
	A.C. Storie	18	6	51	0	–	–	–	–
	M.B.H. Wheeler	34	3	117	1	117.00	1-87	–	–
Nottinghamshire	D.J.R. Martindale	2	0	8	0	–	–	–	–
Somerset	J.C.M. Atkinson	65	9	250	2	125.00	1-36	–	–
	P.A.C. Bail	4	2	4	0	–	–	.	–
	R.V.J. Coombs	93	27	268	16	16.75	5-58	1	–
	R.J. Harden	12.3	5	33	2	16.50	1-4	–	–
	A.P. Jones	37	4	142	3	47.33	1-9	–	–
Surrey	A.H. Gray	524	99	1816	79	22.98	8-40	6	1
	T.D. Topley †	161.1	37	464	17	27.29	4-57	–	–
Warwickshire	D.S. Hoffman	326.4	53	1160	28	41.42	4-100	–	–
	S. Monkhouse	17	2	61	1	61.00	1-61	–	–
	T.A. Munton	9	0	35	0	–	–	–	–
	A.R.K. Pierson	155	30	587	8	73.37	3-92	–	–
Worcestershire	B.J. Barrett	18	7	40	1	40.00	1-40	–	–
	S.J.S. Kimber	20	2	72	3	24.00	3-40	–	–
	S.R. Lampitt	1	0	1	0	–	–	–	–
	S.M. McEwan	177	29	635	16	39.68	3-47	–	–
	M. Scothern	16	6	42	1	42.00	1-42	–	–
Yorkshire	C.S. Pickles	126.3	30	385	6	64.16	2-31	–	–
Cambridge U	J.E. Davidson	80	12	254	4	63.50	3-22	–	–
	S.R. Gorman	117.4	17	465	3	155.00	1-27	–	–
	A.M.G. Scott	243.3	34	879	25	35.16	5-68	1	–
Oxford U	D.A. Hagan	1	0	6	0	–	–	–	–
	P.C. MacLarnon	60.3	10	229	1	229.00	1-18	–	–
	J.D. Quinlan	189	37	635	10	63.50	4-76	–	–
	R.S. Rutnagur	189	25	728	15	48.53	5-112	1	–

† Includes 4 matches for Essex

Obituary 1984-85

Two famous cricketers and many other distinguished ones, besides several whose services to the game lay off the field, have died since the last Year Book went to press. *P.G.H. Fender*, of Surrey, was the oldest Test cricketer when he died aged 92. There has been no shrewder county captain nor many better or more engaging all-rounders. He was one of the first to act on the principle that county cricket needed to be a public entertainment as well as an art-form. *J.H. Wardle* was one of the most gifted of post-war Yorkshire cricketers, as left-arm spinner in two styles and dangerous hitter. Despite competition from Tony Lock, he took 102 Test wickets. If his county had encouraged his wrist-spin, he would have been of even more use at home and quite invaluable abroad.

Next in line come a staunch range of county cricketers: the inimitable *George Cox*, whose service with Sussex along with that of his father, also George, spanned 63 years and more than a thousand matches; *Bernard Quaife*, another son of a distinguished father (W.G.); *Les Berry*, who for countless summers bore the Leicestershire batting on his back; *Len Hopwood*, a highly respected all-rounder who recently became Lancashire's first ex-professional president; *Jim Cornford*, a typical Sussex cricketer in bowling pace and disposition, who emigrated to Zimbabwe and was involved in the game there until his death; *Leslie Compton*, brother of Denis and a great Arsenal footballer, who kept wicket for Middlesex; another Sussex Jim and fast-medium bowler, *Hammond* by name, also a footballer, with Fulham, and after retirement coach at Cheltenham and Brighton Colleges; and *Don Brennan*, who as an amateur kept regularly seven years for Yorkshire and twice in 1951 for England, actually being preferred to Godfrey Evans. *R.E. Bird* was a useful bat in the post-war Worcestershire sides, and was a popular captain, 1952-54.

Several Oxford and Cambridge cricketers who also made a mark with their counties are to be noted, starting with *J.L. Bryan*, the best of the left-handed Kentish brotherhood. Jack Bryan opened the innings in the great Cambridge side of 1921. In making 236 against Hampshire in 1923, he broke not only the St. Lawrence ground record, but a pavilion window, the ball plus bits of glass then bouncing via a table into the famous Chevallier Tayler picture on the opposite wall. *G.A. Rotherham*, also of Warwickshire, was a Cambridge contemporary. *H.W.F. Franklin*, subsequently for 22 years headmaster of Epsom, had an Oxford double for cricket and rugger and played in the holidays for Essex. *A.T. Barber* spent a working lifetime in schoolmastering at Ludgrove, but not before he had, in 1929, led Oxford both at Lord's and on the soccer field at Stamford Bridge, and then gone on, for one memorable season, to captain Yorkshire: a rare character with a multitude of friends. Opposing Barber at Lord's was another schoolmaster and double Blue for cricket and soccer, *A.H. Fabian*, who, also like Barber, was a Corinthian.

Three overseas Test cricketers should be mentioned: *M.E. Chapple* of New Zealand and the Indians *K.M. Rangnekar* and *D.G. Phadkar*. The last-named was one of the stalwarts of Indian cricket after the war, an attractive bat and a lively bowler.

There remain other men prominently connected with the game in a variety of ways. *Jim Fairbrother*, head groundsman at Lord's, lingered on through a summer of ill-health in 1984 before dying within days of his announced retirement. The 5th *Lord Harris*, son of the illustrious cricketer and administrator, died aged 95. He was first in seniority among MCC members, having been elected in 1910. Harris, a patron rather than a player, was twice president of Kent.

Lastly come four men of the media. *Michael Standing* of the BBC was a pioneer of cricket outside broadcasts and an admirable commentator himself. *Gordon Ross* was a jack-of-all-trades, freelance journalist, editor, author, and public relations man, who had much to do with the launching of the Gillette Cup, the ideal prototype for sporting promotions. *John Marshall*, for many years editor of the best-selling though now defunct Evening News, wrote several cricket books and notably the standard work on the history of Sussex. The

Hon. Terence Prittie wrote cricket for the then Manchester Guardian, and during the postwar decade was the author of five books of quality, centred chiefly on his abiding loves, Middlesex and Lancashire.

E.W. Swanton

Career Details (b – born; d – died; F-c – first-class career)

BARBER, Alan Theodore; b Eccleshall (Sheffield), Yorkshire, 17 Jun 1905; d Wokingham, Berkshire, 10 Mar 1985. Oxford U (Blue 1927-28-29, captain 1929) and Yorkshire (captain 1930). F-c (1927-30): 2,261 runs (23.30), 2 hundreds.

BERRY, George Leslie (known as Leslie George); b Dorking, Surrey, 28 Apr 1906; d Great Glen, Leics, 5 Feb 1985. Leicestershire (captain 1946-48). Soccer for Sheffield Wednesday, Bristol Rovers, and Swindon Town. F-c (1924-51): 30,225 runs (30.25), 45 hundreds; 10 wkts (60.60); 181 ct.

BIRD, Ronald Ernest; b Quarry Bank, Staffs, 4 Apr 1915; d Feckenham, Worcs, 20 Feb 1985. Worcestershire (captain 1952-54). F-c (1946-58): 7,700 runs (26.10), 7 hundreds; 23 wkts (48.73).

BRADSHAW James Cecil; b Romford, Essex, 25 Jan 1902; d Minehead, Somerset, 8 Nov 1984. Leicestershire. Brother of W.H. (Leics). Hockey for Leicestershire (6 seasons). F-c (1923-33): 5,051 runs (18.98), 3 hundreds.

BRENNAN, Donald Vincent; b Eccleshill (Bradford) Yorkshire, 10 Feb 1920; d Bradford 9 Jan 1985. Yorkshire and England. F-c (1947-53): 1,937 runs (10.52); 318 ct, 122 st.

BRYAN, John Lindsay; b Beckenham, Kent, 26 May 1896; d Eastbourne, Sussex, 23 Apr 1985. Cambridge U (Blue 1921) and Kent. Brother of G.J. and R.T. (Kent). F-c (1919-33): 8,702 runs (36.25), 17 hundreds; 15 wkts (45.00).

CARROLL, Sidney Joseph; b Willoughby, Sydney, Australia, 28 Nov 1922; d Willoughby 11 Oct 1984. New South Wales. F-c (1945-46 to 1958-59): 2,811 runs (39.59), 6 hundreds.

CHAPPLE, Murray Ernest; b Christchurch, New Zealand, 25 Jul 1930; d Hamilton 30 Jul 1985. Canterbury, Central Districts and New Zealand. F-c (1949-50 to 1971-72): 5,344 runs (28.88), 4 hundreds; 142 wkts (25.06).

COMPTON, Leslie Harry; b Woodford, Essex, 12 Sep 1912; d Witham, Essex, 27 Dec 1984. Middlesex. Brother of D.C.S. (Middlesex and England). Soccer (centre-half) for Arsenal and England (2 caps 1950-51). F-c (1938-56): 5,814 runs (16.75), 1 hundred; 12 wkts (47.41); 468 ct, 131 st.

CORNFORD, James Henry; b Crowborough Sussex, 9 Dec 1911; d Harare, Zimbabwe, 16 Jun 1985. Sussex. F-c (1931-52): 1,357 runs (5.34), 1,019 wkts (26.49); 116 ct.

COX, George; b Warnham, Sussex, 23 Aug 1911; d Burgess Hill, Sussex, 30 Mar 1985. Sussex. Son of G.R. (Sussex). Soccer (centre-forward) for Arsenal, Fulham, and Luton. F-c (1931-61): 22,949 runs (32.92), 50 hundreds, 192 wkts (30.91); 139 ct.

CROSS, Eric Percival; b Handsworth, Birmingham, 25 Jun 1896; d Handsworth 27 Feb 1985. Warwickshire and Staffordshire. F-c (1921-23): 61 runs (7.62); 9 ct, 1 st.

CULLEN. Leonard; b Johannesburg, South Africa, 23 Nov 1914; d Johannesburg 15 Sep 1984. Northamptonshire. F-c (1934-35): 253 runs (8.43); 11 wkts (59.09).

CUNNINGHAM, William Henry Ranger; b Christchurch, New Zealand, 23 Jan 1900; d Christchurch 29 Nov 1984. Canterbury. Toured Australia 1925-26 and England 1927. F-c (1922-23 to 1930-31): 396 runs (11.64); 91 wkts (34.30).

FABIAN, Aubrey Howard; b East Finchley, Middlesex, 20 Mar 1909; d 26 Sept 1984. Cambridge U (Blue 1929-30-31). Toured Jamaica (Oxford and Cambridge Us) 1938-39. Soccer for Cambridge U and Derby County – amateur international. F-c (1929 to 1938-39): 763 runs (26.31); 61 wkts (37.37).

FENDER, Percy George Herbert; b Balham, London, 22 Aug 1892; d Exeter, Devon, 16 Jun 1985. Sussex (1910-13), Surrey (1914-35) and England. F-c (1910-35): 19,034 runs (26.65), 21 hundreds; 1,894 wkts (25.04); 600 ct.

FRANKLIN, Henry William Fernehough; b Ford End, Essex, 30 Jun 1901; d Worthing, Sussex, 25 May 1985. Oxford U (1921-24, Blue 1924), Surrey (1921 – 1 match), and Essex (1921-31). Brother of R.C. (Essex). F-c (1921-31): 2,212 runs (19.23), 2 hundreds; 46 wkts (43.52).

HAMMOND, Herbert Edward ('Jim'); b Brighton, Sussex, 7 Nov 1907; d Brighton 16 Jun 1985. Sussex. Soccer for Fulham. F-c (1928-46): 4,251 runs (18.72), 1 hundred; 428 wkts (28.73).

HAYWOOD, Esme Thomas Lancelot Reed; b East Preston, Sussex, 23 Aug 1900; d Hereford 8 Jan 1985. Somerset. F-c (1925-27): 137 runs (8.56).

HOPKINS, Victor; b Dumbleton, Glos, 21 Jan 1911; d Dumbleton 6 Aug 1984. Gloucestershire. F-c (1934-48): 2,608 runs (14.81); 138 ct, 44 st.

HOPWOOD, John Leonard; b Newton Hyde, Cheshire, 10 Oct 1903; d Denton, Lancashire, 15 Jun

1985. Lancashire, Cheshire and England. F-c (1923-39): 15,548 runs (29.90), 27 hundreds; 673 wkts (22.45); 198 ct.
HUGHES-HALLETT, Lt Col Norton Montresor; b Melbourne, Derbyshire, 18 Apr 1895; d 26 Mar 1985. Derbyshire and Europeans. F-c (1913 to 1926-27): 255 runs (15.93); 17 wkts (18.35).
JOHNSON, Tyrel Fabian; b Tunapuna, Trinidad, 10 Jan 1917; d Caura, Trinidad, 5 Apr 1985. Trinidad and West Indies. F-c (1935-36 to 1939): 90 runs (9.00); 50 wkts (21.50).
MERCHANT, Uday Madhavji; b Bombay, India, 14 Oct 1916; d Bombay 7 Feb 1985. Bombay and Hindus. Brother of V.M. (Bombay, Hindus, and India). F-c (1938-39 to 1950-51): 2,789 runs (55.78), 9 hundreds.
MERMAGEN, Patrick Hassell Frederick; b Colyton, Devon, 8 May 1911; d Ipswich, Suffolk, 20 Dec 1984. Somerset. F-c (1930): 114 runs (11.40).
O'CONNOR, Leo Patrick Devereaux; b Murtoa, Victoria, Australia 1890; d 16 Jan 1985. Queensland. F-c (1912-13 to 1929-30): 3,311 runs (39.89); 9 hundreds; 82 ct, 21 st.
PARKER, John Palmer; b Portsmouth, Hampshire, 29 Nov 1902; d Warblington, Hants, 9 Aug 1984. Hampshire. F-c (1926-33): 1,117 runs (17.45), 1 hundred; 6 wkts (43.00).
PHADKAR, Dattatraya Gajanan ('Dattu'); b Kolhapur, Maharashtra, India, 12 Dec 1925; d Madras 17 Mar 1985. Maharashtra, Hindus, Bombay, Bengal, Railways, and India. F-c (1942-43 to 1959-60): 5,377 runs (36.08), 8 hundreds; 466 wkts (22.04); 92 ct.
QUAIFE, Bernard William; b Olton, Warwicks, 24 Nov 1899; d Bridport, Dorset, 28 Nov 1984. Warwickshire (1920-26) and Worcestershire (1928-37). Son of William (Warwicks and England) and nephew of Walter (Sussex and Warwicks). F-c (1920-37): 9,594 runs (20.02), 3 hundreds; 9 wkts (33.00); 186 ct, 54 st.
RANGNEKAR, Khanderao Moreshwar; b Maharashtra, India, 27 Jun 1917; d Bombay 11 Oct 1984. Maharashtra, Bombay, Holkar, and India. F-c (1939-40 to 1963-64): 4,602 runs (41.45), 15 hundreds; 21 wkts (40.95).
RICHARDSON, John Alan; b Sleights, Yorkshire, 4 Aug 1908; d Scarborough, Yorkshire, 2 Apr 1985. Yorkshire. F-c (1934-47): 343 runs (31.18); 2 wkts (54.00).
ROTHERHAM, Gerard Alexander; b Coventry, Warwicks, 28 May 1899; d Bakewell, Derbyshire, 31 Jan 1985. Cambridge U (1919-20 – Blue 1919), Warwickshire (1919-21), and Wellington (1928-29). F-c (1919 to 1928-29): 1,801 runs (18.76); 180 wkts (28.36).
SHAW, George Bernard; b Treharris, Glamorgan, 24 Oct 1931; d Port Pirie, South Australia, Aug 1984. Glamorgan. F-c (1951-55): 30 runs (4.28); 26 wkts (27.15).
WARDLE, John Henry; b Arsley, Yorkshire, 8 Jan 1923; d Hatfield, Doncaster, Yorkshire, 23 Jul 1985. Yorkshire (1946-58), Cambridgeshire and England. F-c (1946 to 1967-68): 7,333 runs (16.08); 1,846 wkts (18.97). 256 ct.
WATERS, Albert Edward; b Stoke Bishop, Bristol, 8 May 1902; d Bristol Jun 1985. Gloucestershire and Wiltshire. F-c (1923-25): 270 runs (12.85); 5 wkts (75.40).

Their Record in Tests

Batting/Fielding	Career	M	I	NO	HS	R	Avge	100	50	Ct/St
D.V. Brennan (Eng)	1951	2	2	0	16	16	8.00	–	–	–/1
M.E. Chapple (NZ)	1952/3-1965/6	14	27	1	76	497	19.11	–	3	10
P.G.H. Fender (Eng)	1920/1-1929	13	21	1	60	380	19.00	–	2	14
J.L. Hopwood (Eng)	1934	2	3	1	8	12	6.00	–	–	–
T.F. Johnson† (WI)	1939	1	1	1	9*	9	–	–	–	1
D.G. Phadkar (Ind)	1947/8-1958/9	31	45	7	123	1229	32.34	2	8	21
K.M. Rangnekar† (Ind)	1947/8	3	6	0	18	33	5.50	–	–	1
J.H. Wardle† (Eng)	1947/8-1957	28	41	8	66	653	19.78	–	2	12

†Left-handed batsman

Bowling	Type	Balls	R	W	Avge	Best	5wI	10wM
M.E. Chapple (NZ)	SLA	248	84	1	84.00	1-24	–	–
P.G.H. Fender (Eng)	RM/LB	2178	1185	29	40.86	5-90	2	–
J.L. Hopwood (Eng)	LM	462	155	0	–	–	–	–
T.F. Johnson (WI)	LF	240	129	3	43.00	2-53	–	–
D.G. Phadkar (Ind)	RFMorOB	5994	2285	62	36.85	7-159	3	–
J.H. Wardle (Eng)	SLAorSLC	6597	2080	102	20.39	7-36	5	1

Looking forward

England on Tour 1985-86

Tour Party to West Indies

	Age	Caps		Age	Caps
D.I. Gower, captain (Leics)	28	76	B.N. French (Notts)	26	0
M.W. Gatting, vice-capt (Middx)	28	41	G.A. Gooch (Essex)	32	48
I.T. Botham (Somerset)	29	79	A.J. Lamb (Northants)	31	38
P.R. Downton (Middx)	28	21	R.T. Robinson (Notts)	26	11
P.H. Edmonds (Middx)	34	33	D.M. Smith (Worcs)	29	0
R.M. Ellison (Kent)	26	7	L.B. Taylor (Leics)	31	2
J.E. Emburey (Middx)	33	28	J.G. Thomas (Glamorgan)	25	0
N.A. Foster (Essex)	23	9	P. Willey (Leics)	35	21

Tour Manager: A.S. Brown. Assistant Manager: R.G.D. Willis. Physiotherapist: L. Brown.

Tour Itinerary

February	1, 2, 3, 4	Windwards (St Vincent)
	7, 8, 9, 10	Leewards (Antigua)
	13, 14, 15, 16	Jamaica
	18	West Indies (Jamaica), 1st one-day international
	21, 22, 23, 25, 26	**West Indies** (Jamaica), First Test
	28, 1, 2 March	Trinidad
March	4	West Indies (Trinidad), 2nd one-day international
	7, 8, 9, 11, 12	**West Indies** (Trinidad), Second Test
	14, 15, 16, 17	Barbados
	19	West Indies (Barbados), 3rd one-day international
	21, 22, 23, 25, 26	**West Indies** (Barbados), Third Test
	30	West Indies (Trinidad), 4th one-day international
April	3, 4, 5, 6, 8	**West Indies** (Trinidad), Fourth Test
	11, 12, 13, 15, 16	**West Indies** (Antigua), Fifth Test
	18	*Depart for London*

'I Was There'

20 great sporting memories from 20 top writers. The sports correspondents from the *Daily* and *Sunday Telegraph* look back over the last 20 years and pick out the deeds and events that still give them a thrill when they say, 'I was there' . . . the magic of Pelé . . . Ali's 'rumble in the jungle' . . . the miracle of Headingley . . . these and many more – all are brought vividly back to life as the *Telegraph* writers recapture the atmosphere and relive those memorable moments of sporting history.

Available through leading bookshops, the Telegraph Bookshop at 130 Fleet Street, price £7.95 hardback, or by post from Dept. IWT, Daily Telegraph, 135 Fleet Street, London EC4P 4BL (please add 55p for postage and packing).

'B' Team Tour Party to Bangladesh, Sri Lanka, and Zimbabwe

	Age	Caps		Age	Caps
M.C.J. Nicholas, capt. (Hants)	27	0	M.D. Moxon (Yorkshire)	25	0
K.J. Barnett, vice-capt (Derbys)	25	0	D.R. Pringle (Essex)	27	10
J.P. Agnew (Leics)	25	3	D.W. Randall (Notts)	34	47
C.W.J. Athey (Glos)	27	3	S.J. Rhodes (Worcs)	21	0
N.G.B. Cook (Northants)	29	9	W.N. Slack (Middx)	30	0
N.G. Cowans (Middx)	24	19	C.L. Smith (Hants)	26	7
D.V. Lawrence (Glos)	21	0	T.M. Tremlett (Hants)	29	0

'B' Tour Itinerary

In Bangladesh
January	7	Bangladesh (Chittagong)
	9, 10, 11	Bangladesh (Dhaka)
	12	Bangladesh (Dhaka)

In Sri Lanka
January	16, 17, 18	President's XI (Sara Stadium, Colombo)
	20, 21, 22, 23	Sri Lanka (SSC, Colombo), 1st Unofficial Test
	26, 27, 28, 29	Sri Lanka (CCC, Colombo), 2nd Unofficial Test
February	1	Sri Lanka (Sara Stadium)
	2	Sri Lanka (Sara Stadium)
	4	Sri Lanka (SSC, Colombo)
	6, 7, (8)	Nuwara Eliya District Association (Radella)
	10, 11, 12, 13	Sri Lanka (Asgiriya Stadium, Kandy) 3rd Unofficial Test

In Zimbabwe
February	17, 18, 19	Zimbabwe 'B' (Harare)
	21, 22, 24	Zimbabwe (Harare)
	23	Zimbabwe (Harare)
	26	Zimbabwe South (Harare)
	28, March 1, 3	Zimbabwe (Bulawayo)
March	2	Zimbabwe (Bulawayo)
	5, 6, 7	Zimbabwe (Harare)
	9	Zimbabwe (Harare)
	12	President's XI (Mutare)
	15, 16, 17, 18	Zimbabwe (Harare)

The Cricketer
INTERNATIONAL

more depth . . . more variety . . . more antiquity and more topicality than any other cricket magazine

Founded by Sir Pelham Warner in 1921.
Edited by Christopher Martin-Jenkins in 1985.
To open a subscription for 12 months, please fill in below or transfer details to a letter or postcard.

SUBSCRIPTION FORM: Only £12.45 for 12 issues (two of which are the extra large annuals) to join the regular readers of the world's largest selling cricket magazine.

PLEASE OPEN A SUBSCRIPTION (tick appropriate box)
THE CRICKETER (One-year subscriptions): Inland, Ireland, Channel Islands BFPO £12.45 ☐
Airmail £21.70 ☐ Overseas surface mail £13.45 ☐

*For subscriptions to the following countries please send; sterling as above or **Surface mail**: USA $25.04, Canada $30.20, Australia $22.92, New Zealand $31.33, Holland 64.58 guilders, Eire IR £16.72.*
***Airmail**: USA $43.02, Canada $50.92, Australia $37.09, New Zealand $50.70, Holland 104.09 guilders.*

THE CRICKETER QUARTERLY FACTS AND FIGURES: Inland, Ireland, Channel Islands BFPO £5.90 ☐ Airmail £8.70 ☐ Overseas surface mail £5.90 ☐

*For subscriptions to the following countries please send; sterling as above or **Surface mail**: USA $10.69, Canada $12.65, Australia $9.16, New Zealand $12.20, Holland 25.15 guilders, Eire IR £6.51.*
***Airmail**: USA $15.85, Canada $18.76, Australia $13.74, New Zealand $18.78, Holland 38.70 guilders.*
IF THIS FORM IS USED TO RENEW AN EXISTING SUBSCRIPTION PLEASE TICK HERE ☐ AND QUOTE COMPUTER NUMBER IF KNOWN. SUBSCRIPTIONS ACCEPTED FOR ONE-YEAR PERIODS ONLY.

Name ....

Address ....

....

....

I enclose my remittance for £ ....
Payable to THE CRICKETER LTD, Beech Hanger, Ashurst, Tunbridge Wells, Kent TN3 9ST.

The 1986 Season

Times have changed since a season without a visiting team from Australia or West Indies could be expected to produce a one-sided Test series. Both India and New Zealand, who will be coming in 1986, have successes to their name in the last few years that suggest that, given reasonable weather, they can again make even an improved England side work hard.

India, moreover, will be coming with two of the most brilliant young players in the world – Azharuddin, who made a hundred in each of his first three Tests in 1984-85 against England, and Sivaramakrishnan, the leg-spinner who made such an impact against England and later in Australia.

The comparison with Bob Holland, who played in four Tests for Australia against England in 1985, will be interesting. After his initial success at Lord's, when he exploited the rough and played a major part in Australia's victory, Holland was used largely in a containing role, continuing to bowl into rough that was much less helpful to him than at Lord's, and being played comfortably by the best England batsmen. Sivaramakrishnan promises more exciting exchanges, for, though he may not have Holland's unusual accuracy, he does have an effective and well disguised googly.

Successes by visiting leg-spinners are few on low, slow English pitches, but Sivarama's is not the only Indian spin, and the balance of the side is greatly helped by the all-round talents of Ravi Shastri, who won the car awarded to the outstanding player of the so-called 'Mini-World Cup' in Australia in February and March 1985.

In England in 1986, India will have the chance to show whether this 1985 victory and that in the 1983 World Cup were passing triumphs, helped by certain types of pitch on which their medium-pace and spin are peculiarly awkward to attack, or whether they have a genuine new-found flair for the limited-overs game. In any case, they have a variety of good bowling and a depth of batting which make them on paper far stronger than most Indian sides of the past.

New Zealand, on their last visit, won their first Test victory in England, and since then have beaten England in a series in New Zealand. They are the last country to have won a series against West Indies. Their perennial problem is lack of depth in their cricket. But they no longer suffer from the fact that visits to England were so spaced out – sometimes seven years, sometimes nine – that the experience gained on one tour was seldom used on the next. New Zealand, above all, have benefited from the two-tour system introduced in the 1960s. Now they are coming only three years after their last visit, with others beside the redoubtable Richard Hadlee still in their prime. It is worth remembering, too, that though Hadlee had a tremendous tour in 1983 with both bat and ball, he did not take a wicket when New Zealand won at Headingley. It was far from a one-man band.

Fixtures 1986

Duration of Matches (*including play on Sunday)

Cornhill Tests	5 days	One-day Internationals	1 day
Britannic Assurance		Benson & Hedges Cup	1 day
County Championship	3 days	NatWest Bank Trophy	1 day
Tourist matches	3 days or as stated	John Player League	1 day
University matches v Counties	3 days	Other matches	as stated

APRIL 19, SATURDAY
The Parks	Oxford U v Somerset
Fenners	Cambridge U v Leics

APRIL 23, WEDNESDAY
Lord's	MCC v Middlesex
The Parks	Oxford U v Glos
Fenners	Cambridge U v Essex

APRIL 26, SATURDAY
Britannic Assurance Championship
Bristol*	Glos v Glamorgan
Leicester	Leics v Kent
Lord's	Middlesex v Derbyshire
Trent Bridge*	Notts v Hampshire
Taunton*	Somerset v Yorkshire
Hove*	Sussex v Lancashire
Edgbaston*	Warwickshire v Essex
Worcester*	Worcs v Surrey

Other Match
Fenners	Cambridge U v Northants

APRIL 30, WEDNESDAY
Britannic Assurance Championship
Chesterfield	Derbyshire v Somerset
Southampton	Hampshire v Glamorgan
Canterbury	Kent v Northants
Old Trafford	Lancashire v Leics
The Oval	Surrey v Notts

Other Matches
The Parks	Oxford U v Middlesex
Fenners	Cambridge U v Warwickshire

MAY 3, SATURDAY
Benson & Hedges Cup
Chesterfield	Derbyshire v Leics
Bristol	Glos v Somerset
Old Trafford	Lancashire v Yorkshire
Lord's	Middlesex v Surrey
Hove	Sussex v Essex
Slough	Minor Counties v Northants
The Parks	Combined Univ v Hampshire
Glasgow (Titwood)	Scotland v Worcs

MAY 4, SUNDAY
John Player League
Chelmsford	Essex v Warwickshire
Cardiff	Glamorgan v Hampshire
Canterbury	Kent v Glos
Old Trafford	Lancashire v Sussex
Leicester	Leics v Derbyshire
Lord's	Middlesex v Notts
Bradford	Yorkshire v Somerset

Tourist Match
Arundel	Lavinia, Duchess of Norfolk's XI v India (one day)

MAY 6, TUESDAY
Tourist Match
Worcester	Worcs v India

MAY 7, WEDNESDAY
Britannic Assurance Championship
Chelmsford	Essex v Kent
Old Trafford	Lancashire v Hampshire
Lord's	Middlesex v Leics
Northampton	Notts v Glos
Taunton	Somerset v Glamorgan
The Oval	Surrey v Worcs
Headingley	Yorkshire v Sussex

Other Match
The Parks	Oxford U v Notts

MAY 10, SATURDAY
Benson & Hedges Cup
Swansea	Glamorgan v Sussex
Southampton	Hampshire v Middlesex
Canterbury	Kent v Surrey
Leicester	Leics v Warwickshire
Northampton	Northants v Derbyshire
Trent Bridge	Notts v Yorkshire
Taunton	Somerset v Essex
Perth (North Inch)	Scotland v Lancashire

Tourist Match
Cheltenham Town CC	Glos v India

MAY 11, SUNDAY
John Player League
Derby	Derbyshire v Sussex
Swansea	Glamorgan v Leics
Southampton	Hampshire v Northants
Trent Bridge	Notts v Warwickshire
Taunton	Somerset v Middlesex
The Oval	Surrey v Yorkshire
Worcester	Worcs v Kent

MAY 13, TUESDAY
Benson & Hedges Cup
Chelmsford	Essex v Glos
Northampton	Northants v Leics
Trent Bridge	Notts v Scotland
Taunton	Somerset v Glamorgan
The Oval	Surrey v Hampshire
Worcester	Worcs v Lancashire
Walsall	Minor Counties v Warwickshire
Fenners	Combined Univ v Kent

MAY 15, THURSDAY
Benson & Hedges Cup
Derby	Derbyshire v Minor Counties
Chelmsford	Essex v Glamorgan
Bristol	Glos v Sussex
Southampton	Hampshire v Kent
Lord's	Middlesex v Combined Univ
Edgbaston	Warwickshire v Northants
Worcester	Worcs v Notts
Headingley	Yorkshire v Scotland

Tourist Match
The Oval	Surrey v India (one day)

MAY 17, SATURDAY
Benson & Hedges Cup
Swansea	Glamorgan v Glos
Canterbury	Kent v Middlesex
Liverpool	Lancashire v Notts
Leicester	Leics v Minor Counties
The Oval	Surrey v Combined Univ
Hove	Sussex v Somerset
Edgbaston	Warwickshire v Derbys
Headingley	Yorkshire v Worcs

Britannic Assurance Championship
Northampton	Northants v Essex

Tourist Match
Southampton*	Hampshire v India

MAY 18, SUNDAY
John Player League
Leek CC	Derbyshire v Warwickshire
Swindon	Glos v Essex
Leicester	Leics v Lancashire
Lord's	Middlesex v Kent
Trent Bridge	Notts v Sussex
The Oval	Surrey v Glamorgan
Headingley	Yorkshire v Worcs

MAY 21, WEDNESDAY
Britannic Assurance Championship
Chelmsford	Essex v Yorkshire
Lord's	Middlesex v Glamorgan
Trent Bridge	Notts v Leics
Taunton	Somerset v Glos
Hove	Sussex v Surrey
Edgbaston	Warwickshire v Northants
Worcester	Worcs v Lancashire

Tourist Match
Canterbury	Kent v India

Other Match
Fenners	Cambridge U v Hampshire

MAY 24, SATURDAY
Britannic Assurance Championship
Derby*	Derbyshire v Notts
Cardiff	Glamorgan v Somerset
Bournemouth	Hampshire v Glos
Lord's	Middlesex v Sussex
Northampton	Northants v Leics
Edgbaston	Warwickshire v Worcs
Headingley	Yorkshire v Lancashire

MAY 24, SATURDAY
Texaco Trophy (1st 1-day international)
The Oval	England v India

MAY 25, SUNDAY
John Player League
Cardiff	Glamorgan v Somerset
Canterbury	Kent v Surrey
Northampton	Northants v Leics
Hove	Sussex v Glos
Edgbaston	Warwickshire v Worcs
Sheffield	Yorkshire v Essex

MAY 26, MONDAY
TEXACO TROPHY (2nd 1-day international)
Old Trafford	England v India

MAY 28, WEDNESDAY
Benson & Hedges Cup
Quarter-finals

Tourist Match
Ireland v India (two days)

MAY 31, SATURDAY
Britannic Assurance Championship
Derby	Derbyshire v Essex
Southampton	Hampshire v Notts
Tunbridge Wells	Kent v Worcs
Old Trafford	Lancashire v Warwickshire
Leicester	Leics v Glos
The Oval	Surrey v Middlesex
Horsham	Sussex v Somerset

Tourist Match
Northampton*	Northants v India

JUNE 1, SUNDAY
John Player League
Derby	Derbyshire v Essex
Southampton	Hampshire v Notts
Old Trafford	Lancashire v Warwickshire
Leicester	Leics v Glos
The Oval	Surrey v Middlesex
Horsham	Sussex v Somerset

228 LOOKING FORWARD/FIXTURES 1986

JUNE 4, WEDNESDAY
Britannic Assurance Championship
Swansea	Glamorgan v Essex
Bristol	Glos v Warwickshire
Tunbridge Wells	Kent v Sussex
Leicester	Leics v Surrey
Trent Bridge	Notts v Somerset
Worcester	Worcs v Middlesex
Sheffield	Yorkshire v Derbyshire

Other Match
The Parks	Oxford U v Lancashire

JUNE 5, THURSDAY
First Cornhill Test
Lord's	ENGLAND v INDIA

JUNE 6, FRIDAY
Northampton	Northants v Zimbabwe (one day)

JUNE 7, SATURDAY
Britannic Assurance Championship
Chelmsford	Essex v Notts
Bournemouth*	Hampshire v Somerset
Old Trafford	Lancashire v Middlesex
Northampton	Northants v Worcs
The Oval	Surrey v Derbyshire
Hove	Sussex v Leics
Edgbaston	Warwickshire v Glamorgan
Harrogate	Yorkshire v Glos

Other Match
The Parks	Oxford U v Kent

JUNE 8, SUNDAY
John Player League
Chelmsford	Essex v Notts
Old Trafford	Lancashire v Middlesex
Northampton	Northants v Worcs
The Oval	Surrey v Derbyshire
Edgbaston	Warwickshire v Glamorgan
Headingley	Yorkshire v Glos

JUNE 11, WEDNESDAY
Benson & Hedges Cup
Semi-finals

Other Matches
Harrogate	Tilcon Trophy (three days)

JUNE 12, THURSDAY
Tourist Match
The Parks	Combined Univ v India (two days)

JUNE 14, SATURDAY
Britannic Assurance Championship
Ilford	Essex v Hampshire
Gloucester	Glos v Derbyshire
Old Trafford	Lancashire v Worcs
Lord's	Middlesex v Yorkshire
Northampton	Northants v Warwickshire
Trent Bridge	Notts v Surrey
Bath	Somerset v Kent

Tourist Match
Leicester*	Leics v India

Other Matches
The Parks	Oxford U v Glamorgan
Hove*	Sussex v Cambridge U

JUNE 15, SUNDAY
John Player League
Ilford	Essex v Hampshire
Gloucester	Glos v Derbyshire
Old Trafford	Lancashire v Worcs
Lord's	Middlesex v Yorkshire
Northampton	Northants v Warwickshire
Trent Bridge	Notts v Surrey
Bath	Somerset v Kent

Other Match
Ireland v Wales (three days)

JUNE 18, WEDNESDAY
Britannic Assurance Championship
Ilford	Essex v Sussex
Swansea	Glamorgan v Warwickshire
Gloucester	Glos v Kent
Basingstoke	Hampshire v Surrey
Trent Bridge	Notts v Middlesex
Bath	Somerset v Northants
Worcester	Worcs v Yorkshire

JUNE 19, THURSDAY
Third Cornhill Test
Headingley	ENGLAND v INDIA

JUNE 21, SATURDAY
Britannic Assurance Championship
Chesterfield*	Derbyshire v Glos
Swansea	Glamorgan v Lancashire
Southampton	Hampshire v Kent
Lord's	Middlesex v Essex
Luton	Northants v Yorkshire
Edgbaston	Warwickshire v Leics
Worcester	Worcs v Sussex

Other Match
Fenners	Cambridge U v Surrey

LOOKING FORWARD/FIXTURES 1986

JUNE 22, SUNDAY
John Player League
Swansea	Glamorgan v Lancashire
Basingstoke	Hampshire v Kent
Lord's	Middlesex v Essex
Luton	Northants v Yorkshire
Bath	Somerset v Notts
Edgbaston	Warwickshire v Leics
Worcester	Worcs v Sussex

Tourist Match
Arundel	Lavinia, Duchess of Norfolk's XI v New Zealand (one day)

JUNE 25, WEDNESDAY
NatWest Bank Trophy (First Round)
	Berkshire v Glos
	Cheshire v Surrey
Derby	Derbyshire v Cornwall
	Devon v Notts
Southampton	Hampshire v Hertfordshire
Old Trafford	Lancashire v Cumberland
Leicester	Leics v Ireland
Northampton	Northants v Middlesex
	Northumberland v Essex
Edinburgh (Myreside)	Scotland v Kent
Taunton	Somerset v Dorset
	Staffordshire v Glamorgan
Hove	Sussex v Suffolk
Edgbaston	Warwickshire v Durham
Worcester	Worcs v Oxfordshire
Headingley	Yorkshire v Cambridgeshire

Tourist Match
Fenners	Combined Univ v New Zealand

JUNE 26, THURSDAY
Chester-le-Street	League Cricket Conf v India (one day)

JUNE 28, SATURDAY
Britannic Assurance Championship
Bristol	Glos v Surrey
Maidstone	Kent v Glamorgan
Liverpool	Lancashire v Derbyshire
Leicester	Leics v Notts
Hastings	Sussex v Northants
Worcester	Worcs v Hampshire
Bradford*	Yorkshire v Warwickshire

Tourist Matches
Lord's*	Middlesex v New Zealand
Taunton*	Somerset v India

JUNE 29, SUNDAY
John Player League
Bristol	Glos v Surrey
Maidstone	Kent v Glamorgan
Leicester	Leics v Notts
Hastings	Sussex v Northants
Worcester	Worcs v Hampshire

JULY 2, WEDNESDAY
Britannic Assurance Championship
Derby	Derbyshire v Worcs
Cardiff	Glamorgan v Sussex
Bristol	Glos v Yorkshire
Maidstone	Kent v Somerset
Leicester	Leics v Hampshire
Uxbridge	Middlesex v Surrey
Trent Bridge	Notts v Warwickshire

Tourist Match
Chelmsford	Essex v New Zealand

University Match
Lord's	Oxford U v Cambridge U

JULY 3, THURSDAY
Third Cornhill Test
Edgbaston	ENGLAND v INDIA

JULY 5, SATURDAY
Britannic Assurance Championship
Derby	Derbyshire v Kent
Cardiff	Glamorgan v Glos
Old Trafford	Lancashire v Essex
Uxbridge	Middlesex v Warwickshire
Taunton	Somerset v Hampshire
The Oval	Surrey v Northants
Worcester	Worcs v Notts
Middlesbrough	Yorkshire v Leics

Tourist Match
Hove*	Sussex v New Zealand

JULY 6, SUNDAY
John Player League
Derby	Derbyshire v Kent
Cardiff	Glamorgan v Glos
Old Trafford	Lancashire v Essex
Lord's	Middlesex v Warwickshire
Tring	Northants v Surrey
Taunton	Somerset v Hampshire
Worcester	Worcs v Notts
Middlesbrough	Yorkshire v Leics

JULY 9, WEDNESDAY
NatWest Bank Trophy (Second Round)
Hants or Herts v Worcs or Oxon
Somerset or Dorset v Lancs or Cumberland
Berks or Glos v Leics or Ireland
Devon or Notts v Scotland or Kent
Sussex or Suffolk v Staffs or Glamorgan
Warwicks or Durham v Northumberland or Essex
Derbys or Cornwall v Cheshire or Surrey
Yorks or Cambs v Northants or Middx

Tourist Match
Norwich (Lakenham)	Minor Counties v New Zealand

LOOKING FORWARD/ FIXTURES 1986

JULY 12, SATURDAY
Benson & Hedges Cup
Lord's   Final

Tourist Matches
Scarborough*	Yorkshire v India
Edgbaston (or	Warwicks (or Lancs
Old Trafford)	if Warwicks in B & H Final)
	v New Zealand

JULY 13, SUNDAY
John Player League
Chelmsford	Essex v Somerset
Leicester	Leics v Middlesex
Finedon	Northants v Derbyshire
Trent Bridge	Notts v Glos
Hove	Sussex v Glamorgan

JULY 16, WEDNESDAY
Britannic Assurance Championship
Southend	Essex v Leics
Neath	Glamorgan v Worcs
Bristol	Glos v Sussex
Lord's	Middlesex v Somerset
Northampton	Northants v Lancashire
Worksop (?)	Notts v Yorkshire
The Oval	Surrey v Kent
Edgbaston	Warwickshire v Derbyshire

Texaco Trophy (1st 1-day international)
Headingley   England v N. Zealand

JULY 18, FRIDAY
Texaco Trophy (2nd one-day international)
Old Trafford   England v N. Zealand

JULY 19, SATURDAY
Britannic Assurance Championship
Derby	Derbyshire v Middlesex
Southend	Essex v Worcs
Swansea	Glamorgan v Northants
Bristol	Glos v Somerset
Portsmouth	Hampshire v Warwickshire
Canterbury	Kent v Lancashire
Leicester	Leics v Sussex
Headingley*	Yorkshire v Surrey

Tourist Match
Trent Bridge*   Notts v New Zealand

Other Match
Ireland v MCC (three days)

JULY 20, SUNDAY
John Player League
Derby	Derbyshire v Middlesex
Southend	Essex v Worcs
Neath	Glamorgan v Northants
Bristol	Glos v Somerset
Portsmouth	Hampshire v Warwickshire
Canterbury	Kent v Lancashire
Leicester	Leics v Sussex

JULY 23, WEDNESDAY
Britannic Assurance Championship
Portsmouth	Hampshire v Derbyshire
Southport	Lancashire v Notts
Leicester	Leics v Glamorgan
The Oval	Surrey v Essex
Hove	Sussex v Worcs
Scarborough	Yorkshire v Kent

JULY 24, THURSDAY
First Cornhill Test
Lord's   ENGLAND v N. ZEALAND

JULY 26, SATURDAY
Britannic Assurance Championship
Abergavenny	Glamorgan v Derbyshire
Northampton	Northants v Middlesex
Guildford	Surrey v Sussex
Edgbaston	Warwickshire v Lancashire
Worcester	Worcs v Glos
Sheffield	Yorkshire v Notts

JULY 27, SUNDAY
John Play League
Ebbw Vale	Glamorgan v Derbyshire
Southampton	Hampshire v Leics
Northampton	Northants v Kent
Taunton	Somerset v Lancashire
Guildford	Surrey v Sussex
Worcester	Worcs v Glos
Hull (or Scarborough)	Yorkshire v Notts

JULY 30, WEDNESDAY
NatWest Bank Trophy
Quarter-finals

JULY 31, THURSDAY
Jesmond   England XI v Rest of World XI (one day)

AUGUST 1, FRIDAY
Jesmond   England XI v Rest of World XI (one day)

AUGUST 2, SATURDAY
Britannic Assurance Championship
Cheltenham	Glos v Hampshire
Canterbury	Kent v Leicestershire
Old Trafford	Lancashire v Yorkshire
Lord's	Middlesex v Northants
Weston-super-Mare	Somerset v Worcs
Eastbourne	Sussex v Essex

Tourist Match
Derby*   Derbyshire v New Zealand

First Young Cricketers 'Test'
Headingley*   England v Sri Lanka (four days)

LOOKING FORWARD/FIXTURES 1986

AUGUST 3, SUNDAY
John Player League
Cheltenham	Glos v Hampshire
Canterbury	Kent v Leics
Old Trafford	Lancashire v Yorkshire
Lord's	Middlesex v Northants
Trent Bridge	Notts v Glamorgan
Weston-super-Mare	Somerset v Worcs
Eastbourne	Sussex v Essex
Edgbaston	Warwickshire v Surrey

AUGUST 6, WEDNESDAY
Britannic Assurance Championship
Chelmsford	Essex v Middlesex
Cheltenham	Glos v Nottinghamshire
Canterbury	Kent v Hampshire
Leicester	Leics v Yorkshire
Northampton	Northants v Glamorgan
Weston-super-Mare	Somerset v Warwickshire
The Oval	Surrey v Lancashire
Eastbourne	Sussex v Derbyshire

AUGUST 7, THURSDAY
Second Cornhill Test
Trent Bridge   ENGLAND v N. ZEALAND

AUGUST 9, SATURDAY
Britannic Assurance Championship
Buxton	Derbyshire v Lancashire
Cheltenham	Glos v Middlesex
Southampton	Hampshire v Sussex
Leicester	Leics v Essex
Wellingborough School	Northants v Somerset
The Oval	Surrey v Worcs
Edgbaston	Warwickshire v Kent
Bradford	Yorkshire v Glamorgan

First Young Cricketers 1-day international
Chelmsford*   England v Sri Lanka

AUGUST 10, SUNDAY
John Player League
Buxton	Derbyshire v Lancashire
Cheltenham	Glos v Middlesex
Bournemouth	Hampshire v Sussex
Leicester	Leics v Essex
Wellingborough School	Northants v Somerset
The Oval	Surrey v Worcs
Edgbaston	Warwickshire v Kent
Scarborough	Yorkshire v Glamorgan

AUGUST 11, MONDAY
Second Young Cricketers 1-day international
Lord's   England v Sri Lanka

AUGUST 13, WEDNESDAY
NatWest Bank Trophy
Semi-finals

Tourist Match
Old Trafford   Lancs (or Warwicks if Lancs
(or Edgbaston) in NatWest Semi) v N. Zealand

AUGUST 16, SATURDAY
Britannic Assurance Championship
Chesterfield	Derbyshire v Yorkshire
Colchester	Essex v Northants
Lord's	Middlesex v Hampshire
Trent Bridge	Notts v Lancashire
Taunton	Somerset v Surrey
Hove	Sussex v Kent
Nuneaton	Warwickshire v Glos
Worcester	Worcs v Leics

Tourist Match
Swansea*   Glamorgan v New Zealand

Second Young Cricketers 'Test'
Bristol*   England v Sri Lanka
(four days)

Other Match
Scotland v Ireland (3 days)

AUGUST 17, SUNDAY
John Player League
Chesterfield	Derbyshire v Yorkshire
Colchester	Essex v Northamptonshire
Lord's	Middlesex v Hampshire
Trent Bridge	Notts v Lancashire
Taunton	Somerset v Surrey
Hove	Sussex v Kent
Edgbaston	Warwickshire v Glos
Worcester	Worcs v Leics

AUGUST 20, WEDNESDAY
Britannic Assurance Championship
Chesterfield	Derbyshire v Leics
Colchester	Essex v Glos
Bournemouth	Hampshire v Worcs
Dartford	Kent v Surrey
Lytham	Lancashire v Glamorgan
Northampton	Northants v Notts
Taunton	Somerset v Sussex
Headingley	Yorkshire v Middlesex

AUGUST 21, THURSDAY
Third Cornhill Test
The Oval   ENGLAND v N. ZEALAND

LOOKING FORWARD/FIXTURES 1986

AUGUST 23, SATURDAY
Britannic Assurance Championship
Chelmsford	Essex v Surrey
Cardiff	Glamorgan v Kent
Bournemouth	Hampshire v Yorkshire
Old Trafford	Lancashire v Glos
Leicester	Leics v Northants
Trent Bridge	Notts v Derbyshire
Hove	Sussex v Middlesex
Worcester	Worcs v Warwickshire

AUGUST 24, SUNDAY
John Player League
Chelmsford	Essex v Surrey
Bournemouth	Hampshire v Yorkshire
Old Trafford	Lancashire v Northants
Trent Bridge	Notts v Derbyshire
Hove	Sussex v Middlesex
Edgbaston	Warwickshire v Somerset
Worcester	Worcs v Glamorgan

AUGUST 27, WEDNESDAY
Britannic Assurance Championship
Swansea	Glamorgan v Surrey
Leicester	Leics v Derbyshire
Lord's	Middlesex v Lancashire
Northampton	Northants v Hampshire
Trent Bridge	Notts v Kent
Taunton	Somerset v Essex
Edgbaston	Warwickshire v Yorkshire

AUGUST 30, SATURDAY
Britannic Assurance Championship
Derbyshire	Derbyshire v Hampshire
Folkestone	Kent v Essex
Leicester	Leics v Somerset
Hove*	Sussex v Notts
Edgbaston	Warwickshire v Middlesex

Third Young Cricketers 'Test'
Trent Bridge*	England v Sri Lanka (four days)

AUGUST 31, SUNDAY
John Player League
Heanor	Derbyshire v Hampshire
Moreton in Marsh	Glos v Northants
Folkestone	Kent v Essex
Old Trafford	Lancashire v Surrey
Leicester	Leics v Somerset
Lord's	Middlesex v Worcs
Headingley	Yorkshire v Warwickshire

Other Matches
Edgbaston	Warwick Under-25 Final (one day)
Scarborough	D.B. Close's XI v N. Zealand (three days)

SEPTEMBER 3, WEDNESDAY
Britannic Assurance Championship
Derby	Derbyshire v Northants
Cardiff	Glamorgan v Notts
Folkestone	Kent v Warwickshire
The Oval	Surrey v Glos
Worcester	Worcs v Somerset

Other Match
Scarborough	Essex v Lancs (ASDA Cricket Challenge, one day)

SEPTEMBER 4, THURSDAY
Scarborough	Hants v Yorks (ASDA, one day)

SEPTEMBER 5, FRIDAY
Scarborough	ASDA Final (one day)

SEPTEMBER 6, SATURDAY
NatWest Bank Trophy
Lord's	Final

SEPTEMBER 7, SUNDAY
John Player League
Cardiff	Glamorgan v Middlesex
Bristol	Glos v Lancashire
Canterbury	Kent v Notts
The Oval	Surrey v Hampshire
Hove	Sussex v Yorkshire
Worcester	Worcs v Derbyshire

SEPTEMBER 10, WEDNESDAY
Britannic Assurance Championship
Old Trafford	Lancashire v Somerset
Trent Bridge	Notts v Essex
Hove	Sussex v Hampshire
Worcester	Worcs v Glamorgan
Scarborough	Yorkshire v Northants

SEPTEMBER 13, SATURDAY
Britannic Assurance Championship
Chelmsford	Essex v Glamorgan
Bristol	Glos v Worcs
Southampton	Hampshire v Lancashire
Canterbury	Kent v Middlesex
Trent Bridge	Notts v Northants
Taunton	Somerset v Derbyshire
The Oval	Surrey v Leics
Edgbaston	Warwickshire v Sussex

SEPTEMBER 14, SUNDAY
John Player League
Chelmsford	Essex v Glamorgan
Southampton	Hampshire v Lancashire
Canterbury	Kent v Yorkshire
Trent Bridge	Notts v Northants
Taunton	Somerset v Derbyshire
The Oval	Surrey v Leics
Edgbaston	Warwickshire v Sussex

Fixtures are the copyright of the Test and County Cricket Board 1986